Into the Pulpit

ELIZABETH H. FLOWERS

Into the Pulpit

SOUTHERN BAPTIST WOMEN
& POWER SINCE WORLD WAR II

The University of North Carolina Press | *Chapel Hill*

©2012 THE UNIVERSITY OF NORTH CAROLINA PRESS

All rights reserved. Designed by Sally Fry and set in Adobe Caslon Pro and Latienne Swash by Rebecca Evans. Manufactured in the United States of America. The paper in this book meets the guidelines for permanence and durability of the Committee on Production Guidelines for Book Longevity of the Council on Library Resources. The University of North Carolina Press has been a member of the Green Press Initiative since 2003.

Library of Congress Cataloging-in-Publication Data
Flowers, Elizabeth Hill.
Into the pulpit : Southern Baptist women and power
since World War II / by Elizabeth H. Flowers.
p. cm.
Includes bibliographical references (p.) and index.
ISBN 978-0-8078-3534-0 (cloth : alk. paper)
1. Southern Baptist Convention—History. 2. Baptist women—
United States—History. 3. Sex role—Religious aspects—
Southern Baptist Convention—History of doctrines. I. Title.
BX6462.3.F56 2012
262′.1432082—dc23
2011035947

16 15 14 13 12   5 4 3 2 1

For my mother and father,

IVA LOU

and

ROBERT FLOWERS

Contents

Acknowledgments

As a historian of women in American religion, I am well aware that it is those unnamed persons who motivate and enable significant events, most often from behind the scenes. While this book is hardly a major world happening, it is certainly a momentous occurrence in my academic life, and I want to name the individuals whose assistance and encouragement kept me pressing toward the finish.

I am fortunate to have had significant mentors, colleagues, and intellectual inspirations from the outset of my academic career. First and foremost is Grant Wacker, my trusted advisor and friend throughout the past decade. More than anyone, Grant taught me how to study religious subjects empathetically. Reflective of his own everyday kindness, he never let me forget the consideration each person under study deserves. His meticulous eye sharpened this book's argument and historical analysis. Others were also crucial to the project from the start, eventually reading the manuscript in its entirety. Tom Tweed urged me to focus on Southern Baptist women and suggested the theorists who became the book's intellectual scaffolding. Donald Mathews appealed to my fascination for the evangelical South and helped me explore its relationship to American culture. Both he and Laurie Maffly-Kipp pushed me to establish the connections between race and gender, with Laurie offering key insights concerning revision. Jack Carroll assisted me in surveying the contemporary American religious landscape, while David Steinmetz forced me to reflect more critically on my methodology. I benefited firsthand from the knowledge of certain Baptist historians, particularly Curtis Freeman and Keith Harper. Pam Durso and Carol Holcomb offered a wealth of information on Southern Baptist women. They provided essential contacts as well as needed camaraderie. Stephen Berry, Katie Lofton, and Lynn Neal, companions in the field, skillfully critiqued particular chapters. Finally, my dear friend Judy Dodd enlivened my storytelling by reading the manuscript at several different junctures and responding with a keen editorial eye to numerous chapter drafts and mail inquiries.

In testing the waters of university presses, I sent a proposal to the University of North Carolina Press. My eventual editor, Elaine Maisner, called me immediately and then deftly led me through the press's rigorous process, during which three anonymous reviewers offered important suggestions for strengthening the book. I appreciate Elaine's belief in this project from the beginning and her expertise, along with that of the press's editorial board, in seeing it to print. Stephanie Wenzel also served as an assiduous copyeditor. Of course, none of the aforementioned individuals are responsible for errors of fact or emphasis that remain.

I also want to acknowledge those institutions and persons who made available the financial and archival resources necessary for this project. Duke University's Women's Studies Program awarded me its Ernestine Friedl and Anne Firor Scott prizes, which covered early research forays. Texas Christian University (TCU) assisted me in the final stages of research and revision, granting me time and money through both its Research and Creative Activities Fund and Junior Faculty Summer Research Program spearheaded by Dean Andrew Schoolmaster. Bill Sumners and Taffey Hall at the Southern Baptist Historical Library and Archives showed patience and good humor in tracking down almost anything that dealt with Southern Baptists, women, and gender, while Amy Cook and Dianne Baker at the Woman's Missionary Union Library and Archives retrieved vital information from the infamous vault. Likewise, the expertise of Rebecca Sharpless, now a valued TCU colleague, greatly accelerated my research at Baylor University's Institute for Oral History.

Historians often groan at the mention of living subjects. My experience, however, evokes the opposite response, and I would be remiss if I did not recognize the women from both camps of the Southern Baptist controversy who welcomed me into their churches and homes. Twenty-three agreed to formal interviews. These women trusted me implicitly, and several became friends. While I did not necessarily share their theological worldview, they earned my respect as I witnessed their struggle to apply their faith to life's messy verities. As a scholar, I undoubtedly approach the events that they lived and experienced from a different set of convictions. But I feel an abiding, deep appreciation for their sharing their stories, and I hope that I have honored their narratives with the dignity that they deserve. On the conservative side, I would like to especially thank Susie Hawkins and Sarah Maddox, who are both grace-filled and sparkling exemplars of their tradition. The indomitable women connected to (Southern) Baptist Women in Ministry also extended extraordinary hospitality, and several went out of their way to help, particularly Linda Hood Hicks, Anne Neil, Karrie Oertlie, Terry Thomas Primer, and Lynda Weaver-Williams.

The collegiality of the TCU Department of Religion created the ideal environment in which to write. With David Grant and Nadia Lahutsky acting as successive, and extraordinarily thoughtful, chairs, the department did its best to ease the teaching and service components of my position, making completion of the book less arduous. Fortuitously, Jan Quesada's office is located a few steps from mine, and beyond anecdotes of Southern Baptist life, she has supplied kindness and laughter in ample doses. During the process of writing, I have also been enriched by dialogue with the wise women (and man) at TCU who make up the women's studies program, most notably fellow religionists Claudia Camp and David Gunn and colleagues "across the street" Theresa Gaul and Lisa Vanderlinden. My student assistant, Caroline Hamilton, good-naturedly assumed many of the menial tasks that accompany the scholar's life.

Friends and family formed a network of support, too, and they never tired of asking me about my "big paper," as Marnie Williams and Beth Mikeska humorously called it. There are far too many to thank by name, so I will mention those more directly involved. Two breakfast groups of fellow women academics offered a space for discussing work while, at the same time, helping me keep everything in perspective: my North Carolina group with the Jennifers (Graber, Trafton, and Woodruff) and Esther Chung, and my Fort Worth/TCU coterie of Julie Byrne, Judy Dodd, and Edna Rodriguez, who welcomed me to Texas. Edna also gave me two precious goddaughters. A needed week escape to Austin to visit Mity Myhr and work in her family's guest house led to the book proposal's completion. I was also able to connect with my adopted Aunt Whitt, who has long modeled academic success, when staying at her house in Houston for field research, and with Emily Cook during a foray to Alabama. Lynn Eaton functioned as a home away from home for more than two years and often read pieces of my writing.

Upon hearing of my project, the women at my childhood church in Memphis amazed me yet again with their spirited care. Carol Richardson and Margaret Martin provided me with research contacts. Visiting the small archive there, which was crammed with photos, brought back a flood of memories (thank you Beth C., Vivian, Grace, the Loves, and Dawn Grosser). The wondrous women of the Heavenly Council (Holly, Jane, Janet, Merry, Sandy, and Sarah) continued to inspire. My sisters, Anne Tinker and

Lou Martin, along with their families, called to cheer me on during noted absences from holiday gatherings, while my English parents-in-law, Joan and Alan, sent notes of encouragement from Old Blighty. Along with those already mentioned here, Jeanne McCarty, Dorree Jane Smith, and Margaret Weems were, as always, steadfast.

Coming full circle, the scholarly inspiration for this book began well more than a decade ago when Marie Griffith introduced me to the exciting possibilities of ethnography and demonstrated firsthand innovative ways to engage evangelical women. She also guided me toward American Religion, literally opening the door to my academic career. Marie and Andrew Walls expressed enthusiasm for an essay that I wrote on the Woman's Missionary Union, as did Ann Braude when I presented at the Women in Religion in America Conference. The questions of Catherine Allen inspired me to write another paper on the historic women's mission group, which I completed under the able direction of James Moorhead to secure the Torbet Prize in Baptist History. It was because of the attentiveness of these early mentors that I returned to Southern Baptist women as a book-length project.

In closing, my deepest gratitude goes to my parents, husband, and son, all of whom made sacrifices for this project. My mother spent the past six years driving the interstate between Memphis and Fort Worth to assume child care duties so that my husband and I could work. Without complaint, my father endured weeks of her absence. To be sure, my mother's endless patience and optimism alongside my father's abiding humor and cooperative spirit kept me moving forward. They have always offered me comfort and security, and as Baptists, they exemplify their tradition's finest qualities. Honoring them with this book's dedication is a blessing.

My husband has willingly suffered the trials of being married to a wandering historian, and in the process of this book, he often assumed the lion's share of our personal and parental responsibilities. When I experienced frustration, Darren kept my focus on the finale and created the conditions, financially and emotionally, with his characteristic creativity and kindness, which enabled me to persevere. Last, as I was writing this story, my own narrative took a decided turn with the arrival of our son. While motherhood slowed the pace of my prose, it also deepened my understanding. Jonathan's excitement and wonder at the everyday world taught me to appreciate more deeply the faith-filled lives of those women whom I was studying, interviewing, and engaging, and who are the bedrock of this book.

Into the Pulpit

Introduction

On July 12, 1979, more than 15,000 messengers to the annual Southern Baptist Convention (SBC) gathered in the Houston Astrodome to elect the charismatic, conservative, and controversial preacher Adrian Rogers as their denomination's next president. To the dismay of many church officials, Rogers, who stood outside the traditional network of leadership, defeated several senior Southern Baptist statesmen with a 51 percent margin of victory on the first ballot. More significantly, his victory served as the initial step in a carefully calculated plan to overthrow the power base that his opponents represented.

Conservatives like Rogers argued that theological and cultural liberalism had infiltrated the denomination's highest institutions and offices. As they saw it, university professors had abandoned biblical Creationism, women had usurped men's leadership in missions, and feminists now crowded the seminary classrooms. "If those liberals will ever come to the cross of Jesus," proclaimed Rogers on the eve of his election, "then all heaven will break loose."[1] Rogers's words incensed those coalescing around the traditional leadership structure. One SBC executive even assigned Rogers's success to "Satan" and "his efforts" to deflect attention from missions and evangelism.[2] The SBC's outgoing president, Jimmy Allen, urged messengers to resist the temptation of groups intent on dividing the denomination and altering its agenda.[3] Initially seen as SBC loyalists, Allen and his cohorts soon adopted the name "moderates" and argued fervently for compromise.[4]

The contest between conservatives and moderates was fierce. It lasted more than two decades and quickly moved beyond vitriolic rhetoric, annual convention politicking, and media-hyped Disney boycotts.[5] During this period, conservatives radically revised denominational policies, disfellowshipped congregations, and redefined church roles. As they continued to secure the SBC's presidency, they systematically replaced the denomination's leading officials, board presidents, seminary professors, missionaries, journalists, and more. Insiders and outsiders alike characterized the protracted struggle as the "Southern Baptist battles." When the battles finally came to an end, the SBC had been altered irrevocably. Old alliances had been destroyed and new boundaries drawn.

Powerful tensions in both the culture and the church converged to ignite the Southern Baptist controversy. During the immediate post–World War II period, the South underwent tremendous transformation. Economic progress, advances in communication and technology, higher education levels, and greater geographic mobility linked the South to the rest of the nation. Like most southerners, Southern Baptists welcomed the opportunities that accompanied this transformation. In an era of unprecedented prosperity, church leaders grew the SBC into the largest American Protestant denomination. Initially, optimism prevailed. The Americanization of Dixie, however, also introduced certain anxieties. The end of the Jim Crow era gave rise to both white flight and urban blight. Economic progress led to an influx of new labor, first transregional and later transnational. Higher education levels brought greater acceptance of controversial philosophical and scientific concepts. The 1960s also introduced the war in Vietnam, the sexual revolution, rock and roll, and hippie culture. The result was that to many southerners, including Southern Baptists, the enemy no longer resided without, as the "godless North," but had moved within, as secular or liberal America. Tensions, issues, and differences that had often been overlooked or downplayed suddenly became more threatening and less tolerated.

The "woman question," as Southern Baptists frequently phrased it, was one such issue. With feminism sweeping the country and increasing numbers of Southern Baptist women seeking ordination, the rhetoric surrounding women's roles and behaviors became increasingly inflammatory and divisive. Women, conservatives argued, could not occupy that coveted place of power in evangelical life: the pulpit. Nor could they preside at the defining ritual of Baptists: baptism. At one heated point in the struggle, a Southern Baptist Theological Seminary trustee warned, "If you believe that pastors can be women, then you need to go somewhere else, because we're not going to believe it. . . . The gauntlet is down. It's not going to change, so if professors believe that, it's our job to get them out of here."[6] Contrary to popular stereotypes, women responded as active participants in both conservative and moderate life. Some celebrated, encouraged, and even insisted on a posture of submission as "first tier in the realm of salvation."[7] Others felt aggrieved that "there were actually people sitting around discussing what roles women can have, as if they can actually decide what we can and cannot do."[8]

Argument

In this book, I argue that as Southern Baptist moderates and conservatives fought for control of the denomination, the issue over women's changing roles and their bid toward greater ecclesial power moved from the sides to the center of the controversy. This argument unfolds thematically and chronologically, with several related subplots. First, while theological and cultural tensions informed historic Southern Baptist life and culture, genteel Southern Baptist oligarchs kept a broad coalition intact through most of the twentieth century. As they saw it, denominational identity transcended partisan politics. After World War II, newfound prosperity enabled the denomination's rapid growth and development. In trying to maintain the SBC's new status, denominational leaders continued to govern according to the same principle of compromise. Downplaying theological matters, they emphasized financial solvency and organizational restructuring. Second, by the 1960s, the coalition was faltering. The introduction of modern scholarship, civil rights, and feminism, for example, unleashed ideological debates over inerrancy and cultural conflicts involving race and gender. Old tensions assumed new potent forms, bringing about the confrontations that ripped Southern Baptists apart. Third, in a dramatic reversal of previous patterns, party politics trumped denominational loyalty. And finally, as the battles progressed, one of the most divisive issues became women's roles and practices.

As to "why women?," the issue had produced sharp tension consistently running just under the surface of Southern Baptist life. Southern Baptists never had settled on one concept of womanhood. Frontier women exhorted, testified, and prophesied, while their eastern-educated counterparts sat quietly in their pews. One of the fiercest disputes in nineteenth-century Southern Baptist life involved the propriety of women organizing for missions. Once women formed the Woman's Missionary Union (WMU) in 1888, they debated the issues of women giving public speeches, suffrage, and their organizational autonomy. Moving into the twentieth century, state conventions vacillated wildly over whether to seat women messengers, while national leaders pondered women's presence on denominational committees. The debate over women challenged Southern Baptist men and women alike, with most Southern Baptists leaning toward a traditional or "conserving" impulse that prohibited pushing too far the boundaries of dominant social conventions regarding women's roles and practices.[9] At certain transitional moments, a dissenting or progressive impulse within the WMU led some of its women to question particular limitations. In step with their genteel male counterparts, its female leaders successfully mediated these competing understandings. By the 1980s, however, even this cohesive force was faltering.

As for other historic tensions, civil rights legislation brought a measure of social justice. Racism died slowly, but when the Southern Baptist battles broke out, denominational conservatives were as eager as moderates to dispel any racist image. As I show, a more constrained view of womanhood and women's ministry replaced hardened notions of race and attitudes toward racial desegregation, which fell out of favor after the 1960s.[10] Race, then, ceased to be the divisive issue. As for inerrancy, numerous moderate leaders mimicked conservative rhetoric by boasting allegiance to biblical literalism and inerrant principles, and they, too, expressed grave concern over liberal or loose interpretations of scripture. Moreover, as both groups discovered, a large number of Southern Baptists, even denominational officials, proved to be atheological, not willing to dig too far beneath any superficial understanding. Initially an effective rallying point for conservatives, inerrancy seemed increasingly nebulous.[11]

Eventually, the resolutions calling for female submission proved pivotal in capturing imaginations, stirring passions, and energizing followers. In fact, by the end of the conflict, women's actual responsibilities, particularly denominationally related ones, served as the most immediate and at least visible marker of difference between the two camps. A glance at the conservative and moderate meetings from the late 1990s is telling. Women at the moderate-related gatherings appeared alongside men on the central platform, presided over business sessions, served communion, led worship, and preached. In contrast, women at the annual SBC meeting sat primarily on the convention floor, wielding authority only in sex-segregated spaces. When asked what most distinguished them from conservatives, moderate leaders often stated that they accepted women in the pulpit.[12] The title of this book, *Into the Pulpit*, then functions symbolically, as a reference to women's changing roles and the way the issue of women divided Southern Baptists.

Disputes over women's submission and ordination did provide conservatives with a set of universally significant issues to guard and protect, and it gave moderates a range of options for mounting a response.[13] Many denominational officials, conservative and moderate alike, thus persisted in seeing the debate over women as a secondary concern, a litmus test, so to speak, for something greater. This is undoubtedly one way of assessing the role of the woman question in the overall controversy. Nevertheless, for the more than 50 percent of Southern Baptists who were, in fact, women, disagreements that touched on their familial roles and ecclesial authority were not secondary. Moreover, as with slavery a century earlier, biblical hermeneutics frequently serviced cultural understandings of women's roles and behaviors. After the 1960s and 1970s, conservatives could no longer view women's ordination apart from feminism, abortion, the Equal Rights Amendment (ERA), and other liberal causes that the religious right portrayed as antifamily, anti-American, and anti-Christian. As a result, the debate over women drove Southern Baptists to embrace certain biblical interpretations over others.

This is not to say that gendered ideas about women were more important than theological matters, particularly biblical inerrancy, but that the two were inextricably intertwined. The woman question was one strand in a large, complicated story, and cultural dictates regarding women certainly guided scriptural interpretation. The denominational controversy moved between multiple tensions, with certain issues taking precedence and coming to the fore at particular times. The woman question was one issue that moved from the side to the center of the controversy. It played a profoundly decisive role with deep-rooted historical and cultural implications as well as serving more pragmatic functions.

Admittedly, few events in American religious history have been analyzed with as much frequency as the Southern Baptist battles. I persisted in writing this book to address a gap in the prevailing narratives that distorts our understanding of the post-1979 SBC controversy. Namely, when considering this event, most scholars have focused mainly on male-oriented theological and cultural contests. All too often, they have emphasized debates concerning scriptural interpretation and church polity, relegating the argument over women as a mere symbol for substantive biblical and ecclesial concerns.[14] Few historians have examined thoroughly the controversy's impact on women or even acknowledged them as key characters in the story, as protagonists who initiated, resisted, and engaged the denominational struggle. While some studies have explored Southern Baptist women, focusing particularly on the WMU, none have traced ongoing tensions regarding their roles and behaviors into the postwar period.[15] Even historians who argue that gender replaced race as a means to power and otherness have tended to cast their gaze on institutional racism, seeing arguments regarding women's submission as a narrative postscript.[16] By relocating battles over the status and ministry of Baptist women from the margins to the center of the narrative about conservative ascendency, I present women as major characters in the denominational controversy and as the major story of this book. My intention is not to replace other stories but to correct an imbalance in the literature that will further our understanding of this pivotal event in southern, evangelical, and American religious history.

Theoretical Framework

In posing my argument, I take seriously the call of the American religious historian Ann Braude to consider the overwhelming presence of females in most religious communities and to view them as primary players in American religious life.[17] Braude opens her seminal essay "Women's History *Is* American Religious History" with a simple observation: "In America, women go to church."[18] The strong ideological link between piety and femininity mirrors this reality; therefore, religion cannot be separated from gendered ideas about women, she says, if we are to situate either one accurately within the American context. Braude then pushes further, recognizing that women have been mainstays in the same religious traditions that have excluded them from positions of leadership and authority. The paradox of American religious history, she asserts, has been that its "institutions have relied for their existence on the very group that they have disenfranchised," or, inversely, women willingly "participate in the institution that enforces their subordination and provides the cosmological justification for it."[19]

While Braude understands the formative role of religion in establishing and reproducing cultural norms, particularly gendered norms for women, she also sees its churches, synagogues, organizations, and programs as providing the primary arenas in which women have negotiated these norms and located "special meaning for their lives as women."[20] Inherent in her analysis here is the notion of change in relation to power. As most cultural historians would maintain, what appears static and stable is subject to alteration. Contexts, environments, and cultures constantly evolve. Human needs shift, and lives take diverse turns. Changes in women's roles and practices reveal much about the structures of authority and control within certain societies, particularly religious communities. At the same time, change, as Braude indicates, occurs not only from the top down but from the bottom up. It starts with women as well as men, laity as well as clergy. In this respect, change involves both agency and constraint and appears at the interstices between individual subjects, grassroots movements, and corporate institutions. It takes shape as outright resistance, subtle negotiation, or anything in between.[21] Religion, then, particularly as it invokes women, is to be found in this process of change, serving both regulative and transformative impulses.[22]

But change also lacks consistency over time. As the cultural anthropologist Ann Swidler explains, settled periods support varied patterns of belief and practice, while unsettled times demand higher commitments to particular doctrines and ideologies. New forms of pluralism, greater economic disparity, geographic displacement, or shifts in leadership frequently initiate unsettled periods. Differing levels of accommodation inevitably accompany the intrusion of new ideas and ways of thinking. As a result, conflict develops within previously established communities, with boundaries and divisions assuming symbolic form. Almost any tradition, ritual, prejudice, mythologized history, or ideology—including gender, or more particularly, gendered ideas about women—could be used as a divisive issue in the ensuing power struggle.[23]

This understanding of women, religion, and culture frames my study. From about 1910 to 1950, Southern Baptists dominated the South. But after World War II, the southern landscape changed dramatically as the Sunbelt attracted new industry and labor. While this new labor was initially northern, it became increasingly transnational after the Immigration Act of 1965. At the same time, southerners became more educated and middle class, and many left home to pursue careers and jobs in other parts of the country. The SBC followed its members to plant churches outside its former parameters, thereby welcoming nonsoutherners into its fold. Finally, as civil rights legislation dismantled Jim Crow segregation, the old order governing southern society and culture began to crumble. While the South had never been an isolated and bounded entity, a new cultural pluralism began to replace its once-perceived hegemony, diminishing the strength and influence of its social structures. If this were not enough, the various countercultural movements of the late 1960s only added to a general sense of social unrest and anxiety over change.

The controversy between moderates and conservatives resulted in part from this unsettled period. Differences that denominational leaders had managed to downplay were rearranged and reinterpreted to become symbolic tools in a new form of boundary drawing. One of the more pronounced areas of contention centered on women: their roles, practices, behaviors, and functions. At almost every annual convention after 1973, Southern Baptists heatedly debated the parameters regarding women's place in ecclesial and domestic life. Conservative resolutions that directly rejected feminism and dictated women's submission to male authority forced congregations to examine their own assumptions and understandings. Moderates cried freedom against conservatives' restraints but then argued about freedom's actual meaning. Many questioned the extent to which they would accommodate variety regarding women's practices and the reality, rather than the rhetoric, of women's movement into positions of authority. As the struggle progressed, women themselves broke into factions. Once held together by the WMU and missions, they formed their own disparate groups and organizations around competing concepts of womanhood. Conservative women were as much a part of this process as moderate women and those seeking ordination, creating their own religious spaces to achieve a certain degree of autonomy, voice, and power.

In taking seriously the injunction that scholars of American religious history begin with female presence, I present the WMU's fragmentation as the illustrative subplot of the denomination after World War II. Moreover, if we start with women and their experiences, we notice that the narrative shifts. Inerrancy, for example, plays a less dominant and more interactive role, while the wider cultural context, with its varied and contradictory forces, assumes greater prominence.

Southern Baptists, Evangelicals, and Sectarian America

It was no coincidence that Southern Baptists fought their battles at the same time that the culture wars tore evangelical America apart. The two were interconnected, and the party politics that came to dominate Southern Baptist life indicated a growing sectarianism across the wider American religious landscape. The Americanization of Dixie was, in many ways, the Americanization of everything. As the SBC grew to become the largest American Protestant denomination, it functioned as a symbol of both the South and the nation.[24] This book, then, is not simply about the debate over women in Southern Baptist life but also about how the SBC and its subplots signaled trends in modern American religion. While it moves existing conversations regarding Southern Baptists and southern culture in new directions, it likewise interprets Southern Baptists within the wider context of American evangelicalism. Few scholars would question the southern focus. Some, however, might ask whether Southern Baptists really represent American evangelicals.[25]

As I define them, evangelicals have constituted a cluster of groups, traditions, and trends within the wider American religious landscape. Historically, evangelicals were born of the great revivals that swept the country during the second Great Awakening. They emphasized belief in the Bible as the inspired word of God, the experience of individual conversion, the assurance of salvation through the work of Jesus Christ, and the ongoing cultivation of a personal relationship with God within the community of the church. As for everyday practice, they sang hymns like "Revive Us Again," hosted revivals, conducted prayer meetings, embarked on witnessing and evangelism campaigns, and commissioned missionaries to spread the gospel around the world. After the 1970s, many evangelical traditions splintered, though almost all claimed a heritage shaped by these earlier events, beliefs, and practices.

In terms of historiography, studies of twentieth-century evangelicalism have concentrated on its northern, urban, and more sectarian manifestations, painting a portrait that leaves out Southern Baptists.[26] To be sure, Southern Baptists do possess a fairly insular history. After leaving the Triennial Convention in 1845, they shunned any ecumenical associations. Over the next century, Southern Baptists contentedly established their own boards, agencies, and programs. Until World War II, they rarely moved out of the South, eventually dominating the region. And to the chagrin of many evangelicals, the SBC refused to join the National Association of Evangelicals.

But there are, alternatively, significant reasons to view Southern Baptists as part of the larger evangelical world. Nineteenth-century historians have viewed the frontier revivalism that swelled Baptists' ranks in the antebellum South as crucial to American evangelicalism's development.[27] Southern Baptists' historic emphasis on both biblical authority and the born-again experience brought together the Reformed and Wesleyan traditions, which many scholars have seen as evangelicalism's two theological sides.[28] Their evangelistic faith and mission emphasis also place Southern Baptists squarely in the evangelical camp. They could belt out Fanny Crosby with the best of them while revivals, altar calls, and Wednesday night prayer suppers became early staples of church life. If they were less apt to participate in the postwar evangelical parachurch movements and organizations, it was because, to coin a phrase, elephants rarely dance with mice.[29] As a denominational superpower, the SBC viewed such networks as incidental to achieving its goals. More recently, the popular media has portrayed Southern Baptists as diverse as Jimmy Carter and Jerry Falwell to be undeniably evangelical, and the culture war that Falwell initiated as a result of Carter's presidency both influenced and was influenced by the Southern Baptist battles.[30] As a result of the protracted struggle, newer generations of Southern Baptists bristled at denominational labels. In fact, when interviewed for this project, younger conservatives and moderates alike were less apt to question their evangelical rather than their Southern Baptist identity, frequently prioritizing the former while bickering over the latter.

Several differences between Southern Baptists and other evangelicals did, however, distinguish the Southern Baptist controversy from the culture wars and are worth noting. First, Southern Baptists did not experience the modernization debates of the 1920s, or certainly not with the same intensity. This meant that while northern and smaller evangelical groups were long accustomed to their sectarian standing, Southern Baptist conservatives and moderates found any marginal position frustrating. In terms of scholarship, prominent historians like James Davison Hunter have analyzed the culture wars as a debate inherited from this earlier period. According to Hunter, conservatives and liberals emerged from the 1920s modernization debate with competing views of moral authority. Conservatives clung to orthodox notions of "external, definable, and transcendent authority," while liberals agreed to "resymbol historic faiths according to the prevailing assumptions of contemporary life." As conservative evangelicals became increasingly politically engaged after the 1960s, the two views collided, and the culture wars ensued.[31] In contrast, Southern Baptists largely accepted the notion of orthodoxy and rejected liberal tendencies as relativism. It was only when far-right conservatives narrowed the parameters of truth that moderates found themselves left behind. Second, and relatedly, the Southern Baptist battles invoked the often neglected middle ground, and the issue of Christian womanhood dominated this middle ground much longer than outside journalists or scholars recognized.[32] By the 1990s, both the media and the academic world had moved on to groups in which debates over homosexuality and abortion superseded related fights over women. In their view, the Southern Baptist contest seemed old-fashioned and dated. Last, another key difference was that Southern Baptists engaged in a struggle for the SBC in which institutional concerns often took center stage in a way that they did not in the culture wars.

Because of these differences, denominational scholars, especially those from the moderate side, have often presented the SBC's postwar struggles as sui generis. But evangelicals have been both northern and southern, rural and urban, establishment and anti-establishment, sectarian and mainstream. Theologically, they have Calvinist and holiness roots.[33] During the 1980s and 1990s, many could be found at Christian Coalition rallies and even a few at Sojourner-supported social justice events. Moreover, the fact that the two denominational camps understood their relationship to the culture wars differently complicated the link between the Southern Baptist battles and the evangelical culture wars. While Southern Baptist conservatives conflated the religious right's fight for American culture with the denominational battles, moderates were more likely to separate the two. The conservative strategy proved crucial, since those prioritizing partisan identity over denominational loyalty could easily access the passion of the culture wars rhetoric, including its antifeminist invectives. At first, during the 1970s and 1980s, Southern Baptist conservatives were subject to those sectarian evangelicals informing the religious right, but as they ascended to denominational power, they began influencing conservative evangelical rhetoric more directly. For them, the two movements coalesced, and over the 1990s, key figures in the religious right, including Falwell, joined the SBC. Not surprisingly, the major players in Southern Baptist conservative life more frequently overlapped with those of the religious right, and disproportionate numbers in the religious right were also from the South.[34]

In speaking of evangelicalism's diversity, the scholar Timothy Smith uses the metaphor of a mosaic or kaleidoscope.[35] Numbering between 13 million and 16 million, Southern Baptists undoubtedly reflect and illumine the multiple pieces of this evangelical kaleidoscope. To fully understand American evangelicalism in the postwar period as well as the new sectarianism that came to dominate the American religious landscape, it is essential to cast our gaze on Southern Baptists.

"A Story to Tell"

The historians David Steinmetz and Grant Wacker insist that the "goal of the historian is to resurrect the dead and let them speak."[36] While many of my subjects are actually living, making this task both more and less daunting, I attempt in this book to record as honestly and as objectively as possible the manifold voices that informed the SBC and its postwar conflict. The qualification "as possible" remains crucial, for as postmodern theory likewise posits, no scholar works from a neutral location. Impartiality is elusive, and at some point, the historian must consider how context shapes understanding. For me, as an American religious historian also grounded in women's studies, women's experience seemed the fitting starting point to explain the Southern Baptist battles and to heed voices that often had gone unheard. This bit of scholarly self-analysis came easily enough. But equally significant, the focus on women resonated with my own background. Like many scholars, I am writing about the people who shaped my early world. Because such self-disclosure carries certain complications, it is necessary to say more about both my relationship to Southern Baptists and how it informed my telling their tale.

In many ways, this study began in the church of my childhood and youth. I grew up in a Southern Baptist family who, like most loyal and faithful Southern Baptists, attended church several times weekly. My experience then was not, contrary to outsiders' assumptions, one of female limitation. As far as my friends and I were concerned, women led our congregation. Their presence pervaded our every activity. They organized our mission groups, taught our Sunday school classes, conducted our spring Bible drills, planned our summer vacation Bible schools, and chaperoned our youth outings. While men preached the sermons and took the offerings during Sunday morning worship, they remained at our periphery. Church meant piling into Mrs. Richardson's brown minivan to pass out "we care" kits at the local children's hospital or nursing home, listening to Mrs. Hopkins and Mrs. Martin spin fascinating tales of missionary life in Africa, and practicing with Linda Love as she prepared our voices and sewed our costumes for the upcoming youth choir musical. It took years for me to realize that while women operated at the center of my church world, when it came to formal leadership, they remained on the institutional fringe.

Similar to many Southern Baptist congregations during the 1970s, a distinctly women's sphere known as the Woman's Missionary Union existed in my church. More than any other program or activity, the WMU and missions defined Southern Baptist women. All Southern Baptist girls, or so it seemed, moved through the WMU's ranks as Southern Baptist women-in-training. My mother led its Girls-in-Action group. Every Wednesday night we read about Southern Baptist missionaries overseas, wrote them letters on their birthdays, prayed over their lists of requests, sent their children "Christmas in August" boxes, and cooked meals from our limited repertoire of Chinese stir-fried rice, Mexican enchiladas, or Russian teacakes, which represented their countries of service. Sometimes a furloughed missionary visited in costume dress and shared her experience of life overseas. The world outside, however exoticized, filled our imaginations. As an Acteen, a member of the WMU program for teenage girls, I attended every Wednesday night gathering in both eager anticipation and self-conscious trepidation of its spring coronation. In an elaborate ceremony of candles, white dresses, capes, scepters, and tiaras, the church WMU president crowned as Southern Baptist queens those who had completed the specified mission projects. At the close of the coronation service, Acteens joined the younger girls and adult women in singing the WMU hymn, "We've a Story to Tell to the Nations." Its words and music together sounded a rousing anthem: "We've a story to tell to the nations, that shall turn their hearts to the right, a story of truth and sweetness, a story of peace and light."

Southern Baptist women did indeed have stories, and telling them was essential to being a good Southern Baptist woman. As with any story shaped and nurtured within a particular community, the narratives I grew up hearing shared key features. Most involved a call from God—or even more personally, Jesus—to perform a particular task or deed. A few evoked deep drama, especially those whose calls involved life-changing transformations—coming to God's saving grace, for example, or a heart-rending surrender to full-time mission work. Whether it be during a Wednesday night prayer meeting, a special revival service, the weekly morning WMU gathering, or even, occasionally, Sunday morning worship, women delivered their stories in the form of soul-stirring, emotion-filled, public testimony. These testimonies reenacted the paradigmatic story of the Gospel. They were intended to lead others to *the Story*. But they also served as models for other women. As part of their mission training, Southern Baptist girls learned the art of storytelling and testimony. They also learned that God called them, too.

On a more informal level, storytelling filled women's conversations in the sort of gossip we overheard from our church mothers. These stories exacted a strict moral code and standard of conduct. They passed judgment on a woman's success or failure as a Christian exemplar, indicating, much to our delight, that pious, teetotaling Southern Baptists did indeed have their scandals and intrigues. They also exhibited, however, a nurturance and compassion for the community. Women drew on story to elicit prayer chains, arrange dinners for a grieving family, or visit a new mother. They exchanged stories with one another in mission circle meetings, during the Sunday morning coffee hour, while minding the church nursery, or when lingering after a service. These narratives informed a distinct subculture. They filled the nooks and crannies of Southern Baptist women's lives. And they taught us what it meant to be a Southern Baptist woman.

As I grew older and reached high school during the early 1980s, I began to discover greater variation within this world. At denominational camps, regional youth retreats, and national Acteens gatherings, I encountered other stories with surprising differences in backgrounds, beliefs, and practices. Simultaneously, I discovered gaps in my own childhood story, which so naturally had placed women at the center of religious power. As the growing denominational conflict moved into the local church, arguments swirled around women's ordination as deacons and ministers. Our county association disfellowshipped one congregation for calling a woman as its senior pastor. My own church was divided over the issue. During this tumultuous time, I questioned my earlier perceptions of women's ecclesial roles, and over the course of my senior year, I decided to distance myself from my Southern Baptist background.

But as I went off to a Methodist college, then to a Presbyterian seminary, and finally to a secular graduate school, I encountered hackneyed stereotypes of Southern Baptist women. These dormant and submissive housewives hardly captured the feisty women of my youth, and I became convinced— Southern Baptists might say convicted—that their story had to be told. In seminary, I wrote a paper portraying women's missions as the battlefield in a war between male leaders determined to strip Southern Baptist women of any autonomy and the WMU leaders who resisted such usurpation. Despite my best efforts, the story I told failed to capture the complicated tensions among women in Southern Baptist life and was as predictable and lopsided as the stereotyped images that I had encountered.

When I revisited the Southern Baptist story for this project, I turned first to the grassroots women I had known as a child. I listened to their voices and tales. Almost immediately, I discovered that "We've a Story to Tell" was gone in more ways than one. At a superficial level, snazzier tunes prevailed, but more surprisingly, the WMU, while continuing to engage the energies of an aging generation, no longer occupied the center of Southern Baptist women's culture. A variety of discrete organizations and groups flourished in its place. For instance, Women's Enrichment Ministry focused on sex-segregated, women-mentoring-women programs. Global Women, a more youthful-looking mission group, had been created by a few former WMU leaders. There was also Baptist Women in Ministry, an organization supporting women in ordained ministerial positions, along with other grassroots groups who were meeting a wide range of needs.

A significant aspect that emerged from their stories was that the denominational conflict had actively involved women, and its legacy continued to affect them. Not all Southern Baptist women were aware of the struggle, but it informed their alliances, networks, and understandings of Christian womanhood. In many ways, the stories that I discovered in researching and writing this book were messier and more muddled than the ones I remembered as a girl or the one narrated in my original paper. But they also proved to be livelier as they revealed the complexity of human impulses in all their nobility and pettiness. While I began my study as a consideration of contemporary Southern Baptist women, my focus soon became the postwar struggle over women's roles and behaviors—or the story behind their stories.

From "A Story to Tell" to Telling a Story

In writing this book, I drew on both field based and textual research. In most cases, the fieldwork preceded archival work and concentrated on conservative and moderate Southern Baptist women's groups and organizations.[37] Over the course of two years, I attended nine women's conferences and retreats; went to half a dozen national meetings, dinners, and gatherings; and participated in the local manifestations of these organizations. I visited various church Bible studies, luncheons, presentations, and programs, participating for six months in a conservative women's homemaking and mothering group. I also went to one Southern Baptist convention meeting and three Cooperate Baptist Fellowship assembly meetings as representative of conservative and moderate life.[38] During this period, I engaged in hundreds of conversations, conducted numerous informal and unstructured interviews, took copious field notes, and collected surveys.[39] My fieldwork revealed that women had been more active in the Southern Baptist controversy than previously recognized and that the rhetoric informed their self-understandings, even at an unconscious level. While this research involving contemporary women appears primarily in the epilogue, it nevertheless guided my archival study, helping me spot clues that I would have overlooked otherwise. It also provided notions, concepts, and ways of being and doing among churchwomen that I was able to trace historically. Toward the end of my research, I conducted written, e-mail, and phone interviews with twenty-three Southern Baptist women prominent during the embattled years. These interviews proved critical to my interpretation.[40]

As for text-based and archival research, I made several visits to the WMU's Alma Hunt Library and Archives in Birmingham and Baylor University's Institute for Oral History. I also made two extended visits to the Southern Baptist Historical Library and Archives in Nashville, one to the archives at the James P. Boyce Centennial Library at Southern Baptist Theological Seminary, and numerous excursions to the A. Webb Roberts Library at Southwestern Baptist Theological Seminary, which happened to be down the street in Fort Worth. In brief, I consulted any primary source that per-tained to women's roles: state convention newspapers and journals; national SBC publications; accounts of the annual convention; seminary programs; official letters and executive minutes from SBC boards, agencies, and committees, including the WMU; videos; interviews; and select personal correspondence. I also paid careful attention to *FOLIO*, the quarterly newsletter of Southern Baptist Women in Ministry (SBWIM). More than any publication, *FOLIO* followed the debates about women's ordination during the 1980s and 1990s.[41]

In her ethnography of the Haitian Vodou priestess Alourdes, Karen McCarthy Brown writes that "whatever else it is, ethnographic research is about human relationships."[42] While my research was not, for the most part, ethnographic, it involved human interaction, and I devoted a disproportionate amount of my energy to cultivating, maintaining, and managing these relationships. Additionally, my archival work remained personal in nature. As I read through the journals, newsletters, and correspondence of numerous Southern Baptist women and their related groups and organizations, I entered their struggles, felt their sorrows, and celebrated their victories.

Every relationship is two-sided, even in academic fieldwork. For my part, I liked the women that I encountered, and many came to be regular correspondents. For their part, they welcomed me into their churches and homes and included me in their families and friendships. We conversed over meals and coffees, in hotel lobbies and retreat centers, on shuttle buses, and once waiting for a plane. Some exchanges were quick, formal, and polite; others were open and invigorating dialogues lasting into the late hours of the night. They involved both haphazard, spontaneous encounters and deliberate, planned meetings. During some of this research, I was pregnant. Women gave me helpful bits of motherly advice, asked after my health, and included me on their prayer lists. A few even sent me baby gifts.

Relationships also involve similarity and difference. In attempting to understand these women, I exhibited a certain presentation of self. My pregnancy in a culture celebrating motherhood and family undoubtedly made some conservative women more comfortable with me. Growing up Southern Baptist likewise brought certain advantages. I knew the language of call. I could sing the old hymns by heart. I was familiar with the newer praise tunes. I laughed at women's jokes. And I could quickly swap tales of being a Girls-in-Action, Acteen queen, or "Lottie Moon convert" in the annual church Christmas pageant. This camaraderie inclined women to share their stories, but it also carried expectations. Some women assumed that I would write a hagiographic piece, while others wanted me to be clear about my

Southern Baptist leanings and loyalties. One leader questioned my unwillingness to participate more fully in her group, and she interpreted my lack of commitment as heretical to *the Story*. Several women that I contacted for interviews wanted to inspect my writing before they committed themselves to my project.

Ethnographers often speak of the difficult liminal space in which they find themselves when the boundary between participant-observer and informant breaks down.[43] The religionist Thomas Tweed, though, offers an alternate trope. In his study of Cuban Catholic immigrants to Miami, he acknowledges that his own sympathies were far to the left of the exiled community's anticommunist fervor. Moreover, he was white and not actively Catholic. Despite such differences, a few years into his fieldwork he found himself lighting a candle to Our Lady of Charity, Cuba's national patroness, and spontaneously whispering the prayer *Virgen Santisma, salva a Cuba*. In analyzing this surprise occurrence, Tweed questions the notion of in-between or liminal space. "The major difficulty with this view," he says, "is that it freezes the action at a single point in the midst of a complex series of interpretative moments" and thus "confuses one instant with the whole." Because "interpretation is more processive, and more complex," Tweed suggests the metaphor of movement.[44] As he describes it, researchers move back and forth or across, from their own stories to those of their subjects, crossing the terrain "between inside and outside, fact and value, evidence and narrative, the living and the dead, here and there, us and them."[45]

This movement of back and forth and across more accurately portrays my own research, archival as well as field-based. Whether I was reading about a WMU woman in the 1950s or interviewing a woman ordained in the 1980s, I moved from moments of distance and dissonance to moments of collaboration and clarity. The further I delved into my research, the more frequently the feelings of collaboration, even mutuality, occurred. In the movement across, I was forced to reevaluate my own history and relationships. Still, as Tweed also concludes, the scholar, however changed, consistently returns to her or his own position and story, separate from those of her or his subjects. There, I discovered, a sense of estrangement remained. One incident during my research was particularly revealing. A women's ministry leader at a large conservative Southern Baptist church in a small Texas town had taken an entire day to show me her church, introduce me to those active in women's ministry, and talk to me about the development of the program. When I thanked her for her help and commented on her open and welcoming spirit, she responded, "We are so excited that a woman scholar from a liberal institution would be interested in what we have to say." Her words reminded me that the story I was telling was not my own.

Each of us, scholars and subjects alike, possesses a storehouse of stories, symbols, and beliefs that we construct, arrange, and rearrange in various ways. The purpose of my research has not been to place my set of meanings over and against that of my subjects, as placing the understandings of Southern Baptists against one another has been challenging enough. My purpose, rather, has been to move as deeply into the Southern Baptist experience as possible, to listen to voices that have gone largely unheard, and finally, to render moments of illumination in language that would help us see how and why concepts of womanhood functioned as such divisive and threatening truths.

Interpreting the Past

The attack of the emerging religious right of the 1970s on feminism, women's liberation, and the ERA as threats to motherhood and the nuclear family stoked the Southern Baptist debate over womanhood, an age-old debate whose flames had flickered intermittently across the years, only to rage at certain transitional moments. These moments are important to consider.[46] Equally significant, though less obvious, is how Southern Baptists interpreted them, and their different interpretations became a key element in my research. During my interviews and forays into the archives, I discovered that conservatives and moderates were both scrambling to reimagine their past, privileging certain movements, events, and historical periods over others, arranging and rearranging them in various patterns to fit the situation at hand. As the debate over womanhood became more intense, each side elevated particular models as basic to Baptist identity.[47] With close to 400 years of historic Baptist life, there was no shortage of examples from which to glean. How Southern Baptists interpreted and presented their past is crucial to understanding their turbulent postwar story.

Moderates who supported a more progressive stance on women, particularly women's ordination, often focused on Baptists' historic roots.[48] Baptists trace their beginnings to the dissenting movements of early seventeenth-century England. Alongside believer's baptism, "she-preacher[s]" set Baptists apart.[49] Seventeenth-century English clergy complained, for example, not only that Baptists allowed "saucie boys, bold botching taylors, and other most audacious, illiterate mechanicks to run out of their shops into a pulpit" but that "bold, impudent huswifes . . . prate an hour or more."[50] Although in the New World, seventeenth-century Baptist women did not practice the same public roles as they had in England, the Great Awakening revivals led to more egalitarian congregations than that of the Congregationalist majority, and for multiple reasons, including women's roles, Baptists continued to be marked as a fringe movement.

As the number of Baptists in eighteenth-century America increased, they formed multiple groups and movements. Scholars often speak of two dominant factions: Regular Baptists and Separate Baptists.[51] Regular Baptists were theological Calvinists. They were liturgical in worship style, and since they viewed ministry as a professional calling, their clergy was overwhelmingly educated and male. Not surprisingly, women rarely participated as leaders in worship and public church life. In contrast to Regular Baptists, who were mostly part of the Eastern Establishment, Separate Baptists populated the frontier. They, in large part, benefited greatly from the Great Awakening revivals, which became even more distinctive in the South. Like other revivalist groups, Separate Baptists boasted a highly spontaneous and enthusiastic worship. Ministry was charismatic, and women as well as children and slaves exhorted, testified, witnessed, and prayed aloud. In some congregations, women and slaves participated and voted in church business meetings, and records indicate that women were ordained as deaconesses. Moderates often referred to Separatist Baptist women as preachers, a term not used readily in the period itself.[52] In turn, conservatives insisted that moderates' historic claims about women, dependent as they were on feminist interpretations, were greatly exaggerated.

Greatly exaggerated or not, any hints of racial and gendered egalitarianism in the antebellum South did prove short-lived. By the early nineteenth century, the South's plantation establishment was anxious to impose order on the unruly frontier. This desire only intensified as the issue of slavery became more controversial. From about 1790 to 1830, southern evangelicalism underwent a taming process, and as part of this process, Regular Baptists and Separate Baptists merged.[53] Differences remained, fueling underlying tensions, but the hierarchies that came to characterize the South prevailed. Submission, one of the hallmarks of Victorian womanhood, assumed special status in a region whose livelihood depended on slavery, hierarchy, and order, thus giving rise to the myth of the southern lady.[54] In 1845, Baptists in the South split from their northern counterparts over slavery, forming the Southern Baptist Convention.

The story of Southern Baptist women has been told largely as the story of the WMU and missions.[55] Both conservatives and moderates affirmed the significant contribution of women to missions, though they disagreed over the legacy of this relationship. An example is the "auxiliary" in the WMU's full title: Woman's Missionary Union, Auxiliary to the SBC. Conservatives interpreted it to mean submission, so that the WMU, in their view, was intended as a helpmate to the male-led mission boards.[56] Moderates, on the other hand, and especially more progressive moderate women, interpreted the inclusion of "auxiliary" as a necessary ploy by the WMU's founders to gain acceptance from denominational leaders.[57]

There is truth to both interpretations. The SBC male leadership initially resisted any denomination-wide women's mission group. They believed that such an organization would pull too much from the denomination's limited monetary resources as well as assume an independence ill-befitting the female sex. Those women who pushed for a denominational organization assuaged the men's first fear through their fund-raising abilities. From 1845 to 1888, during the first forty-three years of the SBC's existence, women basically kept the convention's Home and Foreign Missions boards financially afloat by networking in local mission circles and state chapters. The women also went to great lengths to counter any accusations toward independence. In contrast to women's mission agencies in the North, they insisted that the male-led boards should continue to appoint and fund missionaries directly. The role of Southern Baptist women, they assured men, would remain one of support. This strategy worked. When the all-male messengers to the 1888 Richmond convention narrowly passed a resolution to "encourage" women in their mission enterprises, the women waiting in the wings immediately voted to form the Woman's Missionary Union, Auxiliary to the SBC. "Disclaiming all intention of independent action," they outlined their primary goals as "stimulating the missionary spirit" and "collecting funds."[58]

The SBC leaned heavily on the WMU. While the SBC entered the twentieth century with few financial resources, no central headquarters, and a president who did little beyond preside at the annual convention meeting, the WMU boasted a Baltimore office, publishing facility, executive staff, and traveling team. The WMU's success, particularly in finances, gave the women leverage. Though they could not appoint missionaries, they started a training school for women and lobbied the mission boards to do their bidding. Despite the SBC's objections, WMU leaders insisted on allocating their women's annual offerings. Scholars have noted also that the WMU pushed much further on social and ecumenical issues than their male counterparts, emulating Methodist and other evangelical women in their bid toward greater usefulness.[59] On behalf of mission education and mission fundraising, Southern Baptist women sometimes gained access to the local church pulpit and, in 1929, the convention podium. It is little wonder that Southern Baptist women seeking ordination looked to the WMU's founders as their foremothers.

But the story was not as seamless as later women sometimes presented it. First, the WMU suffered from internal tensions. Not all women were comfortable with what they perceived to be an increasingly independent, even radical, course. Many early WMU leaders refused to speak in front of men, and as early as 1906, the WMU's longtime secretary and founder, Annie Armstrong, left the organization over its establishment of a training school. Moreover, in contrast to that of Methodist women, who were also far more likely to advocate women's right to vote, the WMU's social programming was fairly anemic and rarely carried out in local circles.[60] The last, and perhaps the least-touted, part of the story was that as the SBC organized, it was no longer as dependent on women's fundraising power; thus the men slowly pulled the reins on the WMU. After the 1920s, the WMU and its women began to downplay their rhetoric of independence and more readily followed the SBC's lead. They handed over the training school to the denomination, relinquished any allocation of offerings, and ceased most ecumenical activities. Like their male counterparts, they assumed a position of compromise by deliberately avoiding any controversial issue, especially related to women.

On one hand, conservatives decried male denominationalists' attempts at compromise as inviting theological and cultural liberalism into the SBC, while on the other hand, they celebrated the position of WMU women as one of female obedience and submission. Too many contemporary Southern Baptist women had veered, in their view, from Baptist tradition, and that number now included the WMU.[61] Moderates, in turn, pointed to an early golden age. What both sides often failed to indicate or emphasize was that in Baptist life, Christian womanhood, or whatever Southern Baptists might call that ideal dictating women's roles and behaviors, was never tied to one fixed and stable historical reality. Baptist notions of womanhood existed in the plural and developed amidst a swirl of debates. They represented a dynamic process, absorbing and reconfiguring different ideologies, movements, actualities, and ideals. Most Southern Baptists heeded a more traditionally conservative or conserving impulse, but when it came to women's roles, even the concept of submission held multiple meanings and realities.

I argue against the conclusions of some historians and about the neglect of others as to how the debate over women interacted far more regularly with other theological, institutional, and cultural conflicts, thereby helping trigger the postwar contest. Nevertheless, the question might fairly be posed as to how I am interpreting Southern Baptists' past as a way to understand the postwar period and their battles. Where might I overlap and agree with conservative and moderate interpretations? More specifically, what were those other conflicts and tensions, and how did they engage the issue of women?

Well into the twentieth century, as I understand it, the SBC persisted as a local, nonintegrated religious vitality in which a degree of variety and difference flourished. While a well-educated minority elite occupied the denomination's highest offices, the vast majority were impoverished, rural folk who worshipped in small country churches and congregations. They possessed neither the financial resources to contribute to the SBC nor the mind-set to access programs as basic as Sunday school.[62] Like other organizations, the WMU had difficulty penetrating rural congregations, many of whom saw the mission circles as representative of the "New Woman." The SBC's convention-style governance also reinforced a certain level of democratic diversity. On political issues, for instance, most Southern Baptists were conservative, yellow-dog Democrats who supported Jim Crow segregation, though social progressives, populists, and others of more dissenting positions, including a few women lobbying for the vote, did make their way into the fold.[63]

Theologically, the bulk of Southern Baptists held to a modified Calvinism, which allowed for a certain degree of human agency. Hard-core Calvinists, however, managed to stand alongside staunch advocates of Wesleyan free will, with the latter flourishing more in the towns and cities of the New South and being more open to women's public roles in the church. In fact, social mobility could have made middle-class Baptist congregations more likely to accept this theology. When it came to related ecclesial matters, Southern Baptists squabbled over almost every aspect of congregational life: the meaning of conversion, the appropriate age for baptism, rebaptism, the adoption and use of confessions of faith, associational involvement, and open versus closed communion. Although they wholeheartedly affirmed the Bible as their foremost authority, they disagreed as to the relationship between the outer witness of scripture and the inner witness of the Spirit. Once again, women lobbying for roles of authority in the church, including missions, emphasized the call of the Spirit and beckoned their daughters to listen. Finally, traditional Baptist ideals concerning soul competency and the priesthood of the believer often clashed with the actual power and authority of charismatic pulpiteers as numerous churches flouted denominational strictures and seminary credentials in favor of a more fervent worship and heart-educated clergy.[64] Only this time around, women called to witnessing, testifying, and prophesying did not always find welcome in these congregations. The past, it seemed, did not always predict the future.[65]

If most of the SBC's organizational efforts during this period failed to reach the local church, officials did lay some groundwork for the postwar era. The SBC's Commission on Efficiency in 1914, for instance, led to a much-needed Executive Board, denominational headquarters, and centralized infrastructure. The WMU's plan for the Cooperative Program, which the Commission on Efficiency adopted, streamlined churches' denominational offerings. Equally significant, in their desire to create a greater sense of denominational identity, SBC leaders stressed personal morality and piety as sources of unity. As the historian Bill Leonard puts it, being Southern Baptist in the early twentieth century meant no drinking, no gambling, and no dancing. It also meant praying, reading the Bible, and memorizing scripture. By elevating these practices, Leonard says, denominationalists presented the SBC as existing primarily on the spiritual level. Likewise, they drew on evangelical zeal and passion in an attempt to keep the churches connected and committed. The SBC, as they represented it, was a vast mission enterprise dedicated to saving souls. Bickering and infighting, church officials emphasized, impeded the work of conversion. It also curtailed financial solvency.[66]

Women were crucial to both. During the SBC's first 100 years, the denomination and its mission boards operated in a constant state of near-bankruptcy. Women saved the day, time and time again. They financially supported the denomination's mission force from home and populated it as missionaries abroad, but as soon as they tried to move outside missions and apply their skills elsewhere, they found the doors tightly shut. Missions was as much a limiting as a liberating impulse for women who acted as creative subjects bounded simultaneously by institutional politics and social trends. As the SBC moved into the postwar era of prosperity, women followed the new domesticity of the period and gave up many of their previous privileges toward autonomy, authority, and power, all, of course, for the sake of missions. To come full circle, this move made the counterculture movements of the late 1960s and 1970s feel even more disruptive and disturbing.

Overview

This book's cultural hinge is the period after World War II. Chapters 1 and 2 consider the years leading to the struggle, from 1945 to 1978. Chapter 1 shows that after the war, Southern Baptists completed their move from a local, nonintegrated religious vitality to a corporate culture of compromise and efficiency. By emphasizing financial prosperity and organizational restructuring, leaders grew the SBC into the largest Protestant denomination nationwide. A period of optimism prevailed. But as modern science, civil rights, feminism, and other changes penetrated the South, a sense of anxiety, fear, and confusion crept into the denomination. During the 1960s, SBC executives found it increasingly difficult to contain tensions. Issues over biblical inerrancy and theological orthodoxy initially seemed to pull the denomination apart, but they were largely driven by a sense of social unrest, which escalated when the first wave of Southern Baptist women were ordained. Chapter 2 looks carefully at several events over the 1970s that served as precursors to 1979, concluding with the 1978 Consultation on Women in Church-Related Vocations, sponsored by eleven SBC agencies. It claims that by downplaying such events and focusing more exclusively on theological issues, scholars have overlooked how gendered ideas about women, particularly women's ordination, helped trigger the post-1979 contest.

Chapter 3 examines the struggle's beginning years, from 1979 to 1984. To conservatives' minds, the calls for denominational loyalty and consensus that had enabled the SBC's growth had also inculcated a dangerous liberalism. Conservatives needed a means to identify and expel those dangerous liberal elements and tendencies. Conservative leaders initially energized their congregations with cries for biblical inerrancy. But as inerrancy proved increasingly ambiguous and the culture wars escalated, they more consciously linked liberal hermeneutics to other social ills, essentializing the feminist movement to resist changing roles for women. At this point, moderates scrambled to organize and mount a defense. While SBWIM organized as a lobbying group for women's ordination and joined the moderate movement by default, many moderate leaders were loath to address the controversial issue. This shows how internally divided moderates were. Some had inherited that tradition of accommodation and compromise; others, like the organizers of SBWIM, saw themselves as dissenters, carrying forth a prophetic vision.

Chapters 4 and 5 explore conservatives and moderates from the struggle's climactic years to the ultimate symbol of conservative victory: the 1998 and 2000 amendments to the Baptist Faith and Message. Chapter 4 reveals how conservatives used women's roles as a primary means to determine otherness and power. It examines the onslaught of forced resignations, firings, and systematic purges. Chapter 5 turns to moderates and their struggle to respond to the conservative agenda. Against conservatives, most moderates argued for freedom. While they cited the Baptist principles of soul competency and local church autonomy, they also interpreted freedom within the new secular context of increasing pluralism and abundant choice. Women's roles, practices, and behaviors were symbolic of this new economy, but moderates' rhetoric of freedom and choice often failed to offer any real opportunity or difference for women.[67]

In each chapter, I highlight women's voices and experiences, weaving the WMU's struggles into the narrative to show how the debate over women coalesced with other theological and cultural issues. Contrary to popular assumptions and stereotypes, women were active in the struggle. As the WMU fragmented, conservative women involved in local women's programs fostered a notion of complementarian womanhood as a means to promote supportive female communities and affirm submission, while also negotiating submission's varied meanings. SBWIM pressed for the ordination and acceptance of women as equal partners in ministry, preaching from the center pulpit, performing the ritual of baptism, and filling diverse positions of authority in congregational life. The shifts within feminism and its transition from the 1970s to the 1980s were crucial to these profeminist Southern Baptists, who avoided the earlier, more confrontational and anticapitalist versions of the movement.

An epilogue draws on my field-based research to examine the status of women after 2000. As I discovered, even after the lines had been drawn, the institutions purged, and victory declared, tensions over women's practices and behaviors in conservative and moderate life persisted, with women both participating in and resisting the infighting. Preaching women still sometimes felt as if they were prodigal daughters, while conservative women continued to negotiate the tenet of gracious submission. In the end, theirs is a story of bold, lively, and colorful characters who experience intense joy and deep sorrow as they search for meaning in the religious roles they have assumed.

1

Into the Center Pulpit

A DANGEROUS DREAM

On August 9, 1964, Watts Street Baptist Church in Durham, North Carolina, ordained Addie Davis to the gospel ministry—the first ordination of a woman by a Southern Baptist church. It came well ahead of many mainstream Protestant bodies and only one year after the publication of *The Feminine Mystique* by Betty Friedan.

Davis was a well-educated, professional, and single woman from a long line of Virginian Baptists. She grew up in Covington Baptist Church, the very church that her great-great-grandfather had pastored. From an early age, Davis felt called to preach. Speaking in the measured Virginian brogue that also characterized her sermons, she later narrated her story: "I was baptized between the ages of eight and nine. I have, as long as I remember, had a very strong religious interest. As a child I felt a call to preach, but women were not preachers so I never expressed this openly."[1] It took Davis years to follow her sense of call. She graduated in 1938 from Meredith College, a Baptist women's college in Raleigh, North Carolina, with a degree in psychology. She served briefly as the education director for a local Baptist congregation and then became the dean of women at Alderson Broaddus College, a Baptist school in West Virginia. When her father died four years later, she left her academic post to help her mother run the family furniture business. During this time, Davis became critically ill and vowed that "if I was permitted to live, I would do what I'd always felt in my heart I should do, which was to be a preacher."[2]

In 1960, at the age of forty-three, Davis matriculated at Southeastern Baptist Theological Seminary. When her home pastor in Covington made it clear that he would not recommend her or any woman for ordination, she turned to Watts Street Baptist. Davis knew Watts Street's pastor, Warren

Carr, as both he and Watts Street had achieved something of a reputation for their civil rights activism. In recalling his conversations with her, Carr said she was actually unaware that no other Southern Baptist congregation had ordained a woman. Davis's strong sense of call swayed Carr, who insisted that "she belonged in the center pulpit, according to our tradition, to proclaim the gospel on the Lord's Day."[3]

One might assume that her ordination would create a storm of controversy across the Southern Baptist Convention (sbc). After all, during their first 100 years, Southern Baptists had debated almost every change in women's denominational and ecclesial status, from their organizing for missions in 1888 to their being seated as convention messengers in 1918. In 1929, the issue of women's public speaking practically brought the annual convention in Memphis to a halt. Reaction to Davis's ordination, though immediate, was also limited. Carr reported about fifty angry letters to Watts Street over the occasion, and Davis puzzled why people as far away as California would bother to write, one even denouncing her as a "child of the Devil." As an unmarried woman, she must have found the letter instructing her to learn from her husband rather humorous. But by and large, the protests ended there. Like Davis, those who participated in the 1964 service remained largely unaware of the event's historic significance.[4] The sbc's official news service, *Baptist Press*, simply ran a single story announcing the ordination with the veiled conclusion that "women graduates of Southern Baptist seminaries usually enter church vocations in education or music, become teachers or are appointed as unordained missionaries."[5] At the 1965 convention in Dallas, the topic was not raised, at least from the floor. Even more astounding, when asked in 1966 about women's ordination, Marie Mathis, president of the Woman's Missionary Union (wmu), insisted, "I've never heard of a woman wanting to be a minister, and I've been connected with women's organizations in this faith since 1938. . . . I think it is women's intuitive feeling that ministers should be men."[6]

Scholars have explained the event as an anomaly or aberration in Southern Baptist life.[7] Davis was an unassuming and modest personality who dreamed of a pulpit rather than a debating chamber, and when she could not find a Southern Baptist placement, she moved to Vermont. Out of sight meant out of mind. Still, one is hard-pressed to accept that the major milestone for Southern Baptist women in the twentieth century could be so easily forgotten. It seems more likely that Mathis and the wmu were intentionally avoiding any hint of controversy. Like their male counterparts, wmu officials operated from the center. If Davis's ordination became the symbol of progress for Southern Baptist women, as it was later touted, its downplaying also embodied the spirit of compromise that marked Southern Baptist life during the 1950s and early 1960s. By 1966, though, compromise was in jeopardy. The sbc was mired in an inerrancy debate, and despite the wmu's best efforts, women were soon to be implicated. In fact, the controversy in 1971 surrounding the second ordination of a Southern Baptist woman by a Southern Baptist church stood in stark contrast to that of Davis's ordination seven years earlier. The second ordination revealed the extent to which compromise had been eroded as well as the presence of the new interpretive lens of feminism.

This chapter considers the years from 1945 to 1972. It shows that the prosperity and nationalization of the South after World War II provided Southern Baptists with newfound wealth and middle-class status. Riding this wave of success, denominational leaders adopted a corporate model of church that kept the sbc growing and expanding. They emphasized financial solvency and organizational restructuring while encouraging the downplaying of theological differences and social tensions. During this period, institutional loyalty usurped democratic diversity and partisan identities. The strategy worked as long as optimism prevailed; however, changes in both southern and American culture eventually brought a sense of anxiety and fear to Southern Baptists. Longtime sbc statesmen as well as wmu officials could not tame the forces of evolutionary science, civil rights, feminism, and the countercultural movements of the 1960s. By the decade's end, they were hard-pressed to pit bureaucratic issues against biblical debates or questions concerning women. The interaction of these ecclesial and cultural dynamics shattered the synthesis that held the denomination together.[8]

Regional Change

Economic prosperity transformed the postwar southern landscape and, with it, Southern Baptists.[9] Two events served as catalysts. First, while southerners had watched falling cotton prices throughout the first part of the century, technological innovations both diversified crop production and revived agricultural production. Second, a large nonunionized workforce alongside a mild climate and low cost of living made the lower states attractive to the developing military industrial complex. Seemingly overnight, the South, which had lagged well behind the North in almost every measurable category of stability and success, found itself a vital part of the burgeoning American economy.[10]

Related developments marked the "newer" New South and the nationalization of Dixie. Industrialization led to the rapid urbanization of the South's population. In 1940, 65 percent of southerners lived in rural areas and 35 percent resided in urban settings. By 1960, more than half, 57 percent, claimed urban residence. The 1970 figures reversed the 1940 ones: 64 percent resided in urban areas whereas 36 percent lived in rural ones.[11] Better modes of transportation that made travel far more efficient were integral to urbanization. The increase in paved roads along with the expanded federal highway system connected southern towns and cities to one another as well as to the rest of the country. Television made southerners more immediately aware of nationwide events and trends. Perhaps even more telling, southerners could actually afford the latest technology and trappings of consumer culture. In 1940, southerners earned 2 cents to every nonsouthern dollar. By 1968, they were receiving 69 cents.[12] As more southerners became part of the American middle class, they also took advantage of educational opportunities, which meant greater status and wealth.[13]

Over this period, migration patterns reversed themselves as well. During the Depression, southerners had left their homes, heading north and west in record numbers. After the war, however, increasing numbers of nonsoutherners moved south to find better jobs. At the same time, southerners continued to leave the region for education and vocational purposes. With the growth of a national economy, physical mobility and movement across regional boundaries increased. Starting in the mid-1960s, the South also experienced transnational migration. As immigration once again opened, Vietnamese and other Southeast Asian refugees frequently chose to relocate in the burgeoning Sunbelt, which included the South with the Southwest. They were soon followed by Hispanics, Middle Easterners, Africans, and others who complicated the divisive dynamics of what had been viewed as a society composed strictly of blacks and whites.

Southern Baptists benefited as much as any group from the postwar boom. As congregations became increasingly white collar and middle class, congregants filled their offering plates. Suddenly, after a century of near-bankruptcy, the SBC and its agencies found their coffers overflowing. Simultaneously, a stately group of silver-haired, golden-tongued, and grey-suited men entered the SBC's upper echelons. They inherited the denomination's highest offices from respected elders like Austin Crouch, James Gambrell, and E. Y. Mullins, who had struggled valiantly simply to keep the SBC afloat. The new generation of leadership acquired a variety of names: genteel oligarchs, organization men, and new denominationalists. Most of them had been educated at Southern Baptist Theological Seminary in Louisville, and together they formed a tight cadre that dominated the SBC's politics, governed its agencies and boards, ran its seminaries, and defined its policies well into the 1970s. Their tenures were extensive and noteworthy: James Sullivan headed the Sunday School Board from 1954 to 1974; Baker Cauthen led the Foreign Mission Board from 1954 to 1979; Porter Routh beat his record, standing as secretary-treasurer of the SBC executive board from 1951 to 1979. He inherited the position from Duke McCall, who then served as Southern Seminary's president from 1951 to 1982, an unprecedented thirty-one years. The tenure of Alma Hunt at the WMU from 1945 to 1974 matched that of her male colleagues, with whom she worked in tandem. Together, they ushered in a new era.

The Corporate Church

Under the governance of this genteel oligarchy, Southern Baptists moved from a local, nonintegrated, lived religious vitality to that of a corporate sect.[14] According to the SBC's sesquicentennial chronicler, Jesse Fletcher, World War II cultivated in American business and industry a "strong organizational awareness and a commitment of corporate efficiency."[15] The South was also central to big business and the burgeoning national economy. Reflecting and accommodating their new cultural environment, denominationalists adopted a corporate model of church.[16] Several strategies proved crucial to their success.

First, they prioritized organizational restructuring. In the fifteen years after World War II, the SBC established a plethora of new commissions, committees, and foundations along with an interagency council to coordinate their varied tasks and services.[17] In the mid-1950s, both the executive committee and the Sunday School Board hired outside management consultants whose recommendations for greater bureaucratic efficiency were far-reaching. One recommendation led to a second related strategy: programmatic unity. Through the Sunday School Board, the WMU, and other agencies, the SBC provided local congregations with a standardized slate of age-appropriate organizations and accompanying program material. It urged them to adopt a convention calendar that filled the weeks and months with events and activities. Unlike in years past, Southern Baptist congregations, eager to compete with their Protestant neighbors, grabbed all that Nashville sent their way.[18] By the 1950s, growing up Southern Baptist meant not only a series of moral no's but Wednesday "Royal Ambassadors and

Girls Auxiliary, revivals in the fall and spring, and Vacation Bible School in the summer."[19] As the sociologist Nancy Ammerman observes, even diversity in worship lessened: "Although Southern Baptists vigorously claimed to be a 'nonliturgical' denomination, there was a liturgy as predictable as in any church with a prayer book. Like the Latin Mass, it provided a universalizing experience for those who participated in it."[20] Southern Baptists could travel from their own church to another sbc-related one and find the "familiar feel of home."[21] During this period, organizational restructuring and programmatic unity became a primary means to keeping the Southern Baptist family connected and intact.

A third strategy of the corporate model, somewhat more vague and difficult to pinpoint, promoted a style of leadership that downplayed any controversy, whether doctrinal or political in nature. While a basic theological and cultural conservatism had dominated Southern Baptist life, Southern Baptists never represented one tradition or persuasion. Variety had posed challenges as Southern Baptists bickered over differences, but in former days, the main struggle was simply to keep the denomination solvent and afloat. Now, as sbc executives expanded the denomination, they felt the pressure more than ever to downplay doctrinal precision and democratic diversity. Compromise, accommodation, and institutional loyalty guided denominationalists' decision-making, and they carefully steered a middle course in all of their endeavors. James Sullivan, president of the Sunday School Board, insisted, "The most basic principle of administration for any [sbc] agency or institution, therefore, is that it must operate at the center of its constituency. A true leader is one with skill who will never identify himself with either extreme group."[22] Denominationalists quite often treated the sbc as a big business. The bottom line was to keep the company growing, prosperous, and moving forward.

And yet these leaders were perceived as more than just organization men. A fourth strategy was that they constructed, in the words of Ammerman, "a remarkable bridge between the world of past and present, between the efficiency of the bureaucracy and the inspiration of the pulpit."[23] As denominational agents, they tirelessly traversed the states of the sbc, addressing local congregations, associational and state meetings, Ridgecrest and Glorieta camp assemblies, various retreats, and the annual convention. When these leaders spoke, they spoke with the evangelistic zeal and missionary passion that Southern Baptists felt to be their own.[24] In other words, the new generation mastered the old rhetoric of personal morality, piety, and evangelism, or what some historians refer to as the language of Zion.[25] As Ammerman describes them, "They were respected as fine Southern gentlemen, looked up to as outstanding pulpiteers, and depended upon for the inspiration that kept missionaries volunteering and support money flowing." They stirred Southern Baptists to response and reassured them of God's presence in their lives.[26] Southern Baptists accepted the new corporate model because in its quest for numbers and growth, they heard the echoes of revivalism.

By almost every measurable statistic, the corporate model demonstrated astounding success, particularly on the financial front, as Southern Baptists gave generously to the Cooperative Program. In 1941, it reported $7.8 million in revenues, representing only a slight increase over the previous decade. Within twenty years, it had jumped to $84 million. By 1971, it was $160.5 million.[27] As a result, programs such as Advance, A Million More in Fifty Four, and the Thirty Thousand Movement touted an incredible number of lives saved, baptisms performed, churches planted, and members gained. Within twenty years, Southern Baptists nearly doubled in number. In 1946, the SBC counted approximately 26,000 churches with 5.8 million members. In 1964, it boasted 33,000 churches with 10.3 million members. By 1972, it was 12 million members strong.[28]

Growth also included geographic expansion. Southern Baptists had participated in the great migration of the Depression. As they moved north and west, few found churches to their liking, so they founded their own fellowships and communities. Initially independent, these churches attempted to re-create Southern Baptist life. As early as 1940, a group of fourteen such churches formed the Southern Baptist Convention of California. In 1942, the SBC recognized the California messengers at the annual convention, an act that inflamed northern Baptists, who saw the SBC as violating long-agreed-upon territorial boundaries. In 1950, however, the Northern Baptist Convention changed its name to the American Baptist Convention, and the SBC moved forward, holding its annual convention in Chicago. By 1960, Southern Baptist churches dotted every state, and by 1972, each state had either its own or a shared convention.[29]

As Southern Baptists grew in members, churches, organizations, programs, and status, they called for more congregational ministers and denominational administrators, demanding not only an increase in numbers but greater professionalization as well. Urban and suburban churches with their middle-class congregations wanted full-fledged church staffs who possessed credentials and specializations. With its increasing revenues, the SBC established two new seminaries. In 1950, Southeastern Baptist Theological Seminary in Wake Forest, North Carolina, opened its doors. Seven years later, Midwestern Baptist Theological Seminary in Kansas City, Kansas, followed. In 1946, the SBC elevated the Baptist Bible Institute in New Orleans to New Orleans Baptist Theological Seminary, and in 1949, it assumed full ownership and control of Golden Gate Baptist Theological Seminary in northern California. Within a decade, the SBC went from two seminaries, Southern Baptist Theological Seminary in Louisville and Southwestern Baptist Theological Seminary in Fort Worth, to six. In addition, two of the four new seminaries fell outside southern borders, with Golden Gate as far west as possible.

In 1955, the "Catholic church of the South," as some dubbed the SBC, became the largest and most wealthy Protestant denomination in the United States. In this respect, Southern Baptists became a national symbol, as much American as they were southern. Their success, prosperity, and optimism embodied the patriotism of the 1950s, an unprecedented time of conservatism and unity in American life. On the flip side, there was also a sense of security, even smugness, that proved tenuous to both Southern Baptists and America at large.[30] And by the decade's end, the SBC was starting to show signs of vulnerability. The spectacular growth, which had enabled unprecedented success, now made the denomination increasingly unwieldy. Its organization men needed to make quick bureaucratic decisions that frequently worked against Southern Baptists' slow-moving congregational policy and democratic-based governance. Those at the top sometimes attempted to bypass the old system, often to their peril. Not surprisingly, grassroots Southern Baptists began to feel disconnected from Nashville.

During the 1960s, as the SBC encountered a bewildering plurality of ideas and movements, the historic penchant for denominational compromise turned to controversy. Questions emerged regarding how much diversity, or as some pronounced it, liberalism, Southern Baptists would tolerate. Differences that had once been minimized assumed new, more menacing forms. At first, the controversies seemed strictly biblical or theological in nature, but it soon became apparent that they were entangled with deep-seated cultural issues involving race and gender.

Biblical Debates

In 1958, Southern Seminary dismissed a group of thirteen dissident professors. The dominant factors appeared to be theological liberalism and the institutional control of scholarly ideas.[31] While Southern's president, Duke McCall, felt that he had prevented a potential maelstrom in letting the professors go, the incident proved as much a beginning as an end, for both the seminary and the denomination. Most of the professors went to Southeastern. One Old Testament scholar, Ralph Elliott, escaped the purge at Southern by leaving a year earlier for the newly established Midwestern. Four years later, however, he found himself embroiled in a much larger controversy.[32]

Friends described Elliott as a gentle scholar and loyal Southern Baptist inadvertently caught in the crossfire of denominational politics.[33] Broadman Press, the publication wing of the SBC Sunday School Board, issued Elliott's *The Message of Genesis* in 1961. In the preface, Elliott announced that he was seeking God's truth in light of the vexing questions posed by scientific advances and evolutionary theory. In the text itself, he endorsed some of the latest historical critical methods, suggesting, for instance, the possibilities of a symbolic reading of Genesis 1–11. As he exegeted the creation stories, he set them in their historical context, concluding that they revealed more about the nature of God as Creator than the creation itself.

Elliott's commentary sparked a debate that grew into a denomination-wide furor, with state convention newspapers fanning the controversy's fires until it consumed the 1962 annual convention, one marked by old-fashioned hooting and hollering. A number of messengers came to the meeting decrying Elliott's book as "poison" and Elliott as having undermined the scriptural integrity and infallibility that Southern Baptists held sacred. Led by Texas pastor K. O. Owen, they demanded Elliott's firing. Rallying to his defense was a smaller cadre of Southern Baptist professors, pastors, and laypeople who felt to Elliott more like "individual faculty here and there."[34] These individuals argued for a degree of modern hermeneutics under the guidance of Christ and the inspiration of the Holy Spirit. They, too, spoke of Baptist tradition by employing the language of soul competency, the theological principle that stresses the individual accountability of each person before God. In the words of one Elliott supporter, though, the "question of justification for a professor in Old Testament was not the agenda of the power people." Organization men worried more over the potential financial fallout that such conflict would cause. As executive secretary-treasurer of the SBC, Porter Routh demanded that Midwestern's president "settle this thing" lest it "cost us millions of dollars in the Lottie Moon offering," the largest source of funding for foreign missions and promoted by WMU women.[35]

This was not the first time that Southern Baptists had encountered a denomination-wide crisis over biblical interpretation. During the early 1920s, when the fundamentalist-versus-modernist debates were tearing many northern Protestant denominations apart, Frank Norris, a fiery, combative, and self-proclaimed fundamentalist pastor from Fort Worth, Texas, claimed that continental liberalism and evolutionary theory had entered the ranks of Southern Baptist institutions. Norris and his followers created something of a stir, exerting enough pressure to have a few college professors fired.[36] To defuse the troublesome situation, several prominent Southern Baptist statesmen charged Southern Seminary's president, E. Y. Mullins, with drafting a confession of faith that outlined Southern Baptists' core beliefs. The 1925 convention voted to adopt the Baptist Faith and Message, basically reaffirming the 1833 New Hampshire Confession, which held to a more modified Calvinism than other Baptist confessional statements. Mullins, however, felt that the real issue of the day was the Bible, and so he made certain adjustments.[37] The first article of the Baptist Faith and Message emphasized scripture as having "God for its author, salvation for its end, and truth, without any mixture of error, for its matter." This emphasis settled the concerns of most Southern Baptists, who viewed modernism primarily as a northern problem.[38] Overall, if the Norris incident was tumultuous, it also proved brief. After the passage of the Baptist Faith and Message, Southern Baptists experienced nearly forty years of relative peace on the matter.

When the 1960s "Genesis crisis," as it was called, swept the SBC, denominationalists worked again for the same peaceful end. Seeking compromise, Porter Routh and his assistant, Albert McClelland, joined Herschel Hobbs, a longtime SBC statesman and Oklahoma City pastor who served from 1961 to 1963 as the denomination's president. First, although they refused to request that Midwestern fire Elliott, they did draft a convention resolution that affirmed the Bible to be "authentic, authoritative, and infallible" as well as historically accurate. Next, recognizing the need for a more long-term solution, they appointed a committee to revise the 1925 Baptist Faith and Message. As a sign of their frustration, messengers to the 1962 convention voted against presidents from the seminaries being on the committee, choosing instead the state convention presidents to work with Hobbs.

Hobbs was the consummate denominational politician and, like his predecessor Mullins, drove much of the process. With Hobbs at the helm, the committee labored diligently to pacify both those who opposed and those who backed Elliott. Regarding the former, for example, they were careful to retain the earlier language concerning the Bible as having "God for its author, salvation for its end, and truth, without any mixture of error, for its matter." To placate Elliott's supporters, the committee also added that "the criterion by which the Bible is to be interpreted is Jesus Christ." Anticipating cries of anti-Baptist creedalism, the committee stipulated that no confession of faith could be binding on the individual conscience. It asserted local church autonomy and warned against using the Baptist Faith and Message as a divisive tool.

When messengers at the 1963 convention affirmed the revised statement, Hobbs, Routh, and other denominational executives believed that they had spirited away future controversies in the same way that the 1925 Baptist Faith and Message had quieted earlier fundamentalists. It quickly became apparent that they had failed. Despite the committee's best efforts, in 1965 the Sunday School Board came under fire again at the convention for selling *The Message of Genesis*. W. A. Criswell, pastor of First Baptist Church, Dallas, the largest church in the SBC, circulated his address denouncing the seminaries for their modernist teachings. As before, the Sunday School Board apologized for its mistakes and pledged publicly to "prevent their recurrence."[39] Nevertheless, the entire Genesis affair was repeated again when, in 1969, some charged that the Sunday School Board's newest Genesis commentary by G. Henton Davies incorporated the latest historical critical methodologies. This was also the year that the convention voted Criswell as president.

The subsequent 1970 meeting in Denver was referred to as a "three-day doctrinal dispute."[40] Messengers, at one point booing Hobbs, voted overwhelmingly to recall the new commentary. The fact that Davies was a British Baptist did little to placate tensions. From the floor, angry messengers made several motions to have denominational employees and seminary faculty sign an annual statement affirming their belief in the Bible as the "authoritative, authentic, inspired, infallible Word of God." The motions failed only when the parliamentarian deemed them unconstitutional. Convinced that the SBC and its academic institutions were peddling theological liberalism, several preachers and their churches left determined to establish alternative institutions for ministerial training. In 1971, Criswell led his members in founding the Criswell Bible Institute, which later became Criswell College. A year later, two former Southern Baptist missionaries launched Mid-America Theological Seminary in Little Rock. It was soon relocated next to Bellevue Baptist Church in Memphis, where Bellevue's dynamic young pastor, Adrian Rogers, assumed the seminary's reins.

Years later, Elliott recalled the naive SBC leaders who thought that they could simply rehearse the events of 1925. The SBC of the 1960s was a transformed entity, and its Genesis crisis occurred within a vastly different context. The southern ways that once had held the denomination and its members intact had eroded, and as a growing number of Southern Baptists perceived it, the enemy no longer stood outside as the liberal North or continental Europe. The enemy had invaded to stand fully within their midst. In the end, Elliott's detractors demanded forthright thinking and decisive action. Compromise could only amount to vagaries and ambiguity, unbefitting the task at hand. After all, they asked, what did claims regarding "truth without mixture" alongside "Jesus Christ as the criterion for biblical interpretation" actually mean? Not surprisingly, nearly seven years later, Hobbs found himself once again arguing against any insertion that would more narrowly define the statement's claims.

The primary reason for the persistence of the controversies was the larger context in which they were being fought. During the 1960s, the nation exploded with the civil rights movement, protests against the Vietnam War, rock and roll, the sexual revolution, and the drug culture. Writing in 1966, the preeminent southern historian Samuel Hill observed, "Everywhere old moorings are breaking loose, deeply entrenched attitudes are being shaken, and traditional patterns of social life are gradually giving way and being replaced by new."[41] For many Southern Baptists, the momentum of change was too great. The inerrancy debates, as they spun out, were as much about the instability of their social and cultural context as they were about the infallibility of scripture, theological orthodoxy, or even the traditional Baptist principles that each side promoted. While feminism and questions regarding women interacted more heavily with inerrancy and theological tensions over time, the most immediate cultural controversy to Southern Baptists during the 1960s was civil rights. Watts Street Baptist Church, for instance, received letters of criticism for ordaining Addie Davis; it encountered bomb threats and vandalism for supporting desegregation.

Racial Matters

In 1954, the Supreme Court delivered its ruling favoring Brown in the landmark *Brown v. Board of Education of Topeka*. This decision marked the beginning of the end of "colored only" bathrooms, water fountains, and waiting rooms throughout the South. It bolstered civil rights activism, which struck at the heart of Jim Crow. Racism lingered, but within two decades, legal segregation disappeared.[42] The civil rights movement and the changes it invoked were swift, violent, and bloody. In the beginning, the movement focused on the South; by the end, it had implicated all of American society.

Throughout the 1940s and most of the 1950s, hard-line segregationist forces dominated the South, and Southern Baptists proved no exception.

Prominent southern politicians who vowed to overturn *Brown* and successive civil rights measures—the noted Mississippi governor Ross Barnett, for instance, or Arkansas governor Orval Faubus—were Southern Baptists who were widely embraced by the denomination's leading churches and pastors. In 1955, from the pulpit of the SBC's largest church, the powerful pulpiteer W. A. Criswell condemned integrationists, calling them a "bunch of infidels, dying from the neck up," and Criswell had his congregation's unswerving support in rejecting the membership of blacks in the First Baptist Church of Dallas. Stories of blacks turned from Southern Baptist church doors became legendary. For the most part, denominationalists hid behind the language of individual piety to avoid making any social statement. Silence ruled the day.[43] Those few ministers who preached against racial hierarchy lost members and pulpits. As Criswell would have it, they were branded as infidels and liberals, representative of the waywardness of modern society. In fact, as Herschel Hobbs worried over the possibility of a growing theological crisis, he and several other denominational statesmen warned Southern Seminary against entanglements with race, advising its faculty in 1961 against inviting Martin Luther King Jr. to campus.[44]

The tides shifted dramatically during the 1960s. Civil rights activists staged boycotts, sit-ins, and marches focusing the nation's attention on the inherent violence of white supremacy. Television screens across the country were filled with white policemen unleashing dogs and aiming water hoses on peaceful black protestors. A dignified Coretta Scott King and her four young children marched silently behind the casket of their assassinated husband and father. These images bewildered and embarrassed white Americans, including Southern Baptists, and as a result, progressive voices became more common throughout the denomination. Some of the more outspoken, such as Clarence Jordan, founder of the interracial Koinonia community, left the SBC. Others stayed and found official expression. In the face of being accused of northern liberalism and procommunism, Foy Valentine and the SBC Christian Life Commission, which Valentine headed, routinely denounced segregation and called for Southern Baptists to become "actively involved in seeking cures for personal prejudice, unfair housing, discriminatory employment, unequal justice, and denial of voting rights."[45] While the WMU and the mission boards did increasingly address the need for Southern Baptists to participate in the betterment of race relations, no agency or institution was as forthright as the Christian Life Commission.[46]

Heartened by such efforts, more preachers and pastors attacked the racial injustices in their midst. Will Campbell, who quit his chaplaincy at the University of Mississippi, was certainly the most noted, but there were many more who often came from surprising and unlikely locations. Harold O'Chester, for example, pastored a small Southern Baptist church in Meridian, Mississippi, with past connections to the Ku Klux Klan. Still, he decided to campaign actively against racial hatred, and he managed to sway nearly 100 of his congregants to commit themselves likewise. Later he recalled moving his children to sleep on the den floor, away from their front bedroom windows, for fear of violent retaliation by rabid white supremacists.[47] Brooks Ramsey served at Second Baptist Church in suburban Memphis, which was one of the fastest-growing congregations in the denomination. To the dismay of many church members, Ramsey became increasingly vocal on civil rights issues. They nevertheless voted to keep him on, even after he marched with black sanitation collectors during the 1968 Memphis sanitation workers' strike.

These examples of progressivism were not indicative of the official party line, but denominationalists did move out of their silence in an attempt, once again, to find the middle and most popularly respectable course. During this period, they denounced racial violence aimed at blacks as well as any massive resistance to desegregation. Unlike progressives, who emphatically connected racial equality to biblical ideas of justice and Jesus's gospel ministry, most SBC officials presented it solely as a matter of good Christian citizenry, avoiding, for the most part, hermeneutical contests.[48] Over and over, they advised calm reason in the midst of chaos. When the Civil Rights Act of 1964 and the Voting Rights Act of 1965 passed, the SBC executive committee guided messengers in a resolution that urged Southern Baptists to "provide positive leadership in their communities toward obtaining peaceful compliance with laws assuring equal rights." It also "deplored open and premeditated violation of civil law, destruction of property, violence, and shedding of blood as a way of influencing legislation or changing social or cultural patterns."[49] Wayne Dehoney, president of the SBC at the time, joined the National Citizens' Committee for Community Relations, designed to foster compliance with civil rights legislation, as a model for Southern Baptists.[50]

Dehoney's plan succeeded mainly because it represented the common consensus of everyday white middle-class southerners and Southern Baptists. Polls revealed that in 1963 more than 60 percent of white southerners opposed school integration; by 1966 only 24 percent reportedly did. By the end of the 1960s, more local Southern Baptist churches held open policies than closed. Letters to state convention newspapers had clearly tipped in favor of those declaring opposition to Jim Crow.[51] To show the extent to which the tide had turned, in 1968 Criswell called his support of segregation a "colossal blunder" and welcomed blacks into his congregation. By the 1970s, few white southern politicians openly admitted any lingering opposition to segregation and civil rights legislation. The same could be said for those in SBC leadership. According to the historian David Chappell, civil rights succeeded largely because white supremacy failed to muster the religious support, particularly of southern evangelicals, it needed to overcome change.[52]

Racism, of course, hardly disappeared. Differences over race remained real, deep, and persistent, and the legacy of the civil rights movement could be seen in ways that influenced both the 1980s culture wars and the related Southern Baptist battles. First, civil rights legislation had introduced a form of government intervention that many white Americans found meddlesome. Despite their acceptance of laws that affirmed basic civil rights, many felt that subsequent Supreme Court rulings during the 1970s crossed a line. These included decisions that dictated busing practices, legalized abortion, and banned religious activities in the public arena.[53] Second, during the process of integration, numerous whites, in the South and other regions, moved to the suburbs, where they relocated their churches, supported separate school systems, and sometimes founded Christian academies. In a 1968 survey, only 127 of 686 surveyed Southern Baptist congregations officially reported to accept blacks actually had even one member. Southern Baptists, like many white Americans, accepted desegregation more as an ideal than as an everyday reality, and in certain matters of race, Sunbelt Baptists differed little from their Bible Belt predecessors.

On the progressive side, feminism could be seen as a legacy of civil rights. As with abolition a century earlier, civil rights drew attention to discrimination against women as well as blacks. Early postwar feminists participated in the civil rights movement, using it as a model for their legal activism regarding women. Feminism also promoted the rhetoric of choice, and in this sense, for many, it seemed to embody the liberal pervasiveness or relativism of modern society. If integrationists, civil rights activists, and racial progressives had been, in the eyes of many Southern Baptists, "a bunch of infidels" and "heathens," feminists now assumed this threatening role. It was not enough to invoke biblical inerrancy. As segregation fell out of favor after civil rights laws were passed, many Southern Baptists demanded that the boundaries regulating women's roles and behaviors be more tightly defined.

but why?

Feminism

The record numbers of Americans who attained middle-class status in the postwar period defined the American dream for a new era. They purchased their own homes, formed tight-knit neighborhoods, and surrounded themselves with the novel trappings of consumer culture. The elevation of the two-parent nuclear family was a by-product of this middle-class prosperity. Professional politicians, educators, psychologists, and clergy alike proclaimed it to be the bulwark of American society and culture; its continuation ensured individual happiness, moral development, and communal stability. During this period, a new class of credentialed family experts guided mainstream white Americans in their newfound familial roles and responsibilities.[54]

New domesticity characterized the virtues of the 1950s nuclear family as they applied to women. Similar to nineteenth-century Victorians, the 1950s nuclear family depended on a gendered division of labor. The woman's role was to cultivate a pleasing domestic space, to promote the professional career of her husband, and to oversee the moral education, health, and happiness of her children. New domesticity celebrated the ideal woman as gentle rather than tough, passive rather than active, and soft and easygoing rather than aggressive and manipulative. Her "inborn proclivity for nurture and love" found its creative expression in the home.[55] Even as social psychologists spoke of companionate marriages in which wives and husbands enjoyed social outings and family vacations, they also counseled wives to affirm their husbands' authority. Women should tend to the everyday running of the home, and men should make the "big decisions."[56]

American society in general reflected the popularity of this new domesticity. Colleges offered their women students degrees in home economics, interior decorating, and child development. Magazines with names like *Ladies' Home Journal* and *Woman's Home Companion* provided recipes, housecleaning advice, and beauty tips, while consumer specialists advertised the perfect products to achieve domesticity and femininity. Television programs such as *The Donna Reed Show*, *Father Knows Best*, and *Leave It to Beaver* showcased the virtues of American family life. Demographics from the 1950s were telling. The average marrying age dropped, fertility rates rose, births increased, and divorce statistics leveled for the first time since the Civil War. Reporting on the growth of the nuclear family, journalists used the term "baby boom."

The rhetoric of new domesticity never quite fit the reality, however, and any resemblances proved short-lived. During the 1950s, an increasing percentage of women actually entered the job market. Despite warnings about maladjusted offspring and harm to society, nearly half of these women had school-age children, and a substantial number came from the white middle class. Moreover, toward the decade's end, the statistics bolstering the nuclear family, with its image of happy domesticity, began to reverse themselves. Birthrates once again declined, and divorce rates were on the rise. The paradigm could not hold.[57]

Historians typically date postwar liberal feminism to Betty Friedan's 1965 publication of *The Feminine Mystique*, in which she severely problematized the prevailing understanding of womanhood tethered, as it was, to mothering and homemaking. As she asserted, the "problem that has no name" was actually that domesticity deprived women of their own voice. Friedan's book sold more than 1 million copies in its first printing. Obviously it reflected a dissatisfaction, which Friedan called ennui, among many white middle-class housewives and homemakers and provided them with the language to express it. Friedan, Gloria Steinem, and other 1960s feminists saw themselves as continuing the work of those nineteenth-century women who had challenged Victorian ideals of womanhood with their call for suffrage. Sometimes called second-wave feminists, they held that the 1950s ideology of family had stalled earlier advances.

Initially, feminism had two branches: women's rights and women's liberation. Women's rights focused on legislative measures and, with the availability of birth control in 1960, issues of reproduction. In 1966, twenty-eight women formed NOW, the National Organization for Women. At first, with NOW, women's rights efforts experienced tremendous success, particularly in the areas of education, health, job discrimination, and family planning.[58] The Equal Rights Amendment represented the pinnacle or culmination of NOW's work, and in 1970, the Senate opened hearings on the amendment. The House followed a year later, and Congress approved it in 1972. Women's rights activists likewise celebrated the repeal of certain abortion laws with *Roe v. Wade* one year later. Feminism's second branch, women's liberation, promoted an awareness of sexism in everyday life, involving everything from family and childbirth to etiquette, language, and literature. Numerous popular feminist writings, such as Kate Millet's *Sexual Politics* and the anthology *Sisterhood Is Powerful*, followed *The Feminine Mystique*. Women's studies grew to be a mainstay of academic life, and women's centers became standard on college campuses. In terms of popular culture, if *Our Bodies, Ourselves* was one of the best-selling books of the 1970s, the *Battle of the Sexes*, the tennis match between Billie Jean King and Bobby Riggs, was one of the most-watched sports events. Finally, in 1972 *Ms. Magazine* grew out of a column by Gloria Steinem to become feminism's official expression.

As feminism gained momentum, it developed in multiple areas. During the 1970s, its leaders worked diligently to attract women of different ethnicities and classes, who often formed their own related groups and organizations.[59] More radical feminist groups, which emerged as early as the mid-1960s, became even more vocal. They spoke not so much of the gender equality and social transformation of liberal feminism but of total revolution. This would involve the abolition of marriage, capitalism, Christianity, and other institutions thought to be irredeemably patriarchal. As a result, radical feminists often promoted lesbian sexuality and exclusively female communities.[60] Finally, while earlier feminists had tried to obliterate gender difference as a form of inequality, some feminists attempted to reclaim gendered notions of womanhood as empowering. The popular mantra "I am Woman" proclaimed womanhood as strong, sexual, daring, and aggressive.

These various groups and manifestations made feminism difficult to define. Additionally, as the movement's leaders increasingly disagreed over its direction, they became embroiled in internal divisions and squabbles, so that feminism was an easy target for critics, who could sling multiple accusations in its direction. Most often, they pointed to the more antiestablishment and confrontational styles, which did dominate the movement and the press throughout much of the late 1960s and 1970s, spawning the "burn the bra" stereotype. Feminism undoubtedly led to strides for women in almost every facet of American culture and society, but at times it seemed more about the promotion of the rhetoric of choice rather than its actual practice. This was also the case as feminism made inroads into religion.[61]

At first, feminism mostly affected women in Roman Catholic and mainstream Protestant traditions. Some academics and scholars, like the feminist theologian Mary Daly, called for a radical departure from historic Christianity. Most, however, sought a rereading of the Bible and church history from the perspective of women's liberation.[62] Women, as well as men, who were actively involved in church life and gravitating toward feminism began to lobby for gender-inclusive language, equal rights for laywomen, and most especially, women's ordination. The pulpit, in some traditions, and sacramental authority, in others, were highly visible and potent symbols that historically had been limited to men, thus making women's ordination ripe for feminist scrutiny and controversy.[63]

Mainstream Protestant traditions that tied ordination to the pulpit ensured women clerical rights earlier than traditions with a higher sacramental authority. Of the larger bodies, for example, the Methodist Church and Presbyterian Church in the United States (North) first ordained women in 1956, while the Episcopal Church and Evangelical Lutheran Church waited until 1976. Many smaller holiness and Wesleyan traditions regularly opened their churches to women's preaching during the late nineteenth century. Ordinations among these and other Pentecostal denominations were common well into the twentieth century. These evangelical movements valued women pulpiteers because the Spirit's call exceeded ecclesial tradition.[64] After the 1960s, however, women's ordination, no matter what the tradition, was interpreted through the lens of feminism and seen to represent a bid toward gender equality. In addition, critics often associated the bid for women's ordination with more confrontational, even radical, versions of feminism, which was certainly how Southern Baptist conservatives essentialized the movement. This meant that the second set of Southern Baptist ordinations in the early 1970s challenged the denomination's stance on compromise, particularly the WMU's. More than any other organization or group, the WMU served as the primary arena in which Southern Baptist women learned and taught, and forged and negotiated their roles and behaviors.

The WMU, Feminism, and Women's Ordination

During the 1940s and 1950s, at a time when women's mission organizations in other denominations were disbanding, the WMU, in tandem with the SBC, doubled in size. Its women's mission circles and children's mission groups became standard in the majority of Southern Baptist churches, and as they grew in number, so too did the WMU. Likewise, the WMU's Lottie Moon Christmas Offering for Foreign Missions capped the denomination's yearly calendar in a grand joint endeavor of old-fashioned evangelical zeal and transformed middle-class prosperity. Clearly, the historic organization remained central to the lives of Southern Baptist women. When asked the reason behind the WMU's success, Alma Hunt, executive secretary, replied, "The answer is simple: our purpose. We have never veered from the purpose of missions."[65]

Hunt's statement, however, was not altogether accurate. During the first part of the century, the WMU had sometimes lobbied for advances in denominational power and authority for women. In 1918, it pushed the convention toward accepting women as messengers. In 1921, it presented a convention resolution requiring greater representation on denominational boards.

Furthermore, the masterminds behind the establishment of the Cooperative Program were the leaders of the WMU. If this were not enough, as the historian Carol Holcomb points out, the WMU risked the ire of SBC officials from 1909 to 1929 by incorporating principles of the social gospel into its local personal service programs.[66] By focusing so exclusively on missions, and interpreting missions more solely as evangelism, WMU leaders like Hunt promoted the compromising spirit touted by denominationalists. Compromise became a convenient means to avoid controversial issues and, thus, the internal squabbles that had challenged the organization in its early years. But practiced by women, it also reflected submission to the SBC's male leadership, and at higher levels than in previous decades.

Two events in the 1950s were indicative of this submission. In 1956, the WMU officially conceded allocation of its special Lottie Moon and Annie Armstrong offerings. The financial significance of these offerings to the mission boards was staggering. The Moon offering provided nearly 50 percent of the Foreign Mission Board's budget, and the Armstrong offering achieved the same for the Home Mission Board. The SBC had long attempted to control the funds' placements; still, WMU officers had resisted, seeing the offerings as a means to support women missionaries paid less than their male counterparts. During the 1950s, however, the WMU focused more exclusively on promoting the offerings, allowing the mission boards to designate the offerings' recipients. The WMU made this official policy in 1956. Then one year later, an SBC executive subcommittee requested that the WMU transfer ownership of the Carver School of Missions and Social Work, formerly the WMU Training School, to the SBC. While the WMU had resisted earlier attempts to turn the school's focus from missions and social work to religious education, in 1957 the women complied, following the route of compromise without asking for any financial reimbursement. Relinquishing control over these institutions and activities lessened their administrative load, a reason sometimes cited by WMU officials for the acquiescence; at the same time, it severely weakened the WMU's independence and its ability to influence directly SBC missions. As a result, both moves represented a loss of power for Southern Baptist women.[67]

Organizationally, the WMU now served exclusively as a helpmate to the SBC mission boards. Moreover, as if to confirm the 1950s understanding of womanhood, its monthly magazine, *Royal Service*, often echoed other popular women's homemaking journals with their affirmations of motherhood and domesticity.[68] When WMU president Marie Mathis was elected in 1963 as the SBC's second vice president, the highest national office any woman had attained, she was careful to tie the position to women's missions rather than any bid to power. A few years later, Mathis attempted to clarify the WMU's position further, writing that "by nature, women are helpers. In the design of God, this role is natural and right."[69] WMU president Helen Fling addressed the denominational convention in 1964, insisting, "A woman's role in the kingdom is not competitive to man's, it is complementary. . . . Woman's function is that of a supporting helper, her position is auxiliary, and her service is essential."[70] According to the WMU historian Catherine Allen, before 1970, the WMU and its publications mentioned neither feminism nor changing roles of women in the church.[71]

In many ways, the WMU was simply accommodating the culture of its times. Compromise seemed the price of survival for Southern Baptist women during the 1950s. And yet, during the 1960s, even as it refused any connection between itself and the feminist movement, the WMU opened the doors for women, albeit often unwittingly and almost always in the name of missions. First, in 1965, WMU leaders determined that women's mission expertise should not be restricted to children but used to educate the entire church. As a result, the WMU encouraged its local circles to sponsor church-wide seminars, book studies, dramas, and mission fairs. In some churches, WMU members spoke regularly from the pulpit, making women far more visible in larger church life and from the primary place of congregational authority and power. Second, the WMU continued to emphasize that God spoke to and called women—and sometimes in unexpected ways. While *Royal Service* ran stories endorsing the popular domestic ideology of the day, its accounts of women missionaries also pushed the boundaries of new domesticity. As laywomen back home were sure to discover, the efforts of women missionaries in the field frequently overlapped with those of their male peers, and in certain contexts, women missionaries even functioned as pastors. Relatedly, and despite Marie Mathis's claim that she had "never heard of a woman wanting to be a minister," women who later pursued ordination almost always cited the WMU in their call to ministry. The language of call that the WMU had worked tirelessly to instill in girls stirred, as Addie Davis put it, their sense of "religious intent." After the 1960s, it was only one small step to transfer that intent from missions to ordained pulpit ministry, particularly as mission service was becoming less appealing to women.

In 1966, the WMU witnessed its first membership decline in decades, and though in the early 1970s its membership settled at 1 million, the organization represented fewer and fewer Southern Baptist women. Cultural factors that prompted the fight for women's rights also led to the WMU's decreasing numbers. As more and more white middle-class women entered the workforce, they found their time limited. Not surprisingly, a denomination-wide group devoted primarily to women's missions seemed increasingly narrow and old-fashioned. Younger women felt that it did little to address the struggles they were experiencing in their daily lives. If compromise had indeed been the cost of survival in the church, that, too, was changing.

On August 22, 1971, Kathwood Baptist Church in Columbia, South Carolina, ordained Shirley Carter to the gospel ministry. News of the second ordination of a Southern Baptist woman quickly circulated throughout the SBC. In May 1972, she made headlines again by marrying a former Roman Catholic priest, Pringle Lee, who renounced his priesthood vows prior to the ceremony. The events surrounding Carter's ordination and marriage turned even more controversial that summer when Carter revealed that she had been three months pregnant when she wed Lee. As the story hit Southern Baptist state newspapers and was circulated in secular venues as well, the Columbia church urged Carter to resign her ordination. She responded by calling Kathwood's decision "hasty" and "grossly unfair" and claimed that the reason behind the public outcry and the church's decision was not "the 'act' itself but that she was a woman." Contrasting her situation with those of "several men who as Baptist pastors were caught in the act of adultery, but were only asked to leave the church," Carter protested that "when a woman minister commits a responsible act of love before the actual wedding ceremony, then her ordination is revoked." Carter ultimately resigned her ordination, citing "censure" and "non-acceptance" rather than any wrongdoing. In fact, she defended herself and Lee by insisting that prior to any formal ritual or ceremony "we had committed ourselves to one another completely" and thus "were married in the sight of God." Nowhere in the Bible, she concluded, does marriage begin "only with the wedding ceremony."[72]

Advocates of women's ordination have virtually expunged Carter from the annals of Southern Baptist history because of the fornication issue. But Carter's ordination carries historical value because the scandal affirmed the growing concern of many Southern Baptists that feminism was liberal values and moral relativity run rampant. Few could have heard about the six ordinations that followed in less than a year without the memory of Shirley Carter fresh in their minds. The details of the scandal faded over time; nonetheless, the fears that it invoked persisted well into the following decade. Opponents of women in ministry would rally support by linking women's ordination to feminism along with the numerous liberal causes and radical images they associated with the movement.

By the 1970s, Southern Baptist women were moving into the pulpit. Although their number was small, they garnered much attention and thus assumed the anxieties of a new age. For a few, this proved too much to bear. Others seized the moment as an opportunity, choosing to see themselves as called of God, following in the steps of Addie Davis, who urged them to "cherish the dream" and "press on." They did this in the face of mounting opposition from those who decried their efforts as anathema to Southern Baptist tradition, biblical authority, and postwar compromise. These women soon discovered, as Davis likewise warned, that "it's sometimes dangerous to dream."[73]

2

Redigging the Old Wells

THE CHRISTIAN WOMAN VERSUS WOMAN'S LIB

Settling on the theme "Sharing the Word Now," Southern Baptists met in Portland, Oregon, on June 12, 1973, for what denominational officials predicted would be a "non-controversial" convention.[1] The northwestern location suggested that times had indeed changed. The Southern Baptist Convention (SBC) was now the largest and wealthiest Protestant denomination in the nation. In 1973 alone, the Foreign Mission Board commissioned more than 170 new missionaries, and the Home Mission Board commissioned a record-breaking 360. Southern Baptists also boasted churches throughout the fifty states. After a rather tumultuous decade, messengers were now ready to celebrate their success and expected the next three days to be a grand reunion. Men would fraternize with old preacher buddies, women would hear the latest advances in the Woman's Missionary Union (WMU) and mission education, and all would engage in old-fashioned hymn singing. More than a few hoped to slip out of the sleepy business sessions for some sightseeing. So when Jessie Tillison Sappington submitted a resolution favoring what she referred to as the "Christian woman" over "woman's lib," the Committee on Resolutions hurriedly revised it to make the language less inflammatory, with the content reflecting benign appreciation for the work of women, including their "leadership roles in church and denominational life."[2] Sappington would not have it.

She hailed from Houston, where her husband, Richard Sappington, pastored the 500-member Cloverleaf Baptist Church. To the surprise of committee members, the fashionable young preacher's wife with a genteel southern accent proved a feisty Texan who was fearless of controversy. Insisting that the new resolution destroyed her original intent, and that it could be interpreted to affirm women's ordination, she motioned for a substitute.

Sappington prefaced her motion with an engaging narrative, relating how, when leading a women's Bible study, she had been asked whether "God is unisex." The woman posing the question was genuinely puzzled, and Sappington said that she could only assume the woman's query resulted from a culture saturated with women's liberation. Rather than merely passing resolutions condemning drugs and alcohol, the sbc, she insisted, must address the growing ideological attack on Christian women, or what she later called the "evil influences of the anti-scriptural aspects of the Women's Liberation Movement on the home."[3]

Sappington's resolution pointed to the "distinct roles of men and women in the church and home" as "recorded in Scripture." It did affirm the words of Kenneth Chafin of the Home Mission Board, who had spoken earlier and called Southern Baptist women to "redig the old wells of mission promotion and education," but the resolution made clear that any redigging that came solely in the promotion of the wmu and women's missions was not enough. It must go deeper. Citing the "great attack by the members of most women's liberation movements upon scriptural precepts of woman's place in society," the resolution's first statement "resolved that we redig or reaffirm God's order of authority for his church and the Christian home." This order intended "Christ the head of every man," "man the head of the woman," and "children in subjection to their parents—in the Lord." As bold as this claim was, redigging the old wells did not stop there. "Be it further Resolved," the resolution continued, "that we redig or reaffirm God's explicit Word that man was not made for the woman, but the woman for the man," "that the woman is the glory of man," and "that as woman would not have existed without man, henceforth neither would man have existed without the woman, they are dependent one upon the other—to the glory of God."[4]

Heated debate followed Sappington's motion. Three men and one woman spoke for her substitute resolution, and two women spoke against. Joyce Rogers, the wife of Adrian Rogers at Bellevue Baptist Church, urged passage, stating that "as a woman" she felt "completely liberated in Christ" and that women should only assume "leadership roles among women and children." Speaking for the other side, Anne Rosser, who was later ordained, adamantly denied the motion's claims and did not see "the Word," as the resolution claimed, to be "explicitly clear on this subject." According to Rosser, "Jesus Christ liberated woman for all time and places in leadership and ministry," so that women were "free to assume leadership roles" without "one sex over another." In the end, Rosser did not speak for the majority. The thunderous applause for those supporting Sappington indicated the crowd's favor. When the moderator called time, the ayes for substituting her resolution were matched by the ayes passing it.[5]

Nearly forgotten after the events of 1979, the Sappington incident initially stood out in a convention otherwise described as "bland" and "non-newsworthy."[6] It was significant to the post-1979 struggle, though, in that it predicted how Southern Baptist conservatives would marry women's submission to the rhetoric of biblical inerrancy as well as conservatives' notion of what the "explicit Word" had to say about women. It also showed that conservatives would have the support, even leadership, of women. Not incidentally, the Baptist Faith and Message Fellowship held its first meeting in Atlanta prior to the 1973 Portland convention. Its goal was to mandate an interpretation of the Baptist Faith and Message Society along inerrant lines. In focusing almost exclusively on the Baptist Faith and Message meeting, later scholars have obscured the importance of the Sappington affair—and thus the early role of the woman question.

This chapter considers the period from 1973 to 1978, highlighting several events that have gone largely unnoticed. Together with the Sappington resolution, these moments reveal how the wider cultural tensions between evangelical feminism and traditional womanhood fueled unease—among denominationalists as well as conservatives.

Evangelical Feminism

Disillusionment defined the 1970s. The military debacle in Vietnam was highlighted by television footage of American atrocities. Race riots raged in Chicago, Los Angeles, and Detroit, exposing inner-city drug abuse, crime, and poverty. The Watergate scandal exposed an illegal cover-up in the Oval Office. Richard Nixon's failed presidency was nearly matched by the crises that marred Jimmy Carter's four years. Inflation, exorbitant gas prices, and the Iran hostage situation ended a turbulent decade.

Many Americans blamed the dismal state of affairs on the moral and political upheaval of the 1960s. Once the controversy over racial segregation had been settled legally in favor of civil rights, the prime target became feminism and its bid for the Equal Rights Amendment (ERA). In 1972, as twenty-two of the necessary thirty-eight states immediately ratified the ERA, Phyllis Schlafly formed STOP ERA. According to Schlafly, the ERA would create a gender-blind society hostile to women and the American family. Women, she insisted, would actually lose certain privileges in society. Schlafly stirred passions by pointing to wife-care benefits under Social Security and exemption from the armed services as well as the more intangible delights associated with being a homemaker. The staunchly Catholic wife and mother, as Schlafly identified herself, made more inroads in the Republican Party and in political lobbying than she did with religious institutions. Only when evangelical feminism developed its own voice and following did a growing number of evangelicals begin to focus on the movement.

At first, the tide of evangelical opinion seemed to favor feminism, with one survey reporting a three-to-one margin of support.[7] Two events proved crucial. In 1973, fifty noted evangelical scholars and leaders, mainly male, gathered in Chicago to form Evangelicals for Social Action. Their Chicago Declaration included a short statement: "We acknowledge that we have encouraged men to prideful domination and women to irresponsible passivity. So we call both men and women to mutual submission and active discipleship." Bolstered by this declaration, Letha Scanzoni and Nancy Hardesty published *All We're Meant to Be: A Biblical Approach to Women's Liberation* a year later. In *All We're Meant to Be*, they boldly claimed that the God of the Bible called women and men to practice gender equality. The dialogue between Scanzoni and Hardesty involved other women, most notably Lucille Sider, Catherine Kroeger, and Patricia Gundry. These women hailed from the smaller, primarily northern denominations, evangelical seminaries, and neo-evangelical institutions affiliated with the National Association of Evangelicals. Together they forged a movement that they called evangelical, or biblical, feminism, with *All We're Meant to Be* serving as its manifesto.[8]

Evangelical feminists coalesced around a core set of convictions drawn from their feminist ideals and evangelical heritage. Like other feminists and feminist theologians, they rejected any form of women's subordination. As they saw it, God called women and men to equality and partnership in the earthly and spiritual, or secular and sacred, realms. They staunchly supported the ERA and called for women's ordination and ecclesial leadership. At the same time, evangelical feminists remained cautious in their pro-choice rhetoric and were less likely than other feminists, including feminist theologians, to challenge notions of gender difference. Instead, they highlighted the language of mutuality, partnership, and fellowship with men. Women and men, evangelical feminists declared, were "joint heirs" in working for the kingdom. Relatedly, evangelical feminists insisted on recognizing the Bible as their highest authority, claiming, again in contrast to many feminist theologians, that no biblical text could be dismissed for its patriarchal tendencies.[9] Finally, they emphasized the necessity of a personal and saving relationship with Jesus Christ.

The influence of evangelical feminism reached well beyond its initial nucleus. In fact, the noted feminist Alice Mathews called *All We're Meant to Be* "a shot heard around the evangelical world."[10] True to their religious heritage, evangelical feminists found immediate ways to proclaim and disseminate their message. They organized the Evangelical Women's Caucus, convened numerous conferences, published relevant material, and circulated several newsletters. Less measurably, they gave other evangelical groups and traditions, including those Southern Baptist women feeling God's call to ministry, a biblical means to support feminism. A sure sign of their success was that they inspired opposition.

Traditional Womanhood

It took evangelical women who shared a discomfort, if not hostility, toward feminism some time to organize a formal outlet for their views. As with Sappington, these women rallied around the concept of Christian womanhood as tied to the traditional role of submissive wife, nurturing mother, and skilled homemaker. Still, even women who supported STOP ERA, with its goal to protect their traditional role as sacred, were not inclined in the early 1970s to become too politically involved. Many women felt politics clashed with their domestic responsibilities, and so they looked elsewhere, finding a more comfortable space in groups like Marabel Morgan's "total woman" movement.

In 1973 Marabel Morgan published *The Total Woman.* According to Morgan, God's primary call to a woman was to please her husband. This meant admiring him, adapting to him, supporting his work, and accepting him as head of the household. It also meant a clean home, well-cooked meals, and well-behaved children. Moreover, in a new, not so traditional twist, it demanded creative opportunities for his sexual satisfaction. After all, "warm sexual love" was one of man's most basic needs. Morgan devoted an entire third of her book to "Sex 201." As a result, she became more noted for her suggestions of sexual play, which included costume ideas from pixie to pirate and cowgirl to showgirl, than for her ideas on organizing the house. Both homemaking and lovemaking, however, fulfilled God's plan for women in marriage and promoted family stability. "Man and woman," she argued, "although equal in status are different in function." Moreover, "God ordained man to the head," and "unless the wife adapts to his way of life, then there's no way to avoid the conflict that is certain to occur."[11] In 1974, *The Total Woman* sold more than 10 million copies, making it the year's leading nonfiction book. Three years later, after the success of the book's sequel, *Total Joy*, Morgan appeared on the cover of *Time* magazine. She soon launched total woman workshops across the country. Evangelical women likewise formed total woman support groups, identified themselves as total women, and enthusiastically endorsed the concept of wifely subordination or submission to their husbands' authority, which posed an essentialized understanding of feminism as intent on destroying all that was sacred in their lives.

As the decade wore on, other evangelical women devoted to traditional womanhood became bolder in their actions. Anita Bryant and Beverly La-Haye, for example, gained tremendous popularity as they literally charged into the political arena. Bryant and LaHaye combined the work of Schlafly and Morgan, insisting that at this dire turning point in American society and culture, Christian women had a responsibility to their husbands and children to involve themselves in the antifeminist campaign. By linking feminism to divorce, abortion, homosexuality, and radical bra-burning types, they provoked passions and provided a template for the Christian right's family values agenda.[12] Bryant, a Southern Baptist who had earned fame as a pop singer, as the runner-up in a Miss America pageant, and in commercials for Florida orange juice, led the way. In 1977, she launched a successful crusade in Florida called "Save Our Children" to repeal a Miami–Dade County ordinance prohibiting discrimination based on sexual orientation.[13] According to Bryant, homosexuality was akin to child abuse and pedophilia because gays recruited children from heterosexual parents and families, hoping to swell the homosexual ranks.[14] By the mid-1970s, James Dobson and Bill Gothard had also entered the antifeminist fray as evangelical family experts. Their hugely popular books and videos reasserted a strict hierarchy between husband and wife as well as parent and child.[15] Moreover, because Jimmy Carter's Whitehouse Conference on Families included homosexual, single, and divorced parents, evangelicals like Bryant, LaHaye, and Dobson viewed it as both profeminist and antifamily, labels they pushed as synonymous.

These early evangelical antagonists toward feminism used the term "traditional" or "Christian" womanhood. And yet, because they fought their battles at the forefront of the daily news and secular world, their inflammatory rhetoric lacked both the biblical emphasis and careful exegesis associated with evangelical feminism. Southern Baptist women who, unlike Bryant, were already working from within the boundaries of the church and congregational life filled this gap by developing a strong biblical basis for their understanding. To them, traditional womanhood was more than Christian womanhood. It was biblical womanhood.

One of the most recognized and influential leaders in biblical woman-hood was Barbara O'Chester. O'Chester was a young pastor's wife who had graduated from New Orleans Baptist Theological Seminary with a music degree. When her husband, Harold O'Chester, took a church in Austin, Texas, Barbara began conducting retreats for pastors' wives. The events soon became so popular that she opened the doors to all women, and through-out the 1970s, hundreds of women, Southern Baptist and otherwise, flocked to what O'Chester sometimes called "Wonderful Weekends for Women." O'Chester led these weekends in churches across Texas, Arkansas, Alabama, and Oklahoma, the geographic home for the future conservative movement. She offered workshops that involved Bible studies and revolved around the themes of wifely submission, child-rearing, and the act of marriage (or sex). The retreats were also significant in creating informal networks of conserva-tive women in the various locations in which they were held.[16]

Joyce Rogers at Bellevue Baptist Church was active in the weekends and close to O'Chester. In 1974, she published a pamphlet titled *God's Chief Assignment to Women*, which indicates the substance of Bible studies at this time. According to Rogers, "To women God has given one very special assignment. It was given at the beginning—in the Garden of Eden. Eve was to be a help—fitting for her husband." Rogers also claimed that "as a result of her [Eve's] sin she was further instructed in Genesis 3:16 that her desire would be to her husband and that he would rule over her." The story of the fall "was the beginning of earthly leadership. The man would lead; woman was to be submissive."

The pamphlet served as biblical justification for submission. After Rogers rooted this mandate in Genesis, she then moved to the Pauline epistles. She pointed to the misinterpretation of Galatians 3:28 ("there is neither male nor female: for ye are all one in Christ Jesus") as having been "used to justify women assuming leadership over men." The Galatians text, Rogers insisted, had "no reference to God's order of authority on earth," teaching instead that "God loves the woman as much as the man" and that woman "has equal access to the throne of God." She further indicated that the "same Paul" wrote that "the head of the woman is the man" (I Cor. 11:13) and directed wives to "submit yourselves unto your own husbands . . . for the husband is the head of the wife" (Eph. 5:22–24). Rogers admitted that there were man-made abuses in carrying out God's order of authority, but she compared the "rebel-lious, nagging woman" to Satan. Modern women, she said, had lost their way and were looking for liberation in the wrong places. "The truly submissive wife finds that her husband and her God release her to a freedom unknown by others."

In the second half of the pamphlet, Rogers addressed what she felt to be two errors in ecclesial life. The first was that women should not speak in church or serve in any leadership capacity. The second was that women could take positions of leadership equal in authority to men's. In correcting these errors, Rogers compared I Corinthians 14:34–35, where women are told to keep silent in the churches, to I Corinthians 11:5–10, which commanded women to cover their hair when praying or prophesying in church. The latter, said Rogers, made it obvious that a woman could speak but that there was a "condition attached to her ministry." I Timothy 2:11–12 clarified this condition: "Let a woman receive instruction with entire submissiveness. I do not allow a woman to teach or exercise authority over a man, but to remain quiet." Rogers dismissed any counterargument to women's submission that might invoke context. In his justification, Paul, she said, referred to Genesis and the Garden of Eden rather than any custom. Rogers concluded her defense of submission with a paragraph on homemaking as one of the most creative callings in life. A woman could pursue other "good things" only if homemaking remained her priority. Of course, any responsibility that demanded she serve as a king rather than a queen violated God's word.

The grassroots movement of these burgeoning women's Bible studies, retreats, and workshops showed how Southern Baptist women supported, even provided and shaped, the rhetoric of submission. This early approving stance from women inspired conservative male leaders. Even as Harold O'Chester grew his congregation into one of the denomination's first megachurches, he credited his wife's retreat ministry to women as a large reason for the church's triumph.

SBC officials did not want to confront the woman question head-on, especially as feminism became increasingly linked to more controversial issues and exaggerated stereotypes. In 1971, Southern Baptists began to pass resolutions condemning abortion and urging "a high view of the sanctity of life, including fetal life." Throughout the 1970s, these resolutions, while conservative, initially did provide for exceptions in cases of rape or incest or to save the life of the mother, thereby acknowledging some moral ambiguity or complexity on the issue. On the other hand, Southern Baptists were unequivocal regarding homosexuality. When Anita Bryant addressed the pastor's conference at the 1977 annual convention, reportedly stealing the show, messengers passed a resolution commending her for her antihomosexuality campaign. That fall, seventeen state conventions followed suit. The antifeminist campaign, as it linked feminism and the ERA to homosexuality, pedophilia, abortion, and the demise of the nuclear family, appeared to be a success. Eight states ratified the ERA in 1973, bringing the number to thirty; three more followed in 1974. But only two states ratified the amendment afterward, and five actually rescinded their earlier ratifications. The tide of favor toward feminism had reversed itself.

At first, the denominational oligarchy attempted to treat the woman issue in the same way they had handled race, which was by cautiously following the winds of change. This time, however, the approach failed. A large reason was that not only were Southern Baptist women, as well as men, becoming more committed to the debate; they were moving in opposite directions. On one side, conservative women like Sappington, Bryant, O'Chester, and Rogers were elevating their submission and the traditionalist understanding of women's expected roles and behaviors. On the other side, a growing number of women at the official SBC seminaries were seeking ordination.

Christian Liberation for Women Conference

Two events, both held as conferences, demonstrated the attempts of Southern Baptists to cultivate evangelical feminism within Southern Baptist life. These gatherings marked the beginning of a Baptist justification or theology for women in ministry. They also indicated the unease with which denominational officials approached the issue.

The WMU proved a surprising ally for the growing number of evangelical feminists within the denomination. In 1974, Alma Hunt retired as the WMU's executive secretary, and a young and enthusiastic Carolyn Weatherford assumed the organization's lead position. "How well I remember when I entered the WMU building as Miss Hunt left," Weatherford wrote more than thirty years later. "She said to me, 'Carolyn, I have had WMU in the glory days. I'm so sorry that you receive it at this time, when things are looking down.'"[17]

Hunt had battled the WMU's precipitous decline in numbers for more than a decade and recognized that old-style mission promotion and education no longer held sway. Women's roles in Southern Baptist life were changing in ways that excited some and disturbed others. It had taken Southern Baptists seven years to ordain two women. From 1972 to 1974, the number increased to thirteen. Four years later, it had reached fifty. These figures, though small, pointed to the increasing numbers of Southern Baptist seminary women who were expressing their desire for ordained ministry.[18] Articles in both of the mission boards' publications extolled women's new roles as ministers, deacons, board members, professors, and social workers. Reflecting once more on those years, Carolyn Weatherford first stated, "I don't think wMU saw itself as an 'advocate for women.' We just moved along doing what we knew best how to do—missions." She then acknowledged, almost as an aftersight, that "a lot of the things that we did . . . related to 'opening doors for women.'"[19]

One of those things was the wMU's involvement with the Christian Life Commission and its push toward "freedom for women." Often the fly in the ointment, according to denominationalists, the Christian Life Commission represented the vanguard in change. After lobbying for civil rights, it turned to women's issues. At the 1974 Dallas convention, the Christian Life Commission proposed adoption of its report "Freedom for Women," presented by Herbert Howard, who, as minister of the affluent Park Cities Baptist Church in Dallas, held clout. Echoing the goals of women's liberation, the first three parts of the report urged Southern Baptist churches and denominational agencies to "bear witness to the rest of society by rejecting sexual discrimination against women in job placement," "providing equal pay for equal work," and "electing women to positions of leadership."[20] The fourth part recommended a bylaw change requiring one-fifth of sBC-appointed board members, trustees, commissioners, and standing committee members to be women. Jesse Tillison Sappington once again interrupted the flow of events by presenting a motion to table the first three parts of the report dealing with women's discrimination. Sappington criticized the ambiguity of the language as open to women's ordination. After parliamentary twists and turns, Sappington prevailed, and messengers voted to table the report. In addition, the latter measure requiring that one-fifth of all sBC boards, commissions, and committees be women failed solidly.[21] And if that were not enough, a motion from the floor was passed to amend the constitution to stipulate that any missionary whose "function should be that of pastor" be male.[22]

Once again, women's issues threatened what most editors of Southern Baptist newspapers agreed was a convention of "unity and harmony."[23] The state newspapers also congratulated sBC leaders for maintaining the middle ground. As C. R. Daley, editor of Kentucky's *Western Recorder*, put it, the convention assumed the "correct course by refusing to endorse the ultra-conservative view or the ultra progressive view on theology and social issues."[24] Jack Harwell, editor of Georgia's *Christian Index*, likewise commented on the "debate about freedom for women and the SBC recognition of female ordination," stating that "Baptists can be swayed by a lot of emotion and oratory, but they can't be led to question or delete Biblical authority."[25]

The Christian Life Commission and its supporters saw the convention in a different light. Not willing to admit defeat, shortly after the Dallas convention, the commission hosted a Glorieta, New Mexico, conference called "Christian Liberation for Contemporary Women." While it was a small gathering, several participants were prominent SBC leaders who went on to represent the moderate movement. The WMU's Carolyn Weatherford was one. A year later, she reconfigured the conference as a seminar for WMU national officers and Birmingham employees—a move that sent a clear signal as to the WMU's direction.

The SBC's Broadman Press published the fourteen conference presentations by Sarah Frances Anders, Harry Hollis, and David and Vera Mace in *Christian Freedom for Women and Other Human Beings*. The lectures addressed a variety of topics ranging from women's liberation and women in church history to concepts of marriage and issues surrounding abortion. They were unified by a particular vision of "Christian womanhood." Quakers Vera and David Mace, for example, affirmed a sexless God who called women and men to multiple tasks regardless of gender. They proposed companionate marriages and declared any form of female subordination to be against God's original intent and Jesus's liberation. Anders, a Southern Baptist sociologist and professor, traced the prevalent sexism of the Western church, and although stopping short of endorsing women's ordination, she described the practice's long history in numerous Protestant, evangelical, and even Baptist traditions.

Hollis, the Christian Life Commission's director of family and special moral concerns, addressed contemporary changes in women's lives, including greater education, reproductive choices, and full-time employment. He insisted that many of the more dangerous social trends, such as divorce, sexual promiscuity, spousal and child abuse, and abortion, resulted from society's failure to accommodate changes in women's roles rather than the changes themselves. Dismissing women's liberation, he said, "ignores the injustices to females which many in women's liberation are trying to correct" and "perpetuates the erroneous view that the Bible teaches the utter subordination of women."[26]

Following on the heels of the events at Dallas, conference participants found the Glorieta retreat invigorating. As one woman stated, "I felt very discouraged when I came. . . . I am now determined to try to raise the consciousness of my fellow church members to improve the status of women. I am not going to leave the church. I am going to help it do right."[27] Hollis was even more forthright as he addressed conference participants: "The messengers may table recommendations but they cannot table rights. . . . Women are going to be free! God requires it. Justice demands it. Our national constitution guarantees it. And many men and women in the Southern Baptist Convention are going to keep on working under the leadership of the Holy Spirit to help churches reflect God's intention that all humans should be free. . . . Freedom for women is a powerful idea whose time has come."[28] Declarations like this for women's freedom and liberation borrowed largely from the women's liberation movement, feminist theology, and most especially, evangelical feminism. It was one small step to connect the concept of freedom in these ideologies to historic Baptist ideas. Still tied as they were to steering the middle course, the denominationalists stalled. The Christian Life Commission did set the ball in motion and persisted in its support, but it was women, as they became increasingly active in lobbying for their equal status in congregational life and church ministry, who made that crucial link. Guided by the WMU, they began with the language of call.

Women in Church-Related Vocations

By the decade's end, women's ordination dominated almost every evangelical debate over the role of women, or Christian womanhood. In September 1978, SBC officials finally confronted the issue. Over a three-day period, the SBC Inter-Agency Council hosted what it formally called the "Consultation on Women in Church-Related Vocations" at the Sunday School Board's Nashville headquarters. Eleven SBC agencies, commissions, committees, and educational institutions formally sponsored the event, with the WMU at the forefront. Its women conceived of the event, steered the planning committees, and ran the meeting.

Nearly 300 persons attended the consultation. Practically every SBC agency head, commission chair, and seminary president was present. Numerous SBC board members, seminary trustees, and college and seminary professors came. Most of these denominational elite were male; however, it was the 202 women crowded into the Sunday School Board's conference rooms who dominated the proceedings. These women were traditional homemakers, denominational workers, WMU leaders, missionaries, college professors, seminary students, and ordained ministers. By design, women presided over the sessions.[29]

The official threefold purpose of the conference was "to define the present situation in the sbc with regard to women in church-related vocations," "to provide a platform for the presentation of a balanced variety of views on the topic," and "to identify options available [to] women and girls in church-related vocations."[30] The unofficial purpose was to discuss the status of women's ordination. As Catherine Allen, both the wmu's associate executive director and the consultation's steering committee chair, reported afterward, ordination was the "hottest topic of the consultation." It "repeatedly came up. People wanted to talk about it. Obviously women are hearing calls from God which in various ways come to involve ordination. Churches are ordaining them. Some are pursuing comfortable and successful careers. Some are having troubles." According to Allen, the challenge was "that some Baptists apparently do not believe that women can be called of God at all. Some do not believe that a woman can be called into nontraditional jobs in the church."[31] In referring to nontraditional jobs, Allen clearly meant those ordained ministerial positions granting women authority and power over men.

In addressing the hard questions of Christian womanhood, the consultation attempted some balance. The banquet menu even matched feminist-inspired "Germaine Greer's Greens" with "Marabel's Total Dough." A southern and Southern Baptist flavor was added with "Scarlett's Salad" and "Lottie Moon's Daily Fare." At the same time, Allen admitted that "balance was not accomplished," largely because "most of the speakers showed a clear predisposition to favor increased numbers of women in nontraditional church-related vocations." As one Southern Baptist state newspaper put it, the conference had a "feminist feeling." Even though the 1974 Glorieta conference had drawn more intentionally on feminism, feminist theology, and evangelical feminism, that event had not been nearly as visible, and women's ordination had not yet seized the imagination with the same intensity.

A glance at the consultation's program, addresses, and findings report supports Allen's assessment. As far as formal presentations, Frank Stagg, a professor of New Testament at Southern Seminary, and Evelyn, his wife, who had a developing interest in the classical world, provided a daily Bible study that echoed evangelical feminism. The Staggs emphasized Jesus as having opened the door wide for women. Christ's eternal principles, they declared, superseded Pauline strictures, Old Testament concepts of order, and any other biblical mandate limiting women's roles, including their full participation in ministry. Southern Baptists, they charged, must choose *that's just not how the Bible works*

Jesus over Paul. Kay Shurden, a high school literature teacher, examined the homemaker-mother role that permeated the Sunday School Board's literature. As she saw it, the dominant homemaker image for women and girls "severely limited role models" and failed to "encourage women to explore their own options creatively and responsibly."[32] Southern Seminary professor Andrew Lester spoke of the psychological issues that surfaced around women ministers. These women encountered emotional barriers involving the gendered nature of authority and competition, and so, too, did their congregants. When it came to sexuality, Lester said, male congregants confessed to particular struggles when encountering a woman minister. Nevertheless, he concluded that women ministers were vital in reshaping destructive notions of authority, competition, and sexuality.

Bolstered by these affirming public addresses, women participants actually pushed ordination as the consultation's "hottest topic." Approximately two dozen ordained women were present, almost half of the SBC's reported fifty. Many female seminarians also attended. To be sure, these women shaped the atmosphere and mood. They shared their stories, expressed their desires, and laughed and cried, often spontaneously from the floor. Over and over, they raised the issue of ordination, whether it was in larger question-and-answer sessions or in the breakout small-group discussions. Women ministers and seminarians claimed a Jesus who spoke to them personally and liberated them to follow God's call.[33] Like Addie Davis fourteen years earlier, these women emphasized that their Southern Baptist churches and distinctly Southern Baptist spaces fostered this sense of ministerial call. Lynda Weaver-Williams, an ordained woman and Southern Seminary doctoral student, told her story. Citing her years in Southern Baptist Sunday School, youth camp, and the Baptist Student Union and her time as a Home Mission Board summer intern, as well as her seminary experience, she issued a moving challenge to her Southern Baptist audience:

> I am where I am because of you. Because you let me learn from you, and because you provided ways for me to respond to God's call, and because you have supported me and encouraged me in every endeavor. At least you have supported me until now. Now that support is gone. Those prayers and smiles and pats on the back, and even the more substantial means of support are gone because I have not answered God's call in the way you wanted—in the way that you believe to be valid. . . . God has called me beyond what people have designed for

me, and I think that you should know that I am not alone. There are more women like me—women who are hearing God call them to all kinds of ministry and who are responding, both because of Baptist encouragement and in spite of Baptist obstinance. If Southern Baptists are not ready to use the women God is calling to ministry—ministry within Southern Baptist churches—then you'll have to purge the ranks of your Sunday School teachers of women and let the men do Vacation Bible School. You'll have to limit the youth camp to boys only, and keep the women and the girls out of the choirs. Eventually you'll have to turn us away at seminary because God is calling us through every avenue of the church. God is making ministers of the women and girls in our churches, just as God is making ministers of the men and the boys. We hear the same call, and we are beginning to respond in the same way. You will have to decide what to do about it because God's call is as much to you to accept women as ministers as it is to me to be a minister.[34]

Williams put the responsibility for God's call squarely in the lap of male SBC leaders, administrators, and ministers. It seemed that she intentionally left the WMU and its cultivation of call out of the picture, not because WMU women were incidental but because she was drawing a line in the sand. She clearly wanted those men present, who represented the corporate church with all of its power and authority, to cross over and be held accountable for the status of women ministers, or lack thereof, in Southern Baptist life. For her, either they accepted God's transformative call or they did not.

In response, men pointed to reality. Few Southern Baptist churches, they warned, would hear God calling them to appoint a woman pastor to preach weekly from the pulpit. In a question-and-response period, Roy Honeycutt, Southern Seminary's provost, revealed that during the ministerial recruitment process, Southern's placement office regularly asked churches if they would accept women's biographical data. Almost none answered positively. As Honeycutt advised Weaver-Williams and the other women present, "Think about marketability. If you have to do so, forget about ordination."[35]

This attitude angered many of the consultation's women. Women seminarians addressed the need for concrete help in the form of better placement services, vocational guidance, and support groups. They pointed to the absence of any woman seminary professor in biblical studies, church history, and systematic theology. Diane Hill, an ordained minister and Southeastern Seminary graduate, challenged what she interpreted as the "defensiveness" of denominational executives and seminary presidents. Responding to claims about women's limited marketability, she said, "I don't think any of us would quibble with that." But she continued: "My direct aim, my hope, and what I am working for is that our seminaries and some of our other institutions will be able to be leaders to make changes."[36] Turning to Honeycutt, she bluntly stated, "It bothers me when I hear that you asked a church, 'Will you consider a woman?' I believe that question insinuates there is a problem here, something is abnormal in having a woman as a minister. I would like for the seminary in some subtle and also in some very obvious ways to lead out—yes, with sensitivity to the constituency; yes, with consideration for not alienating.... I would like for there to be some very conscious steps made to do some leading in that area."[37]

As an added frustration, many consultation participants found words like "call," "ministry," and "church-related vocation" too vague for constructive dialogue. Frank Stagg noted that ordination was neither a New Testament nor a Baptist concept. Some, like Stagg, argued that ordination had garnered excessive attention in recent Southern Baptist life and that all believers were ministers. Stagg's sentiments in this instance indicated a particular direction and an avoidance that only added insult to injury. It was hardly likely that contemporary Southern Baptists would adopt attitudes that had flourished in more sectarian, frontier environments. Qualifications were necessary in the new, postwar denomination. Ordination was vital to full clerical standing in the corporate church, and women felt God calling them to serve as ordained pastors rather than as lay ministers. Scholars have noted that after the 1960s, ordination took on fresh meaning as a bid to equality and power. As a result, the traditional language and rhetoric of call assumed controversy, and conservatives pitted the language of call against faithfulness to the Bible, awakening the tension between the inner witness of the Spirit and the outer witness of scripture.

sbc leaders listened to complaints. Seminary presidents pledged to do more. Since Jimmy Allen served as the current sbc president, his affirmation of women's ordination was monumental. In a consultation-related press interview, he even revealed that he had voted for the era.[38] Allen delivered the consultation's closing address, beginning in a broadly supportive tone by reading Joel 2:28–32 ("And your sons and daughters shall prophesy") and Matthew 8:14 ("And she arose and ministered unto them"). He invoked the civil rights movement, stating that the "same kind of revolution is now happening in the maleness and femaleness question." As sbc president, Allen spoke of the wider church's shared responsibilities: the "responsibility of the family of faith to affirm the gifts of all the children of the family," "the responsibility of the called," and related to that responsibility, "to call the called to respond to the truth of the eternal." Allen began in a supportive vein, saying, "I am concerned that we as a family work to remove artificial barricades for service from all the family members."[39]

But Allen then quickly shifted his focus to those appealing for women's ordination, particularly women themselves, whom he called the barricaded. "Every group, every person who finds himself barricaded finds himself angered," he said. "That anger sometimes twists us, it keeps us from being effective."[40] The first test to their Southern Baptist family, he warned, "is whether or not we will be sensitive to the leadership of the spirit of God." The second, he continued, "is whether or not we will maintain a spirit of unity in the midst of diversity." Allen charged that some consultation participants possessed a spirit of ridicule that contradicted God's grace and destroyed family unity. Comparing them to angry blacks whose tempers had done little for the progress of civil rights, he urged "the right combination of patience and persistence," or compromise. "Change comes," he said, "when the black person who comes to join the church wasn't trying to make the point except that he loved Jesus. And the folks who got up next to him found that out. And then they could change." Allen predicted change "because people have a relational spirit in which the love of God has created a new openness both to him and his love." He ended his address with a "welcome" to "any gifted person anywhere to do anything they're good enough to do. This is the day for it," he declared.[41]

Despite Allen's optimistic conclusion, his comments placed the onus of patience, persistence, and change on blacks, women, and those being barricaded. He even spoke of his being barricaded from preaching early on because of his youth, a comparison few women would find helpful and most would find irritating. Moreover, while he predicted gender would go the route of race, they were not the same issue. Allen, who was vocal in supporting the civil rights movement in the 1960s, failed to recognize that in 1978 few blacks would have felt comfortable entering a Southern Baptist church, no matter what their attitude or love for Jesus. Not surprisingly, women like Weaver-Williams and Hill found the spirit of compromise as represented by Allen to be a stumbling block to women's movement into the pulpit and the empowerment it symbolized.

And yet, they still believed that progress would come. The consultation's conclusions acknowledged that the WMU and missions had served as "good routes" for Southern Baptist women to "make achievements in denominational management professions" and "'ministerial' professional jobs." For nearly 100 years, the WMU had encouraged in girls and women a sense of God's call. Now that they were beginning to attach the feminist rhetoric of freedom and liberation to both their call and their Southern Baptist background, they found God's call taking them to new places. As the 1970s came to a close, these Southern Baptist women felt that the cultural surge against the ERA, feminism, and women's ordination represented the last gasps of a dying patriarchy, and even denominationalists like Allen justified compromise by predicting eventual change and progress. Less than a year later, Adrian Rogers replaced Jimmy Allen as the SBC's president, initiating a chain of events that would prove the cultural surge to be a beginning rather than an end.

3

A Rattlesnake in the House

THE BEGINNING OF THE CONTROVERSY

As the 1978 Consultation on Women in Church-Related Vocations concluded, women felt hope for their future in ordained ministry. The Woman's Missionary Union (WMU) was coming to their side. The Christian Life Commission had adopted their cause. Plans for a women-in-ministry network were under way. While frustrated by the advice of male denominationalists to wait, they celebrated "glimmers of light here and there."[1] For the first time in the denomination's history, some young women actually anticipated an ordained ministerial career in Southern Baptist life. Terry Thomas Primer was one. As a collegian from Baltimore in the early 1970s, she had been a state leader for the Baptist Student Union, published in its student magazine, and worked with the Home Mission Board's Baptist Student Ministries as a summer missionary. It was, according to Primer, an "exciting, creative, intellectually stimulating place to be." Years later, she compared her early experience to a scene in *Mary Poppins* in which Mary and Bert, strolling through the park, came across a beautiful chalk drawing full of color, vitality, and movement and jumped into an "alternate reality." For Primer, the alternate reality invaded the present with promises "for me to have a place and a chance to minister, and to be creative and open and intellectually honest."[2] Afterward, she enrolled in Yale Divinity School to explore a pastoral calling.

Not all women felt enthused by the new developments. After attending the 1978 consultation, a Mrs. Patray reported, "Some of what I have heard . . . sounds like the feminists and that disturbs my spirit."[3] Mrs. Patray voiced the concerns of a growing number of Southern Baptist women and men who sensed that the denomination was losing its way. These Southern Baptists did not celebrate that alternate reality as possessing any glimmer of hope. They feared instead for the future of the Southern Baptist Convention (SBC), particularly if its leaders continued to open the doors to liberals and feminists like Primer. In the word of the conservative preacher James Robison, there was now a "rattlesnake in the house."[4]

In 1979, two events dramatically and irrevocably changed the direction of Southern Baptist life. First, the young, dynamic megachurch preacher Adrian Rogers beat a slate of leading Southern Baptist statesmen for the SBC's presidency. His victory led to a two-decade power struggle between self-described conservatives and denominationalists-turned-moderates. Second, a little-known independent Baptist preacher from Virginia launched a campaign against America's first "born-again" president. Accusing Southern Baptist Jimmy Carter of abandoning his religious heritage for liberal causes like feminism, homosexuality, abortion, and secular education, Jerry Falwell and his Moral Majority laid the foundation for the new religious right and helped Ronald Reagan sweep into the Oval Office. While Rogers's victory more directly affected the SBC's future, Southern Baptists waged their campaigns as part of the larger culture wars that the Moral Majority spearheaded. The SBC's confrontation both influenced and was influenced by the surrounding evangelical and political debate. As a result, Southern Baptists stepped out of their former isolation, forming closer alliances with other like-minded evangelicals. These alliances were based on similar agendas, but because Southern Baptists possessed a distinct history, their struggle followed its own unique path.[5] Unlike other culture warriors, for example, Southern Baptists engaged in a challenge for denominational control, with institutional concerns more often taking center stage. Additionally, though social issues inspired and even drove the Southern Baptist contest, with resolutions addressing abortion and the Equal Rights Amendment (ERA), conservatives' initial attack against denominationalists seemed more theological in its rhetoric.

This chapter considers the years from 1979 to 1983 and examines how "inerrancy" functioned as conservatives' initial rallying call and how "freedom" was the moderates' response. Almost immediately, the terms "inerrancy" and "freedom" became ambiguous signifiers, causing confusion and animosity within each camp. If there was a rattlesnake in the house, who, or even what, was the rattlesnake? And whose house was it in? As this chapter demonstrates, Southern Baptist women gave the denominational dispute a more relevant focus, for as they experienced it, the debate over women's roles and practices was integral to theological concerns. By coalescing around differing concepts of Christian womanhood, they upheld the issue of gender, or gendered concepts of women.

The Conservative Plan

SBC leaders initially interpreted the victory of Adrian Rogers as one of those occasional aberrations in convention politics. To be sure, the conservative Rogers perpetuated the charismatic pulpiteer tradition that Southern Baptists traced back to the Separate Baptists of Sandy Creek, North Carolina, who attracted thousands to their endless revivals with charismatic preaching and evangelical fervor.[6] Under his leadership, Bellevue Baptist Church in Memphis had grown to nearly 11,000 members.[7] But Rogers and Bellevue also stood on the fringes of the SBC. Not only did Bellevue contribute little financially to the SBC and its Cooperative Program; it donated its monies and resources to competing institutions and programs. Since the early 1970s, for instance, Rogers had led Mid-America Theological Seminary—an alternative to what he viewed as the liberalism of the official Southern Baptist seminaries.

Following Rogers's election, many denominationalists pointed out that other ultraconservatives outside the denominationalists' fold had attained the SBC's highest office, including Rogers's Bellevue predecessor, the "silver-maned, silver-tongued orator" Robert G. Lee, who occupied the position in 1950. During the 1960s and 1970s, both the fiery W. A. Criswell and his fellow Texan K. O. White, who led the anti-Elliott contingency, wielded the gavel. None of these men had penetrated denominational politics, nor had they mounted any serious effort. After all, a presidential term lasted only a year, with the usual one-year reelection. SBC insiders hurriedly concluded that it made little sense to become overly alarmed. They were wrong. Rogers's election was not simply the success of a dazzling pulpiteer. As scholars both inside and outside the SBC have endlessly noted in their analyses and critiques, Rogers served as the charismatic face for a conservative network determined to wrest SBC control from longtime denominationalists who held the keys to the Southern Baptist kingdom. Paul Pressler, a prominent Houston judge, and theologian Paige Patterson, the president of the Dallas-based Criswell College, engineered what they referred to as the conservative resurgence.

Pressler and Patterson had struck up a friendship more than a decade before. In March 1967, Pressler, then an up-and-coming judge in his early forties, was attending a layman's conference at New Orleans Baptist Theological Seminary, where Patterson happened to be a fresh-faced doctoral student. The Elliott controversy had greatly disturbed the forceful Pressler, and he believed it indicated a liberal drift in the denomination's seminary classrooms as well as its highest offices. A mutual friend had given "the judge," as Pressler was often called, Patterson's name as a another Texan who shared his concerns. The two met late one night over coffee, hot chocolate, and beignets at Café du Monde, an encounter that has assumed legendary status in Southern Baptist lore. When conservatives experienced their twelfth consecutive presidential victory at the 1990 New Orleans convention, they crowded Café du Monde's outside patio, singing "Victory in Jesus" as homage to Patterson's and Pressler's 1967 rendezvous.

At this first, more intimate Café du Monde gathering, Pressler and Patterson, with their wives, Nancy and Dorothy, discussed their worries. Patterson said that his seminary professors had ridiculed him when he defended the historical accuracy of Genesis. As he later remembered, "The judge asked me one question: 'Who is going to do something about the liberal drift?' And I said, 'Well God will raise somebody,' and he said, 'Why not you?'" Patterson responded, "I am just a student" and said that it would take months of studying the SBC's inner cogs and wheels to effect any action. "That's where I come in," said Pressler. "If you are willing to work with me, maybe with my organizational background and your knowledge of Southern Baptists, maybe together we can do something."[8]

Patterson's agreement forged an enduring partnership, though a decade would pass before the two took any concrete action. Pressler's conversations with Baylor students over what he agreed to be heretical teachings set the ball rolling. Equally significant, by the mid- to late 1970s, the climate seemed right. After a decade of Vietnam, Watergate, inner-city riots, drugs, and escalating crime, many Americans felt disillusioned, and some southerners were raising the question of the nationalization of Dixie. Other, mostly nondenominational, evangelicals were renewing their commitment to theological orthodoxy and biblical inerrancy as they joined the early forces of the culture wars. In 1978, many of these evangelicals formed the International Council on Inerrancy. During the same years, Harold Lindsell's 1976 *The Battle for the Bible* and his 1979 sequel, *The Bible in Balance*, were nationwide bestsellers. In *The Battle for the Bible*, Lindsell warned evangelicals against false teachers who were posing as devout believers. In denying absolute inerrancy, he said, they abandoned basic biblical teachings like heaven and hell. He even devoted one chapter to the SBC, charging that the denomination, once a bastion of inerrantist thinking, was now overrun by false teachers who had succumbed to modern scholarship. Lindsell urged an immediate showdown: "The longer the Southern Baptists wait, the rougher the battle will be, the more traumatic the consequences and the less obvious the outcome in favor of historic Christianity."[9]

While dependent on his local church membership, Lindsell was most often a Southern Baptist who, like Billy Graham, related more to northern evangelical circles and alliances. He had attended Wheaton College, taught at Fuller Theological Seminary, and served as *Christianity Today*'s senior editor. In 1979, he dabbled in Southern Baptist politics, becoming president of the Baptist Faith and Message Fellowship, the organization lobbying for a stricter interpretation of the Southern Baptist statement of faith. Almost simultaneously, Lindsell joined Jerry Falwell, James Dobson, and Pat Robertson in forming the religious right, integrating scriptural concerns with family values. Lindsell never stepped fully into Southern Baptist circles, but he provided a crucial connection, linking Southern Baptists to the larger evangelical world just as some of its once-sectarian leaders were beginning to mobilize.

By the decade's end, Pressler and Patterson were poised to answer Lindsell's appeal for a showdown. Pressler had carefully studied the SBC's constitution and noted that the president single-handedly appointed trustees to the SBC's boards, commissions, committees, and seminaries. The key to reshaping the denomination was to capture the presidency and then hold on to it. For most conservatives, the Baptist Faith and Message Fellowship would have been the natural starting point. Pressler and Patterson, however, were savvy enough to recognize its primarily rural and small-church following as backwoods cousins who lacked the necessary money, influence, and power. Moreover, its North Carolina base was far from their Texas home, where they could run the conservative show. So Pressler and Patterson turned instead to the megachurches of the urban and suburban South, in cities like Houston, Dallas, Atlanta, Orlando, and even Phoenix, those areas that had most intensely experienced growth, prosperity, change, and conflict. This new catchment resonated more deeply with the two men, both of whom combined education, credentials, and clout with a feisty Texan spirit. Pressler, for example, boasted an Ivy League Princeton degree. Patterson held a Ph.D. from New Orleans Baptist Theological Seminary, and as president of Criswell Bible Institute, he held connections to the influential W. A. Criswell and the First Baptist Church of Dallas. The Patterson family name also carried some denominational weight, as T. A. Patterson, Paige's father, had presided over the largest and most influential Southern Baptist state convention, the Baptist General Convention of Texas.

From the urban megachurches of the traditional Bible Belt and burgeoning Sunbelt, Pressler and Patterson developed their own network of powerful pulpiteers. Over the next twelve years, they successfully ran, one by one, their chosen men for the coveted presidential office. After 1990, conservative candidates stood unopposed. By the mid-1990s, trustees representing the Pressler–Patterson network dominated almost every SBC institution. Their strategy for victory surpassed conservatives' wildest dreams and moderates' worst nightmares. To be sure, success required more than simply executing a plan; it also meant rallying the troops. Conservatives won the denomination because they persuaded the vast majority of Southern Baptists that conservative victory would not only save the denomination but rescue American culture as well.

Inerrancy

The initial rallying call of conservatives was inerrancy. During the spring of 1979, Pressler and Patterson traveled across the South and the nation inciting congregations to send messengers to the Houston convention with the aim of electing a president committed to the "unadulterated Word." That same spring, as Lindsell promoted his bestseller *The Bible in the Balance*, he likewise implored Southern Baptists to fight for "historical Christianity," even if it meant a substantial denominational decline in numbers. Conservative preachers responded. With their oratorical skills and folksy styles, they crafted stirring sermons on "the perfect Word of God" and called their congregations to old-fashioned, Bible-believing religion. From 1979 onward, the "infallible Word of God" dominated the annual SBC's Pastor's Conference, the showcase of the denomination's most gifted rhetoricians and, since the mid-1970s, the conservative arena. Throughout the early 1980s, conservative SBC presidents urged messengers, amidst thunderous applause and shouts of "amen," to accept unwaveringly "the Word without error."[10] In 1980, conservatives in power successfully passed their resolution "on doctrinal integrity," which directed SBC seminaries, boards, and institutions to employ only those "who believe in the divine inspiration of the whole Bible, infallibility of the original manuscripts, and that the Bible is truth without any error."[11]

For conservatives, the rhetoric of inerrancy superseded the language of Zion—a tenet that reflected the pietistic and missional zeal that denominationalists had relied on to hold various factions together. According to conservatives, however, missions, evangelism, and revivalism flourished only when they grew from the doctrine of biblical inerrancy. As one preacher put it, proclaiming Jesus without fighting for the Bible was akin to playing baseball without using the ball. Since the Elliott affair, a growing number of conservatives had criticized the language of Zion as theological vagary, claiming that it promoted a denominational compromise that proved "toothless" and ineffective. In many ways, the push for inerrancy symbolized the rejection of institutional stability, with its penchant for compromise over controversy. But despite the desire and demand of conservatives for clear-cut boundaries, ambiguity and confusion also beset talk of inerrancy. As the struggle proceeded, the rhetoric of inerrancy soon posed several challenges: definitional, historical, and functional.

Like many evangelicals, Southern Baptist conservatives abandoned the traditional nuances of meaning among the terms "inerrancy," "literalism," "infallibility," and "plenary inspiration," using them interchangeably. As the conservative megachurch pastor James Draper wrote during his 1984 SBC presidential term, "Those who criticize conservative Christians for using all of this terminology should consider the reason why we have to keep coining new terms to describe our position. It is because unnamed others keep usurping the old terms and twisting them into something totally different from their original meaning."[12] The term "inerrancy" enjoyed a broad definitional usage within the denomination. In fact, during the beginning years of the Baptist battles, many denominationalists-turned-moderates affirmed the conservatives' rhetoric. According to the sociologist Nancy Ammerman, 1985 convention messengers interpreted "inerrancy" as meaning anything from the Bible's scientific accuracy to its moral authority, with some inerrantists, as they called themselves, accepting nonliteralist interpretations of the Genesis account and other biblical stories.[13]

Conservatives attempted to clarify "inerrancy," "infallibility," and other terms describing their hermeneutic by insisting on absolute inerrancy as the historical and scientific accuracy of the Bible, which had God as its author, and then emphasizing inerrancy's connection to inviolable theological orthodoxies, which they identified early as the virgin birth, the physical resurrection, the second coming, Adam and Eve's actual fall from grace, the belief in Satan as a personal being, and the literal concepts of heaven and hell. Conservatives traced these orthodoxies to scripture and believed that renouncing any one meant a rapid downslide into hermeneutical, theological, and moral relativity—what another conservative SBC president, Morris Chapman, named the "dalmatian theory" with "a spot of truth here and a spot of error there."[14] Sounding like Lindsell, Patterson stated, "If you give up inerrancy, the first thing to go is eternal punishment. If hell goes, then Jesus Christ doesn't become nearly important. If heaven is real and hell is real and if a relationship with Jesus is the only way to avoid one and go to the other . . . well, it is the vividness of that in my soul that propels me in everything that I do."[15] Theological belief and everyday practice, then, went hand in hand. Chapman put it more succinctly: "If you believe all of the Word, you're in. If you believe less than all of the Word, you're out."[16]

Chapman's formula sounded easy enough, or perhaps too easy, since distinguishing who believed "all" from who believed "less than all" remained difficult. This difficulty led to a more historical reason for inerrancy's ambiguity. While the mandate for inerrancy among Southern Baptist conservatives connected them to the wider evangelical world, they had not participated in the 1920s debates among evangelicals that had shaped that world's landscape. The premillennial-versus-postmillennial dispute that tore apart northern denominations never fully penetrated Southern Baptist life. Consequently, Southern Baptists had not experienced the same polarization, and after a century of compromise, their boundary lines had yet to be drawn. This lack created other challenges: First, conservatives celebrated the period prior to the Elliott controversy and the edict of compromise as a golden age, a period in which Southern Baptists were united in their opposition to northern liberalism and modern scholarship. The Norris affair in the early 1900s did not have much of an impact because Southern Baptists were a more unified conservative and traditional people. Liberalism did not hold the same threat. At the same time, conservatives could not easily expunge this past of its racism. Southern Baptists had, after all, left northern Baptists over slavery. Cultural factors like race drove the two apart as much as any ecclesial or theological position. Moderates, then, insisted that theological conservatism went hand in hand with the old southern order of Jim Crow politics and racial segregation. Often ignoring the relative silence of the prevailing denominationalists during the civil rights era, moderates saw themselves as rightful heirs of the progressive New South, especially regarding race.

Second, although conservatives tarred denominationalists as liberals, many, if not most, moderates embraced orthodox beliefs. They steadily upheld the virgin birth, the physical revelation, and the second coming, and some even affirmed absolute historical inerrancy. They did not uniformly and indiscriminately embrace modern hermeneutics. And only a handful actually supported wider liberal causes. At the onset of the battles, insiders and outsiders alike found themselves hard-pressed to cite major differences between conservatives and moderates. Many Southern Baptists, including pastors, missionaries, and board personnel, felt unsure as to which camp they belonged in. Some of the most devoted future moderates later remembered worrying alongside conservatives that the mainline Protestant drift toward liberalism might infiltrate the denomination's highest institutions and offices.[17] In the eyes of many outsiders, conservatives appeared to be conducting guerilla warfare against their own.

Finally, the most significant challenge was more functional in nature. No matter how loud conservatives shouted, the scientific accuracy of the Genesis creation did not radically affect the way most people lived. Southern Baptists claimed to be a Bible-believing people. Convention messengers booed and hissed evolutionary theory. They applauded and cheered the seven-day Creation as "truth without mixture of error." Church members voiced their "amens" during sermons lauding the "infallible Word." And yet, despite Patterson's testimony, the scripture's historicity did not propel everything they did. Ammerman's research indicates that as late as 1985, the majority of Southern Baptists still did not see themselves as heavily invested in the inerrancy debate. They might have attended the annual conventions in record numbers, but most went about their day-to-day business without much concern over denominational politics. If conservative leaders were to sustain passions over a long period of time, they needed to make their appeal more relevant. They did not have to search far. The religious right played a key role here, and so, too, did conservative Southern Baptist women.

Women's Concerns Conference

During the 1970s, a group of conservative Southern Baptist women were laying the foundation for local women's ministry programs. Inspired by Barbara O'Chester's Wonderful Weekends for Women, they began establishing church Bible studies independent of the WMU and women's missions. Many of them were joining the growing number of independent evangelical women's Bible studies, while others supported conservative political organizations like Phyllis Schlafly's Eagle Forum and Beverly LaHaye's Concerned Women of America.[18] Like their male counterparts, these Southern Baptist women felt that liberalism had infiltrated the SBC. They touted inerrancy but interpreted it more immediately within the context of feminism and the growing debate over culture wars. As they saw it, feminism was eroding the traditional understanding of Christian womanhood, which laid the foundation for the American family and its flourishing. Abortion, homosexuality, and all sorts of alternative and promiscuous lifestyles affirmed their worst fears, driving them toward what they felt to be a stricter understanding of scripture. They were convinced, furthermore, that the WMU was neither addressing women's pressing needs nor fighting dangerous feminist influences, which they associated with angry, man-hating women and radical antifamily attitudes.

In 1980, Joyce Rogers, Adrian Rogers's wife, and her friend Sarah Maddox brought 4,000 conservative-minded women together in the Mid-Continent Women's Concerns Conference. Women inspired, planned, and led the conference, which was hosted by Bellevue Baptist Church. More than twenty-five years later, Maddox narrated the personal events behind its inception.

In 1978 Joyce Rogers and I were scheduled to attend a family conference in Chicago, IL. Because our plans did not materialize, on the day of our planned departure, we met at my house to pray and exchange ideas. During our discussion Joyce shared about her desire to promote the traditional role of women among Southern Baptists and other Christian women, and I shared about my desire to motivate Southern Baptist and other Christian women to become involved in standing for righteousness in our nation. During our discussion we came up with the idea of having a conference at Bellevue whereby we could encourage women in fulfilling their traditional roles as wives and mothers as well as challenge women to become involved in promoting moral virtue and traditional family values in our society.

Maddox added that the conference was needed because "there were so many competing voices speaking to women about their roles and responsibilities," and she, along with Rogers, desired to "reach as many Southern Baptist women as possible" through this venue. "No church in the SBC had ever hosted such a conference," she added, and "there were no SBC models to follow."[19]

At the time, Rogers and Maddox were young suburban wives and mothers who felt their values and priorities under siege by post-1960s cultural forces, particularly feminism. With a team of nineteen women, they selected the theme "A Wise Woman Builds" (Ps. 14:1).[20] In connection to the theme, Maddox recalled two planning goals: "One of our main purposes was to motivate and help women build stronger Christian homes. We wanted to validate the importance of their roles as wife and mother, with special emphasis on the unchanging Biblical role of women." As a secondary goal, Maddox added that "I personally hoped that we would be able to motivate these Christian women to take a strong stand for righteousness in the places where they lived." The first goal validated traditional womanhood, shaped as it was by new domesticity and the 1950s *Ozzie and Harriet* notion of family. The second goal then recast their purpose by encouraging women's more public and political participation. Joyce Rogers explained that the crisis caused by feminism demanded an active response from women: "Feminism was rising in our country and a great demise in morals and proper priorities for women and the home." Much to her chagrin, "awareness on these issues were [*sic*] not great in Southern Baptist circles."[21]

The event exceeded their expectations. More than 4,000 women from twenty-six states, including Alaska, flocked to Memphis for the three-day spring event. Enrollment closed early, and hundreds were turned away at the door. As women registered, the organizers quickly realized that the meeting had moved beyond any regional gathering and pulled women in from outside the SBC, too. Even if the majority of participants might have been Southern Baptists, most plenary speakers came from other evangelical traditions.

The conference emphasized submission and domesticity as God's design for women. Keynote speakers included the noted evangelical inspirational writer Elisabeth Elliot, Beverly LaHaye, and Vonette Bright, whose husband, Bill Bright, founded Campus Crusade for Christ. All three were leading antifeminist voices committed to traditional womanhood. A total of thirty-five workshops ranged from "Basic Needs of a Man" and "Your Children and Rock Music" to "Biblical and Medical Perspectives on Abortion" and "Combating Moral Pollution." Conference participant Susie Hawkins later described her experience:

> The concerns that the conference addressed were both national and personal. The speakers explained the national issues, such as feminism, and why Christian leaders objected to some of the feminist platform. Those objections would include the priority of marriage in God's plan, the woman's influence in the home versus the workplace, the importance of motherhood and training children. It was meaningful to me because it helped "put into words" or define the evangelical position on current issues and WHY the position was taken. It also gave a voice to the many women who were uncomfortable with the feminist agenda, but not sure how to express that discomfort.[22]

Although the presentations were not archived or published, Joyce Rogers's related book, *The Wise Woman . . . How to Be One in a Thousand*, captured their central message. As in her 1974 pamphlet, *God's Chief Assignment to Women*, she argued that fixed, gendered patterns concerning women were part of God's overarching plan for humanity. In the book, she pushed further, adding that cultivating contentment in womanhood was crucial to women as they worked out their salvation—accepting the tenets of traditional, or biblical, womanhood was to them akin to accepting the virgin birth and the second coming. In outlining these tenets, Rogers again emphasized the biblical basis for women's submission. She reiterated both the order of creation (Gen. 2:18, 22–23) and God's curse on Eve (Gen. 3:17). In a new twist, she encouraged women to celebrate their submission to men as Jesus celebrated his relationship with God, the Father. Jesus, she reminded readers, was constantly submitting himself to the Father's will. In her 1974 pamphlet, Rogers had focused on the submission of women in ecclesial life. In *The Wise Woman*, she addressed submission in family matters, claiming it laid the proper foundation for domesticity and homemaking. Rogers acknowledged that God might call some women to singleness; nevertheless, she insisted that his primary role for women was wife and mother, and as wives and mothers, women should serve their husbands and children through homemaking. With the right attitude and a few "creative homemaking ideas," women could turn their earthly homes into "a little bit of heaven." Discontent, restlessness, and uncertainties over worth and identity—feelings that Rogers admitted to experiencing—resulted from feminism's dangerous assault on traditional womanhood.

The Wise Woman began and ended with submission, and Rogers incorporated several poems that she had written on the subject. One, "Submit to Him? Lord," concluded with a twist on Proverbs 31:28–31:

If I obey, You will lift me up?
    What Lord?
If I am truly submissive my
    children will rise up and
    call me blessed—
My husband will praise me—
And You, Lord—You will honor me?
Then give me a submissive heart
    Oh Lord!
I want to be in your perfect will![23]

Another, "The Blessings of Submission," transformed the Beatitudes into an antifeminist blessing on those "who demonstrate a submissive spirit" and other related virtues. Citing numerous scriptures, the poem blessed those women "who do not seek / to assert their own rights," "who recognize / their God given position," "who do not / accuse God of giving / them an inferior / position," and "who do not seek / to explain away the principles / of God's Word to suit one's / own cause."[24]

In a conference-related interview, Rogers and Maddox sought to answer criticism by arguing that submission entailed difference rather than inferiority. According to Maddox, "We believe we are equal to our husbands . . . but we do not have to be just like the men in order to be fulfilled and to find a purpose in life." They also acknowledged "so many wrongs such as male dictatorial attitudes or wife and child abuse." And yet, the "solution to those problems is not through demanding our rights," said Rogers. She held "that if a woman or child is being mistreated, if they will yield their rights, God will work for them to meet their needs." Once again, Rogers and Maddox were playing with the feminist language of rights and equality, early on reversing the process of liberation. Feminism, they claimed, "helped to generate attitudes leading towards a moral decline in the country." Maddox concluded that seeking a gender-free society "has certainly not helped the situation."[25] As Maddox and Rogers demonstrated in their comments, by the 1980s, conservative women had to define traditional womanhood in relation to what they perceived as a feminist assault.

Ironically, one of the few Southern Baptist plenary speakers resisted privately the conference's overall message. The WMU's executive director, Carolyn Weatherford, delivered the final address as representative of the historic Southern Baptist women's organization. She was invited, it seemed, both to ease the underlying friction that was growing between the national WMU and young conservative women like Rogers and Maddox and to appease older conservative women holding lifelong WMU attachments. Under Weatherford's guidance, the WMU had sponsored the 1978 Consultation on Women in Church-Related Vocations. Recognizing the opposite drift of the 1980 conference, Weatherford had questioned whether she should accept the invitation to conclude the conservative women's venue. A few days before it started, she wrote her executive staff, "Obviously I will not be with my best friends. I will be sharing the platform with folks who do not agree with my philosophy, and vice versa. Pray that I will be usable in presenting missions—and WMU—positively."[26]

Weatherford pinpointed the problem, but her prayer was not answered.

Riding the crest of the conference's success, Rogers and Maddox pressed for a new, more active network for women. Although the WMU had been women's primary arena in Southern Baptist life, Maddox held that "in the seventies the world of women was changing. They seemed to have needs that were not being met. . . . Too many women were having to go outside the church to find programs, Bible studies, and support groups for women. That ought not be! We needed to find a way to address the areas not being addressed by WMU." In 1982, Bellevue dropped the WMU from its programming and launched the first Southern Baptist women's ministry program with its own full-time director. Somewhat intentionally, it seemed, this full-time working woman was single. One women's ministry leader commented that if Bellevue and Adrian Rogers were doing it, others were bound to follow, including the denomination's most prominent megachurches. In fact, a primary characteristic of leaders and churches in the conservative movement was their association with women's ministry.[27]

Women's Ministry

Like Rogers and Maddox, Susie Hawkins was a young wife and mother. During the early 1970s, she lived in the small town of Ada, Oklahoma, where her husband, O. S. Hawkins, pastored a Southern Baptist church. O. S. became a well-known pastor and leading figure among conservatives, ending up at First Baptist in Dallas, and Susie likewise rose to prominence in women's ministry. Like other women activists, early figures in women's ministry have maintained that theirs was an informal and grassroots movement. According to Hawkins, "It just happened! . . . the SBC president, or head of the Missions Boards or Executive Committee did not call for the formation of a 'women's ministry department.' It started at the lay level, gained credibility, and was then recognized as a legitimate need in our churches."[28] In 1992, Hawkins joined Sarah Maddox as cochair of the SBC's women's ministry task force, which did advise establishing women's ministry as a department in the Sunday School Board. The task force eventually succeeded. In these early years, however, Southern Baptist conservative women struggled to write and supply most of the materials, often incorporating other evangelical voices. Feeling disconnected from the larger denomination, they brought the concerns of the Bellevue conference into their local churches, with, of course, the support of their pastor, which was not always forthcoming.

When asked to describe the concept of Christian womanhood dominant in women's ministry, particularly in its early years, Hawkins, Maddox, and other women leaders concurred with Rogers: Homemaking, marriage, motherhood, and submission were integral to what they called the traditional understanding. "Women's ministry sees a Christian woman's primary role as one who serves Christ through her marriage, her children and her community," said Hawkins. "The emphasis on marriage is huge and the woman's responsibility [is] to manage her home according to Christian principles. The limits would include putting her own desires above her husband or children's," though Hawkins did add the caveat "within reason!" She provided an example: "If a woman had young children but wanted to return to her vocation on a full time basis, she would have been strongly encouraged to stay home with her young children, spending valuable time with them, and possibly return to work when they began school or were older." Maddox stated that "all conservative churches would strongly agree" that "mothering is definitely promoted as the primary role for women, if God so chooses to give her children." Once again, submission was foundational to their message. Hawkins saw submission as a "general principle of marriage: that a woman agrees to her husband's leadership on crucial decisions and that the husband loves her sacrificially." She went further than others in adding that this principle of submission should include "great freedom" and never accommodate any type of abuse. Maddox explained that Bellevue's women's ministry firmly taught that "the man is to be the spiritual head of the home" and "he is to make the final decisions."

In spite of the language of submission and traditional womanhood, conservative women saw themselves as making a bold claim for the present life of women in the church. The very designation "women's ministry" was a reaction to the growing number of ordained women in Southern Baptist life. As conservative women insisted, their sex-segregated programs and networks remained valid and vital forms of Christian ministry. They were just not the feminized and ordained forms of Protestant liberalism. They also boasted that women's ministry could not be compared with the old-fashioned and outdated mission circles of yesteryear. To them, women's ministry was innovative, contemporary, and new. It had begun as an initiative of women, and it was women who defined, shaped, and implemented its curriculum and agenda in a wide range of settings, from local church programs and regional retreats to nationwide conferences.

When characterizing women's ministry and evaluating its success, leaders and participants alike stressed flexibility and relevance. Programs were heavy on Bible studies that addressed current issues. They also differed from place to place. A local church's women's ministry program, for example, might as easily have sponsored a seminar on abortion as an arts and crafts class. Some WMU women criticized women's ministry as "fluff," citing self-oriented activities that focused on diet or fashion. Women's ministry advocates countered these claims by maintaining that they were responding to women's varied and wide-ranging needs. Bellevue's women's ministry hosted its Conference on Women's Concerns every few years, and other churches followed suit. As in the 1980 meeting, these conferences placed pressing social issues at the forefront of their agendas, and throughout the decade, the political component remained strong.

Women's ministry flourished as one conservative church after another incorporated the segregated programs into congregational life. Within a decade, women's ministry surpassed the WMU, eventually involving millions of Southern Baptist women. At first, their leaders borrowed heavily from other evangelical traditions. This was soon reversed as conservatives took hold of the denomination, and money became available to provide women's ministry with its own director, budget, and resources. In roughly a decade, the SBC became the leader in conservative women's programming, with the term "women's ministry" being adopted by other conservative denominations as well, demonstrating that as conservatives wrested power from moderates, their influence within the circles of the religious right and the wider conservative evangelical world was growing. In fact, when Southern Baptist Theological Seminary fell to conservative control, leaders in the evangelical right recognized it as a new center of power and elected to move the headquarters of the Center for Biblical Manhood and Womanhood to its campus, a transfer that attested to the increasing dominance of the conservative-led SBC within the wider evangelical world.

As with any new venture, women's ministry experienced its own growing pains, and some of these pains involved men. Women did sometimes complain about pastoral control, resisting what they saw as men's meddlesome interference, and at times, their bold assertions of "ministry" contradicted the everyday realities of female submission. Prominent women's ministry leaders also occasionally felt their efforts were used by the denomination as a moneymaking venture. Of course, critics enjoyed pointing out that conservative pastors and denominational officials were more than willing to give room to a women's ministry group advocating submission. But overall, many women attributed the underlying success of women's ministry to the designation of "women" rather than "ministry." As Hawkins put it, "Women seemed to need the relationship with one another on a spiritual level as well as friendship." For many women, it was the first space in which they could become fully vulnerable. Together, they negotiated their role in the conservative movement, assuming a certain degree of influence and power even though the formal doors of pulpit ministry and denominational authority were closed to them.

The significance of women's ministry to the early conservative cause has been underestimated, largely because women themselves downplayed the significance of their role. Early leaders claimed that neither the 1980 conference nor the grassroots movement originated as a means to promote the Pressler–Patterson political agenda. Still, as Hawkins herself admitted, the "goals of women's ministry were definitely in harmony with the conservative movement, although not expressed or even understood at the time in that way. Part of the interest of women in Bible study was grasping theological truth with daily application and that was certainly part of the conservative movement." This need for daily application undoubtedly brought gender roles and the rhetoric of family values to the foreground of women's ministry. According to Maddox, "Since the more liberal viewpoints were being expressed among Christian women of all denominations, and there was some discussion in our own denomination, we did have a sense that we traditional Baptist women needed to stand strongly for what we believed." If conservatives wanted to make the battles more relevant, women had already found a key.

Why did gender, particularly gendered concepts of women, their roles, and performances, contain such force? As seen throughout Southern Baptist history, theological arguments were often responses to social instability and regional upheaval. Theological tensions were integral to cultural ones, and they often evoked questions regarding the southern order. In fact, controversies over civil rights followed the Elliott debacle and intensified its significance. Elliott's detractors claimed that northern liberalism had invaded Southern Baptist culture through modern scholarship. Their anxieties over this occurrence could not be separated from the seismic cultural shifts that southerners were feeling. By 1979, race was no longer the same issue that it had been, and over the next decade, conservative leaders were keen to distance themselves from racist caricatures. For them, feminism came to embody the liberal impulses of modern American society.

Moreover, women's lives were changing dramatically as even more conservative women throughout the 1970s went to college and entered the workforce; some did so out of choice, while others responded to the lagging economy. Clinging to traditional rhetoric, at least in the realm of religion, provided some women with a source of comfort. In this way, they still fit the perceived norm. One conservative woman active in women's ministry during this period even shared that a prayer concern involved a daughter playing on her school's girls basketball team, obviously formed in the wake of Title IX. For some conservative women, who grew up seeing girls as cheerleaders and homecoming contestants, basketball pushed the limits of femininity and Christian womanhood.

Other issues besides feminism caused havoc in the culture wars, to be sure. By the late 1980s, abortion, homosexuality, school prayer, and the death penalty, to name a few, seemed to overshadow the debate over women. Conservatives still saw these issues as being birthed by, and thus connected to, the feminist movement, but when conservative Southern Baptists rallied against them alongside the religious right, they were nonplussed to sometimes find moderate Southern Baptists by their side. Few moderates wanted to be seen as sympathetic to more extreme liberal causes, particularly homosexuality, and often went out of their way to make known their rejection.

Questions regarding women, then, were both related and different. Competing understandings of womanhood had always been a sharp tension running just underneath the surface of Southern Baptist life, erupting at certain moments of instability and change. The time once again seemed right, as feminism followed hot on the heels of civil rights, the religious right deemed feminism the root of the moral corruption of society, and Southern Baptist women entered seminary in increasing numbers. The Consultation on Women in Church-Related Vocations had just taken place. If women's submission to men's authority functioned for some conservatives as a litmus test for inerrancy, it was not subsidiary to inerrancy. The concept possessed its own conflicted history, potency, and even fear. Many Southern Baptists were likely to accept or reject inerrancy, and the conservative agenda, on the basis of their understanding of women. As a result, the debate over women dominated much of the Southern Baptist contest, particularly by the late 1980s and 1990s, and certainly much longer than it did in the culture wars and religious right at large.

By pushing for women's submission to male authority, Southern Baptist conservative leaders risked gross stereotypes, as they were often ridiculed as antiwomen. Other evangelicals were also resisting women's ordination, but at 13 million, the SBC dwarfed all other groups, thereby receiving most of the media's attention, criticism, and vitriol. At the end of the day, however, conservative SBC leaders could not have succeeded without their female allies. Women were the lay majority, so their support was crucial. Through local women's ministry programs, women rallied around the conservative cause even before moderates formally organized themselves to oppose it. Somewhat ironically, conservative leaders found themselves following the women's lead. As Adrian Rogers put it,

WHAT IS HAPPENING IN AMERICA IS NOT "JUST HAPPENING." It is the result of a well orchestrated plan with Satan waving the flag. FEMINIST THINKERS ARE OUT TO SUBVERT YOUR WOMEN AND TO BRING IN THEIR HEATHEN HEAVEN to do this through a HUMANIST/FEMINIST/SOCIALIST [*sic*]. There is a move to deny God, debase man, destroy the family, the world. Their plan is to free your children from the [*sic*] of their puritanical parents. . . . IN A WORLD GONE MAD I THANK GOD FOR SOME CONCERNED WOMEN WHO ARE SAYING, "BACK TO THE BIBLE." STAND UP AND BE COUNTED BEFORE THE TIME RUNS OUT FOR AMERICA.[29]

Rogers's plea demonstrated, too, that by attacking feminism and presenting it solely in its most radical and extreme forms, conservatives achieved a sense of immediacy, urgency, and fear that the moderates' message simply failed to conjure. They were able to convince the bulk of Southern Baptists that, indeed, they lived in "a world gone mad."

Moderate Response

While most denominationalists dismissed Rogers's presidency as an aberration, a few worried over its implications, perceiving that the 1979 convention revealed a festering tension. At the Pastor's Conference, conservatives consecutively mounted the pulpit and railed against a new enemy within. Indicting the SBC's seminary presidents and professors for their biblical skepticism, James Robison preached, "I wouldn't tolerate a rattlesnake in my house. I wouldn't tolerate a snake of any kind in my house. I wouldn't care how pretty he is. And I wouldn't tolerate a cancer in my body. I want you to know that anyone who casts doubt on the word of God is worse than cancer and worse than snakes."[30] Robison's sermon spelled trouble for denominationalists in power. Not surprisingly, when Rogers spurned the president's usual second term and another conservative pulpiteer, Bailey Smith, easily slid into office, more SBC insiders took notice.

Cecil Sherman was one such insider. He pastored the First Baptist Church of Asheville, North Carolina, a well-established and fairly affluent downtown congregation. Like Pressler and Patterson, Sherman was a native Texan who had attended Baylor and Southwestern. Colleagues and congregants described him as an energetic and confident, if sometimes belligerent, personality who did not fear heated debate, even if it meant standing alone. Unlike Pressler and Patterson, however, Sherman formed part of a new generation of denominationalists groomed to assume leadership from the elder postwar statesmen. From this position of denominational insight and prestige, Sherman became alarmed. He attended the 1980 convention in St. Louis and wrote, "Believe me, it was different. Speakers felt compelled to identify themselves as biblical inerrantists. Speeches and business sessions were filled with digression so that the house could be evangelized to the new orthodoxy. My wife and I had not heard it this way before in our three decades of attending the sbc." It was there, Sherman remembered, "that I saw our predicament clearly. If we did nothing, the sbc would fall to the Fundamentalists."[31]

In 1980, no formal organization or movement challenging Pressler, Patterson, and their conservative cohorts existed. Sherman's "we" simply referred to those denominationalists who viewed themselves as loyal to the sbc. Some, including Sherman, referred to it as a "good old boy" network or politic.[32] Loyalty showed itself in a variety of ways. Denominationalists had almost always attended and supported the sbc's six seminaries. They served as trustees to the convention's varied boards and agencies and filled its bureaucratic offices. Their churches frequently gave the requested 10 percent of their budgets to the Cooperative Program. For these reasons, denominationalists were generally suspect of any parachurch group that took time, energy, and finances from the sbc. Sometimes, with their high levels of official participation and support, denominationalists were distinguished as "loyalists" or "traditionalists." In their view, megapreachers and pulpiteers like Rogers were "lightly invested" in the sbc's inner workings and did not deserve to occupy its elite positions of power.

In the days following the 1980 convention, Southern Seminary president Duke McCall urged Sherman to bring at least some of these loyalists together. Sherman invited twenty-five like-minded friends and pastors to convene in September in Gatlinburg, Tennessee. Seventeen accepted his invitation. In the words of Sherman, "The moderate movement was born." Thus, fairly soon in the contest, denominationalists began describing themselves as "moderates," hoping to fend off accusations of liberalism.[33]

One week prior to the moderates' first gathering, Pressler delivered his legendary "Going for the Jugular" address. Briefly, Old Forest Road Baptist Church in Lynchburg, Virginia, hosted the Conference on the Conservative Move in Our State and Our Convention. During his keynote speech, Pressler announced, "We are going for the jugular," explaining, "We are going for having knowledgeable, Bible-centered, Christ-honoring trustees of all of our institutions, who are not going to sit there like a bunch of dummies and rubber stamp everything that's being presented to them, but who are going to inquire why this is being done, what is being taught, what is the finished product of our young people who come out of institutions going to be."[34] The Gatlinburg group interpreted Pressler's revelation as an aggressive declaration of intent to take over the denomination, so they focused their energies on strategy. They agreed that their initial tactic had to be running a strong presidential campaign against Pressler's and Patterson's chosen pulpiteer. But they also needed a message, a response to conservatives' accusations, and herein lay a problem that plagued moderates. Despite moderates' more elite status within the denomination, the conservatives repeatedly set the terms of the debate, watching as moderates scrambled to respond.

The response from moderates was twofold. First, they answered the charge of theological liberalism with denial, insisting that they, too, clung to a high understanding of biblical truth and theological orthodoxy. To be sure, Southern Baptists had experienced tensions and disputes, but moderates insisted that they remained truth loving, Bible believing, and even conservative. In fact, some felt that conservatives had hijacked the term, and so they referred to conservatives more often as fundamentalists. The liberal drift was a myth. In the words of Sherman, "Southern Baptists have always been a *very* conservative people. We don't have to *get* conservative. We *have been* conservative. Whole movements pretty well passed us by."[35] According to Russell Dilday, the moderate president of Southwestern Seminary, "Baptists, 99% of them, had this high view of total trustworthiness of Scripture and even if they didn't use the word, the idea of inerrancy was the position that Baptists held without any question of confidence in the Word of God."[36] Dilday and Grady Cothen, president of the Sunday School Board, pointed out that they and other moderate leaders agreed to the Chicago Statement on Inerrancy. Written in 1978 by a group of noted conservative evangelicals, including Carl F. Henry, J. I. Packer, and Francis Schaeffer, the Chicago Statement affirmed the historical accuracy of the Bible and asserted that the "whole of Scripture and all its parts, down to the very words of the original, were given by divine inspiration" and that inspiritation "guaranteed true and trustworthy utterance on all matters of which the Biblical authors were moved to speak." Even Randall Lolley, the president of Southeastern Seminary, characterized by conservatives as the most liberal of Southern Baptists, said it was not the statement that he disagreed with but the politics of exclusion that produced it. In fact, almost every moderate leader insisted on his conservative credentials, likewise denouncing theological liberalism, neoorthodoxy, liberation politics, and anything that the Pressler and Patterson conservative camp associated with liberalism—including, in these early years, feminist theology. As the contest persisted, the seminary presidents, especially those who were targets of conservatives, went so far as to sign statements attesting to their belief that the Bible was "fully God-breathed," "utterly unique," "not errant in any area of reality," and of "infallible power and binding authority." In the words of Dilday, "inerrancy was not the issue."[37]

Second, moderates attempted to argue for biblical truth and theological orthodoxy alongside the discourse on freedom. Glenn Hinson, a Southeastern Seminary professor who was a prime target of conservatives, claimed that moderates sought to protect "freedom for the Word of God" from conservatives who attempted to put God in a box. "Boxes get in the way of God's endless effort to break through with God's Word," he warned. "They get in the way of real obedience to the Word."[38] For the most part, Southern Baptists did not buy into this idea or heed Hinson's warning. Freedom as a means to truth and obedience seemed somewhat contradictory, if not insipid or anemic to the task at hand. Amidst the escalating tensions of the culture wars, freedom as a message or rallying cry did not stand strong against inerrancy. Too many Southern Baptists wanted more. If inerrancy suffered from ambiguity and confusion, so, too, did freedom.

Freedom

One reason for the ambiguity of freedom was both definitional and historic in nature. Moderate leaders tied much of their rhetoric of freedom to historic Baptist tensions. They stressed soul competency, for example, over prescriptive scriptural mandates, or the inner Word over the outer Word. To them, soul competency related to the freedom of the inner Word to guide scriptural interpretation and command conscience. Striking out against powerful conservative pulpiteers, moderates affirmed the priesthood of the believer, which they later retranslated as the priesthood of all believers. Individual believers, they said, had the freedom to work out their own salvation before God. In other words, every individual had the right and responsibility to stand before God without any intermediary or interference. Moderates privileged the freedom of the local church body over associational governments and conventionwide dictates. They emphasized religious freedom over conservative notions of Christian citizenship. As moderates saw it, they were fighting for the heart and soul of Southern Baptist identity, or what moderate historian and Southern Baptist professor Walter Shurden identified as the "four fragile freedoms" underlying and holding up the Baptist faith and tradition: Bible freedom, soul freedom, church freedom, and religious freedom.[39]

But in its search for institutional stability, the corporate church had tamed the more radical manifestations of the old impulses—impulses that moderates were now, almost desperately, championing as historic Baptist freedoms. In addition, after the 1960s, many Southern Baptists connected the rhetoric of freedom to the liberal permissiveness of American society and culture. In this new economy of individualism and choice, freedom conjured plurality and relativism. To conservatives, something far greater than denominational identity was now at stake, and the rallying call "freedom" not only failed to answer the moral corruption of American society and culture; it contributed fully to it.

A second reason for the ambiguity and confusion surrounding the discourse of freedom could be attributed to the makeup of the moderate camp. It was one thing to affirm freedom for interpreting the Word of God. It was another thing for moderates to negotiate divergent interpretations of the Spirit at work among them. To be more specific, as the battles raged on, moderates discovered that they understood the application of freedom in Southern Baptist life differently, and these differences reflected the disparate constituencies of the moderate demographic. On one hand, there were those loyalists who had stood at the center of denominational power. This included elder statesmen like Duke McCall as well as up-and-coming figures like Cecil Sherman. Overall, these men—and they were all men—esteemed compromise, believing that it enabled freedom to flourish. When penning the 1963 Baptist Faith and Message, for instance, politic SBC leaders had sought to preserve both denominational unity and theological integrity. Hobbs and his peers recognized that the demands of faith dictated certain boundaries, but they drew these boundaries to satisfy as many constituents as possible. The inheritors of compromise were disturbed by the extent of control, order, and clarity conservatives were now pursuing. It not only destroyed the family of faith postwar denominationalists had worked so diligently to preserve; it threatened institutional stability. To add insult to injury, moderates like Sherman had anticipated inheriting the mantle of Southern Baptist leadership. Once perceived as the inside elite, they now found themselves being pushed to the edges of denominational life.

On the other hand, some moderates were more accustomed to the de-nominational fringe. These moderates esteemed dissent. In their opinion, compromise worked against freedom's flourishing. The SBC had adopted a corporate model of church in its postwar years, with organizational efficiency and growth taking precedence over doctrinal precision, ideals of social justice, and certain historic Baptist principles. Compromise squelched the freedom of individuals like Elliott. It enabled unresolved tensions to simmer. Most significantly, it hindered Southern Baptists in the greater pursuit of freedom for all members of the family of God, particularly blacks and women. Often referred to as Southern Baptist dissenters, progressives, and even radicals, these more left-leaning Southern Baptists had fostered a prophetic, countercultural impulse in Southern Baptist life. Examples included events as well as figures: the 1954 departure of thirteen dissident Southern Seminary professors for Southeastern on the basis of their modern hermeneutics, the Christian Life Commission's pursuit of desegregation and civil rights over the 1960s, Harry Hollis's 1974 declaration for the freedom of women, and Lynda Weaver-Williams's challenge to Roy Honeycutt at the 1978 Consultation on Women in Church-Related Vocations. For these progressives, denominational upheaval represented an opportunity for them to question, reshape, and even radicalize the SBC's power structure. Up to this point, they had failed. Now they were standing alongside those who had denied them authority. It proved an uneasy alliance. In many ways, those from this dissenting tradition were de facto moderates, with nowhere else to go unless they exited the SBC altogether. During the struggle's early years, even as moderate leaders bemoaned the lack of a dedicated constituency, they distanced themselves from the radical fringe of this group, which included women boldly pushing for ordination.

Sherman later commented that "the people we set out to save would not own us."[40] He was right, in a sense. Numerous old-style denominationalists felt the crisis would blow over and so hesitated to create a body politic. Then, as conservatives assumed more power, seminary presidents and agency heads feared for their own job security as well as that of their employees. Pastors who voted moderate often kept silent about their leanings. The situation only grew worse as moderates sought support west of the Mississippi, as willing state organizers in the old frontier territories were few and far between.

When reflecting on their early constituency more than a decade later, few of the moderate leadership mentioned women. None deemed problematic the lack of women at Gatlinburg and subsequent key gatherings. In autobiographical accounts of the movement's first ten years, key moderates—men like Jimmy Allen, Cecil Sherman, and Walter Shurden—included list after list of exclusively male committees and meetings.[41] In his later reflections, Sherman did not ignore women altogether. When citing moderate commonalities, he highlighted the role of women and the belief that the ordination issue be left to the local congregation—a position some women seminarians and pastors dismissed as a convenient way to avoid controversy. Sherman also maintained that numerous women had "left Baptists" because the "heavy handed doctrine of Fundamentalism about women gives them small place to exercise their gifts or their calling."[42] Sherman's claim might have been accurate, but the early moderate politic did not provide any real alternative to women who felt called to pulpit ministry. As a result, these Southern Baptist women began to mobilize against the conservative agenda on their own terms.

Southern Baptist Women in Ministry

As the feminist movement transitioned from the 1970s into the 1980s, it became less confrontational and emphasized female bonding and relationships. This shift was crucial to Southern Baptist women who, as profeminists in support of women's ordination, believed forming a network was even more pressing and certainly wanted to avoid some of feminism's grosser stereotypes and images.[43]

In many ways, the WMU birthed SBWIM. In 1981, prior to the annual convention, the WMU gave a luncheon for women in church-related vocations, which was the first event of its kind at the actual convention meeting. The following year, the WMU sponsored what it called a Dinner for Women in Ministry.[44] After her presentation, the sociologist Sarah Frances Anders encouraged those attending to establish a formal support system for women pursuing ecclesial careers, particularly, she added, ministerial positions involving ordination.[45] Women at the dinner recalled that Carolyn Weatherford immediately jumped up to pledge the WMU's financial assistance. Helen Lee Turner, an ordained Southern Baptist minister and doctoral student at the time, later reflected that the WMU's support was crucial, as it "had a pre-existing stature and with that more clear cut power, influence."[46] The WMU had enough denominational muscle to create at least a small space for these women.

Nancy Hastings Sehested became the driving force for an official organization. At thirty-two, Sehested was a young, five-foot-two, fearless personality. She hailed from a line of gifted Texas Southern Baptist preachers and, as an ordained assistant pastor in Atlanta, carried on the family tradition. Some women believed that her charisma, quick wit, preaching skills, and denominational credentials frightened conservative and moderate leaders alike. Her degree from Union Theological Seminary in New York undoubtedly added to a sense of suspicion on both sides. In 1982, a North Carolina–based group calling itself Southern Baptists for the Family and Equal Rights sponsored a three-day "Theology Is a Verb" conference, which Sehested helped organize and lead. The group did not survive long past the conference, or the failure of the passage of the ERA, but once again its participants identified the overwhelming need of women ministers for formal support.[47] Following the event, Sehested contacted potentially interested women throughout the SBC. Thirty-three responded positively. They gathered in Louisville in March 1983 to "discuss organizing a network of support for professionally employed women in ministry." Two local women, Reba Cobb and Betty McGary Pearce, also proposed a resource center to be loosely affiliated with Southern Seminary. The center would publish a newsletter as a means to encourage and connect women seeking a ministerial career. Shortly after the Louisville gathering, a task force convened at the WMU's Birmingham headquarters to plan the yet-unnamed organization's first meeting.

Advertised alternately as a conference for women in ministry or for women in church-related vocations, the two-day meeting took place the weekend prior to the SBC's 1983 Pittsburgh convention. It involved an introductory session, a formal dinner, and a business meeting and concluded with a woman-led worship service. A surprising seventy-four Southern Baptists, primarily women, showed up. During the business session, those present agreed to the working title Women in Ministry, SBC, which was changed shortly afterward to Southern Baptist Women in Ministry. They also voted to charter the organization as independent, a move to ensure that denominational politics could not directly dictate its course. In addition, it gave Southern Baptist women a space separate from the WMU. Until the late 1980s, the WMU continued to offer its financial assistance, and many WMU women, including Carolyn Weatherford, remained active. At the same time, the conservative women's ministry program was growing rapidly, and the WMU found itself negotiating an ever-widening spectrum of gendered ideologies concerning women. In light of these pressures, some SBWIM women felt that the WMU would check their progress.[48]

Participants adopted a dual statement of purpose: "to provide support for the woman whose call from God defines her vocation as that of minister or as that of a woman in ministry within the Southern Baptist Convention" and "to encourage and affirm her call to be a servant of God."[49] As a support network, the group decided to open its membership to both Southern Baptist women who felt called to ministry and their advocates. On paper, SBWIM included males. In reality, its leaders and participants were overwhelmingly female.

From the start, SBWIM was a barebones operation supported by a scattering of individuals, churches, and the WMU, with its yearly agenda planned by the steering committee during an annual weekend retreat. Some women started state chapters, and the closely related Center for Women in Ministry published SBWIM's newsletter and quarterly journal, *FOLIO*. Unlike the WMU and the evolving conservative women's ministry programs, SBWIM connected women who felt isolated in their ministerial pursuits. Except for campus seminarians, its members lived far apart. *FOLIO* kept communication lines open for them. It celebrated their accomplishments, narrated their stories, offered a space for reflection, and highlighted relevant denominational news. While steering committee retreats provided a more intimate setting, the annual meeting functioned as the only face-to-face encounter for most women. In that first business session in Pittsburgh, participants agreed to convene again during the weekend prior to the convention and to conclude with a Sunday morning worship service. The annual meeting before the convention became an anticipated tradition. Terry Thomas Primer called it a "sort of 'torch in the dark,'" a "way of upholding and having people cling together in friendship and in solidarity, knowing that they would go back to face the rest of the world pretty much alone with only a few male colleagues."[50] Many women came for the worship service alone. According to several ordained participants, SBWIM's annual worship service counted as the one time during the year when they heard another Southern Baptist woman preach from the center pulpit.

Women gloried in the experience of SBWIM. Nearly twenty-five years later, their exuberance remained palpable, leaping off the pages of their written interviews and narratives.[51] As one steering committee member from the period wrote, the "creativity and energy was wonderful and exciting. The worship, publications, information flow, etc, was 'new' in the way it was not bound to tradition."[52] After the 1983 Louisville gathering, another said, "I was riding the wave; I couldn't believe we as Baptist women had finally found our voice and begun to act. I didn't know then that Baptist women had such a history of doing this. So, I lived and breathed it for several years."[53] If much of the enthusiasm came from the women finding one another, it also came from a high sense of divine calling. From the start, SBWIM's founders insisted that in coming together, they functioned as something more than a therapeutic group, prayer network, or even yearly worship team. Part of finding their voice meant developing a uniquely Baptist theology of women in ministry.

A Baptist Theology of Women in Ministry

In developing a distinctively Baptist theology of women in ministry, SBWIM women predictably highlighted scripture and piety. They also drew on feminist theology, biblical feminism, and more liberationist concepts of social justice to offer a new interpretation of Baptist freedom and Southern Baptist history. Their theology, it turned out, was as much a critique of the corporate church and its "good old boy network" as of conservative power.

First, then, as faithful Southern Baptists, the women grounded their ministerial call in scripture. Sermons included in *FOLIO* and preached at the annual worship emphasized the gospel liberation of women as a biblical principle. In *FOLIO*'s second issue, Molly Marshall-Green, a doctoral candidate in theology at Southern, announced that the "longer I study Scriptures, the more convinced I become of the bedrock theological support for women being afforded equal access to all positions of vocational ministry." Echoing other evangelical feminists, Marshall-Green maintained that feminist understandings of equality were first and foremost biblical. Three "enduring theological principles" in the Bible, she wrote, overrode "Paul's purple passages" and testified to women's egalitarianism in ministry. First, "all persons bear the image of the Divine." Both Genesis and the Apostle Paul revealed not only that woman was created as man's "equal in power and glory" (Gen. 1:26–28) but also that Adam shared culpability for the fall (Gen. 3; Gal. 2:20; Col 2:12). This interpretation of the fall directly contradicted Joyce Rogers's understanding of submission, which put sole responsibility on Eve. Second, "equality reigns in Christ's body the church." Here, Marshall-Green highlighted Galatians 3:28 and pointed to those New Testament stories of women as church leaders (Rom. 16:1; Phil. 4:3; Luke 2:36). Most significant, though, were the "culture-transforming attitudes and behavior of Jesus Christ" in "his uninhibited acceptance of women as 'theology students,' his calling women to serve, and his commission of women as primary witnesses to the resurrection" (Luke 10:38–42; John 4:23ff; Matt. 28:10; John 20:17). Last, the "Holy Spirit gives gifts for ministry—not according to gender—which each recipient must exercise faithfully." The primary scriptural references to spiritual gifts (Rom. 12:1–8; 1 Cor. 12:1–11; and Eph. 4:7–13), Marshall-Green stressed, "do not ascribe certain prominent gifts for leadership to men and 'lesser' gifts to women." In conclusion, Marshall-Green asserted that the argument affording women equal access to vocational ministry was not simply self-interest, as Joyce Rogers charged. It was the means to holistic church renewal.[54]

Marshall-Green's last charge was significant. On one hand, her hermeneutic was neither novel nor uniquely Baptist. For the most part, she leaned heavily on the work of feminist theologians. And yet, as a Southern Baptist, she recognized the tremendous import of both scripture and piety. In framing a Baptist theology of women in ministry, SBWIM women balanced biblical authority with holiness fervor, evangelical zeal, and old-fashioned piety, the sources of which they carefully located in Southern Baptist life. Time and time again, they reminded supporters and critics alike that in Southern Baptist Sunday school, church worship, training union, summer camp, and most particularly, Girls Auxiliary, they had been instructed to listen for God's call. The music and lyrics of gospel hymns like "Just As I Am" and "Wherever He Leads" had stirred their souls. They had walked the aisle, invited God into their hearts, and experienced the waters of baptism. Theirs was the language of Zion. Now, they testified, God was leading them down new paths, to new callings. As Marilyn Mayse, an ordained minister and early SBWIM steering committee member, put it, "My calling would never have come except through GA's and years of preaching about following God's will and hearing God's voice. My rising understanding of myself was shaped by the Journeymen program and my two years in Nigeria. . . . My academic freedom was fostered at a SBC college (Oklahoma Baptist University) and my theological freedom was nurtured at SWBTS [Southwestern] and SEBTS [Southeastern] (before the 'fall') in spite of the preacher boys in the Student Union who would have had it otherwise."[55] Women ministers frequently recollected that as young girls they had assumed a call to missions, and though the specifics had changed, their sense of call remained firm. Baptist piety had taught them the language of call and the necessity of response.

For some women, the Baptist part of this call was as significant as the ministerial component. Betty McGary struggled for more than a decade to be ordained a Southern Baptist minister, overcoming the barriers of both gender and divorce. When asked why she persevered, especially when another denomination would have been willing to accept her credentials, she immediately responded, "I would have given up on ministry before giving up being Baptist."[56] Elizabeth Bellinger felt the same conviction. Bellinger was an ordained Southern Baptist woman living in Waco, Texas, who discovered SBWIM through *FOLIO* and later served as the group's president. Despite challenges in finding a ministerial placement, she stressed that she never considered abandoning her Baptist identity. A "Southern Baptist by birth," she declared that "I am very Baptist. I believe in the priesthood of all believers. I very strongly believe in an adult baptism and immersion . . . and I prefer the Baptists—Baptist policy. I believe in the autonomy of the local church. I think that is something to fight for. So I think that, probably, they'll leave me before I will leave them."[57]

Like most moderates, Bellinger and other SBWIM women prized the traditional tenets of Baptist freedom, defining them in various places and venues as soul competency, the priesthood of the believer, and local church autonomy.[58] They also pushed further than other moderates, drawing attention to Baptists as a movement of dissenters and claiming that freedom should guarantee their ability to pursue God's call regardless of gender. In later *FOLIO* publications, for example, they emphasized Separate Baptist history as prior to the SBC's formation and Separate Baptists as a movement that elevated those lacking power: women, slaves, the poor, and the disenfranchised. The Baptist tradition was forged by those on the margins of society, and true Baptist freedom meant giving voice to the voiceless. In their call to ministry, Southern Baptist women felt that they were also being called to this earlier, more radical Baptist notion of freedom. At the first SBWIM meeting in Pittsburgh, Debra Griffis-Woodberry, an associate pastor in Raleigh, North Carolina, warned women against learning the rules of the SBC system. In her words, the "good-ole boy grapevine affords those who are a part of it opportunities for speaking, for changing pastorates, for being selected to boards, and so on."[59] Women, she reminded them, would never be a part of that exclusionary system, nor should they. For the women of SBWIM, at least, it contradicted gospel liberation as well as Baptist history and heritage.

SBWIM founders and leaders were adamant that a Baptist theology of women in ministry introduce new forms of leadership, authority, and power. When interviewed more than twenty years later, Lynda Weaver-Williams, who was during the 1980s both a copastor in Indiana and a doctoral student in ethics at Southern Seminary, reported, "Those first few years on the Steering Committee included discussions of how to use power. Many of us had been abused by the hierarchical use of power by men. . . . And so on the Steering Committee, we discussed the nature of power and how we wanted to exercise it differently."[60] Well afterward, women like Weaver-Williams distinctly remembered Nancy Sehested's plea at their initial Louisville gathering: that this group could not be about gaining power simply for Southern Baptist women but, rather, gaining power to address the injustices suffered by oppressed persons worldwide. In *FOLIO*'s first issue, Sehested considered the "manipulation, domination, subjugation, and control" that too often accompanied authority. She offered the ancient Jewish rabbi and the modern community organizer as "examples of ministry that are grounded in empowerment for people—not control over them." Turning to the new organization, Sehested asked that its women explore new leadership paradigms, and so she concluded with a more feminine image: that of the midwife "educating, coaxing, encouraging, rejoicing—all through great labor and pain. And all in the name of enabling the process of new birth. That's empowerment!" she concluded.[61]

As the first president of SBWIM and active in its early formation, Anne Thomas Neil attempted a new vision of leadership. Neil was in many ways the paragon of South Carolina womanhood, complete with an elegant southern drawl. Her father, a wealthy farmer and businessman, had served in the South Carolina senate and house of representatives. After nursing school, Anne married Lloyd Neil, the son of her family's Baptist minister. Then, her life took a different route from that of the traditional southern homemaker. In 1952, the Neils were appointed by the Foreign Mission Board as career missionaries to Nigeria and then Ghana, West Africa. Anne served as a working mother of two daughters in a variety of mission roles, from schoolteacher and nurse to relief worker and campus minister. She and Lloyd retired in 1983, after a yearlong furlough during which she began reading feminist theology and making parallels between Western colonialism, biblical patriarchy, the Jim Crow South, and the southern order.

Anne Neil delivered one of the addresses at the SBWIM Pittsburgh meeting. Quoting from the feminist theologians Valerie Saiving and Letty Russell, she passionately argued that while men had been guilty of prideful will to power, women had been guilty of soul-numbing servitude. As a result, women suffered low self-esteem, passivity, and all too often, a willingness to remain weak. This should not be the case, she cried. Christ had liberated women to be his servant-partners, and servant leadership, she said, was an energizing, empowering, and creative outpouring of one's self for others.[62] Participants at the meeting remembered being moved and energized by Neil's address. Her vision made her a natural choice for their president, and as a respected Southern Baptist missionary, she could bridge the gap between SBWIM and the SBC. In her sixties, Neil, then, embarked on a new career as a leader, confidante, and role model to young female seminarians and early SBWIM participants.

Women like Neil, Sehested, Marshall-Green, and Williams nurtured a Baptist theology of women in ministry, bringing insights from feminist theology, evangelical feminism, and liberation politics together with insights from Baptist history and Southern Baptist life. *FOLIO* consistently advertised conferences hosted by the ecumenical Church Women United and Evangelical Women's Caucus alongside WMU retreats and SBC-related seminary events. *FOLIO*'s resource section recommended readings by noted feminist theologians as well as books by well-respected Southern Baptist professors. Despite SBWIM's best efforts, however, these worlds did not easily coalesce. And while servant leadership functioned as an animating theological force in the organization's formation, its actual practice became fraught with conflict, much like early feminism.

Internal Tensions

Nearly a quarter of a century later, women looked back to the early years of SBWIM with a mixture of emotions. They easily recalled their exuberance over finding one another, in dreaming together of an alternate vision, and in trying to embody a new, more inclusive reality. They also remembered the frustrations, anxiety, and even despair of what often seemed an insurmountable task, and how, almost immediately, tensions emerged within the group and among its women.

Some saw the tensions as the challenge of diversity. SBWIM may have been mostly white, middle class, and southern, but women still differed in age, regional location, educational background, seminary loyalties, and clerical status. Older women, for instance, did not always push as far and as fast as younger ones. They were less likely to be ordained, and even though they supported women's place in the pulpit, they nonetheless felt undermined in their own roles and functions. Women seminarians from Southwestern were less likely to have encountered feminism and feminist theology than seminarians from Southern and Southeastern. Gender-inclusive language was valued at the latter two institutions, while Southwestern seminarians viewed it cautiously. During the 1970s, Nancy Sehested had studied at Union Theological Seminary in New York—a center of feminist thought, liberationist politics, and neoorthodoxy, which many Southern Baptists simply lumped together as liberalism. In 1986, Anne Neil attended Garrett-Evangelical

Theological Seminary in Evanston, Illinois, the home of evangelical feminism. Not surprisingly, while Sehested, Neil, and other key leaders had an all-encompassing vision of social justice and likewise recognized the nuances of feminism, many participants came to SBWIM's meetings and worship simply desiring a place at the table, including some who were also scared of the word "feminism" and wanted to avoid controversy. Whether SBWIM would serve as a support network, a lobbying group for women in ministry, or a catalyst for broader social issues was frequently debated, along with tactics and how quickly change could come. In addition, WMU leaders worried that in pursuing the pulpit, Southern Baptist women might abandon their historic commitment to mission. According to Lynda Weaver-Williams, the challenges of diversity exceeded her expectations:

> As we met and tentatively began to know each other in those early days, I sensed how very disparate we were. That would be our paramount challenge. . . . Although we said we wanted to bring together a diverse group, when we had WMU women, missionaries on furlough, female seminarians from SWBTS who were more conservative, female seminarians from SEBTS who weren't, ordained women who were in the pastorate, etc, it was an interesting mix. Women would sometimes leave a worship service unhappy because they thought things had gone too far; the service hadn't been traditional enough. And then we'd also have the other, opposite response.

As the tensions and differences became more apparent, women entered their own power struggle, despite their rhetoric to the contrary. They disagreed, for example, on the relationship between the Center for Women in Ministry, whose main task was to publish *FOLIO*, and SBWIM.[63] Some SBWIM leaders feared connecting the organization to a center or publication that SBWIM could not fully control. Others resisted any alliance with the WMU. While some worried over the dominance of particular seminaries, Helen Lee Turner indicated an insider-outsider dynamic. Those more deeply immersed in Southern Baptist institutional life, whether through Southern, Southeastern, a particular agency, or a prominent church, had more influence than those like herself, she said, who were affiliated with a non–Southern Baptist divinity school and university. Suspicions between laity and clergy also surfaced. As a church clerical assistant, Linda Hood Hicks often felt excluded from the early negotiations. "At one meeting, at my table, I was asked in what area of ministry I served," she recalled. "I replied that I was

Assistant to the Pastor in my church. After being asked if I did weddings and funerals or ever got to preach, I responded that I was not ordained and that my responsibilities were largely clerical. The group fell silent until one woman uttered 'Oh.' After that I was completely out of the conversation." In both a playful and serious twist, Hicks added that "church secretaries can get pretty pissy, too, since they minister not only to the church members, but to the ministers—but the job isn't recognized as ministry—even by Baptist Women in Ministry." Regional differences also played a role in exacerbating tensions. Although some participants in the 1982 Louisville gathering, for instance, traveled from as far as Iowa and New York, the majority of SBWIM's early founders and leaders hailed from Kentucky and North Carolina. These were, of course, the home states of Southern and Southeastern, historically the most progressive seminaries in Southern Baptist life. A smattering of women came from Alabama, Georgia, Virginia, and South Carolina, but no one on the initial task force and steering committees called any state west of the Mississippi her immediate home.

Negotiating the internal conflicts sometimes felt overwhelming to SBWIM leaders. Betty McGary compared SBWIM and its women to a herd of hens in the yard, "all pecking for one piece of corn—so little to go around." She believed the underlying reason for the internal conflicts and tensions was women's historic lack of power in wider denominational life. Because they had been victimized by power, she said, they were opposed to it, had not come to terms with it, and struggled with how to achieve a "shared power model." As the 1980s progressed, the situation for women in ministry, particularly ordained ministry, only became more dire.

In the late 1970s, Terry Thomas Primer stepped into an alternate reality in which she, as a woman, experienced Southern Baptist life to be "a place and a chance to minister, and to be creative and open and intellectually honest." She compared that reality to the colorful chalk drawing Mary and Bert jumped into and embodied in *Mary Poppins*. The movie, however, did not end there, which made the comparison for Primer such a potent one. When Mary and Bert emerged from the drawing, Primer commented, "rain washes away the place that they had been such that it looks like it never existed before." In the movie, they are left, abandoned by the others in the park, to face a cold, bleak, and rainy day. During the 1980s, said Primer, she and other women underwent a "total disenfranchisement" in Southern Baptist life. As with Mary and Bert, their alternate reality disappeared, lingering simply as a magical dream or distant memory that others around them heard of with increasing incredulity and doubt.

4

First Tier in the Realm of Salvation

GRACIOUS SUBMISSION

In March 1984, Southern Baptist Convention (SBC) president James T. Draper announced that Southern Baptists were now less likely to "kill each other." The conservative Texas preacher also went on to say that women's ordination might become "the most emotional and explosive issue" that the denomination faced.[1] Less than three months later, as 17,000 messengers gathered in Kansas City for the annual convention, Draper's prediction about the explosiveness of women's ordination came to pass, intensifying the contest between conservatives and moderates.

Throughout the spring, word had leaked that conservatives might be planning a resolution against women's ordination. At their second official gathering, the women of Southern Baptist Women in Ministry (SBWIM) prepared to speak against any such mandate. On Thursday morning, June 14, Carl F. Henry introduced Resolution No. 3: "On the Ordination and the Role of Women in Ministry." Few realized that Henry was affiliated with the SBC through his church membership.[2] Henry, who had attended Wheaton College, served as the first editor of *Christianity Today*, and helped found Fuller Theological Seminary, was noted as the intellectual voice of northern evangelicalism. His presence and introduction pointed to conservatives' crucial link with that outside evangelical world and how much more subject to it Southern Baptist conservatives were than moderates in the beginning years of the battles.[3] Later known as the "Kansas City Resolution," Resolution No. 3 encouraged the "service of women in all aspects of church life and work other than pastor functions and leadership roles entailing ordination."[4]

The carefully ordered convention floor turned into a chaotic uproar. As Henry was introducing the resolution, messengers thronged the aisles, forming crowds around the three official microphones. From the convention's platform, which appeared to be a sea of dark suits, former SBC president and moderate minister Wayne Dehoney ardently called for a point of order. In a booming voice, he declared the resolution unconstitutional because it interfered "with something that is the affair of the local church entirely." Conservative leaders huddled around Draper, who if diminutive in size was strong in personality. Draper proceeded to rule against Dehoney, admonishing him and warning others that "you're not telling us anything that we don't already know." In characteristic Texas fashion, he announced that they would discuss the resolution with "no hollerin'" but, rather, "order, kindness, and consideration."[5] Almost immediately, though, another messenger challenged Draper's ruling against Dehoney. Messengers voted to sustain the ruling. Then, quite abruptly, time was called on discussion of this resolution, since messengers had agreed earlier to limit debate over any resolution to eight minutes. Amidst boos and hisses, attempts to extend the time failed. When the microphones were turned off, messengers began shouting from the floor. Without any substantial dialogue on the resolution's content, Draper put Resolution No. 3 to an oral vote and then a paper ballot. It passed by 58 percent, with 4,793 yes votes to 3,460 no votes.

Moderates expressed outrage over the entire affair. As an ordained minister and SBWIM participant, Susan Lockwood Wright reported that twice she attempted to speak, and both times she was turned down or silenced. "Women," she emphasized, in referring to the process, "feel shut out."[6] Often seen as a conciliatory spirit, Draper attempted to appease opponents, reiterating that convention resolutions were nonbinding. Likewise, he earlier warned fellow conservatives that women's ordination should not become a "test for fellowship."[7]

In spite of Draper's warning, Resolution No. 3 was a considerable step down that road. The following year, more than 45,000 Southern Baptists traveled to Dallas for the convention. If not prepared, in Draper's words, "to kill each other," they were ready for a good, old-fashioned fight. For many, compromise had seen its day, and the Peace Committee appointed in 1985 proved largely symbolic. In retrospect, the struggle had just begun.

The Kansas City Resolution functioned as a turning point in the Southern Baptist struggle between conservatives and moderates. After 1984, conservatives increasingly focused on gendered ideas about women, particularly women's ordination, as the means to determine otherness and power. Conservative politics mandated that women could not and should not wield power from the pulpit. The practice was rare, but even acceptance of the concept carried a risk of expulsion from the conservative camp and the institutions they controlled. At first, the incidents were subtle, but when all six seminary presidents, most of whom conservatives had accused of liberalism, signed the 1986 Glorieta Statement affirming inerrancy, conservatives needed a more visible marker of difference—and one that inflamed passions. If feminism inspired inerrancy, as the previous chapters argue, then inerrancy likewise inspired the debate over women. The two issues were thoroughly intertwined. This meant that as inerrancy faltered as a determinant for liberalism, conservatives looked increasingly to women's roles and practices. Throughout the next decade, Southern Baptists fought mercilessly over whether women could enter the pulpit, perform baptisms, practice ecclesial authority over men, and assume leadership in missions. At several conventions during the late 1980s, boos, hisses, and catcalls accompanied attempts to reverse the 1984 decision. One conservative woman remarked that at the start of the Southern Baptist battles, the woman question seemed a second-tier issue; but with the failure of the passage of the Equal Rights Amendment (ERA) and the success of Ronald Reagan, the culture wars rhetoric escalated, and the debate erupted from underneath the surface of Southern Baptist life. Over the next few years, conservatives placed women's submission on a par with the virgin birth and physical resurrection, making traditional womanhood, in the words of this same woman, "first tier in the realm of salvation."

This chapter is arranged both thematically and chronologically. It first examines the 1984 resolution and the 1986 Glorieta Statement as together representing a turning point in the contest. After considering women's ordination as a local church conflict, it then concentrates on institutional controversy, demonstrating how women's ordination functioned as a test case for fellowship, employment, and funding at the mission boards and seminaries. Next, the chapter examines how conservatives pushed beyond women's ordination, calling more generally for "womanly submission" and the "end of the feminization of mission." It shows that under the tutelage of key women's ministry leaders, like Dorothy Patterson, historic notions of traditional womanhood were reshaped into a contemporary theology of complementarianism. As part of this process, conservative women formed strong links to the larger evangelical world. While these links proved crucial to conservative victory, conservatives still had to confront the legacy of race. Before revising the Baptist Faith and Message to include women's gracious submission, Southern Baptist conservatives apologized for their racist past. The final pages of this chapter, then, examine the relationship of scriptural inerrancy, race, and gender.

Turning Point

Conservatives viewed women's submission in ecclesial matters as equal to women's submission in the home. In fact, many argued that submission in church emanated from submission at home, and of course, family values figured prominently in the wider culture wars debate that Southern Baptist conservatives supported. Organizations like Focus on the Family grew to 1,000 employees in little more than a decade. With several million devoted followers, it became as formidable as the Moral Majority and the Christian Coalition among the religious right. As advocates of the religious right during the Reagan era, Southern Baptist conservatives were crucial in transforming the South into a Republican stronghold.[8] Nonetheless, as they ascended to power in the SBC, male conservative leaders initially marshaled their denominational energies around the issue of women's ordination.

There were several reasons for this internal strategy. First, submission in institutional matters was simply more tangible than submission in domestic matters—and thus easier to dictate. Conservatives undoubtedly realized that try as they might, they could not dictate the everyday lives of Southern Baptist women and men. Even as passage of the ERA failed, feminism and other cultural factors had ushered in a host of changes concerning women's lives: women's increasing employment outside the home, no-fault divorce, and Title IX, to name a few. Like other evangelicals of the religious right, Southern Baptist conservatives tied homosexuality, abortion, and moral promiscuity to the advent of feminism, dismissing it as antireligious and antifamily. Amidst this bewildering sea of changes, almost all of which harkened back to women, conservatives first sought order within parameters they could control.

Second, women's ministry was already addressing submission in marriage and family, with conservative women taking the initiative in promoting wifely submission. Through women's ministry, these women became a more vocal force in the larger evangelical world, not only as leaders in organizations like the Council on Biblical Manhood and Womanhood and Focus on the Family but in providing the templates, literature, and speakers for women's ministry groups in non–Southern Baptist settings.

Third, after the surge of feminism in the 1970s, many Protestants, mainstream and evangelical, viewed women's preaching and ordination more as a bid to equal authority with men than as a sign of the Spirit's calling. Simultaneously, Southern Baptist conservatives were assigning increased power to their pastors. In 1988, for example, they passed a convention resolution on the priesthood of the believer, a doctrine that not only had been "used wrongly," according to the resolution, but had been given more emphasis recently than historically justified. Highlighting the "command to the local church in Hebrews 13:17, 'Obey your leaders and submit to them,'" conservatives claimed that the doctrine had "been used to justify" both the "attitude that a Christian may believe whatever he so chooses and still be considered a loyal Southern Baptist" and the "undermining of pastoral authority." As conservatives began to view the local church minister in a more hierarchical relationship with the laity, women's ordination became even more threatening.[9]

Finally, in concrete terms, conservatives felt that they had reason to worry. From 1964 to 1974, Southern Baptist churches ordained 15 women. On the eve of the 1984 convention, the number had risen to 200. Moreover, numerous female seminarians expressed a desire for ordination and a pastoral vocation. Southern and Southeastern had added women to their theological faculties and were preparing for a major convention on women in church and society. SBWIM had recently formed. In short, a tiny trickle was becoming a steady stream. To conservative eyes, the SBC was starting to resemble other Protestant denominations, and if this similarity grew, they believed they faced an oncoming deluge. Conservatives were determined to stop the rising tide, so in Kansas City they penned a resolution on the ordination of women.

Much to their surprise, Resolution No. 3 incited a media circus not only inside but outside the denomination. For the first time since 1979, a resolution captured more press than the heavily fought presidential election. Some journalists even claimed that it eclipsed SBC president Bailey Smith's infamous 1980 statement, "God Almighty does not hear the prayer of a Jew."[10] In this sense, the resolution represented a turning point that led beyond the issue of women. As with Smith's statement, Southern Baptists were jarred into the awareness that they were now on a national stage. What they said and did held import beyond the denomination and even the South.[11]

For most outside the SBC, the controversy centered on the resolution's reference to the Edenic fall. In typical Southern Baptist fashion, Resolution No. 3 began by affirming the "authority of the scripture." It benignly listed several New Testament teachings upholding women's ministry and witness. Ironically, Molly Marshall-Green had highlighted the same biblical references with similar arguments in writing for the fall 1983 issue of *FOLIO*, the SBWIM publication.[12] The New Testament, the SBC resolution stated, "enjoins all Christians to proclaim the gospel" and "emphasizes the equal dignity of men and women" (Gal. 3:28). It indicated "that the Holy Spirit was at

Pentecost divinely outpoured on men and women alike" (Acts 2:17) and that "women as well as men prayed and prophesied in public worship services" (I Cor. 14:33–36). Like Marshall-Green, it celebrated Priscilla and Phoebe as women who performed valuable ministries (Acts 18:26; Rom. 16:1). The resolution then took a very different turn, emphasizing that the "Scriptures attest to God's delegated order of authority (God the head of Christ, Christ the head of man, the man the head of woman, man and woman dependent one upon the other to the glory of God), distinguishing the roles of men and women in public prayer and prophecy" (I Cor. 11:2–5). Additionally, it stated, the "Scriptures teach that women are not in public worship to assume a role of authority over men" and that Paul "excludes women from pastoral leadership" (I. Tim. 2:12).

At this point, the resolution resembled other conservative evangelical arguments against women's ordination. But the claim that Paul excluded women from pastoral leadership "to preserve a submission God requires because the man was first in creation and the woman was first in the Edenic fall" (I Tim. 2:13ff) incited even greater fury. Conservative attempts to counteract negative reaction by adding that "the scriptures are not intended to stifle the creative contribution of men and women as co-workers in many roles of church service" and that "women are held in high honor for their unique and significant contribution to the advancement of Christ's kingdom" were fairly useless. The Edenic fall statement overshadowed any caveat.[13]

For many critics, the reference to the Edenic fall conjured up the centuries-old notion of women's innate moral depravity: Tertullian, Augustine, and Martin Luther had cited the Genesis story in tracing sin and evil to woman. Seventeenth-century Puritans often portrayed women as easier prey than men for the devil and therefore temptresses not to be trusted. Even as Victorians downplayed, if not countered, the Edenic fall argument by elevating women's piety, the concept persisted. In fighting the formation of the Woman's Missionary Union (WMU), nineteenth-century Southern Baptist male leaders referred to the Edenic fall as the reason for women's inherent weaknesses. And in the wake of woman suffrage, 1920s fundamentalists revived the debate.

After the 1960s and feminism, however, the justification did not sit well with most Americans. Joyce Rogers had called on the argument but from a more limited, exclusively female venue, which was not covered by the outside media. The widespread and overwhelmingly hostile reaction to the reference to the Edenic fall caught conservative Southern Baptists off guard. In fact, when the Council on Biblical Manhood and Womanhood affirmed women's submission to men's authority three years later, it was careful to reject the argument, stressing instead God's establishment of order in the Genesis Creation. "Adam's headship" it stated, "was established by God before the Fall, and was not the result of sin."[14] The difference in this interpretation showed that even among conservative evangelicals, the resolution's argument represented an extreme.

The resolution disturbed moderates for various reasons. A few went on record denouncing the hermeneutical process at work. Southeastern Seminary president Randall Lolley called the resolution "bad exegesis, bad hermeneutics, bad theology, bad Christology," and more.[15] Southern Seminary professor Bill Leonard compared conservatives' reliance on the Edenic fall to slaveholders' use of the Curse of Ham myth.[16] *FOLIO* published several articles critiquing the underlying exegesis and countered the conservative interpretation of the Greek word for head.[17] And yet, as if to avoid any accusation of biblical infidelity, moderate leaders by and large focused on ecclesial politics rather than on the hermeneutical process—or even the issue of ordination. Like Dehoney, they insisted that the resolution violated the Baptist principle of local church autonomy. After all, the resolution announced the "authority of Scripture in all matters of faith and practice including the autonomy of the local church." Moderate speakers argued that although a resolution might address delegates' views on broad cultural issues, it should not interfere with individual church practices—especially divisive ones. This sense of division was key, for in post–World War II sbc life, "local church autonomy" often functioned as a code phrase for compromise. For many denominationalists-turned-moderates who still sought to avoid the emotions stoked by women's ordination, the turning point in Kansas City was its rejection of compromise. The Glorieta Statement, with its strong case for inerrancy, was another case in point.

At the Dallas convention the following year, a task force backed by state convention presidents proposed establishing a peace committee to promote peace and reconciliation.[18] The nineteen members named in the motion represented conservative, moderate, and neutral positions. All were male. During discussion, a woman named Eileen Rasco queried, "Women in ministry is an issue. How can you address it without a woman on the committee?"[19] The motion was quickly amended to include two women—Christine Gregory, the well-recognized wmu president, and Jodi Chapman, the lesser-known wife of conservative Texas megapastor Morris Chapman. At this point, both conservatives and moderates steered well clear of an ordained woman more representative of SBWIM. They also avoided the question of women in ministry altogether.

Much has been written about the Peace Committee's failure. Most denominational insiders interpreted it as a fiasco for moderates, especially the related Glorieta Statement. Members of the Peace Committee visited each SBC agency, board, and seminary, interviewing personnel and taking notes on procedures and policies, with the result that anxieties only heightened. The Peace Committee seemed particularly concerned over the variant interpretations of Article 1 of the Baptist Faith and Message, which stated that the Bible has "truth without any mixture of error for its matter." Conservatives held that the article referred to all areas of knowledge and experience, including history and science. They also insisted that most Southern Baptists intended that meaning as well.

In the fall of 1986, after completing most of its visits, the Peace Committee invited the agency heads, seminary presidents, and other various SBC officials for a prayer retreat at the SBC's Glorieta Conference Center in New Mexico. As they tried to protect their institutions against accusations of liberalism, the presidents of the six seminaries conferred, prayed, and signed a joint statement of what they called "commitments regarding our lives and our work with Southern Baptists." In this document, they declared that "Christianity is supernatural in its origin and history." They promised to "repudiate every theory of religion which denied the supernatural elements in our faith." They affirmed the "miracles of the Old and New Testaments" as "historical evidences." Covering the range of acceptable vocabulary, they called the sixty-six books of the Bible "fully God-breathed," "utterly unique," "not errant in any area of reality," and of "infallible power and binding authority."[20] The Glorieta Statement left little room for dispute. Cecil Sherman resigned from the Peace Committee in furious disgust, denouncing the Glorieta affair as both "shameful" and a "betrayal." In his words, "Now the people under attack were coming to terms with their attackers. And they were abandoning their Moderate friends."[21]

The Glorieta Statement was clearly written to mollify conservatives, but in truth it also failed to serve their agenda. If conservatives wanted to purge the seminaries, particularly Southern and Southeastern, of any liberalism, the Glorieta Statement gave them little leeway for action. The Peace Committee acknowledged diversity of opinion on the interpretation of Article 1 of the Baptist Faith and Message, yet in language echoing Glorieta, it concluded that most Southern Baptists were more conservative in their understanding and that the sbc's agencies and seminaries should reflect the larger Southern Baptist constituency. Largely on the basis of this particular mandate, conservatives celebrated the Peace Committee's final report. Initially opposed to the proceedings, Paul Pressler expressed jubilance over the report's adoption. At the same time, though, the Glorieta Statement served as a warning to Pressler and his conservative colleagues. It predicted that many moderates, ranging from those in the highest positions of denominational power to those serving small local pastorates, would heed the Peace Committee's advice, bowing to inerrancy while blurring the lines if necessary. The debate over women became more pronounced not only as a result of the Kansas City Resolution but because of Glorieta as well.

Disfellowshipping

On at least two counts, conservatives were correct. First, as they emphasized, Southern Baptists overwhelmingly opposed women's ordination. Second, as they were often less apt to acknowledge, the minority supporting it was increasing. Because of their concern over this growing minority, however, conservatives were eager and anxious to announce that public sentiment was against the practice. After all, a crucial part of their rhetoric was that conservatives were more in touch with the people in the pew and better represented their beliefs and practices. Surveys during the 1970s did indicate that the vast majority of Southern Baptists supported inerrancy and opposed women's ordination to pastoral ministry.[22] For the most part, the same small network of churches ordained women. Even as late as 1986, for example, more than 60 percent of the recorded 232 ordained Southern Baptist women were credentialed in the same four states: North Carolina, Kentucky, Virginia, and South Carolina, respectively.[23] Over the 1980s, the few churches that ordained and called women experienced escalating tensions and alienation, especially as attitudes also began to change. If the majority of Southern Baptists disputed women's ordination, the minority was, nevertheless, growing more substantial, and conservatives were right to worry. According to a 1986 survey conducted by Nancy Ammerman, 45 percent of Southern Baptists favored hiring a "qualified ordained woman" to their church's ministerial staff, though, many indicated, not as the senior pastor; 26 percent of church leaders actually affirmed women's ordination to the pastorate, though again only 11 percent felt their church would accept the practice.[24] As Ammerman pointed out, these figures were not quite the 95 percent of Southern Baptists that conservatives sometimes quoted. While conservative leaders did, for the most part, keep their concerns more private, at certain moments they used the escalating numbers to strike fear in the minds of the majority of a "world gone mad," a phrase used by Adrian Rogers.

In most cases during the 1980s, disfellowshipping accompanied the ordination of a woman or the hiring of her as pastor. Disfellowshipping involved expulsion from the local association, an organized affiliation of Southern Baptist churches from the same county, metropolis, or region, and the practice most often occurred as the refusal to seat a particular church's messengers at the associational meetings.[25] Historically, associations voted to disfellowship a church they deemed guilty of a contentious practice or unorthodox doctrine, which usually translated into a church that found itself at odds with the prevailing religious culture. There is a dearth of material on the subject, but disfellowshipping as a form of neighborly interchurch discipline had declined considerably over the twentieth century, with the development of a more corporate denominational structure.[26] Some associations practiced it from time to time, but local conservative churches resumed the habit more regularly over women's ordination, including their ordination as deacons, which most conservatives viewed as being one step from the pulpit. In 1985, for example, eight churches near San Francisco formed a new association when the Redwood Association refused to seat messengers from three churches ordaining women as either deacons or ministers.[27] The Enon Baptist Association in Ardmore, Oklahoma, disfellowshipped Northwest Baptist Church in 1986 when it ordained Katrina Pennington. Some, like Oklahoma City's Capital Baptist Association, went back and forth over whether to seat messengers from ordaining churches, seating them one year, refusing them the next.[28]

The most publicized fracas occurred when an ordained woman minister moved into Adrian Rogers's backyard. In August 1987, Prescott Memorial Baptist Church of Memphis called SBWIM founder Nancy Sehested as its head pastor. With approximately 200 members, Prescott was small but still one of the largest metropolitan churches to call a woman to this position. Moreover, it was in the same local association as Bellevue Baptist Church. That August, the Shelby County Baptist Association passed a resolution calling for an investigation of the church's "doctrinal soundness," which was, by all accounts, tied to Sehested's position. Messengers then motioned for an immediate vote on whether to refuse to seat Prescott's delegates at the fall association meeting.[29] When Sehested went to the microphone to speak, the association suddenly "called the question," meaning closed the discussion. Sehested said,

I was stunned because this was against all my Baptist upbringing. The one thing I did know about being Baptist was you had a voice. Now, we are a democratic organization and so, we believe in majority rule, but you did have voice in a Baptist church in my growing up. So, I was surprised when they called the question. When they took the vote to call the question, the majority did agree to go on to the motion on the floor and vote on that. As I was standing there stunned that my Baptist heritage was being overrun and that they were not going to allow me to speak, I blurted into the microphone and said, "Mr. Moderator, since I am at the center of this controversy, then I request that I be allowed to speak." The moderator said, "I am sorry but the vote has been taken. We will do the will of the body and we will go on to the motion [to refuse Prescott seating] that is on the floor." There were voices from around the room yelling out to me, "too late, too late, too late."

Conservatives felt that they were in the right, acting on the will of the majority and according to democratic procedure. Ironically, it was Rogers who petitioned the moderator, stating, "I think that in the name of Christian courtesy we should allow this lady to speak." The meeting was in the sanctuary of a local church, so when the moderator bent to Rogers, Sehested made a bold move. As she told it, "I took off down the aisle and went up to the podium. The men on the podium rose, as good gentlemen do, when a woman walks past, and I went straight to the main pulpit." From the pulpit, and not the floor, she proclaimed her authority to preach as given by Jesus Christ alone. After she sat down, about 75 percent of those present rose again, this time against Sehested and Prescott, voting to disfellowship the congregation.[30]

Disfellowshipping undoubtedly caused intense pain. Sehested remembered the spirit of hostility in the meeting as oppressive, and the antagonism and opposition lasted well past the event. "It has been hard," she concluded, when asked about the lack of immediate Baptist support.[31] Local churches like Prescott soldiered on as before. Many of these churches were of the dissenting tradition and had experienced previous tensions with neighboring Southern Baptists over civil rights and other issues. Overall, their congregations were accustomed to struggling alone, forming community relations where they could. Their monies and self-interests were tied more to the national scene, to the seminaries, and to organizations like SBWIM, a setup that meant that events at the higher levels of denominational life proved far-reaching.

The disfellowshipping incidents involved only a handful of churches and their related associations.[32] At the end of the day, few Southern Baptist churches ordained women, and fewer still called them as senior pastors. Moreover, some women felt that certain congregations were now less likely to invite them into the pulpit, even as guest preachers. For the most part, women ordained in Southern Baptist churches served in non–Southern Baptist settings, as chaplains, for instance, or in staff positions that historically had almost always been filled by women anyway.[33] Well into the 1990s, the struggle over women's ordination had more to do with promotion, even acceptance, of the concept rather than the reality of its practice. The disfellowshipping events, however, drew a great deal of attention and created worry for moderates, particularly in the late 1980s. To argue publicly for local church autonomy against the practice of disfellowshipping Prescott and other churches was, in the eyes of conservatives and their potential followers, a means of espousing women's ordination. Where, conservatives asked, would moderates draw the line? Disfellowshipping at the local level also demonstrated that women's ordination might be used as the test for fellowship at even higher levels. It seemed fairly natural that as conservatives formed majorities on SBC boards and agencies, they increasingly turned to the debate over women as a means to purge their respective institutions.

Institutional Change

The conservative plan hinged on the SBC president's appointive powers. SBC presidents selected the Committee on Committees, which then nominated the Committee on Boards. In conversation with the president, this committee put forward a list of trustees to the denomination's various agencies and institutions, and as a formality, all names were presented and approved at the annual convention. From 1979 on, conservative SBC presidents named their men (and, later, a few women) to these positions of authority and argued that, rather than representing an institutional entity, these trustees represented the broader constituency of the convention—a constituency that was likewise conservative. In all, there were approximately 1,000 trustees serving staggered four-year terms, which meant that by the mid-1980s, conservatives had begun to form sizable board presences.

While conservative trustees introduced a sea of changes related to policies, publications, and personnel, one of the most immediate involved hostilities toward ordained women. In the midst of these changes, the Southern Baptist Seminary professor and ethicist Henlee Barnette accused conservatives of selectively picking and choosing their biblical passages in a way that demonstrated a deep-seated "prejudice against women."[34] Conservatives obviously had a different view. In a newfound appeal to denominational policy, they cited the Kansas City Resolution as truly representative of Southern Baptist opinion. If the sbc's boards and agencies were to represent the practices and beliefs of its constituents, then placing women in ordained ministerial positions was definitely not acceptable.

The first recorded incident of women's ordination serving as a test case seemed to have occurred when *Student*, the Baptist Sunday School Board's magazine for college and university students, ran its February 1985 issue: "The Bible and Women . . . When God Calls." The issue began by highlighting the positive changes feminism had brought to women's lives. In one article, women shared the joys and difficulties of balancing career and family life. In another, marriage therapist David Edens warned that men should recognize women's needs for activities other than "dishes, diapers, and dirty clothes." Bill Leonard highlighted women in Christian history, indicating that they had ministered formally as pastors, while retired Southwestern ethics professor T. B. Maston argued that Southern Baptist churches could actually ordain anyone, females included, who had a special call from God to perform a particular task. The magazine then concluded by celebrating the ministry of three ordained women.[35] Conservative Sunday School Board trustees, who were not yet in the majority, fumed. Even though the mission boards had addressed women's ministry in their respective journals, and conferences had certainly explored the issue, this was the most public support in any official widespread circulation to date, and conservatives believed that publications should toe the denominational line. As a result, the *Student*'s editor, W. Howard Bramlette, was soon relieved of his duties.[36] Overshadowed by the upcoming convention, the incident largely went unnoticed, but it did foreshadow a pattern. As conservatives made clear, denominational monies should not promote in any form or fashion women in ordained ministry, especially since 99 percent of Southern Baptists, they estimated, opposed the practice.[37]

Few were surprised when, in 1988, conservatives ousted the Christian Life Commission's Larry Baker, who openly supported women's ordination and limited abortion rights, and replaced him with conservative Richard Land, who became a leading spokesperson for the religious right and its family values agenda.[38] After all, the Christian Life Commission, headed until 1984 by Foy Valentine, had even needled postwar denominationalists.[39] There were other debacles, well documented, in which a multitude of tensions surfaced. None, though, disturbed Southern Baptists quite as much as the struggle over the mission boards and seminaries, in which women's ordination, and women themselves, figured prominently and any compromise failed.

Mission Boards

For many Southern Baptists, missions were the SBC, and the mission boards were the denomination's reason for being. Even after the struggle had been settled in favor of conservatives, moderate churches refused to abandon the SBC completely, citing the need to assist Southern Baptist missionaries who were, in many moderates' opinion, innocent victims of the politics back home.

Conservatives began to form a majority of the Home Mission Board's trustees fairly early in the conflict. In 1985, the board of trustees' personnel committee voted against appointing Janet Fuller, an ordained woman who was also the daughter of Southern Baptist missionaries, to serve as a Yale University campus student worker. The full board reversed the decision but named an Ordination Study Committee to develop guidelines regarding ordination issues and missionary appointments. By 1986, conservative trustees outnumbered moderate ones. Almost immediately, citing the 1984 Kansas City Resolution, Southern Baptist majority opinion, and scriptural authority, the board voted to withhold funding from any Southern Baptist church with an ordained woman pastor. The following meeting that October was dramatic. As both a woman and a moderate trustee, Beth McGhee stood up and passionately pleaded for compromise and toleration. A conservative woman trustee, Linda Principe, responded that the Bible forbade women's preaching. As Principe spoke, McGhee suffered a fatal heart attack. Surely with McGhee's death in mind, conservatives conceded that the board's decision would not affect existing arrangements. In the future, however, no ordained woman would be appointed as a missionary and no church supporting her ministry would be funded.[40]

In light of this turn of events, when trustees named Larry Lewis, a conservative inerrantist and vocal antiabortion advocate, as the Home Mission Board's new president in 1987, moderates predicted an institutional showdown. They had to wait. Even as Lewis restructured the agency by reassigning departments and personnel and prioritizing evangelism and church plants over other professional tasks, the Home Mission Board continued without the anticipated shake-up. In fact, no one was fired, partly because Lewis focused more on bureaucratic efficiency. His one doctrinal mandate came in the form of a memo, asking those who had difficulty with the Baptist Faith and Message to report to him. Of course, quite significantly, the issue over ordained women had already been decided, and the Baptist Faith and Message, at this point, was the 1963 version that contained no references to women's submission. Not surprisingly, it appears that no one on record wanted to risk losing his or her job by reporting to Lewis. Existing employees may not have liked the changes that Lewis initiated, but at this point they could coexist with them. As Ammerman notes, Lewis focused his harshest scrutiny on incoming hires who did change the tenor of the agency, albeit more gradually than moderates had feared.[41]

Events at the Foreign Mission Board followed a different route. Overall, it survived much longer, primarily because of a slower turnover in its larger board of trustees, and in spite of their worry over liberal missionaries on the field, conservatives also might have been loath to touch the SBC's greatest success story. Spanning the globe in 1980 with 3,059 field personnel in ninety-four countries, the Foreign Mission Board represented the SBC's postwar rise to power.[42] If the SBC functioned as a corporate organization, with Home Missions as one of its agencies, Foreign Missions was its global empire. Foreign Missions generated a great deal of denominational support, and the board's enthusiastic, sociable, and larger-than-life president, Keith Parks, was a popular, charismatic presence who traveled from congregation to congregation, keeping the funds flowing. Elected in 1980, Parks followed the Foreign Mission Board's long-standing tradition of neutral statesmanship. This meant that as conservatives began to fill the board's trustee positions, he worked diligently at compromise. Initially, Parks seemed fairly successful. It helped that he was known to be theologically conservative with stringent doctrinal requirements. Additionally, in keeping with the conservative vision, he upheld and implemented a mission policy prioritizing evangelism and church plants, a position that some career missionaries resented because it meant pastors and evangelists were appointed over teachers, medical personnel, and social workers. His strategy of compromise, however, became increasingly difficult, especially regarding women.

In 1988, Parks defended the board in firing missionary appointee Michael Willett. Willett had received a doctorate from Southern before his missionary appointment to Venezuela. During Willett's required missionary training, a fellow Southern Baptist appointee, who had graduated from Adrian Rogers's Mid-America Seminary, wrote Parks. In his letter, he stated that Willett did not believe that Christ performed certain biblical miracles. Parks initiated an investigation that concluded in asking Willett to resign because of "doctrinal ambiguities." Against such accusations, and in a complicated series of events that resulted in his dismissal, Willett maintained that the underlying reason for the requested resignation was his recent article, titled "Opposition to Women in Unpardonable Sin," in the moderate-leaning *SBC Today* that supported women in ordained ministry. Willett and others apparently believed that Parks and the board were hiding behind theological language and the doctrine of biblical infallibility. Parks insisted to his critics afterward that Willett's firing remained an isolated incident, unrelated to the conservative agenda.[43]

While the role played by conservative politics and women's ordination in Willett's firing was questionable, these issues were assuredly the reason for the rejection of Katrina and Greg Pennington as missionary applicants a year later. Both Penningtons had graduated from Golden Gate Seminary, had spent ten years preparing for foreign missions, and were serving on the ministerial staff at Northwest Baptist Church in Ardmore, Oklahoma. Their missionary credentials appeared to be stellar, and they anticipated appointment until Katrina's ordination came in to play. Northwest had caused a stir in the local association when the church ordained Katrina. As a result, the association urged the Foreign Mission Board to reject the Penningtons' application. "It is our conviction," the association wrote, "that the ordination of Mrs. Pennington violated clear Bible teaching."[44] When Parks and the Foreign Mission Board heeded the association's request, Northwest demanded a hearing. Attempting to downplay ordination as the primary reason, Parks and the board cited the discord caused by the Penningtons, trying this time to hide behind ecclesial politics. To calm moderate critics, who called the act everything from a "shame and disgrace" to "non-Baptistic," Parks led the board in hiring an ordained woman shortly afterward.[45] Patricia Lee was appointed along with her husband to Japan. But while his assignment involved developing churches, hers was to work with women and children, and Lee herself noted that ordination was not necessary to her work. In reporting the story, SBWIM underscored these details.[46] Despite the board's claim that ordination was a local matter and did not disqualify a candidate, Lee was the last ordained woman hired during Parks's tenure.

The incident clearly showed that compromise when it came to women and gender was unattainable. Parks held on to the reins, somewhat ineffectively, for a few more years. He retired three years early, after weathering battles over missionaries' seminary credentials, the boards' allotment of funds, and his hiring of moderates. With Parks gone, the board formalized its unwritten policy of avoiding ordained women, and it became the official stance for both mission agencies.[47] Not surprisingly, the number of professional women appointed as missionaries to the Home and Foreign boards declined. As SBWIM, the WMU, and other critics pointed out, the new policies privileging direct evangelism and church plants, activities inherent to preaching, overturned the social ministries traditionally more open to women.[48] Moreover, fewer girls were nurtured in the WMU to hear God's call to missions. The status of missionary wives, often ambiguous, also became more clearly defined with a 1990 Foreign Mission Board policy statement. Affirming them "in their biblical role of Christian homemakers and in their God-called responsibilities as missionaries," it stipulated that "adequate care and attention for children is of primarily spiritual importance," and that this "will be given full weight in assisting all missionary parents, especially mothers, in defining the use of their time."[49] Historically, missions had been the realm of Southern Baptist women; this was not the case in the seminaries, which had traditionally been male bastions.

Seminaries

Conservatives viewed the SBC's seminaries as the chief source of Southern Baptist liberalism. Their 1980 resolution calling for "doctrinal integrity" and biblical "infallibility" indicted seminary trustees, administrators, faculty, and staff. Almost immediately, conservative SBC presidents sought to penetrate the seminary boards as a means to transformation and change. But conservatives recognized that not all six SBC seminaries were equal.

Founded in 1859, The Southern Baptist Theological Seminary in Louisville was the most historic. Its grand southern architecture and sprawling green lawns bespoke its position as the "mother seminary." Often referred to as the "crown jewel" of Southern Baptist educational institutions, it produced the denomination's most recognized statesmen, who insisted on the capitalization of the definite article "The" in the seminary's title. Not surprisingly, most denominationalists-turned-moderates called Southern home. Southern's rival in both age and size was Southwestern, founded in 1908, in Fort Worth. By the early 1980s, Southwestern stood as the world's largest Protestant seminary, boasting nearly 5,000 students. Both location and tradition made it more conservative than Southern. In fact, a majority of conservative leaders had graduated from Southwestern, with New Orleans running a close second.[50]

In the area of academic prowess, Southern's rival was the much smaller Southeastern in Wake Forest, North Carolina.[51] Founded almost a century later, in 1951, Southeastern quickly became home to a group of renegade

Southern professors. They had left Southern over a host of issues. One was that they felt the seminary's curriculum changes bowed too far in the direction of professionalization, and Southern's turn to the new "applied" areas of learning lacked academic rigor. Some of these faculty members had also run afoul of Southern's administration by protesting greater levels of institutional control. Finally, they were more likely to adopt modern hermeneutics and progressive social attitudes.[52] As a result of this more left-leaning cadre, Southeastern did not always follow the tradition of diplomacy and compromise. Its administrators, faculty, and students often saw themselves as progressive, even dissenting, in both cultural and theological matters. The seminary had stood at the vanguard of Southern Baptist life in civil rights, and not surprisingly, Addie Davis articulated her calling to ordained ministry as a Southeastern student. Like Southwestern in Fort Worth, its geographic location played a key role. As the historian Samuel Hill notes, Southeastern's mid-Atlantic placement promoted "openness to 'foreign' currents of thought in biblical and theological studies."[53] Conservatives agreed that Southeastern was the most liberal of the six SBC seminaries, with Southern running a close second. Southeastern also had fewer trustees, approximately thirty to Southern's sixty, making it easier to capture.

Acquiescence to the Glorieta Statement suggested compromise in their biblical hermeneutic, but support for women's ordination clearly marked the two schools. At times, the amount of energy conservatives invested in controlling each SBC seminary seemed to parallel the seminary's record regarding women's ordination. Southern and Southeastern were the only seminaries with resource centers dedicated to women in ministry. Each had hosted a major conference on women in church and society with a decided slant toward biblical feminism. SBWIM had active chapters on both campuses, and the two schools had begun appointing women to their theology faculties. According to a 1986 poll, of the 232 ordained Southern Baptist women, 44 percent had graduated from Southern and 24 percent from Southeastern. Despite its size, Southwestern trailed a distant third with only 9 percent, and SBWIM complained that it could never garner enough support to establish a related chapter on its campus. The other seminaries—Midwestern, Golden Gate, and New Orleans—did not even make the list.[54]

Southwestern did suffer conservative attack. Russell Dilday, who served as Southwestern's president from 1978 to 1994, was described by his followers as tall and handsome, with an affable, charming, and gentlemanly personality. Conservatives saw him more as a fickle and beguiling character. He had begun the battles as neutral, opposing the politics of Sherman and the

Gatlinburg group, but as the years progressed, he gradually moved in their direction. Finally, after he delivered several "anti-fundamentalist" diatribes, conservatives had had enough. The story is told that when trustees finally voted to fire him in 1994, they immediately changed the locks on his office, literally shutting him out. Still, according to the Baptist historian David Morgan, they were more concerned with Dilday and a handful of faculty members than with the overall institution.[55] Midwestern went the way of Southwestern, with conservatives focusing on several individuals. Golden Gate and New Orleans, long considered conservative strongholds, went through the 1980s and 1990s largely untouched. Overall, day-to-day life at these institutions remained largely the same.

Unlike their peer institutions, Southeastern and Southern felt the fight's ferocity. In 1987, Southeastern fell swiftly to the conservatives. Southern followed much later, in 1995, after experiencing nearly a decade of tensions. Other differences between the two besides timing indicated changes in the larger denominational contest. Reflective of earlier years in the conflict, the struggle at Southeastern, or at least the prevailing rhetoric, was generally that of biblical inerrancy and historic Baptist freedom. By the mid-1990s, the discourse of the overall battles more readily and openly invoked cultural issues. As a result, the final showdown at Southern focused more on women, particularly women in authorial positions over men as both professors and ministers.

The Liberal Nexus

For the women of SBWIM, Southeastern president Randall Lolley served as the early exception to the indifference and even fear other moderates had shown toward their cause. Described by these female supporters as an engaging, affirming, and persuasive leader, Lolley vehemently denounced the 1984 Kansas City Resolution. At the school's following fall convocation, he nailed his colors to the mast, preaching that women were "First at the Cross, Fast at the Tomb" and worthy of full ministerial status. In his closing spring address, Lolley declared that "one of the saddest sights on this earth is a man forfeiting his own wholeness in the gospel by denying a woman the partnership which the gospel requires."[56]

Largely because of Lolley's refusal to compromise, Southeastern fell quickly to conservative control. Admittedly, Lolley had signed the Glorieta Statement, which he soon afterward denounced. "It was," in his own words, the "one thing out of all the things I did as a president that I think was a mistake in retrospect."[57] Accused by friends and foes alike of "selling out," he soon took a more hard-line stance. Lolley had the solid endorsement of Southeastern's administration, faculty, and students as together they expressed frustration over the Peace Committee process. In addition, Southeastern had a legacy of bucking denominational compromise and functioned in many ways as the educational counterpart to the Christian Life Commission. In 1987, seminary trustees approved the appointment of Elizabeth Barnes to serve as assistant professor in theology. Barnes was a seminary alumna who held a Ph.D. from Duke and was active in SBWIM as a regular *FOLIO* contributor. The hiring of Barnes disturbed the growing number of conservatives on the board. As one put it, "She is not an inerrantist. And I do object to a woman teaching theology. I don't think it is biblical."[58] Her status with SBWIM obviously did not help.

As with the Christian Life Commission, conservatives worked hard and quickly to shift Southeastern's board so that after the 1987 convention, they held a slight majority of the thirty-seven trustees. In typical fashion, Southeastern refused to kowtow. In his fall convocation address, Lolley threw down the gauntlet. He first described Southeastern's tradition as "a free conscience, free church, free country way of doing theological education." Then he proclaimed that if Southern Baptists desired a seminary "different and destructive of the ideas which this school has sought through its history to incarnate, then this president will give not one moment of the time or one millibar of the energy he has left to producing that kind of school."[59]

The address created an uproar among conservative trustees. At their October meeting, which went into a closed session, they voted to place faculty hires in the hands of the board, a move that nearly cost the school its accreditation. Some students dressed in prison attire and surrounded the trustees in attendance. Bound and gagged, they knelt in prayer. When the trustees demanded their removal, Lolley said, "It is a free country and all they are doing is praying. And that's what you tried to get me to do just recently with you."[60] As the meeting progressed, the campus erupted in protests, and seminarians draped the trees with yellow ribbons. Within ten days, Lolley had resigned, making the surprise announcement to a stunned seminary community during Southeastern's regular chapel service. A third of the faculty followed his lead, and student enrollment subsequently plummeted. Seemingly overnight, the liberal nexus of Southern Baptist life had vanished. It took nearly a decade for the seminary's numbers to recover.

While women's ordination figured only indirectly in the October events, it had needled conservatives and became more prominent in their aftermath.

First, Lolley made it, along with questions over biblical inerrancy and power politics, a chief issue in his resignation statement: "Southern Baptists, how long will you go on calling young girls and women to faith in Jesus Christ; telling them to dedicate all their gifts to his Lordship; removing them from your churches to your seminaries; and then upon their graduation refusing to consider them as your pastors? Do you realize that you are requiring us in your seminaries to be duplicitous with your daughters? That you may be muscling in on the calling of God?"[61] Second, women's ministerial formation was, in the eyes of alumnae, the most immediate and recognizable area of change. One of the new administration's first acts was to terminate the Women's Resource Center, which housed SBWIM's local student chapter.[62] When Paige Patterson arrived in 1992 to assume Southeastern's presidential reins, he appointed his wife, Dorothy Patterson, as the unpaid director of the newly established Women's Studies Program. The program attracted a new group of women committed to women's ministry, as opposed to SBWIM or women in ministry. Under Patterson, the women adopted the Council on Biblical Manhood and Womanhood's "Danvers Statement" endorsing women's submission to men's authority as the program's official statement of belief. Once the stronghold for women seeking ordination, Southeastern Seminary became the leading proponent of traditional—or what Dorothy Patterson was calling biblical—womanhood.[63] In less than a few years, Southeastern was producing godly wives and submissive servants.

The Crown Jewel

In contrast to Southeastern's quick and decisive battle, Southern's conflict was long and drawn out. As tensions escalated, debates over women, particularly their ordination, figured front and center. There were other differences with Southeastern. While increasingly progressive when it came to women, Southern did not have the same level of acceptability for their role in ordained ministry. Susan Shaw's collective memoir reveals that women seminarians from this period remained conflicted over their Southern experience. On one hand, Southern had introduced them to feminist theology and thought. Their callings frequently moved from the more typical female routes of mission service or children's director to that of preaching and pastoring. They felt encouraged in this direction by professors, chapel programs, women speakers, and other female peers. On the other hand, they sensed the pressures of the "good old boy" network and the suspicions of their male student colleagues. Shaw, herself a Southern student in the early 1980s, was told by one male classmate, "Susan, I'll be praying for you that you don't get messed up with the women in ministry stuff."[64] As the struggle progressed, the hostilities escalated, with women reporting such things as open verbal confrontation and anonymous written messages, all with the same resounding message that one female seminarian found on an unsigned note in her mailbox: "You don't belong here. As a woman, you don't belong in a Southern Baptist leadership role. You don't need a seminary degree. You need to find yourself a good husband and then be a good wife."[65]

The story of Southern at this turning point reflected its women's sense of confusion. Some moderates felt that because of its substantial endowment, Southern could have possibly charted a more independent course. Honeycutt had originally been the most vocal of seminary presidents, calling in 1984 for a holy war with Patterson and Pressler over their accusations toward Southern. It was a surprise, then, when Honeycutt took the route of compromise.[66] With more than sixty trustees, Southern did have a larger board, so conservatives would need more time to become dominant, and perhaps Honeycutt felt that he had the advantage of time. Even into the 1990s, moderates still felt that they had a chance to win the struggle.

As a sign of compromise, in 1987 Honeycutt hired David Dockery, an avowed inerrantist from Patterson's Criswell Institute, as academic dean. At the same time, he ushered Molly Marshall-Green through tenure. A polished and articulate scholar, Marshall-Green troubled conservatives for multiple reasons. She was an ordained woman teaching theology to men as well as women. An extraordinarily popular professor, especially among female seminarians, she also advocated gender-inclusive language and, according to some, universalism, the view that all persons will ultimately receive salvation, independent of any relationship with Jesus Christ. She additionally served on SBWIM's executive board, preached, regularly contributed to *FOLIO*, and was active in constructing a Baptist theology of women in ministry from a Southern Baptist context. Because of Dockery's appointment, a winning margin of conservative trustees voted of Marshall-Green's tenure, despite their grave concerns.

By the early 1990s, conservatives held a slim majority on Southern's board of trustees. To appease this new constituency, Honeycutt and select faculty penned the Covenant Renewal between Trustees, Faculty, and Administration. Borrowing heavily from the Peace Committee's final report, the document mapped a coexistence plan for moderates and conservatives. As it stated, the seminary would strive to achieve theological balance in the faculty's makeup by hiring "conservative evangelical scholars" who held that

"Scripture is true and reliable in all the matters it addresses, whatever the subject matter."[67] It said nothing about women.

Under the Covenant Renewal, conservative evangelicals from both inside and outside Southern Baptist life joined the faculty. Carey Newman, for example, was a cradle Southern Baptist who had graduated from Southwestern and Baylor, while Timothy Weber was a Conservative Baptist who had been teaching at Denver Seminary. David Gushee spanned both worlds. He had attended Southern and then completed his doctorate at Union in New York and worked for Evangelicals for Social Action. In spite of their different backgrounds, all Covenant Renewal faculty members passed their interviews as inerrantists, so that existing faculty sometimes dismissed them as "fundamentalists."[68] While the hires caused underlying faculty tensions, compromise held the seminary intact until Honeycutt's resignation. Honeycutt actually resigned a year early, so that moderates had a better chance at retaining the presidency. "With the shifting of the board, I could see the handwriting—next year would be worse," he said. "We had a good [search] committee and I thought they could make the best choice."[69]

In 1992, a thirty-three-year-old named R. Albert Mohler Jr. replaced Honeycutt as Southern's ninth president. Highly inexperienced, Mohler nonetheless seemed a candidate that moderates could affirm. Known in Southern's circles as a serious, somber, and astute scholar, he had recently received his doctorate from the seminary and was serving as editor of the *Christian Index*, Georgia's state convention newspaper. His bass voice and confident demeanor made up for his youthful look, thus lending him a much-needed air of authority. He had served also as Honeycutt's assistant, and Honeycutt endorsed his candidacy.[70] Equally significant, Mohler had actively protested the 1984 Kansas City Resolution, and many saw him as moderate-leaning. Honeycutt later claimed that as a sign of progression, Mohler's wife, Mary, "had the double name," meaning that she hyphenated her maiden name, "Kahler," with "Mohler."[71]

Fairly soon into his tenure, then, Mohler sent shock waves throughout the moderate camp by revealing his conservative loyalties. Moderate-leaning faculty and students compared him to the seminary chapel's weather vane, which topped its steeple because of a previous controversy concerning the donation of a material cross. Even Honeycutt asked where this Al Mohler came from.[72] In a later interview, Mohler attempted to justify his move and defend himself against crass rumors that accused him of expediency and a hunger for power. He explained that what might have appeared an abrupt transformation was actually the result of an awakening process nearly ten years in the making. As a seminary student, he struck up a friendship with Carl Henry when Henry visited the campus at the request of students. In a moment that proved pivotal, Henry challenged Mohler's support for women's ordination:

> When the 1984 resolution came down from the Kansas City Convention on women, I actually helped to lead a movement to put an ad in the *Louisville Courier Journal* to oppose the resolution out of a sense of righteous indignation. Well, somehow Dr. Henry became aware of that. I don't know how. And he made a comment to me as we were walking across the Josephus Bowl, which is the lawn out here, that literally—I mean, it's just like sticking a dagger in me—he said, "Where did you get that?" more or less. You know, "What biblical justification do you have for that position?" . . . He kind of stabbed me to the core, and that's the first time I'd ever met him.[73]

Mohler delved into Henry's works, and eventually Henry became a personal mentor. Beginning in the 1950s, Henry had powerfully called northern evangelicals to renew their commitment to theological orthodoxy and biblical inerrancy against cultural accommodation. Mohler viewed Henry's call as applicable to the post–civil rights South. According to Mohler, southern society had unraveled over the 1960s and 1970s, and the modernist debate that had once divided northern Protestants now confronted Southern Baptists.[74] Like many conservatives, by the 1990s Mohler emphatically applauded civil rights. He stated that 1960s progressives were "certainly right, for instance, on the racial issues" and the "danger of the commingling of the church and the culture," or what he also termed the "cultural Christianity" that prevailed in the pre–civil rights South. But Mohler also believed that "liberals in the SBC drew some bad lessons on being right on those two areas." As he said, "I think they grew blind to how antiseptic the public square was left once—once you remove cultural Christianity, the question is what—what was left." By the 1970s, SBC liberals were "increasingly committed to a worldview largely shaped by a secular establishment, especially the academic community."[75] According to Mohler, women's ordination was a concrete example of how some Southern Baptists had accommodated secular culture and refused to confront the moral crisis at hand. While he expressed regret that women's ordination became central to the final Southern showdown, Mohler's insistence that faculty reject the practice became the deciding factor in hiring, tenure, and promotion at Southern.

Tensions exploded over two events involving women in authorial positions. First, in the fall of 1994, Mohler requested that Molly Marshall, formerly Marshall-Green, come before administrative officials.[76] Allegedly, the hearing would involve her use of gender-inclusive language and defense of universalism. Even though Marshall resigned before the encounter took place and the allegations remained speculative, faculty and students interpreted her departure as forced, and of course, conservative trustees wanted her out. Marshall was not the only theology professor espousing so-called liberal views, but she was the only woman doing so.[77] When asked about his vision for women on the theological faculty, Mohler said that he "would like to see every teaching position in the School of Theology as tantamount to a pastor position"; thus accepting women as professors there became difficult.[78] The professor's podium, it seemed, functioned as a preacher's pulpit.

The second event occurred in March 1995 and has been documented in detail.[79] Briefly, Diana Garland, dean of the Carver School of Social Work, recommended David Sherwood for a tenured opening at Carver. Sherwood was a conservative evangelical teaching social work at Gordon College. According to Garland, Sherwood met all the criteria for a position at Southern, including the Covenant Renewal's call for biblical inerrancy. Each member of the faculty search committee supported his hire. Mohler, however, asked Sherwood to provide an additional statement addressing questions about abortion, homosexuality, the gospel's uniqueness, inspiration of the scripture, and the role of women in ministry. Sherwood proved acceptable in all areas bar the role of women in ministry. When Mohler told Garland that he rejected Sherwood's candidacy, she was irate and went public with the news the following day. Southern's faculty responded decisively and overwhelmingly in Garland's favor. It issued a collective report indicting Mohler for failing "clearly [to] communicate what he understood to be the true parameters of employment at the seminary for a period of two years." While the faculty had long known the Covenant Renewal's conservative stance on scripture, they had not seen women's ordination as a test for employment. Mohler disagreed with the report, later stating that the policy had affected previous faculty searches and that Sherwood was not the first to be denied appointment for affirming women's ordination.[80] One day later, on March 20, 1995, Mohler asked for Garland's resignation.[81]

The campus exploded in protest. Faculty and students donned T-shirts with the biblical passage "Let Justice Roll down Like a River" and staged a candlelight vigil, singing "Keep Your Eyes on the Prize, Oh Lord, Oh Lord." References to civil rights were clear. From a pulpit placed on the stairs of the library and wearing her academic gown, Molly Marshall compared the racism of the past to the misogyny of the present: "Southern has been prophetic at times, never often enough. Usually, it has suffered for it. When Martin Luther King Junior was invited to preach here, some racist donors were offended and the seminary lost money—money well spent." Amidst shouts and cheers from the crowds, and with her finger pointed, Marshall raised her voice in conclusion: "And now with the departure of my gentle colleague Pam Scalise, my forced resignation, and Denise Massey's undaunted claim to pastoral calling, the School of Theology is without a tenured woman and probably will be as long as the misogynistic forces are unabated. In fact, the faculty looks more and more like it did in 1859, and that is blasphemy."[82] As Marshall and other moderate faculty and students viewed it, the Old South had once again descended on the mother seminary. The issues of race and gender, they realized, were interconnected and integral to the doctrinal disputes at hand, if not in the exact way that Marshall presented it. What she and others failed to recognize, though, was also what most denominational moderates neglected: Mohler was moving Southern closer to the evangelical right, with its more sectarian tendencies. The change at Southern was indeed a harkening back to the past, but it was also movement outward, with conservatives like Mohler making alliances in ways Southern Baptists never had.

Both the Baptist and secular media descended on the campus. Behind closed doors, on March 22, Mohler met with the faculty as students and press crews crowded the hallways outside. According to all accounts, the exchange inside was heated. Both sides remembered the day as "Black Wednesday." When Jim Chancellor, another Covenant Renewal hire, and Timothy Weber asked Mohler directly if their acceptance of women in ministry was not acceptable to the new administration, Mohler responded, "That's right." According to one faculty member, a woman professor immediately ran from the room to become sick in the hall.[83]

Southern's board of trustees immediately announced its support for Mohler's position. In an open letter to Kentucky's state convention newspaper, the *Western Recorder*, board chairman Richard D. White stated, "As for the underlying issue behind the conflict: Dr. Mohler does not oppose women serving in ministry. He does believe that the New Testament pattern of local church leadership is for men to serve as the senior pastor, and that is a position shared by the overwhelming majority of trustees and, we believe,

Southern Baptists. We believe that new faculty members being hired should share that view held by the overwhelming majority of the denomination that supports the seminary." Answering those who insisted that the issue of women ministers was not in Southern's traditional statement, its Abstracts of Principles, White retorted, "Well racism isn't in the Abstract, but I would hope Dr. Mohler would not present a racist to the trustees for election of the faculty. Homosexuality isn't in the Abstract, but I trust Dr. Mohler to refuse to recommend a candidate who advocates homosexuals serving as ministers in our Baptist churches." White accused Mohler's detractors of promoting a secular agenda and concluded that "they have rightly perceived Dr. Mohler as one who opposes their efforts to transform our culture and have attacked him at every opportunity for his faithful adherence to the values many of us hold sacred."[84]

The evangelical scholars hired under the Covenant Renewal expressed disbelief. All had been grilled on inerrancy, but women in ministry, they maintained, had not been an issue. Chancellor, Gushee, Newman, and Weber felt particularly alarmed because all four affirmed women's ordination. Each now saw his days at Southern numbered. Newman quoted Mohler as having told him that he had an "A-plus" in research, teaching, and scholarship and could "go down in the annals of this school as one of its finest teachers." On the other hand, Mohler said, "unless you change your public position on women in ministry, you'll never be tenurely promoted here and you cannot teach here."[85] Having come to Southern from non–Southern Baptist life, Gushee and Weber argued that other evangelical institutions like Gordon Conwell Theological Seminary and Fuller Theological Seminary managed to exist with differing opinions over the matter. With Newman, they thought that Southern had been headed in a similar direction. Again, Mohler disagreed, stating that the Covenant Renewal hires were actually compromises made by conservatives, not moderates. According to Mohler, "When they did elect professors Chancellor and Weber, they [conservative trustees] said, 'We are not happy—not at all happy about this compromise we're being asked to make on the issue of women in the pastorate, and we do not intend to make it again.'"[86]

Mohler was also rejecting the new evangelical center and places like Fuller, which later became a moderate refuge, for those more attached to the political right: Jerry Falwell's Liberty University, Pat Robertson's Regent University, and even Bob Jones University in South Carolina, the home to several new Southern trustees. The accuracy of Mohler's recollection was no longer the point, as the days ahead were clear. Latitude over women in ministry may have defined Southern's past; it would no longer describe its future.

Mohler and the trustees had thrown down the gauntlet—and quite effectively. The majority of faculty members present during Black Wednesday, including the Covenant Renewal group, followed Marshall and Garland the next year in leaving Southern. As many female seminarians felt abandoned in their struggle for women in ministry, they, too, departed. In their wake, Mohler and his wife, Mary, established both the Women's Ministry Institute and the Seminary Wives' Institute, each with its own degree programs, as well as other women's ministry initiatives. An emphasis in women's ministry was also offered to women pursuing the master of divinity degree. These programs quickly joined Southeastern in reconstructing traditional womanhood for both Southern Baptists and the larger evangelical world.

With their successful takeover of the Foreign Mission Board and The Southern Baptist Theological Seminary, conservatives captured the heart and soul of the denomination. As Mohler and younger conservative leaders like Richard Land joined the ranks of Pressler, Patterson, and Rogers, SBC leaders merged with American culture warriors, and the rhetoric of Southern Baptist conservatives became more recognizably that of the religious right. Symbolically, after years as an independent Baptist, Moral Majority founder Jerry Falwell led his church into the SBC. Conservatives poured their energies into condemning abortion, homosexuality, evolution, and what they regarded to be numerous liberal movements accelerated by both Bill and Hillary Clinton. That President Bill Clinton was a moderate Southern Baptist only intensified their zeal. Under conservative SBC presidents like Charles Stanley, Ed Young, and Jim Henry, the SBC passed resolutions boycotting Disney, supporting capital punishment, affirming Americans' right to bear arms, and calling for prayer in schools. Oliver North and George W. Bush made debut convention appearances to thunderous applause.

Some, though not all, of these incidents were directly related to the conflict with moderates. Moderates were more internally divided politically than conservatives. While some favored the Republican agenda, many did not. In contrast to conservatives, few moderate church leaders actively joined the culture wars. Overall, during the 1990s, the dividing line between conservatives and moderates thickened over women. In tandem with the new thriving women's ministry programs and prompted by the resounding family values rhetoric of the religious right, conservative leaders moved outward from ordination to address more fully women's roles within the home and in wider culture.

Toward a Complementarian
Understanding of Womanhood

Women conservatives often seemed invisible during the controversy. The percentage of women on SBC boards and commissions, which peaked at 13 percent in 1975, fell as low as 8 percent during the 1980s.[87] When conservatives attempted to boost these numbers, often by appointing the wives of prominent conservative leaders to various agencies and committees, their moderate critics cried tokenism. Appearances, however, could sometimes be deceiving, since conservative women did feel that they had something both institutionally and culturally at stake. Many conservative women worked behind the denominational scene in building powerful local women's ministry programs. Although the upper echelons of denominational and church life were closed to them, women active in founding women's ministry refused token status. Barbara O'Chester, Joyce Rogers, and Sarah Maddox, for example, were highly educated, well versed on the issues at hand, and extraordinarily dynamic speakers. In 1992, they helped lead a group of conservative women to successfully petition the SBC's new conservative leadership for a full-fledged denominational women's ministry program that would have its own director, speakers, and publishing opportunities. The result, Women's Enrichment Ministry, became a multimillion-dollar industry under Lifeway, which was formerly the Sunday School Board. And with the financial success of Women's Enrichment Ministry, a least a few women gained some denominational sway.

Women's Enrichment Ministry was buttressed by the women's programs conservatives established at the SBC's six seminaries. In formulating the theology of Christian womanhood undergirding these programs, particularly in their beginning years, most directors looked to Dorothy Patterson. Patterson worked with other leading evangelicals outside the Southern Baptist context to construct a more nuanced understanding of biblical womanhood called "complementarianism." While not all conservative women accepted her creative applications of the concept, for conservative evangelicals both inside and outside the SBC, the spirited and highly visible Patterson reigned throughout the 1990s as the "matriarch of complementarianism," becoming as well known and as controversial as her husband, Paige.

Dorothy Patterson hardly seemed the most likely candidate for the job of promoting women's submission and the joys of homemaking. In fact, few women, conservative or otherwise, could surpass Dorothy Patterson in professional credentials. In 1968, at the age of twenty-five, she graduated with a

Th.M. from New Orleans Baptist Theological Seminary, where she was the only woman student studying theology. In 1970, she left the doctoral program, a decision, she later insisted, she made not because of family duties but for health reasons. In 1978, she received a D.Min. from Luther Rice Seminary in Georgia, and twenty-four years later, in 2002, she earned a D.Theo. from the University of South Africa, where she wrote "Aspects of a Biblical Theology of Womanhood."[88]

While many women studying theology during the 1970s and 1980s at Southern Baptist seminaries and institutions advocated biblical feminism, Dorothy Patterson stood at the vanguard of the conservative movement. When asked many years afterward about her sense of women's ministerial calling during those seminary days, she reported having no memories of such inclinations. She said that, encouraged by Paige, she pursued her education to help him first as a pastor and then as a seminary professor and administrator. She and Paige had been childhood sweethearts, growing up together in the First Baptist Church of Beaumont, Texas, where Paige's father served as pastor. In public venues, she introduced herself as the wife of Paige and mother of Armour and Carmen. She was, in her words, "primarily a wife, mother, and homemaker," with grandmother added in years to come. Despite her rhetoric, though, Dorothy was comfortable in multiple roles and realms. Outside the home, she was a passionate scholar and debater. A colorful Texan, she often quipped that God had instilled within her a love of hats—and she sported one for every occasion—to remind her of woman's proper place in the hierarchy. Dorothy devoted her writing and teaching to promoting this place with, of course, Paige's permission and blessing, as she assured supporters and critics alike. Along with Paige, she became a lightning rod during the conflict, inspiring intense loyalty among conservatives and bitter ridicule among moderates. Women both valorized and caricatured her, and some more contemporary conservative women came to resent the backwoods portrayal her approach invited. Formal avenues of denominational and ecclesial authority over men were denied her, but she possessed an incredible amount of power and clout.

The Southern Baptist Historical Association invited Dorothy Patterson to present a paper on women's ordination at its 1988 annual meeting, charging her with representing the conservative Southern Baptist viewpoint. In reality, Patterson informed conservative rhetoric on the matter as much as she reflected it. Her paper pushed well beyond women's ordination to articulate what she saw as a biblical theology of women's submission to men's authority. The Southern Baptist Historical Association organized its meeting as a debate, so Patterson actually responded to Jann Aldredge Clanton.[89] Clanton was a forty-two-year-old Southern Baptist woman who, like Patterson, was a married mother of two. A fellow Texan, she, too, was described as spirited, passionate, even persuasive and, like Patterson, had attended seminary to study theology. Clanton, however, was committed to SBWIM, and similar to other SBWIM women, her argument for women's ordination rested on scripture, history, and most significantly, a personal call. Clanton herself had experienced this sense of call and was ordained. Unable to find a Baptist placement, she was serving a Methodist church in Waco, Texas, at the time of the 1988 meeting.

Patterson quickly dismissed Clanton's arguments for history and call. Focusing on the evangelical feminists and moderate Baptist scholars who informed Clanton's understanding, Patterson argued that historical claims for women's "teaching/ruling positions in local churches" stretched the truth. Pointing to Letha Scanzoni's interpretation of Priscilla as Paul's coworker as a case in point, Patterson accused Scanzoni and other like-minded academics of "jesuitical casuistry or historical hanky-panky in order to create a female Mt. Everest out of an anthill to prove a point." Patterson also charged moderate Southern Baptist professors like Leon McBeth, who had argued for women's ecclesial authority in his book *Women in Baptist Life*, with distorting evidence. "Historically," she claimed, "one is hard put to present a case for women in teaching/ruling positions in Southern Baptist churches." In her paper, Clanton contended that Southern Baptists who opposed women's ordination were rejecting the traditional Baptist distinctives of soul competency and the priesthood of the believer. Patterson replied that those women who "left Southern Baptists in a quest for pastoral authority" bore "eloquent testimony that their commitments to Baptist doctrine were superseded by their desires to attain a particular ecclesial office." Even more importantly, insisted Patterson, history and tradition did "not possess absolute and unquestioned authority."[90] Likewise, "practical considerations," such as women's gifts, their ministerial successes, and an accepting culture, meant little against the timeless dictates of the Bible.[91]

Patterson then pitted women's sense of personal call, what she called "emotional and intuitive impulses," against biblical dictates. "Service to God," she reminded, "can never be a purely private matter. The church does have a right and responsibility to examine the call of another." But this examination must firmly rest on scripture. For "if God indeed has spoken," she said "we must examine what he has said and how it has been interpreted for nearly two millennia."[92]

Patterson focused on one New Testament passage that Clanton briefly considered, 1 Timothy 2:8–15, giving it far more exegetical attention.[93] Clanton had argued that Paul's dictate in 1 Timothy 2:11–12 bidding women to keep silent and practice submission paralleled the previous verse (2:9) forbidding women to wear braided hair, gold, pearls, and expensive clothes. According to Clanton, both verses were cultural proscriptions, and no interpreter took the concluding verse (2:15), "women will be saved through bearing children," literally. To heed one verse and not the other was, Clanton said, "selective literalism."[94] In interpreting scripture, one had to distinguish contextual conditions from timeless principles.

Patterson was cleverly challenging moderate Baptists and feminist theologians at their own game by accusing them, in turn, of "selective literalism," a charge often brought against conservatives. According to Patterson, biblical feminists were more guilty of "this process of hermeneutical gymnastics." It was conservatives, she said, who grasped the significance of timeless principles as they sought to "preserve the pure Word of God as enduring across cultures and throughout history and as appropriating itself from age to age with vigor and relevance." Paul's dictate forbidding braided hair, for example, embodied a more general premise. In the verse's first part, Paul urged women to modesty. Afterward, he indicated that women should dress themselves in "good works" and "with reverence for God." The underlying principle for women was "to focus attention upon the inner self and the development of godliness with its pursuant outward manifestation of good works—a timely word for women in any generation." Paul drew on a similar understanding, Patterson insisted, when calling for women's silence and submission. Patterson translated silence as "quietness" and saw it as neither an "absence of sound" nor a "surrender of mind or conscience or private judgments" but a "gentle and tranquil manner which goes hand and hand with submission." Submission, she interpreted, was a "willingness to acquiesce to the will of another," and biblical submission was "forever a self-imposed discipline." "Men," Patterson claimed, were "not directed in scripture to force or require submission."[95]

Patterson added several caveats, which proved noteworthy for the future. First, she challenged any comparison of female submission to slavery. Clanton and other feminists had often made this charge in dismissing submission, and other moderates were soon to follow. If Paul did condone slavery, which Patterson questioned, his instruction for the behavior of slaves did not justify its continuance. The opposite proved true of women because Paul declared their submission part of the created order. Second, Patterson maintained that Paul did not intend women to avoid teaching altogether. Certain New Testament passages urged women to teach children, instruct other women, and "even occasionally privately share understandings with men."[96] And last, Patterson insisted that women's submission did not result from the fall. In fact, Eve's sin was "not only a violation to the divine command concerning the forbidden fruit but also a reversal of divine order."[97]

After Patterson read her paper, one participant asked if she, Patterson, had violated the principle against women teaching men by speaking at the meeting. Patterson answered that she was "sharing" her insights. "My apologies to all the gentlemen here if you thought that [teaching] was my purpose," she added.[98] The audience chuckled. Despite the heightened tensions in the denomination, the meeting was fairly good-natured. It was attended primarily by people interested in church history and was, so to speak, under the radar. Nonetheless, for those paying close attention, Patterson's paper not only reflected conservative sentiment on the matter of women but predicted how conservatives would argue for their submission. Moreover, in addressing slavery, she signaled the need, and willingness, to tackle the related question of race.

Like most conservatives, Patterson engaged scripture, and hers was a far more detailed and nuanced exegesis than Clanton's. It also revealed that although conservatives claimed the Bible to be timeless, conservative interpretation was not. Without being explicit, Patterson rejected the more extreme interpretation of submission expressed in the 1984 Kansas City Resolution and certainly the stricture associated with the iron fist of southern patriarchy. Women's submission, she emphasized, did not result from the Edenic fall but from the created order. This interpretation undoubtedly reflected a growing relationship between Southern Baptist conservatives and the outside evangelical world. In 1987, the Council on Biblical Manhood and Womanhood organized and shortly afterward issued its "Danvers Statement." Patterson had served on the committee that wrote the statement. The Southern Baptist Historical Association meeting was held less than a year afterward and clearly showed the influence.

The "Danvers Statement" advocated a softer form of patriarchy, or what was eventually labeled complementarianism, for its claim of "complementary differences between masculinity and femininity." The statement actually reversed Joyce Rogers and the 1984 understanding of the fall by holding that submission was not intended as a punishment but as a joyful manifestation of the divine order. The fall, it stated, "introduced distortions into the relationships between men and women." In the home, for example, "the husband's loving, humble headship tends to be replaced by domination or passivity; the wife's intelligent, willing submission tends to be replaced by usurpation or servility." It also added that in the church, "sin inclines men toward a worldly love of power or an abdication of spiritual responsibility, and inclines women to resist limitations on their roles or to neglect the use of their gifts in appropriate ministries." The Council on Biblical Manhood and Womanhood was committed to addressing a particular type of male headship and female submission more acceptable for contemporary times. It had the support of numerous evangelical groups, denominations, and organizations, both within and outside the South, but the SBC quickly became one of the largest, most visible, and most powerful. As a sign of their partnership, the council moved its offices to Southern Seminary in Louisville, signaling that the Southern Baptist conservatives were now more directly influencing, rather than being undergirded by, the evangelical subculture.

On one hand, Patterson articulated a less extreme interpretation of submission and patriarchy; on the other, she advocated something far more comprehensive. Rather than a particular argument against women's ordination, she provided an all-encompassing biblical justification for women's submission. "Nothing in scripture," she insisted, "infers that women assume positions of authority over men in either the church or home." Conservatives followed Patterson's example here as they, too, moved beyond women's ordination, focused on the WMU, and supported segregated women's ministry programs as an alternative that did little to usurp, at least formally, the established ecclesial order. For conservatives, the WMU represented the "feminization of missions" and thus resistance to the new male leadership.

An End to the "Feminization of Missions"

When Dellanna O'Brien assumed directorship of the WMU in 1989, she asked about the principal cause for falling numbers. "Death," retorted Carolyn Miller, the WMU's feisty president. A longtime Southern Baptist missionary known for her calm and gentle demeanor, O'Brien soon realized the stark reality behind Miller's statement: "As elderly members passed on, few younger women filled their places."[99] Overall, women felt little enthusiasm for joining a century-old organization populated by their grey-haired grandmothers, but WMU officers like Miller and O'Brien undoubtedly recognized that more recent denominational factors had contributed as well to the WMU's diminished appeal. These factors involved hostilities between the historic women's group and the new SBC hierarchy.

The reasons behind the hostilities varied over time. During the early 1980s, for instance, the WMU birthed SBWIM. And conservative churches began dropping the WMU as "radical." According to Carolyn Weatherford, who served as the WMU's executive director from 1974 to 1989, "there were all kinds of talk that 'WMU leaders are gay,' etc." The WMU's support of SBWIM certainly fed such rumors. A few women later questioned whether it was the WMU or Weatherford who needled conservatives; nevertheless, as the conflict escalated and conservatives moved beyond women's ordination to promote, more generally, women's submission, the WMU became a natural target. One incident proved telling. When introducing Weatherford to speak at a state convention evangelism conference, a male minister stated, "Brethren, my Bible tells me to let the women keep silent in the church, and if they have questions, ask their husbands." Not one to hold her tongue, Weatherford took the podium and quipped, "Brother, I have no husband at home so I shall speak." Weatherford's marital status soon changed. In 1989, at age fifty-eight, Weatherford retired from the WMU and moved to Indiana as a newly married pastor's wife. There, apart from the WMU, she immersed herself in the moderate movement and increased her denominational activism as Carolyn Weatherford Crumpler.

Under O'Brien's directorship, the WMU severed formal ties with SBWIM. O'Brien was not as boldly forthright as Crumpler, which some WMU insiders felt might be beneficial in working with conservative leaders and local churchwomen. None of these factors helped significantly, though, as the new denominational hierarchy still suspected the WMU of moderate sympathies. O'Brien's husband, Bill, had been the Foreign Mission Board's vice president, resigning when Dellanna became the WMU's executive director. While conservatives recognized Weatherford Crumpler's convictions, many conjectured that the O'Briens also leaned toward moderates and that they were uncomfortable with the mission board's movement toward the opposition. Dorothy Patterson, for one, expressed her disapproval over a husband following his wife, saying that it was "putting the cart before the horse."[100] Then, in 1990, Weatherford Crumpler's run for the vice presidency on the moderate ticket with Daniel Vestal led even more conservatives to accuse the WMU of moderate sympathies as they continued to link her with the organization.

Beyond any individual, however, what was most offensive to conservatives and their agenda was the WMU's independence. According to conservative leaders, local WMU groups often challenged, even usurped, their pastor's authority. Moreover, the WMU's constitution stipulated that since it was an auxiliary to the denomination rather than an official agency, the SBC could not name the women's officers or spend their monies. In 1888, Southern Baptist men had insisted on these stipulations to ensure that the organizing women would not become a burdensome entity. One hundred years later, the arrangement meant that while conservatives captured the head of every SBC agency, board, and seminary, they could not touch the WMU. The women's auxiliary was the only SBC-related group that completely resisted conservative control. This situation, and its irony, drew the ire of conservatives.

At first, they acted tentatively, realizing the sacred status the WMU held in Southern Baptist lore. Even as the group had become rather old-fashioned, its women, nevertheless, were regarded as saintly. Many Southern Baptists remembered the devotion of their mothers and grandmothers to the historic organization, and some of these women had been buried wearing their WMU pendants. To criticize the legacy of missionary heroine Lottie Moon, namesake of the WMU's special offering for foreign missions, was anathema. At the same time, newer Southern Baptists felt far less nostalgia over the women's mission group, and as conservative churches grew, many dropped the WMU for women's ministry programs. This, too, created problems for conservatives, since the WMU's special offerings funded more than half of the mission boards' budgets.

Hostilities between the historic women's organization and the new SBC leadership came to a head when, in 1993, the WMU supplied mission literature to moderates who were meeting independently of the SBC. Adrian Rogers immediately announced the end of the "feminization of missions," demanding that the WMU be "hard-wired" into the denomination's structure.[101] The accusation of feminism, of course, would have been a tactic to scare many conservative Southern Baptists. The charge, coming from Rogers, was a condemnation that placed the WMU not only on the side of women's ordination but in the company of bra-burning radicals and moral relativists. Hardwiring the WMU into the denomination's structure would have given conservatives appointive power over the leadership of the women's organization as well as control over its budget. The WMU responded by "politely declining" the SBC's "gracious" invitation to become an official SBC agency. Conservatives fumed. According to Morris Chapman, president of the SBC's executive committee, "When an organization gets a program of its own, it ceases to be an auxiliary" and "becomes its own entity."[102] As a result of the incident, the WMU found itself in an awkward position. An open dispute would feed rumors of feminist aggression and alienate the organization from many of its local church groups and women. Behind closed doors, WMU officers did successfully lobby to keep the Lottie Moon and Annie Armstrong trademarks, to which the WMU's special offerings for missions were attached. At the same time, they recognized that many local WMU women held conservative loyalties. According to O'Brien, at the individual church level, the "WMU's understanding of the role of women in church life would vary from little to no involvement in the church (except that of women and children's work) to the perception of those on the other extreme that women were free to fill any office of the church, including the pastoral role."

Once again, the WMU carefully negotiated competing impulses. As O'Brien said, "Aware of the discrepancies in the areas of gender under-standing, WMU attempted to take the middle road in dealing with these various discrepancies in all publications and venues." In other words, the WMU "avoided those areas that would be controversial." As a publisher of mission material, for example, it had "to exercise caution and care." WMU editor Barbara Massey recalled the contested story of a woman missionary performing a baptism and how afterward they had to carefully screen reports regarding "what some woman missionaries were 'allowed' to do on the field in other cultures." As for SBWIM, O'Brien "determined that any commenda-tion I might receive from some for personal involvement would hinder my support of women's involvement in missions as a whole." Furthermore, the WMU backed away from Carolyn Weatherford Crumpler as she campaigned in 1990 for the SBC's vice presidency, an office that WMU leaders commonly held, as part of the moderate ticket. In assessing the WMU during the 1990s, Weatherford Crumpler concluded that it moved from "being a mission or-ganization for women to a women's organization for missions. It spent its energy and resources promoting mission and service activities for men and women, boys and girls."

In former days "the middle road" ensured that the WMU would survive and flourish, but times had changed. WMU executives no longer worked alongside old-style denominationalists, and "caution" and "care" did not characterize the new era. Dorothy Patterson, for example, complained that the WMU made no "clear, strong statements" on a number of cultural issues. "I do not see in their publications," she said, "a real lifting up of homemaking. That concerns me." According to Sarah Maddox, the prominent women's ministry leader from Bellevue Baptist Church in Memphis, it was extremely important that women's ministry incorporate missions as a part of its pro-gramming. To her chagrin, as missions increasingly became a part of the church, and not simply the realm of the WMU, that did not always happen.

Established in 1992, Women's Enrichment Ministry also strengthened during this period. Denise George, the part-time director, struggled with the job's numerous full-time demands, but by the late 1990s, Women's Enrichment Ministry was a multimillion-dollar enterprise with a full-time staff. It sponsored denomination-wide forums, seminary training, certificate programs, regional retreats, pastors' wives seminars, and more. As part of Women's Enrichment Ministry, a new group of conservative Southern Baptist women sold out coliseums and conference centers across the country. They called themselves Bible teachers, mentors, and leaders for women, and they supplied most of the Bible studies, videos, and materials produced for local churchwomen's ministry programs. Some, like Texan Beth Moore, were cradle Southern Baptists. A vibrant, folksy, and sparkling blond, the Houston-based Moore possessed a natural stage presence. She also made sure that her audience knew that she had her husband's permission to travel, speak, write, and make videos. Others, like Canadian Mary Kassian, had gravitated to Southern Baptists because of their commitment to women's submission. A professor of women's studies at Southern who wrote extensively on women's roles, Kassian had little, if any, connection or loyalty to the WMU.

Over time, in conservative congregations, women's ministry programs either replaced the WMU or put it under a larger network. Stories circulated of older WMU loyalists switching church affiliations over the introduction of women's ministry. One woman lamented the thought of her life without the WMU at its core. At certain points, friendships were ripped asunder. And yet, as new concerns replaced aging passions, these WMU loyalists were increasingly the minority. As Sarah Maddox put it, women's ministry was successful because "it scratched where women itched." The WMU, on the other hand, was not what most women desired or felt that they needed, nor was its middle road.

Submission possessed a magnetism that both repelled and attracted women. According to Carol Richardson, a sixty-year-old WMU executive committee member, church deacon, mother, and grandmother simultaneously studying for ordained ministry, "The WMU's mindset had always been 'don't become involved in the non-essential. Stay focused on the main thing which is mission and the great commission.'" In heeding the first injunction, the lifelong WMU leader actually discovered that submission, at least for herself, "was not a non-essential." Conservative women like Patterson and Maddox concurred. Overall, the Southern Baptist conflict forced women to reexamine their own sense of identity and self-understanding. Many admitted that they had simply accepted the roles handed to them without much thought. Southern Baptist women who underwent this process of self-discovery spoke of new convictions and callings. As a result, the middle road no longer held appeal, and Southern Baptist women fragmented, forming numerous networks and groups. Ultimately, as the debate over women became central to the denominational struggle, the tensions between the SBC and the WMU seemed less relevant to women's lives. Race, however, was another matter entirely.

From Racial Order to Gendered Submission

By the mid-1990s, conservative dominance seemed assured. Conservatives had experienced consecutive SBC presidential victories and now directed almost every agency and board, bar the WMU. Moderates were hurriedly forming their own organizations. Overall, women's submission had largely succeeded as a test for fellowship. And yet, the issue of race lingered as a blot on the Southern Baptists past; to inherit the SBC was to assume this legacy. To the surprise of many moderates, conservatives took time from the contest to address the matter of race.

During the 1990s, various white Christians collectively apologized for sins past.[103] On the 500-year anniversary of Columbus's coming to America, groups ranging from the far-reaching National Council of Churches to the small midwestern-based Mennonite Church apologized to Native Americans for pillaging their land. Lutherans apologized to Jews for Martin Luther's anti-Semitic "Christ-killer" remarks. The United Church of Christ apologized to Hawaiians for Congregationalist missionaries' complicity in the U.S. military's overthrow of the Kingdom of Hawaii. Under Pope John Paul II, Catholics apologized to individuals, movements, and cultures on a range of issues, including the Catholic Church's exploitation of Latin America. Racial reconciliation also became a theme in the wider evangelical world. The National Association of Evangelicals promoted it as one of the organization's central goals. So, too, did Promise Keepers, which integrated its national office and actively recruited more black men to its rallies.[104]

Following this growing trend, in 1995, on the 150-year anniversary of their denomination's 1845 founding, Southern Baptist conservative leaders presented a resolution that apologized to black Americans for the SBC's support of slavery and its racist legacy. In contrast to more recent resolutions, discussion on the Resolution on Racial Reconciliation was minimal and overwhelmingly positive. When messengers at the Atlanta convention affirmed it by a 95 percent majority, Gary Frost, a young black Southern Baptist minister from Ohio, joined SBC president Jim Henry at the podium for prayer. As a white Mississippi and Tennessee pastor very active in championing the civil rights movement and integration, Henry had watched his children be bussed amidst protesters and had received harsh criticism from a bitterly divided denomination and region. Now, more than twenty-five years later, convention messengers joined hands in solidarity with one another on the matter. Frost proclaimed, "On behalf of my black brothers and sisters, we accept your apology. And we extend to you our forgiveness in the name of our Lord and Savior Jesus Christ."[105] Those present regarded it as a highly emotional experience and a lesson in forgiveness and redemption.

The resolution was extensive. In a lengthy preamble and series of "whereas" clauses, it first named the role of slavery in the SBC's founding and the role of Southern Baptists in perpetuating the institution. Acknowledging the failure of Southern Baptists to support civil rights, it also condemned their segregation of worship and their exclusion of African Americans from church membership and leadership. Interestingly, the one scripture that women most often referenced in lobbying for ordination was likewise highlighted in the resolution: "There is neither Jew nor Greek, there is neither slave nor free, there is neither male nor female, for (we) are all one in Christ Jesus." In conclusion, the resolution resolved that Southern Baptists "apologize to all African-Americans for condoning and/or perpetuating individual and systemic racism in our lifetime," "ask forgiveness from our African-American brothers and sisters," "commit ourselves to eradicate racism in all its forms from Southern Baptist life and ministry" and "pursue racial reconciliation in all our relationships."[106]

The SBC received mixed reviews for its action. Some outsiders praised the resolution as a first step toward healing the wounds inflicted by the SBC's legacy of racism.[107] After all, the content of the resolution addressed most racial injustices. The resolution found its share of critics, most of whom focused on what they considered to be the SBC's hypocrisy.[108] They pointed to the decidedly conservative turn of the denomination and its close partnership with groups like the Moral Majority, the Christian Coalition, and the Family Research Council. They charged that these political heroes of the overwhelmingly white religious right pushed against many of the measures intended to correct racism—measures that were supported by black Americans. The black journalist Bill Maxwell asked, "If Southern Baptists are serious about atoning for their historical sins, how can they also join Republicans in destroying affirmation action?"[109] More cynically, the Pulitzer Prize–winning Les Payne wrote that "next century, perhaps, the Southern

Baptists might consider denouncing the 'curse of Ham' or even supporting the 14th Amendment."[110] According to the *Philadelphia Times*, some black Americans would dismiss the resolution as "late by more than a century."[111] The prominent Dallas preacher and National Baptist pastor Caesar A. W. Clark suggested that Southern Baptists were trying to recruit black Baptists away from their historically black conventions.[112]

Inside the denomination, criticism was minimal. Some moderates grumbled that they were the rightful heirs of progressive racial politics, but overall an unusual solidarity prevailed. Eight of the sixteen persons charged with writing the resolution were black, and they gave the process high marks. Gary Frost remembered that during the one-day consultation "something remarkable happened." As he recounted it, "Blacks weren't involved in making the resolution. They were involved in hearing it, receiving it, and making sure that it really dealt with the issues."[113] At the meeting, Eugene Gibson, an older black Chicago minister, "shed tears," realizing that "we were the sons of slaves and the sons of slave owners sitting down together."[114] He even acknowledged that several of the white committee members wanted to push further than the black contingency.[115] Emmanuel McCall, the first black Home Mission Board executive who had also sided with moderates in the Baptist battles, marveled that those who would be considered "far right" politically would be taking the lead on racial reconciliation.[116]

The resolution came about as a younger generation of conservatives, such as Richard Land, who drove the initiative, joined the battles and assumed key leadership roles. Al Mohler also served as a key member of the sixteen-person consultation. According to McCall, Land and Mohler drafted much of the resolution and took responsibility for seeing it peacefully affirmed. There were multiple reasons for their commitments. In contrast to Depression era seniors like Pressler and Rogers, both Land and Mohler were baby boomers, born in 1946 and 1959, respectively. Mohler, in particular, came of age in the post–civil rights South, and each held strong links to northern evangelicals who were publicly committing themselves to interracial dialogue and projects. Mohler even went on record praising 1960s progressives and liberals for their countercultural position in fighting Jim Crow. Because the conservative movement did not summon up progressive politics, Land thought that the support of the denomination's conservative leadership increased the resolution's chance of passing. "It's like maybe only Nixon could go to China," he said, "and only the Democrats can reform welfare."[117]

Conservatives like Land and Mohler seemed genuinely committed to racial reconciliation, yet there was another, subtler factor in the conservative push. Although none addressed it directly, conservatives had to realize how difficult it would be to continue promoting women's submission without evoking ready associations with southern patriarchy, the southern order, and ultimately racial matters. The accusations and comparisons had come already from SBWIM women and other critics. Never mind that racial prejudice was a nationwide phenomenon. Other conservative evangelicals involved with the Council on Biblical Manhood and Womanhood simply did not face the same scrutiny over the issue. It was one thing for conservative Mennonites, for instance, to argue for women's submission and male authority; it was another for Southern Baptists. When northern evangelicals spoke, their words did not conjure the same violent images associated with southern slavery, Jim Crow segregation, and civil rights. Having been schooled at Princeton and Oxford, Land certainly knew the images outsiders held of the South. In arguing for women's submission in the earlier Southern Baptist History and Heritage debate, Dorothy Patterson also felt that she had to reject slavery and racism. After all, apologists for slavery had appealed to the same household codes as those now espousing submission of women. Moreover, when conservatives spoke nostalgically of an era that preceded liberal politics, theology, and hermeneutics, a pre-1960s era in which the South, indeed the American heartland, was "saturated with Christianity," they intended to invoke an image reminiscent of a Normal Rockwell painting.[118] But to many they were invoking a racially ordered, white-dominated world. Thus, the more sophisticated side of conservatism felt the urgency for a formal statement on race, and the SBC's 150th anniversary offered the ideal occasion.

In at least one significant respect, the Resolution on Racial Reconciliation succeeded. As Southern Baptist conservatives began reaching out to historically black congregations, the congregations responded positively. While the tangible programs and resources related to the SBC certainly motivated their response, the resolution also paved the way to their acceptance. Subsequently, throughout the 1990s, large numbers of National Baptist churches dually aligned with the SBC, the Home Mission Board planted numerous predominantly black congregations across the country, and seminaries recruited black students as potential Southern Baptist pastors. These new phenomena enabled Southern Baptist growth. In 1951, the SBC had one black church affiliate. In the early 1990s, the number had grown to around 1,500. By 2000, some 3,000 black churches had affiliated with the SBC, and the National African American Fellowship of the SBC functioned as one of the denomination's more active and thriving groups. According to Richard Land, by the twenty-first century approximately 20 percent of Southern Baptists claimed some form of ethnic heritage.[119]

As hardened ideas about racial segregation fell out of favor with Southern Baptists, a more constrained view of women's ministry did subsequently emerge, shaping and reshaping notions of power and otherness so that women's roles became central in the struggle for control of the denomination. The role of women served as a boundary, separating one side from the other. Race had once functioned similarly. During the late 1950s and 1960s, for instance, "progressive" in relation to Southern Baptist life and culture readily referred to support of integration and civil rights. Now, by the 1980s and 1990s, the descriptor signified support for women in ordained ministry along with a rejection of their submission. During this period, moderates became more progressive in terms of women, thereby more easily defining themselves against conservatives.

But gendered ideas about women did not simply function as a postscript to or replacement of racial order. The controversies played out differently, and earlier divisions did not necessarily predict the battle lines. One example was that of Harold and Barbara O'Chester, who received many threats when they actively campaigned against racism and violence during the 1960s. At the time, Harold pastored a small church in Mississippi whose members had Klu Klux Klan connections. Harold went on to become a conservative megapastor in Austin, Texas, and Barbara became a leading antifeminist voice. Jim Henry was another example of an integrationist and activist who became a leading conservative voice and decided antifeminist. So, too, was Jerry Vines, the SBC's conservative president from 1988 to 1990. On the other hand, denominationalists who were in power from the 1950s to the 1970s compromised on race and did little to challenge dominant prejudices. While most Southern Baptist progressives on race eventually proved progressive regarding women and gender, joining the moderate camp, no absolute blueprint prevailed.

Another substantial difference between the issues of race and women's submission was the number of Southern Baptist women who actually upheld the tenet of submission. One is hard-pressed to think of civil rights succeeding without the activism and backing of the vast majority of southern and northern blacks. Suffrage, the ERA, and feminism were far more contested among women, and especially white southern women. Thus Southern Baptists were able to remain more countercultural in regard to women's issues.[120]

Mandating Submission

In the end, having settled the score on race, whether consciously or not, Southern Baptist conservatives could turn more freely to women's submission. Three years later, in 1998, they amended the Baptist Faith and Message by adding a section on the family to reflect their position. Dorothy Patterson was instrumental in writing Article 18: The Family, as well as the accompanying commentary that explained it. The most controversial part of the article, at least for moderates and outsiders, involved the relationship between husband and wife. The line most often quoted was that concerning gracious submission: "A wife is to submit herself graciously to the servant leadership of her husband even as the church willingly submits to the headship of Christ." As the commentary likewise indicated, the article espoused the complementarian view. In fact, the amendment and commentary borrowed liberally, often word for word, from the "Danvers Statement." Both emphasized the wife's spiritual "equality" to her husband and negated the 1984 Kansas City Resolution's justification of submission by stating that the "complementary relationship between husband and wife is presented as part of the pre-Fall perfect setting." The commentary used the same wording of the "Danvers Statement" in addressing abuses and distortions of the complementary relationship that resulted from the Genesis story. It called on husbands to "forsake harsh or selfish leadership and to extend loving care to their wives" and then for wives to "forsake resistance of the authority of their respective husbands." In two further parts titled "Husbands" and "Wives," it expanded on the complementary nature of their roles and the expectations of servant leadership as well as gracious submission. The commentary on wives closed by boldly stating that "as the realities of headship and submission are enacted within loving, equal, and complementary male-female roles, the image of God is properly reflected."[121]

As with the 1995 resolution on race, the 1998 amendment regarding the family passed easily. A motion to replace the wording of "women's submission" with "mutual submission" was quickly defeated, and the section, as it stood, was supported by a sea of hands, "amens," and final thunderous applause. Clearly the amendment, which received harsh external critique, had the overwhelming approval of conservative messengers. In contrast to years past, few moderates were present. By 1991, they had stopped endorsing a candidate for president and were organizing their own quasi-conventions and fellowship groups. Moderates did join with the secular media, however, in making their disapproval known. President Bill Clinton, speaking as a Southern Baptist, joked that "he might call it to the attention of the first lady."[122] One conservative-turned-moderate pastor, Joel Gregory, famous as the brief heir to W. A. Criswell's pulpit, threw his own punch: "All the men involved in crafting that have some of the most formidable, aggressive, dominant wives I've met in my life."[123]

Of course, the most formidable wife was Dorothy Patterson, whom Gregory failed to recognize as one of those actually crafting the amendment. Conservatives went on to elect her husband, Paige Patterson, as the SBC's president at the same 1998 meeting. Pictures of the Pattersons circulated in the news media, which presented them in stereotypical fashion as emblematic of the new SBC. One such photograph emphasized Paige's double chin and girth as he sat alongside Dorothy, who sported a wide-brimmed hat bedecked with ribbons and flowers. The result was a misleading hillbilly-like caricature of the two. While they did display a homespun humor and folksy manner, the Pattersons were also well educated, well traveled, and politically astute—hardly the simple folk the media seemed bent on presenting. To be sure, it was often difficult to know what to make of the Pattersons. In interview after interview, they glowingly detailed the ways in which male authority and female submission had worked so successfully in their marriage and household. Paige spoke admiringly of Dorothy, ironically saying, "She has the mind of a corporate executive," while Dorothy insisted that Paige "nurtured her mind" and "made her who she is."[124] The images and rhetoric associated with the Pattersons often led to exaggerations and misconceptions that were likewise applied to conservatives, including conservative women.

In 2000, Southern Baptists once again amended the Baptist Faith and Message.[125] This time, the changes were more substantive to the 1963 document. The outcry was not quite as public, in that many of the changes dealt with traditional Baptist theology, practice, and distinctives. Moderates were more upset, though, for these reasons precisely.[126] Some, for example, felt that the transition from the "priesthood of the believer" to the "priesthood of all believers" diminished the Baptist doctrine of soul competency, with its emphasis on the individual's final accountability and responsibility before God. Almost all lamented the deletion of several passages highlighting the role of Jesus Christ in the interpretation of scripture. Particularly objectionable was the replacement of "The criterion by which the Bible is to be interpreted is Jesus Christ" with "All scripture is a testimony to Christ, who is himself the focus of divine revelation." They also questioned the commitment of conservatives to local church autonomy with their substitution of the passage "A New Testament church of the Lord Jesus Christ is an autonomous local congregation" for the original and more simply stated "The church is an autonomous body."

While these changes were subject to interpretive battles over Baptist distinctives, the position of women was not. The new version asserted, as did the 1984 resolution, that "the office of pastor is limited to men as qualified by Scripture." For some moderates, this addition became even more problematic in light of the assertion that in Baptist life and history, confessional statements were meant as "instruments of doctrinal accountability" and that the amended Baptist Faith and Message was intended as a show of the "doctrines we hold precious and as essential to the Baptist tradition of faith and practice." If the 1984 resolution had been used a test for fellowship, how would an instrument of accountability be implemented?

When these resolutions passed almost unanimously at the convention meeting in Orlando, the conservative leadership made its intentions clear. Seminaries held elaborate penning ceremonies as robed faculty signed their names to the Baptist Faith and Message 2000. SBC boards and agencies required employees and job candidates to affirm the statement, and as these institutions had been purged of vocal moderates already, most of their personnel agreed to the process. Many celebrated it as too long in coming. Missions became the one hotly contested area when the International Mission Board, formerly the Foreign Mission Board, required all of its field missionaries to sign the new confession of faith as well. At least a few career missionaries felt that the rules had been changed on them. In the end, 77 missionaries refused to sign the Baptist Faith and Message. The board fired 13 who had a total of 246 years of service among them. The rest resigned or took early retirement. The loss of 43 missionaries on May 7, 2003, the final date to sign, represented the largest mass exodus in the history of the board. Still, as one agency executive put it, 77 represented a small fraction of the approximately 5,500 serving.[127]

The SBC entered the third millennium as a conservative-controlled institution. The amended Baptist Faith and Message symbolized the finality of the conservative resurgence and its transition of power. That conservatives began with women's issues in making amendments signified the increasing dominance of the debate throughout the conflict. In fact, as Russell Dilday put it, "To the surprise of many, the committee did not insert the controversial language of inerrancy in the section on Scripture, further dividing the constituency. It does seem curious, however, that since so much of the twenty-year controversy centered on the use of the term 'inerrancy' to describe the nature of the Bible, it was now apparently deemed unimportant."[128]

Once again, even as lines were drawn around the concept of submission, the significance of women as a defining issue in the controversy failed to be recognized and was seen only as a curious substitute for something deeper and more meaningful.

5

Behold a New Thing?

MODERATE LIFE

When Adrian Rogers won a second presidential victory in 1986, moderates despaired. They recognized that after five consecutive losses, their chances to regain control of the Southern Baptist Convention (SBC) were beginning to diminish. The dramatic events unfolding at Southeastern Baptist Theological Seminary only added to their perception of a conservative takeover. A few began to feel the need for a network whose goals involved something more meaningful than election politics, and that September sixteen moderates gathered at Meredith College in Raleigh, North Carolina. They called themselves the Southern Baptist Alliance. Most were from North Carolina, Virginia, and Georgia. Many were connected to Southeastern Seminary and expressed dismay, even horror, as the nexus of Southern Baptist progressivism was soon transformed into the center of Southern Baptist conservativism.

As both geography and background indicated, the Alliance represented those who had been most critical of SBC traditionalism, even under denominationalists. They certainly seemed most likely to accept women's ecclesial authority and accompanying issues of social justice. But despite their purported progressivism, of the sixteen moderates who initially gathered at Meredith, only one was a woman.[1] A year later, when the Alliance convened again at Meredith for its first convocation, Anne Neil attended, anticipating change. "Imagine my surprise," she said, "when I walked into this large conference room filled with men, mostly clergy. It looked like 'business as usual.' . . . To further undergird my apprehensions were several remarks made by men from the podium that were supposed to be humorous but were demeaning to women. I remember thinking, 'Here is a giant job of consciousness raising.'"[2]

During the next year, several women came aboard who were "thankfully," as indicated by Neil, long accustomed to "consciousness raising." Nancy Sehested and Susan Lockwood Wright served as ordained pastors and had helped Neil found Southern Baptist Women in Ministry (SBWIM). What these women lacked in numbers, they made up for in passion and zeal. Over the next two years, they argued long and hard for women's inclusion in the moderate movement—and not simply as tokens.[3] Alliance leaders listened enough to designate a task force, with Neil as its chair, on women in the church. A furloughed Southern Baptist missionary as well as a registered nurse, wife, and mother of two, Neil was studying at Garrett-Evangelical Theological Seminary with feminist theologian Rosemary Radford Reuther. Twenty years later, Neil's Alliance and SBWIM peers remembered her revolutionary vision, her contagious enthusiasm, and her genteel South Carolinian speech. One described her as the true steel magnolia. In narrating the events of this period, Neil claimed that the task force on women in church became the most active—and radical—of any moderate group. Its suggestions over the following months sparked heated debate and considerable resentment.

One incident stood out in her mind. On November 20, 1987, the executive committee of fourteen men and three women gathered to discuss the Alliance's formal incorporation as an organization separate from the SBC while also of Southern Baptist heritage. During the morning session, the task force on women in church presented two major proposals: a contribution of $15,000 over three years to SBWIM, or $5,000 annually, and an inclusive language policy. Neither proposal passed. In fact, they created an atmosphere of hostility. Rather than the $15,000, the men present voted to send $1,000 from the missionary fund, which Neil interpreted as a "demeaning, condescending, patronizing gesture."[4] Later in the day, after a Southeastern faculty member reviewed the seminary's situation, the majority present pledged $5,000 on the spot, without question, to its recently organized American Association of University Professors chapter, apparently formed to protect Southeastern's faculty from the new conservative administration. Despite having taught at Southeastern and being close to many professors there, Neil immediately protested. After all, the committee had earlier complained that the women's task force demanded too much. Someone angrily interrupted Neil: "Can't you see the blood of these faculty members flowing here on the floor?" Neil immediately responded, "Yes, I can; but can you see the avalanche of blood of women that has been flowing for nearly 2000 years?"[5] A "painful" silence followed, but in the months ahead, the Alliance made a tangible shift in SBWIM's direction. For many Alliance advocates, Neil's startling observation marked a turning point.

During the Southern Baptist battles, this scenario played out time after time. Moderates continued their rhetoric of freedom, tying freedom to historic Baptist distinctives like soul competency (soul freedom), the priesthood of the believer (freedom of the believer), and local church autonomy (free church tradition). Almost every formal statement, vision, and mission emphasized freedom. Still, in dealing with real-life, on-the-ground issues, moderates reacted quite differently. As the contest increasingly invoked women's roles, inheritors of compromise wanted to proceed cautiously and maintain the middle ground. In contrast, inheritors of dissent wanted to act quickly and decisively. The women of SBWIM were part of the latter and frequently critiqued the hesitancy of moderates. They believed that too many moderates wanted the old SBC restored. Grey-haired preachers in black suits were willing to sacrifice women in ministry for the sake of compromise and unity—often translated as money, size, and power.

Over time, even this moderate response began to change. As conservatives pushed in one direction and SBWIM pushed in another, traditional denominationalists awoke to a new reality—and culture. By the mid-1990s, postfeminist America saw womanly submission to male authority as outmoded and outdated. After a long period of hesitancy and compromise, moderates proudly promoted their support of women's ordination as the most visible difference between themselves and conservatives.

This chapter examines the struggle of moderates to respond to what they called the conservative takeover. As with previous chapters, it is arranged both thematically and chronologically. It first focuses on SBWIM and the Alliance as carrying forth what had been called alternatively the progressive, dissenting, or prophetic tradition among Southern Baptists. In developing a distinctly Baptist theology of women in ministry, SBWIM women tied historic notions of Baptist freedom to dissent. Despite its fitful beginning, the Alliance soon promoted this notion of dissent as crucial to fighting sexism, racism, and other Southern Baptist "sins." It was composed, however, of a minority of moderates. The chapter then turns to the majority of moderates who engaged the rhetoric of freedom as a means to unity, compromise, and unrealized victory. As these moderates lost power over the denomination's major agencies and seminaries, they eventually established new fellowship groups, networks, and even seminaries. They touted a "new thing," even though women did not always "behold a new thing" in their approach.

The final pages of the chapter consider continuity and change within the ongoing moderate movement as they related to the debate over women. Undoubtedly, the 2000 election of an ordained woman, Donna Forester, as moderator of the largest moderate organization, the Cooperative Baptist Fellowship (CBF), contrasted with the Baptist Faith and Message as revised by conservatives earlier the same summer to exclude women from pastoral leadership. For some women, however, the election of Forester felt more like a "knee-jerk" reaction. Progressives mourned the dearth of women ministers in moderate pulpits. In charting a centrist position, inheritors of compromise might articulate an acceptance of women in ministry, but few called them into their pulpits. In terms of women, talk of Baptist freedom seemed more often about merely promoting a discourse of choice for women, or even local churches, than any concrete push for their actual ordination and placement.

Dissent: A Baptist Theology of Women in Ministry

Throughout the 1980s, SBWIM continued bringing women together through occasional retreats, planning meetings, and—the highlight for many—its annual convention worship service. SBWIM's quarterly newsletter and periodical followed denominational events diligently. Most significantly, SBWIM participants together deepened their understanding of women in ministry. In 1986, *FOLIO* published a six-article series that undergirded what Molly Marshall-Green called the women in ministry movement with an explicitly Baptist theological foundation. The work was representative of SBWIM during this period. While the authors continued to draw from other feminist scholars, SBWIM's theology of women in ministry also became more innovative, mature, and consciously Baptist. Additionally, SBWIM's theology reflected the context of the culture wars with its partisan, even sectarian tendencies, for SBWIM supporters clearly preferred fragmentation over what they considered to have been the high costs of compromise and denominationalism. This attitude put them at odds with the greater part of moderate life.

Southern Seminary's Molly Marshall-Green began the series by highlighting what she considered Baptists' central affirmations and exploring their "catalytic impact on women in ministry." As before, Marshall-Green started with scripture, noting that this procedure was Baptist tradition. She stated that contrary to conservative opinion, women were searching the Bible as they determined God's claim on their lives. She emphasized that the Baptist tenet of soul competency upheld each individual's right to deal directly with God's call. Like most moderates, she championed local church autonomy as a Baptist hallmark and argued that unity in diversity had long been crucial to Baptist life. "Even if one Baptist church decides against encouraging women in ministry," she stated, "it has no right to make this a test case of fellowship with a sister church."[6]

Marshall-Green and other advocates of women in ministry had previously incorporated feminist and liberationist perspectives into their theological vision with subtle connections to historic Baptist life. In making her final points here, Marshall-Green tied those feminist and liberationist perspectives more directly to an earlier tradition of Baptist dissent. "Baptists have always been characterized by their social concern," she observed, "yet as Baptists climbed the socio-economic ladder, much of our concern for the disenfranchised of society has ebbed." Marshall-Green then argued, "Because women have been among the oppressed historically . . . the theological vision informing women in ministry is acutely sensitive to the brokenness all around us." Marshall-Green concluded with the Lordship of Christ as the "keystone to the Baptist theological structure." The church's leadership must be Christocentric, she said, and Jesus modeled ministerial authority as a servant. Marshall-Green reminded readers that "women have long emulated this ministry style," serving as "heralds today of the need to link authority with service rather than domination." Because early Baptists had experienced tremendous ecclesial censure and persisted in their vision, Baptist women in ministry were "in step with their courageous forebears."[7]

Subsequent articles in the series elaborated on Marshall-Green's concluding two points. Elizabeth Barnes, Marshall-Green's theological counterpart at Southeastern, pointed to God's self-giving power. Western theology had modeled God's sovereignty after the "male characteristics of dominance, impassibility, immutability and might," whereas the New Testament witness portrayed God as "Authorizer," "Energizer," and "covenant partner" to women as well as men.[8] Sociologist Sarah Frances Anders argued that God called believers to "turn the existing disorder and injustice of the world 'upside down.'" For too long, the church had committed itself to providing personal spiritual security, thereby ignoring God's call to combat physical suffering and tyranny. According to Anders, the Baptist Faith and Message had underscored the "healing and the redemptive role of the Christian in the world," and through their missionary organizations, women had managed to "tilt the world, if not turn it upside down."[9] As she saw it, a prophetic impulse in Southern Baptist life, which had begun with the Woman's Missionary Union (WMU), now called them to push further.

Like conservatives, Marshall-Green, Anders, and other SBWIM women assumed a golden age in Baptist life. But while conservatives emphasized postwar liberalism and feminist ideas as corrupting traditional ideals and practices, SBWIM's narrative pushed further back. These women read Baptist history through the lens of feminist theology and liberationist principles. They held that beginning in England and continuing in colonial America, Baptists stood prophetically against the status quo, creating a place for the marginalized and oppressed. As for Southern Baptists, southern prejudices had crept into early nineteenth-century Baptist life, downplaying dissent and transforming the SBC into an agent of the status quo in both the slave-holding and Jim Crow South. Jann Clanton argued in *FOLIO* that Southern Baptists had violated their history first in racist practices and then continued to violate it by oppressing women.[10]

In articulating a distinctly Baptist theology of women in ministry, SBWIM was speaking not only to conservatives. Its women directed their remarks to denominationalists-turned-moderates, imploring them to action. Clanton, for example, was an ordained Texas Baptist serving a Methodist church in Waco. She ended her *FOLIO* article by saying that moderates' problem, or "sin," was tolerance—a tolerance of intolerance. Caution had rendered them fearful to speak, dissent, and act prophetically. Conservatives were winning because they instilled passion, and passion, said Clanton, "comes from seeing a need for change." In constructing a Baptist theology of women in ministry, SBWIM urged moderates to instill passion through "righting the wrongs in our Baptist institutions" and becoming a "prophetic statement for human rights in our larger community."[11] Such changes would move SBWIM women closer to early Baptist roots. At the same time, their notion of authority in terms of "service" and "human rights" was clearly a contemporary interpretation of empowerment. To effect such change, particularly in an increasingly fragmented and politically charged environment, they knew that they needed greater monetary and institutional assistance.

Answering the Call

The Alliance's early agreement to support SBWIM, both ideologically and financially, cemented a relationship between the two. Still, as Neil and other SBWIM affiliates made clear, advocacy of women's ordination should signal a concern for broader social justice issues. They resented how the contest's increasing focus on women was moving moderates away from the larger fight for social justice. As they saw it, those in positions of denominational authority were once again using women as tokens and pawns. In one early Alliance meeting, Susan Lockwood stunned the men present by stating that she objected to their using the women's issue, particularly women's ordination, as a "means to larger ends." She then proceeded to explain that their promotion of women's ordination had to be something other than a politically astute maneuver in the ongoing denominational conflict.[12] Women like Neil and Lockwood believed it to be their role to help the Alliance define itself as an alternative to "business as usual."

If the Alliance truly saw itself as a moderate group dedicated to something other than convention politics and business as usual, one of its most crucial tasks was to determine "what should be that glue that could hold itself together."[13] Early leaders of the Alliance wrote its covenant in a series of meetings over late 1986 and 1987. They conceived it as a series of seven "historic Baptist principles, freedoms, and traditions." In defining these, the covenant first spoke of the "freedom of the individual" as "led by God's Spirit" to "read and interpret the Scriptures, relying on the historical understanding of the church and the best methods of modern biblical study." In addressing the "freedom of the local church," it specifically cited those "gifted for ministry" as "male and female." The covenant upheld the Alliance's support for theological education, defining it as both "reverence for biblical authority" and a "respect for open inquiry and responsible scholarship." Pushing further, it cited certain tenets not readily associated with Southern Baptist life. It celebrated ecumenism as the "larger body of Jesus Christ" and affirmed the "servant role of leadership within the church." It reinterpreted evangelism as the "calling of God to all peoples to repentance and faith, reconciliation and hope, social and economic justice." Finally, it insisted on the "principle of a free church in a free state." As the Alliance sought to explain itself and its covenant to the wider public, particularly Southern Baptists, it published the small book *Being Baptist Means Freedom*. Each chapter defined the Alliance by interpreting traditional Baptist principles as well as new concepts in terms of freedom.[14]

The discourse of freedom appeared everywhere, serving as a contrast to what moderates and Alliance members viewed as conservative control. Similar to SBWIM's theology of women in ministry, the Alliance placed freedom historically in early Baptist life. As former Southeastern professor and missiologist Alan Neely explained, the Alliance was the progeny of those seventeenth- and eighteenth-century marginalized, ridiculed, imprisoned, and free-church Baptists.[15] Reflective of its cultural context, the Alliance also interpreted freedom in terms of civil rights. At their fourth convocation meeting, Alliance advocates acknowledged themselves "as members of the

Southern Baptist family" and issued a statement of repentance to African Americans for "condoning and perpetuating the sin of slavery prior to and during the Civil War" as well as the "continuing pattern of racism, segregation, and prejudice."[16] Unlike conservatives, they viewed women's submission to male authority as a form of sexism related to southern patriarchy and racism.

From the start, the Alliance also quite vocally repudiated the SBC's new political alignment with the religious right, whose policies, Alliance supporters felt, deeply violated their own covenant and sense of Baptist identity. On this front, the Alliance broke from the SBC's historic position of silence or neutrality on divisive political matters, eventually making statements that went against the religious right on everything from opposing the death penalty to defending the right of Palestinians to form their own state.[17] Relatedly, in its understanding of freedom, the Alliance did not simply target conservatives. It separated itself from Southern Baptist denominationalists who had run the SBC too often as a corporate elite dedicated to keeping the organization growing in finances and membership. In other words, the Alliance did reject "business as usual."

Women like Neil, Lockwood, Sehested, Marshall-Green, and other SBWIM supporters quickly found a home in the Alliance. When she read its covenant, Neil knew that she had been waiting since "early childhood for this moment."[18] The Alliance's covenant dovetailed with these women's understanding of Baptist identity, their interpretation of freedom, and their sense of social justice. Equally significant, the Alliance advanced beyond rhetoric to action. A few months after that painful November 1987 meeting, the Alliance voted to become SBWIM's major contributor, designating $5,000 as the minimal payment to the women's group. It deemed that there be equitable gender balance on the executive board and that a woman be named one of its two vice presidents, a stipulation guaranteeing that a woman would serve as the Alliance's president every three years. Over the next twelve months, the Alliance also agreed to fund local churches that had been refused Home Mission Board support because of women's ordained ministry. It published a primer to help churches better understand a Baptist theology of women in ministry. And it mandated the use of inclusive language. Finally, the task force on women in the church became a standing committee to address issues of justice affecting women locally and globally.[19]

SBWIM and the Alliance came to echo each other rhetorically largely because the organizations shared the same leadership and their members attended the same circuit of churches and had graduated from the same seminaries.[20] They had been shaped within that dissenting, or progressive, context, and both now devoted themselves to carrying forth this tradition. Not all SBWIM women celebrated Alliance causes. Some of the tensions that plagued SBWIM led some members to question Alliance concerns. But by the late 1980s, the Alliance was the only moderate voice beyond SBWIM vocally rejecting women's submission and endorsing their ordained ministry as crucial to the organization's identity and self-understanding.

To be sure, the Alliance was a small, even regional, organization. In 1988, it had only 2,000 individual and about forty church members. Some Alliance leaders, like Alan Neely, were intellectual stars in the Southern Baptist firmament. Numerous others functioned as well-recognized progressive voices. Its first president, Henry Crouch, for example, had served as executive director of the SBC's Christian Life Commission. At the same time, Neely and Crouch did not represent the majority of moderate leaders, who rejected the Alliance on two grounds. First, most moderates still hoped to regain control of the SBC, so they remained unwilling to endorse any seemingly schismatic group—and that is certainly how they viewed the Alliance—that took time and attention away from the larger denominational struggle. As the moderate Texan pastor and 1985 SBC presidential candidate Winfred Moore claimed, "I haven't heard the fat lady sing yet, and she's not singing in my part of the country."[21] Second, for moderates like Moore, victory meant maintaining the Southern Baptist center, and the Alliance went too far to the left in its theology, politics, and practice, particularly with its active stance involving women in ministry. It was one thing to support the freedom of the local church to ordain women; it was another to fund churches that did and to make women's empowerment central to Baptist identity. Many of those in the centrist position believed that mandating gender-inclusive policies violated Baptist freedom, and they remained uncomfortable with any hint of feminism. Despite SBWIM's protestations, then, the woman question initially defined differences among moderates.

Looking at the battles from afar, the feminist theologian Letty Russell warned that women might "pay the price for restored unity in the Southern Baptist Convention." She feared that "if the two groups of men struggling for power in the convention work out a compromise, they may agree not to ordain women."[22] The extent of compromise demonstrated by moderates in the Peace Committee and the Glorieta Statement came dangerously close to proving Russell correct, and soon afterward, the Alliance decided that unity would not be worth any cease-fire agreement. On one hand, dissenters had functioned as initial targets for conservatives; on the other, those who had touted the prophetic voice in Southern Baptist life had almost always found themselves pushed to the denomination's fringes anyway. For them, the post-1979 denominational conflict provided a catalyst for change, so they found the hesitancy of moderates to be as frustrating and maddening as the politicking of conservatives. Contrary to Moore's assessment, the fat lady had been singing, quite loudly, for a very long time. Although they struggled financially as a small network, many Alliance members felt that finally they had been liberated. So they watched from the sidelines as the bulk of moderates carried on.

The Moderate Campaign

The majority of moderates, men as well as women, continued their struggle for the SBC, with the goal of electing a moderate to the denomination's presidency. As much as they might resent the religious right's intrusion into SBC life, they denied what some Alliance members referred to as a "death in the family" or, more drastically, a "death of the family." According to Cecil Sherman, the SBC was "not dead." The problem, as he defined it, was that "we've been put outside the house."[23] Throughout the 1980s, Sherman and his Gatlinburg cohorts labored mightily to regain entry.

In 1984, these men launched the SBC Forum. Conceived as an alternative to the conservatives' Pastor's Conference, the Forum met as part of the preconvention events. To the organizers' surprise, more than 2,000 attended the first year's afternoon gathering. The following year, the Forum became a two-day meeting of speeches and sermons. Despite their failure to win a presidential victory, moderates initially viewed the annual Forum as a success. Numbers consistently exceeded expectations, and until they formed a more formal organization in 1988, the Forum kept a counterpolitic alive.[24]

While some personnel initially overlapped between the Forum and the Alliance, the overall goals of those involved diverged. In terms of compromise, the Forum would be far less decisive on gendered issues involving women. It did, though, demonstrate a willingness to discuss women's ordination. In the Forum's first year, for example, its program planners contacted several prominent conservatives to debate the subject. None responded, so the debate was reduced to an affirming paper by the mission executive Sara Ann Hobbs. Numerous women also attended the Forum's meetings and supported its cause, but in terms of their formal involvement, or any full endorsement of women in ministry, the Forum fared little better than the Gatlinburg crowd. From 1984 to 1988, the Forum's most active years, only nine of the roughly seventy or more Southern Baptists who either served on its steering committee or participated regularly in its annual meeting were women.[25] Of the nine, only two were ordained pastors. Most were WMU women reporting on missions. As before, the WMU and missions opened the doors for women even as they limited their entry. In addition, the Forum named no woman to the original steering committee, and no more than one ever served at a time.[26] If, ideologically, many of the Forum's leaders affirmed women's ordination, their collective actions failed to signal any strong commitment. An outsider looking at the Forum's platform would be hard-pressed to distinguish it from its competitor, conservative Pastor's Conference, crowded as both were by the same dark-suited, silver-coiffed white males.

Of course, these moderates also felt trapped. Unlike dissenters, they were still in the campaign, desperate for victory. They recognized that Southern Baptists had been fairly conventional for most of the century, and they did not want to alienate potential advocates. In addition, many Forum leaders pastored traditional congregations who were not well-versed on the issues. These ministers feared losing their pulpits. In the end, they could not win for fear of losing. The rhetoric of compromise fit neither the Southern Baptist conflict nor the surrounding culture wars, both of which demanded decisive action. To add fuel to the fire, dissenting moderates viewed compromisers as those who had sold their souls to the enemy camp for the sake, once again, of more money and more followers and who were committed to resurrecting an outdated, sometimes harmful entity. One SBWIM advocate later referred to the moderate leadership during the 1980s as the "Lukewarm" (Rev. 3:15). Many concurred with that assessment.[27]

By the late 1980s, the Lukewarm realized that they needed a more active network, so they formed Baptists Committed to the Southern Baptist Convention, better known as Baptists Committed. While their purposes were somewhat different, Baptists Committed took the energies of those who had been involved in the Forum, which continued for a few years as a convention event before it simply petered out. The name alone, Baptists Committed to the SBC, distinguished these moderates from those associated with the Alliance. The main objective of Baptists Committed was to elect a convention president—a task that the Alliance had deemed not only untenable but undesirable. There were other contrasts as well. In 1988, the Alliance stipulated that half of its executive committee be female. Of the roughly eighteen or so persons serving on the executive committee of Baptists Committed, none were women.[28] Regionally, the majority of the Alliance's leadership came from the East, whereas the largest numbers of Baptists Committed hailed from Texas.[29] One Alliance member, a former Southeastern professor, joked that it was difficult to tell a Texas moderate from a North Carolina or Virginia fundamentalist. The implication, of course, was that the farther west the Southern Baptist, the more socially and theologically conservative he or she became. Moreover, Texas boasted the largest and wealthiest Southern Baptist state convention, the Baptist General Convention of Texas.

After ten failed bids, moderates put tremendous effort into the election of Daniel Vestal.[30] Vestal seemed their most promising candidate for victory largely because he boasted many conservative credentials. He was a tall, diehard west Texan who possessed a gentle, folksy humor and definite crowd appeal. A young, enthusiastic pastor, he had held the pulpit in several prominent Texas churches, with at least one eventually siding with conservatives.[31] Like many conservatives, he graduated from Southwestern and called himself an inerrantist. As for women's ordination, Vestal had admitted to being torn over the issue. He conceded to a local church's right to ordain whomever it chose; however, he remained personally uncomfortable with the practice.[32] Both conservatives and moderates had vied for Vestal's support throughout the past decade. For the most part, Vestal had kept a low profile. SBC conservative leaders had appointed him to the Peace Committee officially as a neutral member, assuming he held conservative convictions. Then, in February 1989, he surprised everyone by attending a Baptists Committed press conference. As he later told it, his participation on the Peace Committee had convinced him that "only one side really wanted reconciliation." "Fundamentalists" he determined, "only desired control, total control, absolute control" as well as "no participation except with those who had the same desire."[33] Vestal had come to view the conservatives bid for power more as a "take-over," as moderates saw it, than what conservatives insisted on calling their "resurgence."

Moderates like Sherman felt that Vestal would appeal to the Southern Baptist center. They assumed the majority of Southern Baptists wanted unity, and Vestal's ability to see each side's perspective appealed to this sensibility. Sherman and other key moderates hurriedly convinced Vestal to run for the 1989 presidency. He lost. But with only three months of campaigning, votes far exceeded moderates' expectations. Finally, they had found their "man," and elated moderates convinced Vestal to run again. For the first time in a decade, they anticipated victory. Vestal himself believed that he could win: "I felt that if I could have nine months to get out the message of hope, inclusivity, and cooperation, I could surely be elected in New Orleans in 1990."[34]

For the next year, moderates concentrated their energies on Vestal's presidential campaign. The WMU's former executive director, Carolyn Weatherford Crumpler, ran alongside Vestal for the SBC's first vice president. While the offices were voted on separately, moderates clearly viewed Vestal and Crumpler as a team. For nine months, they traversed the South, speaking at local Baptist Heritage rallies and symposiums. In some ways, Crumpler's nomination signaled a shift among what many considered the less progressive moderate group. Vestal may have been hesitant on women's ordination; however, Crumpler was not. At the same time, denominationalists had often nominated prominent WMU women to the vice presidency. Crumpler had only recently left her position as the WMU's executive director to marry an Ohio pastor, so she carried clout as a well-recognized mission leader. In fact, the WMU president, anxious that the SBC would interpret Crumpler's candidacy as the WMU backing moderate forces, was quoted in a newspaper stating that "WMU has not endorsed Mrs. Crumpler." Revealing the multiple tensions at work, Crumpler later noted that she had "not asked for it [the endorsement]."[35]

More than 38,000 messengers attended the greatly anticipated New Orleans convention, an increase of nearly 18,000 from the previous June. Voters packed the convention center. Once again, despite their most organized effort yet, moderates lost—and in Vestal's words, "decisively."[36] It was a devastating blow. After a year of hard campaigning, Vestal actually received a lower voter percentage in 1990 (42.32) than in 1989 (43.39). Ecstatic over their win, jubilant conservatives headed to Café du Monde. Crowding the porch where the fiery Judge Paul Pressler had first met the fresh-faced young seminarian Paige Patterson more than twenty years prior, they joined hands and sang "Victory in Jesus."

At this point, moderates had lost eleven elections. The only election they had not lost was one in which they had not run a candidate. The initial belief that extreme conservatism would run its course was proving an illusion. The moderates of Baptists Committed rallied around the leadership of Cecil Sherman, Daniel Vestal, and Jimmy Allen, who, within two months, organized a consultation regarding their denominational future. Allen presided. Besides overseeing the SBC Radio and Television Commission, he had served as the last nonconservative SBC president, making his authorial position during the gathering highly symbolic. More than 3,000 attended the consultation held in Atlanta in August 1990. More than 6,000 showed up for the second consultation the following summer, at which point they voted to form the Cooperative Baptist Fellowship. For many, the CBF seemed a shadow denomination of the SBC, but with Southern Seminary and the

Foreign Mission Board still hanging in the balance, moderates were not prepared to sever their ties completely. It took time for the CBF to form an identity, but eventually it came to function as a denomination, with its own member churches, headquarters, executives, missionaries, and related seminaries, which were separate from those of the SBC.

Quite naturally, the Alliance and the CBF engaged in dialogue, even contemplating a merger. This discussion stalled almost immediately. Anne Neil, representing the Alliance as its president, remembered, "After hours of talking in circles, we were getting nowhere. Everyone was acting so polite." Tired and frustrated, she asked CBF representatives, "Are we too liberal?" According to Neil, everyone breathed a sigh of relief as CBF personnel nodded in the affirmative. The Alliance was far more comfortable claiming the descriptive title "liberal" than was the CBF, which viewed the term more as an accusation. CBF leaders' fear of the liberal label made them more hesitant regarding women's issues, particularly ordination and feminism. As Neil understood it, women's ordination was a primary reason that the Alliance continued as a separate organization. When she encouraged CBF leaders to promote women's ordination, one prominent CBF spokesperson revealed that such a move would require a transformation of his theology and convictions. Another said that the CBF needed another decade to adapt. Cecile Sherman referred to Alliance leaders during these meetings as "Fundamentalists of the left," particularly in their insistence that "every church should have a place for women in leadership."[37]

By the early 1990s, conservatives were increasingly using the debate over women as a test case for hires and fires. Associations disfellowshipped local churches over women's ordination. Missionary boards refused to appoint women in ministerial positions over men. Women's studies programs in seminaries had become inculcations in complementarianism. The culture wars added to an overall sense of siege and hostility. At the same time that southern Democrats Bill Clinton and Al Gore, both Southern Baptists, were elected to national office, the white South joined the American heartland as a bastion of conservative politics. From the congressional floor, Republican Speaker of the House Newt Gingrich led his controversial contract with America. Rush Limbaugh took to the airways denouncing Hillary Clinton as a "femi-nazi," a term he popularized during this period to further the stereotype of feminists as aggressive radicals. In the midst of such fragmentation, some moderates urged the newly formed CBF and its leaders to take more decisive steps, and many women, particularly those associated with SBWIM, accused them of perpetuating the SBC's "old boy network." Women looked at CBF banners announcing a "new thing" and still saw the same old story of compromise and indifference. In 1994, Nancy Sehested claimed that women seeking ordination and ministry opportunities "had even a better time ten years ago."[38]

Behold a New Thing?

Women seeking ordination felt that they had several reasons to be concerned.[39] First, they did not behold a new thing in the CBF's top leadership. Texans Jimmy Allen, Cecil Sherman, Daniel Vestal, and soon, Keith Parks, were its most visible spokespersons. Sherman served as the organization's first coordinator, and in 1997 Vestal assumed the mantle. Sherman, of course, had initiated the moderate politic. And as certain SBWIM leaders later indicated, he had not seen the necessity of including women. Moreover, Vestal had not been vocally committed to women in ordained ministry, struggling with the issue himself. As a former SBC president and agency head, Allen was a stalwart member of the old guard. So, too, was Parks. In 1992, after thirty-eight years of service, Parks resigned as the Foreign Mission Board's president. The CBF immediately asked Parks to become its first global missions coordinator. Many, if not most, moderates celebrated Parks's acceptance as a tremendous coup, but others' worst fears were confirmed. After all, men like Allen, Sherman, and Parks had struggled mightily against conservatives as denominational loyalists. They mourned the passing of the SBC of their boyhood and seminary days. One CBF enthusiast pressed the need to "dream the Southern Baptist dream again" and went so far as to compare Atlanta 1991 to August 1845, though citing the questionable conditions of the SBC's origins.[40] Sherman even called the CBF a "continuation of the old SBC," especially in its avoidance of hot-button issues.[41] While SBWIM and the Alliance likewise lamented conservative control of the denomination, they saw the old SBC with its exclusionary agenda and compromising spirit as equally problematic.

Second, just as the old story began around missions, the CBF made missions and evangelism its highest priority. Akin to the SBC in 1845, the CBF's first concrete action involved formation of a mission enterprise called Global Missions. The CBF's newsletter, *Fellowship!*, focused on mission-related items while downplaying controversial news. The CBF wanted to gain as many traditional Southern Baptists as possible, and of course, the most effective way to lobby the Southern Baptist center was through missions. As Parks argued, missions had been the cohesive force that held the SBC together from the start, so CBF leaders saw missions as serving a similar purpose. Sherman even referred to the CBF as a "missions organization."[42] Few SBWIM women would dispute the significance of missions in their evangelical faith. After all, the WMU had nurtured their callings. And few would trade what they felt to be the dogmatism of conservatives for the missional emphasis embraced by moderates.[43] At the same time, Southern Baptist denominationalists had too often emphasized the language of Zion to avoid divisive theological and cultural issues, thereby enabling dangerous tensions to fester. Missions had also proved ambivalent in helping women gain denominational power, opening some doors and closing others. As the CBF pulled recognized WMU women into its fold, it seemed that the new organization might be more comfortable with the old model of women in missions than the new one of women in ministry.

Third, in contrast to the Alliance covenant, the CBF's identity, mission, vision, and core values statements failed to mention women outright. Intentionally vague, they offered little to really distinguish the new CBF or set it apart. Few Baptists, for example, would disagree with its identity, a "fellowship of Baptist Christians and churches that share a passion for the Great Commission of Jesus Christ and a commitment to Baptist principles of faith and practice"; its mission, "serving Christians and churches as they discover and fulfill their God-given mission"; and its vision, "being the presence of Christ." In its core value statement, the CBF, like the Alliance, first celebrated Baptist principles as a series of freedoms: soul freedom, Bible freedom, church freedom, and religious freedom. In defining these freedoms, however, the CBF did not move nearly as far as the Alliance, so the new organization appeared indecisive. The CBF also affirmed justice and reconciliation, lifelong learning and ministry, and trustworthiness in a similar ambiguous fashion. Under trustworthiness, the CBF stated that it prized "gifts of diversity" but failed to name what these gifts or diversity might entail. Not surprisingly, the CBF was most specific in outlining the value of "biblically-based global missions" and its accompanying plan of salvation.

Admittedly, the CBF's first address to the public, written by Cecil Sherman and Walter Shurden and presented by the CBF's interim steering committee, did include a section on women and argued that the more liberating Galatians passage superseded Pauline references to submission.[44] But there the CBF seemed to stop. Several women later suggested that certain parts of the address smacked more of Shurden and the Alliance than the CBF and its leadership. The section on women, for one, seemed an ephemeral point of light compared to where the CBF actually was.

Finally, as the CBF established itself, many SBWIM women felt that the organization and its leaders deemed their voices, and their theology, too divisive. Karrie Oertli, an ordained woman and SBWIM executive board member throughout the 1990s, captured the sentiments of several other SBWIM advocates when contemplating the CBF's relationship to SBWIM:

> My sense was that CBF wanted BWIM [SBWIM] to fit into the way that CBF had determined its leadership would function, rather than asking BWIM leaders to assist CBF in changing its practice to be inclusive, truly inclusive, of women. . . . CBF leaders seemed to resist wholescale system changes that would be required to integrate women fully into the leadership of the organization—in other words, to make space for the changes that would happen inevitably if women were full partners. . . . I *felt* as though it was the responsibility of us *women* to make a place for ourselves. At times, that seemed a lot like having to conform to the decisions already made about how leadership would take place, to forego being in leadership at all, or to be thought of as the "pushy broads" who would never be satisfied. Thinking back, what would have been more welcoming would have been the experience of a sense of full partnership if folks from the moderate organizations had taken a stand to say something inviting, such as, "We know women haven't been equal partners during Baptist history—tell us what you think we might do differently so that you can be full members of the work we're doing. We're willing to change the organization to make this right."

According to Oertli, "that invitation was never made."[45] Oertli's description of the CBF's perception of SBWIM as "those pushy broads" is telling, demonstrating the same sorts of assumptions toward feminism as those held by Southern Baptist conservatives.

Oertli characterized the tensions between SBWIM and the CBF as "that of an opposing force [S/BWIM] challenging the status quo of the folks in leadership [CBF]," and leadership did remain a final issue in women's feeling slighted. While the CBF's choice of a woman, Texan Pat Ayres, as its second moderator was deliberate, some felt that supporting a laywoman rather than an ordained woman was deliberate as well, as if in the view of the moderate leadership a laywoman did not count as a feminist, or "pushy broad." Although she appreciated the CBF's attempted inclusion of women, Linda Hood Hicks, an early S/BWIM participant and later board member, wrote that "some of this was nothing more than a knee-jerk" reaction. Other women used stronger rhetoric. According to one Southern Seminary alumna, "You know, they're supposed to be more open to women. They're supposed to be the ones who are going to provide more ministry opportunities for us. And you look at the Cooperative Baptist Fellowship offices, and it's a man in every single position. . . . So I feel like, you know, you're lying to us still. You're perpetuating the same old shit that the fundamentalists did."[46]

In 1991, the CBF posed the often-asked question to SBWIM: "Just what do you women want?" SBWIM's president, Cindy Harp Johnson, answered loud and clear:

> What SBWIM and our supporters want is an absence of reneging on our denominational heritage of the autonomy of the local church, and the right of those churches to ordain and call women as ministers, to be represented by those ministers who act as worship leaders at Southern Baptist meetings. What SBWIM and our supporters want is an absence of reneging on the denominational dream of celebration of diversity as a tool through which a lost world might be won to Christ. In short, our desires echo the longings of all who have been disenfranchised throughout the existence of the SBC, including the fundamentalists of recent history and the moderates of current times. We want to be recognized as valid and vital members of the Body. And this is not a request for a quota-system mentality. It is a challenge to capture a vision of all the components of our denomination, and to allow the leaders and the language of our gatherings to reflect that true identity.[47]

If the CBF really wanted a "new thing," women desired full partnership in shaping its reality.

Not all SBWIM women were equally critical of the early CBF. Sarah Frances Anders, for example, expressed immediate liberation as she compared the CBF to the conservative-controlled SBC. Carolyn Weatherford Crumpler worked long and tirelessly as a CBF insider and acknowledged its struggle. Reba Cobb was one of the younger SBWIM women at the time who also appreciated the new organization. Active from the beginning, she claimed that "a little known fact is that behind the scenes and off the radar screen the women on both the Interim Steering Committee and the Steering Committee of CBF were engaged in setting strategies for influencing policy decisions, and the vision and direction of CBF." In light of Cobb's comment, the reluctance of the CBF's early male leaders to espouse openly a "new thing" could have had more to do with outsiders' perception of the CBF, and fear of that perception, rather than outright hostility toward the women and goals of SBWIM.

While praising the Alliance and contrasting it to the CBF's "old boy network," Terry Thomas Primer conceded that some SBWIM women "demanded more from the Organization of Cooperative Baptist Fellowship than it seemed reasonable to give back, given what they had and the politics involved." Early on, Nancy Sehested predicted that it would be a difficult relationship: "I think that because the CBF wants to embrace a wide group of churches that it is going to be difficult for CBF to be real direct about affirming women in leadership positions in the church because they may risk losing some churches. I think that they will be happy for women to exist among CBF but they may not be in a position to be serious advocates for women in ministry." Sehested defined the alliance between the two "more as a passive willingness to live together."[48] For inheritors of denominational compromise, SBWIM was "not," as Primer concluded, "an easy collaboration."

Struggle for Identity

Conservatives, moderates, and scholars alike have quibbled over the exact year or event signifying the end of the controversy over the SBC's direction. Some have viewed the period from 1991 to 1993 as marking its conclusion. During this time, moderates mobilized around the CBF, Parks left the Foreign Mission Board, and Mohler assumed Southern's presidency. Perhaps most significantly, moderates ceased running a candidate for the SBC presidency. Several name changes also reflected a sense of defeat, with the elimination of "Southern" indicating a more thorough severing from the SBC. *SBC Today*, the flagship moderate publication launched in 1983, became *Baptists Today*, and the Southern Baptist Alliance became the Alliance of Baptists. Moderates also established an independent Baptist news agency, the Associated Baptist Press, and an autonomous publishing house, Smyth and Helwys, whose motto was a "free press for Baptists." Others, in speaking of the conflict, have extended its endpoint to 2000, since it took most of the decade for conservatives to secure and reorganize the denomination. During this period, conservatives and moderates shifted the locus of the contest to state conventions, local associations, and church-related colleges and universities. Although they no longer sent messengers to the annual convention, most moderate congregations continued to send money to the SBC, qualifying them for membership, so that they held dual membership in denomination-like organizations, most usually the SBC and the CBF. Moderates, these congregations realized, still remained in SBC ranks as seminary professors, midlevel administrators, and missionaries endeavoring to survive until retirement. And well after the battles, moderates asserted that the rightful Southern Baptist history and heritage was theirs. With these various factors in play, it can be said that the years between 1991 and 2000 functioned as both a beginning and an end.

Moderates struggled to define their course during this interim. As for the relationship between dissenters and compromisers, the Alliance and the CBF continued to overlap. Many churches contributed to both the SBC and the CBF, whereas others supported both the Alliance and the CBF. At this point, the moderate elite had left SBC circles, making the moderates' leadership distinct from the conservatives'. A few individuals and entities continued to serve both the Alliance and the CBF. For the most part, though, as a dissenting voice, the Alliance accepted that it would remain the smaller moderate body. Indeed, the CBF, steering the middle course, grew more quickly than the Alliance, and within a decade, 1,700 churches were contributing to its coffers. Relative to the roughly 15 million members in the SBC, the CBF remained a shadow organization. Relative to the Alliance, it represented the greater part of moderate life.

Because the Alliance answered polarization with polarization, its identity was forthright and clear. The SBC aligned itself with Focus on the Family, the Council on Biblical Manhood and Womanhood, and other right-wing evangelical organizations, while the Alliance reached out to more liberal mainline Protestants, eventually joining the National Council of Churches and forming alliances with the United Church of Christ and the Christian Church (Disciples of Christ). These more liberal bodies may not have been growing, but their stance was clear. The CBF, in contrast, lacked the same bold sense of identity. CBF personnel often claimed that unlike the SBC and the Alliance, which Vestal dubbed "enemies on the right" and "friends on the left," respectively, the CBF represented "mainstream" Baptists. Conservative and moderate critics dismissed compromisers as taking the easy way out, but finding the center or mainstream of Southern Baptist life was not easy. As the CBF discovered, the historic Southern Baptist mainstream held multiple movements, currents, rivulets, and eddies. Theirs, then, was a challenging course, which must have often felt more like swimming upstream than moving with any main current.

The story of moderate life over the mid- to late 1990s involved both continuity and change, and one locus where moderates spent much of their energies was women and gender. Like Southern Baptists of old, mainstream

Baptists eventually followed their host culture in attitudes and practices, and as the cultural center shifted, so, too, did they. While SBWIM leaders critiqued the CBF's early performance, many agreed that the moderate group had made substantial progress by the end of the decade.

In terms of leadership, for instance, the CBF's first moderator, Daniel Vestal, fully reversed his resistance to women in ministry. When he became the CBF coordinator in 1997, Vestal described his acceptance of women's ordination as resulting from "God's grace and Fellowship friends." Referencing his past position, Vestal said that "I've had to repent and ask God to forgive me."[49] As many former SBC stalwarts migrated to the CBF, men remained in the organization's highest-paid offices. But moving into the twenty-first century, women did compose nearly one-third of the CBF's governing body, or Coordinating Council. During the CBF's annual assembly, they regularly led worship and preached in what was called the great hall. Not until 2000 did the CBF elect an ordained woman as moderator, and it was 2006 before a woman serving as senior pastor was chosen. These events were too long in coming for some, though others were willing to celebrate them as major milestones. Overall, the presence of women on the platform of the great hall contrasted with not only the annual SBC convention but the Southern Baptist Forum.

The CBF made other strides beyond leadership. During the decade, the organization became SBWIM's major contributor, and SBWIM moved its annual meeting and worship service to the CBF's assembly. Likewise, the divinity schools and seminaries that the CBF helped fund, called CBF partner institutions, reported that growing numbers of their students were women, and the CBF reportedly awarded scholarships to female seminarians in numbers equal to those of male seminarians.[50] On countless occasions, Vestal contrasted the CBF's stance on women in ministry with that of the SBC, citing the CBF's sympathetic attitude as a primary difference. As at least one SBWIM participant commented, the CBF had "come a long way, baby."[51]

Some women still dismissed these changes as superficial. The assembly platform might appear inclusive to an outsider, but underneath the surface of moderate life, little had changed, they noted, especially in terms of congregational culture. Throughout the 1990s the relationship between SBWIM and the CBF remained rocky. That many SBWIM women preferred the Alliance to the CBF, however, was becoming irrelevant. Numbers and money stood on the CBF's side, and SBWIM increasingly needed its resources.

During the 1990s, a gap in funding threatened SBWIM's survival. Although SBWIM belatedly dropped "Southern" from its title, becoming Baptist Women in Ministry (BWIM) in 1995, the change in name did little to ease the organization's struggle. Even though the CBF donated the largest portion of BWIM's budget, the $30,000 it gave barely covered operating expenses. BWIM leaders characterized their steering committee meetings as regularly producing creative ideas that were struck down due to lack of time and money. Over the mid- to late 1990s, the annual meeting was reduced to a business session and luncheon following worship. *FOLIO* was floundering. Paid office management was hired and then let go. And BWIM's headquarters and archives were moved to Central Baptist Seminary in Shawnee, Kansas, associated historically with northern Baptists. While Molly Marshall taught at the seminary and it was considered a CBF partner institution, in terms of both tradition and geography, Central placed BWIM further from its constituency, and Central, too, faced financial hardship. Admittedly, BWIM suffered from an inconsistent and diffused leadership, but some women interpreted BWIM's financial straits, disorganization, and wandering status as indicative of an overall lack of moderate commitment.

One BWIM woman described the organization during this period as the "CBF's red-headed stepsister," and many continued to feel stereotyped as "those pushy broads." According to these women, the CBF feared that if it opened its doors to BWIM fully and embraced its women as family, then homosexuality, goddess worship, abortion rights, and other divisive issues—issues that the religious right had deemed antifamily and that the SBC lumped with stereotyped understandings of feminism and feminist theology—would come rushing through.[52] As the CBF saw it, BWIM could bring bad publicity. Sherman himself was blunt on the matter of BWIM, if not irritated by its women's demands: "A minority has tried and continues to try to co-opt CBF. They want CBF to carry the flag for their cause. An illustration: To some extent CBF has become the voice for Women in Ministry. This has been done willingly, but leaving congregations free and serving the Women in Ministry agenda has created problems. Some of the strongest, longest support for CBF comes from West Texas. They are not too keen on women in church leadership."[53] As Sherman's remarks revealed, freedom in terms of women had more to do with the idea of local church autonomy, with its accompanying rhetoric of choice, than any active realization.

In 2000, the CBF's worst fears regarding BWIM were realized. In a widely circulated six-article series, Baptist Press, the SBC's media outlet, accused the CBF of promoting homosexuality. As evidence, it first cited the CBF's financial contributions to BWIM and the Baptist Peace Fellowship. Baptist Press then quoted BWIM's 1999 president, Becca Gurney: "In terms of God calling gays and lesbians, when we start limiting God's call we're in dangerous territory."[54] Gurney's comments reflected a pattern among BWIM presidents, claimed conservatives. They pointed out that a pro-homosexual group named Equal Partners in Faith listed BWIM's 2000 president, Ray Nell Dyer, as a spokesperson. The Baptist Press series also highlighted another past president of BWIM, Kathy Manis Findley, who was serving an Arkansas church that had taken a pro-gay stance.

After careful consideration, BWIM decided against answering Baptist Press. Its board felt uncomfortable speaking for BWIM's wider constituency, even though BWIM's primary leadership might be tolerant of homosexuality. Instead, BWIM took the route of compromise and affirmed disagreement on the issue. As later BWIM officers stated, the organization had never taken a formal position regarding homosexuality. But because they did take the route of compromise, they felt even more betrayed when the CBF denounced the practice. The CBF placed many of BWIM's leaders, particularly those like Gurney and Findley, who had been more vocal in their advocacy, and often their churches, which expressed acceptance, on the fringes of moderate life.

In October 2000, the CBF's Coordinating Council issued a statement. It started with a veiled condemnation: "As Baptist Christians, we believe that the foundation of a Christian sexual ethic is faithfulness in marriage between a man and a woman and celibacy in singleness." Then, it announced that the CBF would "not allow for the expenditure of funds for organizations or causes that condone, advocate, or affirm homosexual practice." And finally, it passed an exclusionary clause prohibiting the "purposeful hiring of a staff person or the sending of a missionary who is a practicing homosexual." Trying to stall any more controversy, Vestal himself announced, "I do not want, one, for us to fragment over this" and "anyone to leave over this." He emphasized, rather optimistically, that the "difference between us and other bodies is we can and should have differences among us and still be committed to Christ and our common cause."[55] Not surprisingly, some did not interpret the statement as an acceptance of differences. And the effort from within the Coordinating Council to rescind the policy on the day before the 2001 general assembly began—an effort led by Dixie Petrey—should have spelled trouble.[56]

Despite efforts by Vestal and others to discourage detractors from bringing the matter to the full assembly, a determined contingency proceeded. Some of them compared the policy to previous Southern Baptist prejudices against blacks and women in ministry, while others saw it as testing the CBF's commitment to diversity of opinion. Women argued more vociferously than men against the CBF's statement, certainly from the CBF's assembly floor and, rumor had it, in the preceding council meeting as well. During the debate, at least, those who spoke for the motion were primarily female, while those who spoke against it were overwhelmingly, if not exclusively, male. This did not mean, of course, that the majority of moderate women were in favor of homosexuality. And many moderate men, particularly those active in the Alliance, also took umbrage at the CBF's action. Approximately 700 delegates voted to uphold the policy, while 500 voted to overturn it. The motion, then, failed, and the policy statement remained. Nevertheless, as the CBF was discovering, including women's voices as equals in every aspect of ecclesial life was not simply a matter of balancing numbers. Celebrating gendered forms of diversity meant acknowledging different experiences and ideologies.

This diversity obviously strained the CBF's ability to appeal to the center. According to Bill Sherman, brother to Cecil and a CBF pastor in Nashville, "Churches out there are not going to support a pro-gay and pro-lesbian group sending missionaries." Bill Sherman and others had predicted the CBF's demise if the motion to rescind had passed.[57] Compromise functioned as a means to keep the center intact. It faltered as a means to maintain the fringe. If determining the boundary between the two proved difficult, particularly from the upper echelons of leadership, the larger Baptist controversy had, at least, demonstrated the limits of congregational acceptance and tolerance. As a result, CBF personnel worried about the organization's acceptance in local church life. By all accounts, moderates were politically as Republican as they were Democrat, and few beyond the Alliance viewed homosexuality as morally acceptable. According to Cecil Sherman, "For all the good or evil in the current 'hot button' issues that tear at our churches, CBF is not a 'hot button' organization. . . . The Alliance of Baptists can take on any issue they want; they don't have to go to Baptist churches and meet a missionary payroll." In contrast, he persisted, "CBF has to stay close to ordinary Baptist churches because ordinary Baptists give the money that sustains missionaries."[58] Vestal was probably correct when he observed that "few CBF-related churches would ordain a homosexual to the ministry or conduct a same sex union." Sherman, not surprisingly, was more aggressive. Speaking of a decline in growth, he stated, "I think that the main reason CBF has slowed in growth is right here. We've not been willing to answer our critics. The lies have piled up. If we don't tell the truth, error will come to be public perception. If CBF doesn't believe the Bible . . . if CBF is soft on abortion . . . if CBF is FOR homosexuality . . . if these things be so, CBF is different from most Baptist churches. Those churches do believe the Bible, have a question about abortion, and are opposed to homosexuality."[59] Of course, these were concerns that conservatives lumped with feminism, and thus, de facto, women's ordination. As Sherman's remarks made clear, maintaining the center and accommodating difference were not the same.

Since conservatives accused moderates of using the historic Baptist principle of local church autonomy to trounce key scriptural mandates and adopt an anything-goes mentality, denouncing homosexuality became a means for CBF officials to assure those at the congregational level that their rhetoric of freedom, even when promoted as individual church autonomy, did not lead to all-out liberalism. It also demonstrated the persistent power of the local church in determining compromise over gender policy. For most churches of Southern Baptist background, the more contested gender issue in day-to-day congregational life still involved women's role in ministry. Despite what might have appeared as change in moderate rhetoric, women continued to confront an unofficial, on-the-ground, and silent but powerful exclusionary policy. And it did not apply only to the West Texas churches that Sherman invoked.

Women in Local Church Life

Southern Baptist women seeking ordination were answering God's call to shepherd a flock—to preach, baptize, visit the sick, and comfort the grieving. In good Baptist tradition, women who successfully found ministerial placements shared their testimonies in *FOLIO* and other publications as well as from the pulpit itself. When telling their stories, few women cited the desire to serve on denominational committees or assume agency positions. Testimony after testimony demonstrated that ordained women found vocational meaning and fulfillment in their local congregations as well as in hospital and hospice settings. Their testimonies of ministry expressed joy, passion, and thankfulness. As in other denominations, Baptist women found themselves laboring in rural hamlets, small towns, and crumbling inner cities, as well as in prisons and psychiatric wards. More often than not, they served in the least desirable pulpits, with small elderly congregations. As Bill Leonard wrote of Cindy Johnson's ordination into the ministry at Wolf Creek Baptist Church, "Wolf Creek Baptist Church is no liberal, urban congregation peopled with seminary professors and other theological pinkos. It is country—situated on Kentucky Route 228 just above the Ohio River. Its congregation is hard-core Southern Baptist, meeting in a nice brick building with a picture of the Jordan River painted behind the baptistry. The members are farmers, homemakers and retired people—and to the last one they voted to ordain Cindy Harp Johnson to the gospel ministry."[60] Esther Tye Perkins was called to be pastor of the Pine Bluff Baptist Church in Southern Carolina, a "383 member basically rural church." Perkins found herself preaching the sermon the week of her husband's death because, quite literally, she said, "there was nobody else."[61]

The testimonies and stories shared by these women were unlike the usual pastor memoirs detailing frustration, rejection, and depression. Southern Baptist women ministers clearly embraced everyday pastoral life. As Betty Winstead McGary, president of BWIM exclaimed, "There is so much love for us to share and there are so many who need it."[62] Twenty years later, women still expressed satisfaction, meaning, and purpose in following their sense of call. For those who found placements, ministry was energizing and life-affirming. After coming close to being fired as a Southern Baptist missionary for both her ordination in Brazil and her refusal to sign the 2000 Baptist Faith and Message, Ida Mae Hays took early retirement and became pastor of the small Weldon Baptist Church in North Carolina at the twilight of her church career. If she experienced any disappointment over her newfound situation, it was certainly not evident. Despite obvious difficulties in her journey to the pulpit, she expressed nothing but joy in her position: "I love my church and all its members. I love Weldon, North Carolina. I love the pastoral ministry. . . . Each week there are new challenges, new goals, and new ministries. The Lord has richly blessed me. I am experiencing more fulfillment and satisfaction as a pastor than I ever experienced in all my years as a missionary."[63] When asked about her experience copastoring Glendale Baptist Church in Nashville with April Baker, Amy Mears laughed. No one told her and Baker that they would be having so much fun; even they could not believe it. Another woman minister said that serving a church as pastor "feels like being a fish put in the water for the first time."[64]

Because of the Baptist power struggle, changes regarding clergywomen in moderate church life could be seen. A surge of women's ordinations actually followed every conservative resolution or policy against women in ministry.[65] During the late 1980s, that flurry usually occurred in Alliance-based churches, but as the CBF became more inclusive, the network did expand. By 1997, approximately 1,200 women had been ordained. In 1979, only one woman served as senior pastor of a Southern Baptist church. In 1997, sociologist Sarah Frances Anders recorded 85.[66] Granted, that number represented less than one-tenth of 1 percent of SBC, CBF, and Alliance-affiliated churches. And women usually held less popular placements such as small rural or dwindling inner-city congregations. The next study was not done until 2005. According to its numbers, 102 women served as either pastor, copastor, or church planter. As for percentages, roughly 22 percent of Alliance churches featured a woman as senior or copastor, and 5.5 percent of CBF churches did so.[67] Moderate churches were also inviting ordained women to serve in traditionally male staff positions, such as associate pastor or Christian education minister. And women serving in paid roles traditionally filled by females, such as children's director, were more likely to be ordained, represented on church staffs, and recognized by the title "minister."[68]

A church did not change its beliefs and practices overnight. First Baptist Church, Memphis, modeled the usual route. With about 1,000 attending members, First Baptist neighbored the much smaller Prescott Memorial Baptist Church and the mega Bellevue Baptist Church, led by Adrian Rogers. Earl Davis, First Baptist's minister from 1976 to 1994, belonged to the original Gatlinburg gang and became a state CBF organizer. When Prescott called Nancy Sehested to be its pastor in 1987, First Baptist voted in the association meeting against disfellowshipping the congregation. Yet it did little else to defend or even encourage Prescott and Sehested. In the controversy's early years, First Baptist avoided gender and other divisive issues for the most part. Financially, it supported both the SBC and the CBF. As the battles wore on, however, it moved closer to the CBF, and in the mid-1990s, with a smaller congregation and a new young minister, it began ordaining women as deacons.[69] In 2000, it ordained its first woman minister, Carol McCall Richardson. A longtime member of the church, Richardson had risen through the WMU's ranks, even serving as the state president. In numerous testimonies, she shared that as a young girl she had felt a call to missions, and while her brother served as a career medical missionary to Nigeria, she responded to God's call through WMU service. At age fifty-two, Richardson decided to attend divinity school, where she began to feel a call to ordained ministry. When First Baptist called Richardson as its associate pastor, she agreed that her duties should incorporate preaching and leading worship. This visibility, not only Richardson but other First Baptist women noted, was needed for their daughters and granddaughters, the girls of the church, so that they could see themselves represented in the pulpit.

Though the process was gradual, First Baptist's congregation came to a different understanding and practice of women in ecclesial authority. Part of this acceptance could have been attributed to the accomplishment, in the nation at large, of many of the practical goals of the feminist movement regarding women in education, politics, employment, and society. At places like First Baptist, at least, to support these goals was now not necessarily seen as a uniquely feminist or radical move. Also, the feminist movement itself had been trying to assume a less confrontational and more relational style. Despite the rhetoric of the religious right and accusations of pundits like Limbaugh, feminism had moved beyond the National Organization for Women to enter some formerly hesitant circles. Those once dismissed as strident had softened, accommodated, or been accommodated. Thus in 2000, when the SBC revised the Baptist Faith and Message, prohibiting women from occupying ministerial positions over men, First Baptist sponsored a community worship service mourning its passage and celebrating women's diverse gifts. This was a far cry from its hesitation to ordain women as deacons only ten years earlier.[70] At the same time, the church also became more attuned to social justice issues, holding, for example, a Martin Luther King Jr. Remembrance Day service and calling attention to AIDS by placing wooden crosses, one for each local victim, across its front lawn. As gay persons began attending the church, they became both active participants and congregational leaders, though the congregation was still unwilling to make any formal statement on homosexuality.

By the late 1990s, the board members of BWIM wondered if it might be time to disband the organization. The struggle between conservatives and moderates seemed to have ended. Looking at churches like First Baptist in Memphis, some questioned whether the organization's financial straits were not so much a lack of commitment as an indication that the issue of women in ministry had run its course. They asked if other matters of social justice should now demand their attention. As they met, dialogued, retreated, and "reimagined," the women of BWIM discovered an overwhelming desire to soldier on. Some women's reasons were sentimental—a nostalgic feeling, for instance, that the group had been too essential to their journey to abandon. Others desired to keep the annual worship service and fellowship time as an opportunity to share one another's stories as well as burdens. The most compelling reason, though, was simple: "Things were better, but not better enough."[71] The CBF might have "come a long way, baby," but as they moved into the twenty-first century, moderates still had farther to travel on the journey of women in ministry.

Epilogue

Baptist Women in Ministry (BWIM) observed its twenty-fifth anniversary in 2008. On June 18, the night prior to the yearly assembly of the Cooperative Baptist Fellowship (CBF), 160 women and a scattering of men gathered at the Memphis Southern History and Heritage Center to celebrate. Sitting around large circular tables, they feasted on a traditional fried chicken meal, complete with turnip greens, biscuits and gravy, and peach cobbler. It was Wednesday evening, the traditional time for Southern Baptist prayer meeting and supper, but on this occasion women were front and center. Recognizing key BWIM founders was its coordinator LeAnn Gunter Johns, a young graduate from Mercer University's McAfee School of Theology and associate pastor at Peachtree Baptist Church in Atlanta. "We remember and celebrate these women who were and who are Baptist pioneers in the cause of women in ministry," she said in a clear, ringing voice. "They paved the way for our own ministries." Johns also unveiled BWIM's special anniversary T-shirt. Women cheered when she held one up, revealing the slogan, "This Is What a Baptist Preacher Looks Like."[1]

Guitarist and folksinger Kate Campbell supplied the entertainment. Between ballads, she shared her own story of being reared in a traditional Southern Baptist family. She spent her childhood in Sledge, Mississippi, a small Delta town where her father pastored a church of about 200. The family then moved to Nashville, where he served as senior minister to a much larger congregation. Campbell graduated from the Southern Baptist–affiliated Belmont College in Nashville and studied history as a doctoral student at Vanderbilt before embarking on a full-time music career. A middle-aged blond dressed casually in jeans, Campbell was clearly one with the BWIM women. They roared with laughter when she sang her tribute to that longtime Southern Baptist custom of "Funeral Food." They clapped and hummed along as she celebrated the churchwomen of her childhood and youth. They nodded in understanding when she recounted the confusion, disjuncture, and sorrow she felt upon realizing she had moved outside the theological and cultural worldview of her parents. And they wept when she sang "In My Mother's House."

Not everyone realized that Campbell's father was the noted megachurch preacher Jim Henry. After growing Two Rivers Baptist Church in Nashville, Henry moved to First Baptist Church of Orlando in 1977, which became one of the largest churches in central Florida and the denomination. During this period, he was a significant voice in the leadership of the conservative movement and even served as president of the Southern Baptist Convention (SBC) from 1994 to 1996. While more in the background to her husband's ministry, Henry's wife and Campbell's mother, Jeannette, was recognized by conservative Florida women with the Clyde Merrill Maguire Ministers' Wives Award and seen by other conservative ministers' wives as a model. Whether or not those present at BWIM's anniversary celebration knew these particulars, many shared Campbell's story of feeling like the "prodigal daughter" to her more conservative parents. When she finished singing the final stanza of "In My Mother's House,"

> In my wandering
> I have found
> There is
> A wideness in mercy
> And there'll always be
> A place for me
> In my mother's house

there was a silence, interrupted only by the sound of gentle crying.

I find it interesting that in my field notes for this anniversary celebration, I wrote "In My Father's World" rather than "In My Mother's House." I made the notes, which I admit were more scribbled than usual, during the event. Yet even as I reread them that same evening, I doubted my memory and put a question mark to the side. I was fairly certain that she had not sung the popular hymn. As I begin writing this epilogue, I contacted others who had attended the event to see if Campbell might have included "This Is My Father's World." They, too, did not have any memory of it, and Campbell herself confirmed that it was not in her repertoire. It must have been "In My Mother's House," one woman suggested.

Mine was a rather telling slip. Having grown up Southern Baptist and having spent the past few years immersed in the Southern Baptist conflict, I well knew that these women had experienced the old SBC as a world ruled by men. No matter how active their mothers had been in their congregations, in running their households, and in nurturing and giving both realms vibrancy and color, it still had been a very patriarchal world. The women at BWIM's anniversary that night had rejected and violated SBC patriarchal dictates. Many BWIM women carried the scars of the previous decades along with the pain of leaving Southern Baptist life. At the same time, they could never fully leave, even if the returning only existed in their hearts and minds. Each was, in her own way, a prodigal daughter. The story of the prodigal son has been told and retold, while that of the daughter has not. Unlike the son in the biblical story, these daughters attained their prodigal status by simply following a call from God.

I immersed myself in field-based research to find out what the world of these women looked and felt like after the contest. To what extent, I asked, was it still their "father's world" and "mother's house"? What of the younger women who had grown up in moderate life? Had they escaped the proscriptions of the old SBC? Did they, too, feel like prodigal daughters? As for conservative women, where did they go when they dreamed of preaching from the center pulpit? How did they negotiate submission? What happened when a Jim and Jeannette Henry found themselves with a wandering Kate Campbell? Campbell still experienced or sang of a mercy, a sense of place, and a connection, even though she had broken away in many of her beliefs and practices and charted a very different path from that of her mother. Did others?

Over a two-year period, I attended nine women's conferences and retreats and half a dozen national meetings, dinners, and gatherings; participated in numerous local church groups, Bible studies, fellowships, and mission meetings; and went to one annual Southern Baptist convention and three CBF assemblies.[2] After writing the manuscript, I returned to some of these venues and talked to conservative and moderate women once again, women active in the Woman's Missionary Union (WMU), women's ministry to women, and BWIM, as well as some newly formed networks. I discovered, first, that many women had wearied of fighting. Also, while their groups and networks still advanced a particular gendered understanding of women, change had occurred. New questions were being asked, and internal tensions, particularly in conservative circles, were increasing.

A Pandora's Box

The WMU, my starting point for this story, clearly had failed in its attempt to straddle both conservative and moderate worlds. Its financial situation tied it to the SBC, so its appeal to moderates was limited; but even in conservative churches, a thriving WMU program was rare. Most were composed of aging women meeting under the umbrella of women's ministry, which firmly remained women's ministry to women. Sex-segregated women's ministry programs flourished in conservative life, replacing the local WMU as the primary space in which women learned, reshaped, and passed on their gendered understanding of what it meant to be a Southern Baptist, evangelical, and Christian woman. These conservative women clearly championed submission and complementarianism in describing their roles. Still, as one women's ministry leader admitted, submission did not fully define her life. Women, she said, needed more to sustain their spiritual lives.[3]

The literature, speakers, and programs associated with Lifeway Women's Enrichment Ministry often affirmed her conclusions.[4] Beth Moore, for example, became Southern Baptist women's most prominent Bible study leader in the late 1990s. By the early 2000s, Moore's was the most popular and recognized name in Lifeway Women's Ministry. Her books, Bible studies, and videos accounted for a multimillion-dollar industry, and her Living Proof Live tours sold out coliseums and convention centers throughout the country.[5] In 2010, she drew the largest crowd Springfield, Illinois, had ever hosted, outselling Elton John. A folksy Texan who poked fun at her own bouncy blond "Southern Baptist hair," as she called it, Moore captivated her audiences by weaving humorous and intimate stories of her childhood, marriage, two daughters, and even her dog with popular biblical narratives.

In September 2004, I attended one of her Living Proof Live weekends at the main coliseum in Little Rock, Arkansas. The women sitting around me came from a variety of churches, identifying themselves as Southern Baptist, nondenominational, United Methodist, and Evangelical Presbyterian. Many came with their churchwomen's ministry group. All identified as evangelical. Throughout the two-day event, Moore avoided more controversial topics, though she did praise the Republican governor of Arkansas, former Southern Baptist minister Mike Huckabee, as a man of God who had invited her for breakfast at the governor's mansion and poured out his heart in prayer. That said, she claimed to "know no [political] parties" and focused on women cultivating a personal relationship with Jesus.

Moore depicted Jesus as a woman's best friend and ideal companion. In his role as savior, Jesus was a knight in shining armor, ready to rescue her from sorrow, depression, disappointment, and suffering. Moore spoke of healing in the midst of marital challenges, whether it be recovering from divorce, infidelity, financial woes, or boredom. She addressed heartache with parents and children. She talked of cancer and death. Women laughed at her funny anecdotes of family life, and some sobbed when Moore dramatically dropped to her knees in anguish over her own sins and shortcomings. As with other Living Proof Live events, she intertwined her intimate experience of Jesus with an explication of selected biblical texts, which on this occasion included Isaiah 26 and the book of Hebrews. Her exegesis was unlike the politically charged interpretations of Joyce Rogers or Dorothy Patterson, devoted as she was to helping women develop a heartfelt and passionate relationship with Jesus.[6]

At the close, Moore called the women forward to dedicate their lives to a Christ who functioned like an ideal husband and lover, a gentle but manly presence who would sweep each of them into his strong embrace. Women thronged the aisles, making their way forward to the center platform, creating a scene that conjured the vision of a female Billy Graham crusade. Like Graham, Moore represented a less aggressive form of conservative evangelicalism than her Southern Baptist counterparts of the previous decades or earlier evangelical leaders such as Anita Bryant or Beverly LaHaye. And, akin to Graham, she was forging a different, broader path.

Along with the larger venues like Living Proof Live, I visited three conservative women's ministry retreats and conferences, including a discipleship week at Ridgecrest, North Carolina, and four local women's ministry small group studies, which I often attended several times. I participated in one of these, a homemaking and mothering group, for six months. As with Moore's events, a primary focus in all of these was cultivating a more personal relationship with Jesus, but talk about domesticity, children, and family life also prevailed in both the formal presentations and informal conversations. Many of the women in these groups worked full time, and they swapped common stories of hectic schedules, mounting housework, inattentive husbands, and rebellious teens. At the discipleship conference, a cheerful woman opened the first early morning session by reading from a 1970s book that sounded like Marabel Morgan's *Total Woman*. According to the passage, every tired husband should arrive home from work to find a clean home, manicured wife, the enticing aroma of dinner, and calm children. The woman reading the passage did look as if she could pull the scenario off, polished as she was, but she then cast the book aside, saying "no way." This scenario might have been the ideal in another age, she exclaimed, and "hooray" to those who managed it, but this conference was going to be about moving beyond images, getting real, and becoming vulnerable about failures and disappointments. The fifty or so women present laughed and cheered.

While talk of submission did not dominate these sessions, when asked about women's roles within the family, the women here and at other events overwhelmingly agreed with the concept. In survey after survey, women typically stated that "within the marriage relationship, the husband is to be respected as the leader"; that "when women take over a man's role, it is detrimental"; and that "women are not to be the head over men." One woman wrote in fluorescent pink that "I am submissive to my husband and then those areas where I have difficulty submitting, I pray harder." When women were asked to elaborate, almost every one of them was eager to emphasize that submission had been misunderstood, that it did not mean that women were not spiritually equal to men, but that their role was different from men's. Though not all women knew the term "complementarian," most of the women's ministry directors and leaders did and preferred to speak of the complementary relationship between husband and wife, especially in the home. As one woman put it, "The roles of men and women should compliment [complement] one another," and in this respect, they "are equal before God" even though "women should not lead."[7] Complementarianism did not downplay submission as much as cast it in a more favorable light.

In keeping with their support for complementarianism and submission, the women involved in these programs generally agreed to the 1998 and 2000 amendments to the Baptist Faith and Message. Almost all middle-aged women admitted that their lives were dramatically different from that of their mothers, many of whom had stayed at home. Clinging to the tenet of submission seemed to give them a sense of normalcy as they navigated new and unfamiliar terrain. When one participant shared in the women's homemaking group that the amended version made her feel affirmed in her life choices, the others nodded in agreement, even those who were working outside the home. Some women laughed and said the committee could have omitted "graciously" in the injunction that a "wife is to submit herself graciously to the servant leadership of her husband"; nonetheless, serious controversy over the dictate seemed to exist mainly outside these women's circles.

Still, not all agreed as to how complementarianism and submission worked in everyday life, particularly marriage. None gave examples in written surveys, and when asked in conversation how to apply the concept, many women struggled to respond. A few joked that they submitted to their husband when they agreed with him. More seriously, some claimed that it was something akin to his making 51 percent of the decisions, while others interpreted it to mean that his was the final word when all else failed and they could not agree. A large number of women believed that it meant a husband should leave the homemaking decisions to his wife and that she should likewise bow to her husband's authority in spiritual matters. Beth Moore seemed to side with this interpretation of spiritual leadership, while admitting frustrations about the setup. Speaking of her husband, she said, "Keith wasn't always a man of faith. In the past, he would go to church as often as he wouldn't. But God told me to treat Keith as though he were already the spiritual leader of our home. When I needed advice, I'd think, 'I don't even know if Keith has a prayer life. And I'm to ask him what to do'? And God would say 'yes.'"[8] At another time, she insisted, "My husband wears the cowboy boots in our family," likewise bragging that she prioritized home life and Keith's needs over her work, speaking engagements, and travel. "My man demanded attention and he got it, and my man demanded a normal family life and he got it."[9]

As for ecclesial life, only a few women privately revealed that they had no difficulties with women serving in ordained ministry positions over men. One stated in a survey, after affirming the importance of submission to her husband in every aspect of their family life, that she was a prophet, which was little different from a preacher. "Southern Baptists say it's wrong for a woman to preach," she wrote, "yet I have the spiritual gift of prophecy. Preachers are supposed to have this gift, but preachers are supposed to be men." After sharing that she had preached to women in the county jail, she said that for the time being, she would remain with Southern Baptists because she liked their "doctrine, concept of church, teachings, and worship style." And yet, she concluded, "If ever the burden to preach became overwhelming, I would go find an appropriate, acceptable outlet. I believe that, if the Lord gives a person a spiritual gift or assignment, that person is meant to use the gift, fulfill the task."[10] Along this same line of thinking, several more claimed in private conservations that although they believed in submission, if God called their daughters to an ordained ministry that obliged them to preach to and shepherd men, then they would support them. These women, however, were the exception; almost all of the women I met, surveyed, and spoke with felt that the practice violated traditional family values and biblical dictates. Even Moore, whom many outsiders viewed as an intense and passionate Billy Graham–like evangelist, was careful to announce herself as a Bible study teacher, not a preacher, and even then, as one who directed her message to women.

Other than senior minister and preacher, women were not as certain about church ministerial positions, particularly in areas such as music, missions, or education, and they insisted that women's ministry to women was a full and equal program in congregational life. In conferences for local women's ministry leaders, women frequently grumbled and complained about "chauvinistic pastors" who undermined the significance of women reaching out and ministering to women, and they strategized how to ensure that churches and their ministers met women's needs and listened to their concerns. While some conservative men indicated privately their reluctance over Moore's ministry, no conservative woman did, celebrating her instead as powerful testimony for women. One session at the discipleship retreat was titled "How to Get Along with Male Staff." During that session as well as more informal question-and-answer times elsewhere, women emphasized that "pastors cannot make a godly woman" and that churches "need to have women doing that." Women believed that the directorship of a churchwomen's ministry program should be a paid position, since women's ministry was just as vital and equal to the ministry of male staff members. The challenge, one longtime women's minister director admitted, was breaking into the "good old boys network" that defined male church staffs and their meetings, especially because, she was quick to add, "we [men and women] live in two different worlds." In the end, she encouraged patience and a gentle demeanor.[11] The more significant issue to these women, and one worth strife and struggle, was that they had their own space to come together, form relationships, share their lives, and speak vulnerably, without men to intervene.

When queried, either by me or other women participants, about working women, homeschooling, and divorce, almost all women's ministry leaders skirted the issues and admitted that they were wary of pushing any agenda on such personal matters. Most women's ministry programs, they acknowledged, were working diligently to attract women who had made different and difficult choices about family and employment. In many ways, the language of inner piety, as exemplified by Beth Moore and her popular studies, replaced the wmu and missions as a means of holding women intact. At the small group studies, women sought comfort, prayers, and guidance for a range of matters, from staying on a diet and disciplining temperamental toddlers to battling boredom in marriage and handling the diagnosis of cancer. Among those who knew each other well, discussions often turned deeply personal. When I asked one Bible study leader in Fort Worth, Texas, about the stance of her women's ministry program on mothers working full time outside the home, she said that even though she was privately against the practice, there were just some things that they, as a leadership team, could no longer claim if they desired more women to participate.[12] "It's just all so muddy," exclaimed one participant at a regional Women Reaching Women retreat. She was a pastor's wife who insisted that women should listen to God rather than denominational officials.[13]

Not all conservatives were comfortable with this ambiguity and believed that women's ministry was in danger of watering down the basic tenets of traditional, evangelical, or biblical womanhood, terms they still used interchangeably along with complementarianism. Southern Baptist seminaries, with their accompanying women's programs, as well as prominent denominational officials showed themselves as working diligently against this trend.[14] Not surprisingly, Dorothy and Paige Patterson, who had moved from Southeastern Seminary to Southwestern Seminary, where Paige occupied the presidential office, led the charge. As director of the women's studies program, Dorothy Patterson was grooming a number of young women scholars, one of whom, Heather King, had helped write the 2000 Baptist Faith and Message. Younger women like King were becoming more vocal in pushing Dorothy Patterson's ideology of submission.[15]

In 2005, Al Mohler invited best-selling author and scholar Mary Kassian to join the women's studies program at Southern Seminary. Kassian was as vehement as the Pattersons in her attack against feminism. A Canadian, she helped initiate the True Womanhood conferences, in which a traveling group of women evangelicals spoke to crowds of more than 6,000 women with the goal of championing the True Woman Manifesto. The manifesto was intended as an updated "Danvers Statement," more fitting for the postmodern, twenty-first century and initiated and promoted by women. It claimed, "We believe that we live in a culture that does not recognize God's right to rule, does not accept Scripture as the pattern for life, and is experiencing the consequences of abandoning God's design for men and women." At the conference itself, Kassian walked in to the sound of Helen Reddy's "I Am Woman." At one point, she danced to the beat, raised her hands, and seemed to be having fun as she invited women to remember Reddy's lyrics. Then, as the music died, she denounced all that the song symbolized. In her diatribe against feminism, Kassian compared June Cleaver of *Leave It to Beaver* to the sexually promiscuous and narcissistic female characters in *Sex and the City*, announcing that we've "really come a long way, baby," and then counted all that had been lost in the name of woman. Feminism, she emphasized, "has taken us from the ideal of a happy, fulfilled woman who serves and exalts her children and her husband and her community to one who serves and exalts herself," and she warned against a watered-down and unaware evangelicalism.[16] Her teaching, scholarship, and books constituted a visceral attack on the forces of feminist culture, including evangelical feminism, inclusive language, goddess worship, and feminine concepts of God, which Kassian lumped together with the radical wing of the 1970s as well as the more recent third wave of the movement.

Thus, after a brief period of relative quiet in the SBC that included some talk of a "kinder, gentler conservatism," passions erupted once again.[17] In December 2006, Southwestern Seminary terminated the tenure-track contract of Sheri Klouda. Klouda's conservative credentials were impeccable. A graduate of Criswell College and holding a doctorate from Southwestern, she had been teaching Old Testament and Hebrew language classes for several years before the Pattersons arrived. While they initially refused any formal statement on the matter, the Pattersons did not hide their belief that women should not be teaching men, especially in biblical studies and theology. According to T. Van McClain, who chaired the seminary's board of trustees, the institution desired "to have only men teaching who are qualified to be pastors or who have been pastors in the disciplines of theology, biblical studies, homiletics, and pastoral ministry," and Klouda's hiring constituted a "momentary lax of the parameters."[18]

The decision, of course, was in keeping with earlier ones made by conservatives, including the forced resignation of Molly Marshall at Southern Seminary in 1994. Now that the denominational contest was over and moderates had left the SBC, the Pattersons and other prominent conservatives probably did not expect too much internal debate. They were wrong. Even as the lines had been drawn, institutions purged, and victory declared, the infighting continued, with conservatives and complementarians on both sides of the fence. As many of her supporters pointed out, Klouda had signed the 2000 Baptist Faith and Message. According to Oklahoma minister Wade Burleson, who was at the time a trustee of the International Mission Board and an increasingly notorious blogger, the "seminary is not a church and Klouda is not a pastor. And neither the Bible nor the convention forbids a woman from teaching Hebrew and theology."[19] In defending her case, Klouda said, "You can't take the role of pastor and superimpose it to the role of professor in the academy."[20] Burleson also caused debate in trying to distinguish the role of "pastor" from that of "preacher," accusing Susie Hawkins, the prominent women's ministry leader as well as a member of the Baptist Faith and Message committee, of conflating the two.

In spite of McClain's comment, the parameters governing the roles and behaviors of conservative Southern Baptist women were far from settled. As I had discovered in my fieldwork, much of it in Texas, conservative women disagreed on the everyday application of submission and complementarianism, sometimes taking issue with the Pattersons and other denominational officials. Some, for example, rolled their eyes over Dorothy Patterson's insistence that a single or widowed woman find a close male relative to whom they should submit. One seminary wife treated the establishment of a new homemaking degree at the college at Southwestern as yet another embarrassment, though other young women enthusiastically signed up.

Denominationally, the questions kept coming, public queries about roles and performances that went well beyond ordained ministry over men and struggled with the nature of submission to male authority in varied settings and capacities: women teaching men in coed Sunday schools, women serving as hospital and military chaplains, women seminarians in preaching classes, the nature and extent of women working outside the home, divorce, physical and emotional abuse, and more. Some conservative women pointed to differences between the seminaries' women's ministry programs and disagreements over the application of complementarianism. Conservative bloggers had broken the Klouda story and became busy again in September 2008 when Lifeway instructed its stores to pull the current issue of the popular conservative evangelical magazine *Gospel Today* from its shelves. The front cover showed five women ministers dressed in black with the bold headline "Female Pastors: Breaking the Glass Ceiling!" A Lifeway spokesman stated that the story contained beliefs contrary to official SBC teaching. This angered the magazine's editor, a woman, who claimed that the article was reporting on a significant trend, not taking a stance, and accused SBC executives of treating *Gospel Today* and the women on its cover as porn.[21]

With instances like the Klouda affair and *Gospel Today*, conservatives had opened a Pandora's box on the issue of women. Even as Southern Baptist complementarians cheered women like Republican vice presidential candidate Sarah Palin as an evangelical mother who refused an abortion to have a son with Down syndrome and who counseled her pregnant unwed teenage daughter likewise, it seemed a stretch to present her as a submissive wife and even more so as one joyful in homemaking. How could she heed Dorothy

Patterson's persistent warning that "a salaried job and titled position can inhibit a woman's natural nesting instinct" or former SBC president Tom Elliff's marital advice that the wife "not be burdened with the necessity of working outside the home"?[22] One young independent evangelical pastor pointed to the SBC's contradictory stances on women as partial explanation for why he left the conservative Southern Baptist fold: "How odd I find it that so many of the people who don't believe a woman should speak from behind a pulpit have no problem with a woman leading an entire nation."[23]

As president of the SBC's Ethics and Religious Liberty Commission, Richard Land maintained that only an "absurd reading" of the 1998 Baptist Faith and Message family amendment would say that wives should not work outside the home. Of course they could, he exclaimed, pointing to his own wife's professional counseling practice. Still, his subsequent counsel that "if a husband doesn't want his wife to work outside the home, then she shouldn't" must have struck many as absurd in itself.[24] When Moore started any public event by telling the crowds of women waiting to hear her speak that she had called her husband before coming onstage and he had given her permission to teach, the caveat came across as a rehearsed formality and certainly at odds with her presentation. The same could be said of other prominent evangelical women like Dorothy Patterson, Mary Kassian, and even more recently, the 2012 presidential candidate Michele Bachmann, each of whom claimed her husband's permission, even urging, for embarking on her public life. When asked in 2008 if his support for vice presidential candidate Sarah Palin contradicted his argument for women's submission, Al Mohler distinguished between the realms of home, church, and politics, stating that the Bible did not directly speak to women in political life. He did admit, however, with more candor than Land and others, "It would be hypocritical of me to suggest that I would be perfectly happy to have Christian young women believe that being Vice President of the United States is more important than being a wife and mother."[25]

As gendered policies over women became increasingly muddled, other tensions resurfaced as well. The conservative resurgence, for instance, had brought about a reemergence in Calvinist beliefs, pitting at certain moments a new generation of Al Mohlers against an older generation of Paige Pattersons. The question of charismatic gifts, particularly speaking in tongues, together with the rise of Pentecostalism led to the departure of missionaries who practiced "private prayer language." None of these issues came close to creating the rifts of the 1980s and 1990s, and none was as internally divisive as the debate over women in ordained ministry. Nevertheless, they pointed to the challenges conservatives would have to face in maintaining a denomination. In 2009, baptisms dropped to a twenty-year low, and memberships decreased almost as rapidly. Admittedly, most Protestant denominations and institutions, including those of moderate Baptists, were suffering losses. But conservatives had not participated in denomination building and, in fact, had treated institutionalization with suspicion. It remained to be seen how long they could maintain their more strident countercultural positions alongside a 16-million-member denomination.

This Is What a Baptist Preacher Looks Like

Conservatives sometimes wondered how countercultural their opposition to women in ordained ministry actually was. At the 2008 CBF General Assembly, BWIM sponsored two sessions on the topic of women in ministry. One involved that year's *State of Women in Baptist Life* report, and the other included a panel of women ministers intended to encourage congregations in considering a woman pastor. At both sessions, the same elderly male pastor from South Carolina recounted the story of a college-age woman who had visited his office to discuss her call to seminary and ordained ministry. His advice was for her to examine her sense of call and, if fully convicted, to join another denomination. "Did I give her the wrong response?" he honestly asked. Many of those present recoiled. Some expressed anger over his advice. "Why not affirmation," one cried. In self-defense, he pointed to the status report and wondered if, thinking of her vocational well-being, he really could have told her anything else.[26]

On at least one count, some women agreed, he was correct. Her current odds of finding a pulpit in moderate Baptist life were slim. According to the first status report in 2005, only 5.5 percent of CBF-related churches reported women as senior pastor or copastor. In 2007, the percentage was 5.9. As expected, the Alliance scored higher, with 22 percent in 2005 and 24 percent in 2007. Interestingly, those state conventions that had not been taken over by conservatives performed lowest, with the Baptist General Convention of Texas reporting only .19 percent in 2005 and .196 percent in 2007. The Baptist General Association of Virginia was not much better, with 1.1 percent in 2005 and 1.3 percent in 2007.[27] These percentages were well out of proportion with the demographics of the fourteen CBF-affiliated seminaries, divinity schools, and Baptist studies programs, whose female students ranged from 23 percent to 53 percent, with eight schools reporting more than 40 percent. In light of the few churches calling women to pastor or copastor, where would they serve? The status reports did indicate that far more moderate churches were inviting ordained women to serve in other traditionally male staff positions, such as associate pastor or Christian education minister, though they did not show the exact numbers. And women serving in paid roles traditionally filled by females, such as children's director, were more likely to be ordained, represented on church staffs, and recognized by the title "minister."[28]

Still, when recounting their seminary experience, some female seminarians sounded frustrated and not unlike their predecessors at the Consultation on Women in Church-Related Vocations in 1978. The women's studies scholar Susan Shaw, also an ordained Baptist pastor who had attended Southern Seminary, interviewed a group of female students at Truett School of Theology at Baylor University in Waco, Texas. Truett was founded in 1994 as an alternative to the conservative-controlled Southwestern, and by 2005, the year of Shaw's interview, it had 385 students. Of these, 32 percent, or 125, were women. Two years later, Truett had 401 students, and of these, 118 were women, making them 29 percent of the student population. Despite Truett's vocal commitment to women in ministry, and Truett's percentage of female students did remain above that of the six official sbc schools, its percentage was among the lower half of the fourteen moderate institutions.[29] Women found the rhetoric of acceptance troubling when measured against the reality of their experience. The school, said LeAnne Gardner, "may pat women on the back and offer affirmation" but nevertheless "doesn't actively encourage churches to call these women as pastors." It was, she said, "like there's one step missing; there is a lot of lip service, and it's not taken one step further." When Melissa Browning complained that she was never called from Truett's pulpit supply list, the staff told her that "a lot of churches don't want a woman." Brown immediately asked, "Well do you try to persuade them?"[30]

Additionally, despite the rising numbers of women in moderate seminaries as well as doctoral programs in theology and church history, only 22 percent of faculty at the cbf's ten Baptist seminaries and schools were female. When we consider all fourteen partner schools, forty of ninety-six women faculty members, almost half, were at the adjunct, visiting, or instructor level, with some holding more administrative positions.[31] Gender equity was clearly lacking.

Many of the early founders, leaders, and participants in bwim had already taken the elderly South Carolina pastor's advice and joined other denominations. Few pioneers from the mid-1980s attended the twenty-fifth anniversary dinner. There were the natural attritions of age and death; for instance, Anne Neil, at eighty-eight, was past travel. But years of struggle and controversy had also taken their toll, especially as women's bodies literally became the final denominational battleground. Years earlier, Addie Davis had warned women that "it's sometimes dangerous to dream." A large number of BWIM's early visionaries, having pursued their dreams to minister, now felt too exhausted, battered, and bruised to persist in any form of Southern Baptist life, moderate or otherwise. Several politely refused participation in interviews about this period because doing so would "open old wounds that had taken years to heal." One BWIM founder celebrated having left for Episcopal ordination. While she found it "hard to leave," she also emphasized that "never have I regretted my move." In her words, "I have been privileged to MINISTER rather than to FIGHT FOR THE PRIVILEGE OF MINISTERING." Quite a few of her Southern Baptist and SBWIM colleagues, she said, now ministered in other denominations as well. She mourned that "so few" of those who stayed "have been able to claim full visibility at the 'front' of the church."[32]

When I spoke with some of the pioneers of BWIM, even those who had moved on, they still expressed enthusiasm that a new generation of young female seminarians and pastors was willing to pick up the dream, as dangerous as it had been; revive BWIM; and breathe new life into the organization. These younger women might not have lived through the battles, but they had grown up hearing the stories. The mythic stories of women like Molly Marshall and Nancy Sehested coupled with the reality of status reports had given these women enough righteous indignation to press on rather than becoming discouraged. At the 2008 CBF assembly, their energy was palpable. "This Is What a Baptist Preacher Looks Like" T-shirts were everywhere and sold out quickly. The women participated equally in the assembly worship, preaching, serving communion, commissioning missionaries, and reading from scripture. Their women in ministry sessions were packed to standing room only. Coordinator LeAnn Gunter Johns awarded a freshly minted M.Div. graduate, Bailey Edwards Nelson, with BWIM's Addie Davis Award in preaching and announced the results of the first Martha Stearns Marshall Day of Preaching, a newly established tradition in which BWIM designated a day for moderate churches to invite a woman to preach from the pulpit. Bolstered by such enthusiasm, the CBF added to its identity, mission, vision, and core values a set of strategic priorities that included "honoring race, gender, and generations." Under this initiative, it pledged to "heighten understanding of women in leadership."

In 2009, BWIM hired a full-time executive director, Pamela R. Durso. Durso was described by her friends and colleagues as a gentle personality, a good listener, an able administrator, a strong speaker, and one who had an eagerness and passion to shine the spotlight on women ministers. She had attended Southwestern and had received her doctorate in church history from Baylor. Although not ordained, she had taught, researched, and written extensively on Baptist women, highlighting their ministries. As executive director, she worked tirelessly to reinvigorate the twenty-five-year-old organization. She also recognized, as coauthor of the status reports, that while doors were opening, the statistics for women in ministry had not progressed significantly over the life of BWIM. In speaking at a gathering of moderate leaders, she addressed the challenge of that South Carolina pastor: "What do we say to our Baptist daughters who feel called and who are gifted to serve as pastor?"

Durso gave two options. The first, she said, "is that we tell young women to stop waiting for existing churches to change. We encourage them to move outside the traditional framework for their future in ministry. In essence, we advise them to give up on looking for open pulpits and existing churches that will embrace their gifts. And instead, we call out young women to plant new churches, churches which from their very foundation will be inclusive of women, affirming of their gifts." The second option, she continued, "is to challenge our young women to stay in their churches, to be proactive and make change happen, to be reformers, revolutionaries. We advise our daughters to work from within our existing churches but to be vocal and strong in their call for change."[33] This second option was the age-old tactic of waiting, a tactic that had not taken Baptist women too far. The first, however, presented a radical vision that threw the challenge back to moderates themselves, and Durso asked the CBF leadership to put finances and training behind it.

Southern Seminary's Al Mohler called moderate support of women in ministry "hypothetical" and "symbolic," a "theological trajectory rather than genuine openness." After reading the status reports, he concluded, "The bottom line is that moderates, while registering strong opposition to the 2000 revision of the Baptist Faith and Message, and while offering strong words of encouragement to women seeking to serve in the pastorate, appear to be extremely reluctant to call women to serve in these positions."[34] Previous generations of BWIM women had come to the same conclusion, experiencing firsthand the reality of reluctant churches. Some in the new generation of moderate women struggled with the same reality. They would be the ones to discover whether "lip service" would give way to change.

Addie Davis delivered the sermon at the 1985 BWIM worship service.

"Cherish the dream God has given you," she proclaimed to the woman who dared to feel called, like Davis, to "serve in the center pulpit of her tradition."[35] Twenty-five years later, this call remained for most moderate Baptist women just that: a dream. Indeed, the BWIM T-shirts were so effective because Baptist preachers still looked like men.

Conclusion

The WMU, once the space that held women together, fragmented after 1979, and in its wake came varied women's networks and programs. While women's ministry and BWIM were more prominent, there were others. Most conservative women did form groups under the umbrella of Lifeway Women's Ministry or their church's women's ministry programs, and these ranged from Mothers of Preschoolers to groups focused on public speaking or divorce recovery. Moderate women worked more independently, but their organizations and networks were also wide ranging. Global Women, for example, addressed social justice issues as they affected women worldwide. They sponsored conferences on topics like AIDS and sex-trafficking and raised money for birthing kits.[36] A group of college-age women initiated weekend retreats called "Freedom Conferences," which encouraged other female students to ponder God's callings beyond the traditional roles they were expected to fill. Oklahoma Women in Baptist Life met annually for moderate women to discuss different theological topics and cultural issues as well as to worship and to hear women preach. At one of their meetings, a couple of women, still frustrated by what they felt to be the "misogyny of moderate life," told me about forming a women-centered house church.[37]

Throughout my research and writing, I was struck by an ongoing persistent paradox. On one hand, through numerous venues women had found their voices and negotiated prevailing gendered assumptions, including those invoked by women's submission. In this sense, they emerged from the two-decade denominational struggle to discover inner vitality and strength, sisterhood, and self-empowerment. On the other hand, the contest between conservatives and moderates had left deep wounds, and like their male counterparts, women wore these scars—sometimes secretly, other times blatantly—with internal debates continuing to evoke their roles and behaviors. Additionally, women were now far less likely than before to cross boundaries or foster alliances between conservatives and moderates. They lived for the most part in tight clusters of information and relationships. This deep polarization among women illustrates the SBC and its two-decade controversy. But the struggle of Southern Baptist women and the Southern Baptist struggle over women also constitute a "story within a story," which is postwar American religion and culture.

With its overflowing coffers, vast infrastructure, mission empire, and numerous megachurches, the SBC after 1945 was no longer about southern failure but about the transformation of Dixie, American prosperity, and evangelical success. As it entered the 1970s, the SBC was one of many evangelical denominations and subcultures that began to fight over women's roles and behaviors. It was ultimately torn apart by the rhetoric, reality, and confusion of pitting the Christian woman against woman's lib, June Cleaver against "This Is What a Baptist Preacher Looks Like." There were other tensions, too—crucial differences concerning doctrine, ecclesiology, denominational relations, social issues, and cultural matters—which interacted heavily with the debate over women in Southern Baptist life. But it is the story of the prodigal daughters along with the savvy submissive mothers and wives that history has persistently downplayed and neglected. These pivotal female characters served as Southern Baptist missionaries, preachers, woman-to-woman mentors, WMU leaders, and Sunday school teachers and included such strong, passionate, and faith-filled personalities as Addie Davis, Dorothy Patterson, Jessie Sappington, Nancy Sehested, and Anne Thomas Neil. Together they bear powerful witness to how gendered ideas about women's roles, behaviors, and performances promoted sectarian religion in the SBC, evangelical life, and postwar American culture.

Notes

The following source abbreviation is used in the notes.

SBHLA   Southern Baptist Historical Library and Archives, Nashville, Tenn.

Introduction

1. Charlie Warren, "Criswell Endorses Adrian Rogers for President," *Baptist Press*, June 11, 1979.

2. Orville Scott, "Concern Expressed over Groups Dividing SBC," *Baptist Press*, June 11, 1979.

3. "President Allen's Address," *Baptist Press*, June 12, 1979.

4. I use "conservative" and "moderate" as labels that each faction most often applied to itself. While moderates frequently referred to conservatives as fundamentalists, conservatives decried this term and its negative connotations. In turn, conservatives characterized the opposing moderate camp as liberal. A few Southern Baptists did define themselves by this marker, but as "liberal" had negative stereotypes in Southern Baptist life, those who opposed the conservative shift in leadership primarily identified themselves as moderates. As a result of the controversy, defining Southern Baptists has also become a complicated process. According to denomination officials, Southern Baptists have been those who belonged to a church that sent a certain amount of money to the SBC's centralized budget, thereby making that congregation eligible to send messengers to the annual convention. Historians and sociologists have traditionally used that criterion to number and analyze Southern Baptists. However, for many Southern Baptists at the grassroots level, particularly women, "Southern Baptist" connoted something that went beyond institutional boundaries. Additionally, as moderates left the denomination in the wake of the conflict, they formed organizational offshoots that claimed to represent "true" Southern Baptist beliefs and practices. While some eschewed the label "Southern Baptist," they celebrated their Southern Baptist heritage. Moderate women often spoke of the Woman's Missionary Union as their mother. Historically, these women had been an integral part of a Southern Baptist women's culture. In light of these considerations,

I define Southern Baptists culturally as well as institutionally, counting moderates as part of the historic Southern Baptist fold.

5. Scholars argue over the endpoint to the controversy. Some put it as early as 1991, when moderates formed the Cooperative Baptist Fellowship, while others extend it to the 2000 revision of the Baptist Faith and Message. Well into the twenty-first century, conservatives and moderates continued to battle over state conventions and their affiliated colleges and universities.

6. David Miller, as he appears in the documentary *Battle for the Minds*. Miller was a Southern Baptist pastor who served as vice president of Southern Seminary's board of trustees.

7. A prominent conservative woman made this comment as we chatted during an informal coffee together. She noted that for many conservatives after 1979, belief in womanly submission joined other orthodoxies like the physical resurrection and virgin birth as essential to salvation.

8. *Battle for the Minds*. The woman seminarian quoted here is unnamed in Lipscomb's documentary.

9. In her study of the Woman's Missionary Training School, Laine Scales refers to a "conserving" principle guiding the female students' roles and behaviors. See Scales, *All That Fits a Woman*.

10. I appreciate the comments of an anonymous reviewer who helped me strengthen the connection between race and gender.

11. For an extended analysis of the term "inerrancy," see the eponymous section in Chapter 3. I am using the term historically, tracing how conservatives and moderates understood it and how their use of the term changed over time. I conclude that while there is no one fixed definition, the doctrine of inerrancy in Southern Baptist life did, for the most part, refer to the belief that God inspired the writers of sacred scripture in such a manner that their words were marked by historical and scientific accuracy on all matters of truth that the Bible affirmed. The challenge was that even these truths shifted according to Southern Baptists' context. As a result, conservatives within the SBC often identified themselves as inerrantists more in opposition to those purposefully drawing on any form of historical critical analysis in their biblical interpretation. As moderates sometimes indicated, this understanding was not always shared by other evangelicals who likewise called themselves inerrantists.

12. Ordained women sometimes added, though, that despite moderates' rhetoric of acceptance, only a small number of their congregations actually called women to occupy this place of power.

13. Again, I acknowledge the insights of an anonymous reviewer here.

14. Insider moderates have analyzed the Southern Baptist battles prolifically. See, for example, Cothen, *What Happened to the Southern Baptist Convention?* and *The New SBC*, and Shurden, *Struggle for the Soul of the SBC*. These works focused primarily on institutional concerns and basically regarded the conflict as a doctrinal dispute entangled with denominational politics. In their respective studies, both Bill J. Leonard and David T. Morgan considered theological, institutional, and cultural concerns. Leonard, though, saw the controversy as theological in nature. See Leonard, *God's Last and Only Hope*, 66, and Morgan, *New Crusades*. Conservatives joined the conversation with James and

Dockery, *Beyond the Impasse*. See also the narrative accounts of Hefley, *Truth in Crisis*, and Sutton, *Baptist Reformation*, as well as the memoir of Pressler, *Hill on Which to Die*. These conservatives interpreted the controversy as a dispute over doctrine. Moving beyond insider accounts, Arthur Emery Farnsley II explored denominational polity and politicking in his more institutional account, *Southern Baptist Politics*. Carl L. Kell and L. Raymond Camp examined conservative and, to a lesser extent, moderate rhetorical strategies in their collaborative work, *In the Name of the Father*. Nancy Tatom Ammerman and Barry Hankins both cited the debate over women in their respective studies of the controversy as a social and cultural struggle, with Hankins placing it within the larger context of the culture wars. While insiders to Southern Baptist life, Ammerman and Hankins each attempted a more neutral scholarly perspective. See Ammerman, *Baptist Battles*, and Hankins, *Uneasy in Babylon*.

15. As for women in Southern Baptist history, two general surveys have been written: McBeth, *Women in Baptist Life*, and Morgan, *Southern Baptist Sisters*. Both H. Leon McBeth and David T. Morgan explored women's organizational roles within the denomination. See also Allen, *Century to Celebrate*, a heavily documented study of the historic WMU. More recently, Susan Shaw interviewed approximately 150 contemporary Southern Baptist and former Southern Baptist women, weaving their narratives into a collective memoir, *God Speaks to Us, Too*. Most studies of Southern Baptist women have concentrated on the WMU in its early years. Only Scales, *All That Fits a Woman*, has been published as a book, though numerous dissertations fall into this category. See, in particular, Holcomb, "Mothering the South," and Tew, "From Local Society to Para-Denomination."

16. See, for example, Harvey, *Freedom's Coming*.

17. I use the rhetoric of women and women's studies over gender and gender studies intentionally. The shift from women's studies to gender studies during the late 1980s and 1990s was a crucial scholarly development. Joan Scott is often credited for this transition. According to Scott, gender is, first, a "constitutive element of social relationships based upon perceived differences between the sexes" and, second, a "primary field within which or by means of which power is articulated" ("Gender," 1067–69). As I interpret it, gender studies systematically compares cultural constructions of female and male roles, or concepts of femininity and masculinity, as they delineate and invoke power. While I heed Scott's claim that "historians need to examine the way that gendered identities are constructed and relate their findings to a range of activities, social organizations, and historically specific cultural representations," particularly as these are related to power, I still find myself more concerned with the social roles assigned to women than men and examine the discourse in Southern Baptist life accordingly. To this end, I respond to the urging of American religious historian Catherine A. Brekus to write about women and see gender history as a supplement to women's history, which insists on highlighting women's agency as a form of power. See Brekus, "Searching for Women in Narratives of American Religious History," 32–33. Finally, I use the category "woman" in reference to not only bodily difference but the historical processes that have produced a sense of collective female identity and shared experience. Again, see Brekus, "Searching for Women in Narratives of American Religious History," 11–12.

18. Braude, "Women's History *Is* American Religious History," 87.

19. Ibid., 90.

20. Ibid.

21. To examine Braude's thesis in relation to conservative evangelical women, see Brasher, *Godly Women*, and Griffith, *God's Daughters*. In their ethnographic studies, both written in the late 1990s, Brasher and Griffith lamented the flattened image often afforded women in conservative religious traditions, particularly contemporary forms of evangelicalism. Earlier feminist scholars from the 1970s and 1980s had likewise questioned the basic paradigm of patriarchal power and female oppression. Exploring women in early modern France, Natalie Zemon Davis discovered ways they manipulated, subverted, and undermined restrictive gender ideologies; see Davis, *Society and Culture in Early Modern France*. Postcolonial feminist critics questioned the dominant paradigm in their examinations of human practice and agency as well. See Abu-Lughod, "Romance of Resistance," and O'Hanlon, "Recovering the Subject." As Rosalind O'Hanlon argued, Western scholars have dismissed strategies that do not take the form of outright rebellion and aggressive resistance. She urged scholars to look beyond the political to consider different forms of resistance, including feminine tendencies that have been suppressed as passive retreat and silent withdrawal; see "Recovering the Subject," 214–16, 220–23. Focusing on the American context, as early as 1966 Barbara Welter demonstrated how Victorian understandings of women as more naturally pious and morally pure than men relegated white, middle- and upper-class women to the domestic or private sphere. See Welter, "Cult of True Womanhood." While accepting Welter's basic analysis, others began to explore how nineteenth- and early twentieth-century women created powerful spaces for themselves within seemingly limited structures. Most influential was Carroll Smith-Rosenberg, who argued that the close emotional ties of a female Victorian world gave some women inner security and comfort, while their status as maternal caretakers and moral exemplars provided justification for more public reforming roles. See Smith-Rosenberg, "Female World of Love and Ritual" and "Beauty, the Beast, and the Militant Woman." Subsequent works from the late 1980s and early 1990s explored the ways that religious women used the rhetoric of domesticity to enable their benevolent and mission work. These included Epstein, *Politics of Domesticity*; Ginzberg, *Women and the Work of Benevolence*; Hill, *World Their Household*; and Hunter, *Gospel of Gentility*. Linda Kerber, however, claimed that the concept of a women's sphere reflected more a rhetorical construction than an everyday reality, and she questioned historians' slippery use of sphere language. See Kerber, "Separate Spheres, Female World, Woman's Place." Though sphere language was called into question, its claims about women's power persisted. Brasher and Griffith advanced the debate to address the current day. And they went further in demonstrating how some women have actively chosen to participate in ideologies that might appear to weaken their authority and self-determination. According to Kathryn Lofton, in her study of Oprah, the challenge of subsequent scholarship, as it then moved to "cajole tales of liberation from every subject," has been a diminishing of those broader themes in religious history and the neglect of "structural contours that surround, determine, and occupy that subject" (Lofton, *Oprah*, 16). Early on, Lofton urged me to heed those far-reaching structural limitations placed on Southern Baptist women as well as the liberating impulses connected to their circles and spheres.

22. For the purposes of this study, I define religion as a dynamic symbolic system

simultaneously produced by and imposed on individuals and communities to guide their behaviors (restoration and order) as well as to give their lives meaning (transformation). This understanding of religion builds on Clifford Geertz as well as his critics. According to Geertz, religion is "a system of symbols which acts to establish powerful, pervasive, and long-lasting moods and motivations in men by formulating conceptions of a general order of existence and clothing these conceptions with such an aura of factuality that the moods and motivations seem uniquely realistic." Geertz explains that symbols convey particular ideas that have a public, communal existence. They invoke "conceptions of a general order of existence" or "world view." Religion, then, guides people to act according to particular values. In this respect, says Geertz, religion is the attempt to account for the "threat of disorder" (Geertz, "Religion as a Cultural System," 90). I also heed Talal Asad's warning that Geertz neglects the historical processes through which religious symbols are constructed and the heterogeneous elements, like work, politics, power (and, I would add, gender) included in their construction; see Asad, *Genealogies of Religion*, 27–54. Moreover, as scholars of women's history remind us, women in religion act as agents of change, often invoking disorder and upsetting the structures of dominance and control. Religion, then, as a meaning-making system is ever in flux and embedded in conflict, contestation, and issues of power.

23. Swidler, "Culture in Action." See also Mach, *Symbols, Conflict, and Identity*.

24. Some scholars have argued more for the southernization of America than the nationalization of Dixie. One of the first was Egerton, in *Americanization of Dixie*. In this 1974 work, John Egerton claimed that as southerners moved north and west, they took a distinct worldview and religious sensibility with them. The Americanization of the South led, in turn, to the southernization of American Christianity and culture. Nearly twenty years later, in *Resurgent Evangelicalism in the United States*, Mark Shibley questioned Egerton's thesis. Shibley argued that while southern religion has undoubtedly influenced American culture, southern religion has also been irrevocably changed in the process, and certainly more than Egerton acknowledged—or could have foreseen. See also, more recently, Gregory, *Southern Diaspora*, and Dochuk, *From Bible Belt to Sunbelt*.

25. For the history behind this question, see, first, Garrett, Hinson, and Tull, *Are Southern Baptists "Evangelicals"?*, then Dockery, *Southern Baptists and American Evangelicals*. Historians outside the SBC have found the question puzzling. Leonard I. Sweet called the debate as it appeared in the Garrett, Hinson, and Tull volume "one of the stranger exchanges about whether a denomination is 'evangelical'" (Sweet, "Evangelical Tradition in America," 84 n. 306).

26. George Marsden is most frequently cited when it comes to defining twentieth-century evangelicalism. Marsden rejected the consensus view of evangelicalism dominant through the 1960s and 1970s. According to the consensus view, evangelicals represented those who after the 1920s failed to adapt to modern technology, evolutionary science, and higher biblical criticism. Scholars upholding the consensus view saw evangelicals as a largely rural, uneducated, sectarian, and culturally irrelevant group. Conversely, Marsden contended that evangelicalism was an intellectual system dominated by Princeton orthodoxy and Calvinist theology. Its prime leaders held to the pre-Romantic, commonsense realism of Baconian epistemology and Reformed theology. See Marsden, *Fundamentalism and American Culture*. Joel Carpenter extended Marsden's thesis into the post–World

War II period as he traced the emergence of new evangelicals like Carl Henry, Harold Ockenga, and Billy Graham. See Carpenter, *Revive Us Again*. In what some scholars called the Reformed approach, Marsden, Carpenter, Mark Noll, and others emphasized evangelicalism's northern, urban, and sectarian roots. But while they successfully combated gross stereotypes made popular by the consensus view, they neglected evangelicalism's nineteenth-century southern and frontier roots, overplayed early twentieth-century fundamentalism's role in the overall movement, and dismissed issues of women and gender.

27. Most influential to my understanding were Mathews, *Religion in the Old South*, and Heyrman, *Southern Cross*. According to both, the evangelical tradition could not be understood without reference to both women's prominence and its constant reshaping of gendered patterns and symbols.

28. Donald Dayton vigorously decried the Reformed interpretation of Marsden and others, instead calling historians to heed the Wesleyan side of the story with its holiness themes, Arminian underpinnings, and frontier characters. See Dayton, "Yet Another Layer of the Onion." In "Wise as Serpents, Innocent as Doves," Leonard I. Sweet likewise focused on evangelicalism's Wesleyan features. Women figured more prominently in both Dayton's and Sweet's analysis. Approaching their critique of the Reformed analysis from another direction, both Margaret Lamberts Bendroth and Betty A. DeBerg argued that fundamentalism was a gendered movement. As turn-of-the-century women entered the industrial workforce, pushed for suffrage, and exchanged Victorian fashion for bobbed hair and flapper dress, evangelical men constructed an aggressive, manly Christianity promoting male spiritual headship and patriarchal family structures. See Bendroth, *Fundamentalism and Gender*, and DeBerg, *Ungodly Women*.

29. I appreciate Grant Wacker for making this observation and giving me this phrase.

30. Following Jimmy Carter's election as president, both *Newsweek* and *Time* named 1976 the year of the evangelical. More recently, the religious right's support of George W. Bush has resulted in an increased media focus on evangelicals. But while popular journalists have portrayed Southern Baptists as evangelical, they have made little distinction among the various evangelical traditions and their particular theological, political, and cultural constituencies. Few realize, for example, that Falwell began as an independent Baptist. It was only as a result of conservatives' rise to power in the SBC that he moved his church, Thomas Road Baptist, into the Southern Baptist fold. Liberty University, which he founded as Lynchburg Baptist College in 1971, remained independent.

31. Hunter, *Culture Wars*, 44–45. The literature on the religious right and culture wars is vast. Some of the more influential works consulted in this study include Bivins, *Fracture of Good Order*; Dowland, "Defending Manhood"; Lienesch, *Redeeming America*; and Martin, *With God on Our Side*. See also, more recently, Flippen, *Jimmy Carter*, for the role of Carter's presidency in the rise of the religious right, and Hankins, *Jesus and Gin*, for a more extensive historical perspective. In *Jesus and Gin*, Barry Hankins sees the unity of 1940s and 1950s American religion and culture as something of an aberration amidst the religious foment of the twentieth century. The culture wars era simply revived the unrest, scandal, temperament, and polarization of the 1920s. For studies that focus more on conservative evangelical women, see Brasher, *Godly Women*; Gallagher, *Evangelical Identity and Gendered Family Life*; and Griffith, *God's Daughters*.

32. For an examination of this middle ground, see Groothuis, *Women Caught in the Conflict*. As for evangelical feminists, see Ingersoll, *Evangelical Christian Women*, and Cochran, *Evangelical Feminism*.

33. See Dayton and Johnson, *Variety of American Evangelicalism*.

34. See Dowland, "Defending Manhood."

35. Smith, "Evangelical Kaleidoscope and the Call to Christian Unity."

36. David Steinmetz, as quoted in Wacker, *Heaven Below*, xi.

37. These included Baptist Women in Ministry (formerly Southern Baptist Women in Ministry); Global Women; the Woman's Missionary Union; Women's Enrichment Ministry, with its local women's ministry church programs; and Women in Baptist Life. They ranged from highly coordinated programs involving thousands of women to small informal groups and networks. Whereas the SBC sponsored Women's Enrichment Ministry as an organization under Lifeway Christian Resources (formerly the Southern Baptist Sunday School Board), Women in Baptist Life was independent. Most of the groups associated with or received funding from either the conservative or the moderate faction. Some involved weekly gatherings, while others functioned as a yearly meeting.

38. See the epilogue for a more detailed explanation of these venues and events. See the Bibliography for a list of the conferences, retreats, and meetings attended.

39. During larger public venues I remained anonymous, though in personal encounters I always explained who I was and the purpose of my research. I also handed out business cards with this information. At smaller meetings or retreats, particularly those involving groups that I attended more regularly, the main leader introduced me and had me tell my reason for being there. If permitted, I passed out surveys. Sometimes leaders requested that I instead take the names of interested women and mail or e-mail them the surveys later. The surveys had a snowball effect. Women frequently forwarded them to friends through e-mail. A few volunteered to pass them out at future gatherings and return them to me in bulk. Many supplied me with the names and addresses of other potential participants. In the survey, a woman marked basic demographic categories such as race, age, income, marital status, children, and educational background, but most questions were open-ended. They asked about a woman's interests and activities, her involvement in a particular women's group, and her understanding of women's roles in church, home, and community life as well as her sense of herself as a Southern Baptist and evangelical woman. Respondents remained anonymous, and I divided the surveys by organization and group. Overall, 106 women completed surveys. Breaking this number accordingly, I received 49 from WMU members; 38 from local women's ministry participants; 5 from Baptist Women in Ministry, primarily board members; and 14 from Women in Baptist Life. Many of the latter were also Baptist Women in Ministry participants. However, I record them here as the women self-identified. Interviews pulled more heavily from (Southern) Baptist Women in Ministry leaders.

40. Most of the women I had met previously, and the questions came from our conversations. Some interviews focused on a particular event. Others dealt more generally with the conflict. A majority of the women were leaders of a particular women's organization or program such as (Southern) Baptist Women in Ministry, the WMU, or local women's ministry programs, and my questions often asked after that group's involvement in the controversy as well as its particular successes and challenges.

41. In 1995, Southern Baptist Women in Ministry changed its name to Baptist Women in Ministry. I will use the name or abbreviation appropriate to the date under discussion.

42. Brown, *Mama Lola*, 12.

43. Orsi, "Snakes Alive," 112; Brown, *Mama Lola*, 12.

44. Tweed, "On Moving Across," 270. See also Tweed, *Crossing and Dwelling*.

45. Tweed, "On Moving Across," 253.

46. For an overview of this basic history, see Allen, *Century to Celebrate*; McBeth, *Women in Baptist Life*; and Morgan, *Southern Baptist Sisters*. Morgan depends heavily on McBeth. My understanding pulls from these works, as well as Brekus, *Strangers and Pilgrims*; Mathews, *Religion in the Old South*; Heyrman, *Southern Cross*; and my own archival research.

47. Most representing a more moderate viewpoint drew from McBeth. Women involved with the organization (Southern) Baptist Women in Ministry, for example, often cited McBeth and followed his interpretation in their newsletter *FOLIO*. Conservative interpretations were more difficult to locate, as conservative scholars had not written as prolifically on women in Baptist history. My sense of their interpretation, as presented here, comes primarily from my field-based research as well as conversations with Southern Baptist historians and scholars. One of the most revealing written sources was Dorothy Patterson's "Why I Believe Southern Baptist Churches Should Not Ordain Women," a paper delivered at the annual meeting of the Southern Baptist Historical Association in 1988. In this paper, Patterson accused H. Leon McBeth and other moderates of distorting history to favor their own support of women's ordination and preaching. Later conservative women scholars like Mary Kassian at Southern Baptist Theological Seminary or Rhonda Kelley at New Orleans Baptist Theological Seminary would have agreed with Patterson.

48. Beyond McBeth, see Molly Marshall-Green, "Toward Encompassing Theological Vision for Women in Light of Baptist Tradition," *FOLIO*, Autumn 1986, 1. Marshall-Green's argument was typical of Southern Baptist ministry during this period. See also Neely introduction, v–vi, or Aldredge-Clanton, *Breaking Free*, esp. chap. 9.

49. See Freeman, "Visionary Women among Early Baptists." As Curtis Freeman notes in this study of early English Baptists, General Baptists were more open to women's preaching than Particular Baptists, but nevertheless, either as prophetesses or writers, Particular Baptist women demonstrated remarkable ministries that made them central to the movement. The term "she-preacher" was used derogatorily by a seventeenth-century English Presbyterian minister to describe Mrs. Attaway, a member of a Baptist congregation who reportedly preached to crowds of a thousand. See Durso and Durso, "Baptist Women Ministers," 5.

50. McBeth, *Women in Baptist Life*, 31.

51. Other groups included Freewill Baptists, Seventh Day Baptists, and General Baptists. Primitive Baptists soon followed.

52. H. Leon McBeth refers to Separate Baptist women as preachers. Catherine A. Brekus, on the other hand, avoids this label, viewing women's speaking as exhorting, an informal type of witnessing and testifying to be distinguished from the authoritative nature of expository preaching. Brekus insists that although numerous accounts from the

period referenced young boys and male slaves as preachers, the extent to which women assumed this role remains unclear.

53. There were other reasons for their coming together: the fight for religious liberty as well as the beginnings of denominationalism.

54. In her seminal 1966 essay "The Cult of True Womanhood," Barbara Welter wrote that the "attributes of true womanhood," or Victorian womanhood, "could be divided into four cardinal virtues: piety, purity, submissiveness and domesticity" (152). Of course, the work on southern womanhood has been immense. One of the earliest scholars to explore true womanhood in its southern manifestation was Ann Firor Scott in *The Southern Lady*. Published in 1970, Scott's work deconstructed the southern belle of moonlight and magnolias by showing that even for plantation mistresses, life in the Old South was filled with toil and labor. Twelve years later, in her groundbreaking study *Within the Plantation Household*, Elizabeth Fox-Genovese then tied southern gendered constructions of women to the slave system. Other scholars built on her thesis. See Friedman, *Enclosed Garden*, and Wolfe, *Daughters of Canaan*. Later historians likewise argued about the effects of the Civil War on southern gendered codes regarding women. Catherine Clinton claimed that while elite women found the demands of war galling, they succumbed to a stoic endurance and experienced no significant shift in their beliefs and values; see Clinton, *Tara Revisited*, as well as her earlier work, *The Plantation Mistress*. In contrast to Clinton, Drew Gilpin Faust argued that the Civil War completely disrupted southern gendered assumptions of women. Attempts to reclaim old patterns afterward failed largely because women could never be the same. See Faust, *Mothers of Invention*. Faust actually followed Scott's much earlier argument that the war initiated a revolution in women's self-understandings. Scott concluded that this revolution was not readily apparent until after Reconstruction. See also Holcomb's outline of true womanhood in its southern and Southern Baptist contexts, in "Mothering the South," 57–73.

55. For a history of Southern Baptist women and missions, see Allen, *Century to Celebrate*.

56. Conservative leaders raised the issue of auxiliary status during the 1990s. See, for example, Chapter 4 at n. 102.

57. I encountered this interpretation consistently during my fieldwork and interviews with moderate women.

58. WMU Constitution, adopted May 14, 1888. For an account of this meeting, see "Organized!," *Baptist Basket*, June 1888, 100; Organizational Minutes, May 11, 1888, Hunt Library and Archives; and Allen, *Century to Celebrate*, 42–46.

59. Carol Holcomb argues that national WMU leaders adopted the social gospel and Progressive Era reform by establishing a Department of Personal Service. Holcomb explains this primarily as the influence of southern Methodist women and their social reforming efforts. See also Flowers, "Southern Baptist Evangelicals or Social Gospel Liberals?" There is much literature tying Protestant women's social reform to nineteenth-century ideas of evangelical usefulness, particularly in the Methodist church. See, for example, Hardesty, *Women Called to Witness*. Holcomb speaks of evangelical womanhood as standing between two poles, with Victorian or southern womanhood on one end and women's rights, in its more radical Seneca Falls manifestation, on the other. Together,

they represent three nineteenth- and early twentieth-century archetypes. Holcomb's outline is helpful, though I would argue for less fixed or stable points of reference.

60. Holcomb indicates that the efforts of the WMU lagged well behind those of their Methodist counterparts, while Laine Scales concludes that their goodwill centers for the urban poor often provided inculcations in traditional understandings of Victorian and southern womanhood. Allen notes that by 1927, fewer than 37 percent of local societies reported participating in personal service; see Allen, *Century to Celebrate*, 215. The more progressive rhetoric seemed to have come from a few national leaders, and most notably Fannie Heck, the WMU's president from 1892 to 1899 and again from 1906 to 1915.

61. See Patterson, Oral Memoirs, 29–34, and *Christian Century*, April 21, 1993, 424. See also "Chapman: SBC Needs Clarification from WMU," *Baptist Press*, January 11, 1993, 3, and "Rogers Is Critical of Persons Speaking for Him," *Baptist Press*, March 11, 1993, 7.

62. In 1922, almost 75 percent of Southern Baptist churches lacked regular activities for young people, and 20 percent had no Sunday school. Of the more than 2 million rural Southern Baptists, only 31 percent were enrolled in Sunday school, and a mere 20 percent attended regularly. See Flynt, "Southern Baptists," 24–25.

63. See, for example, Stricklin, *Genealogy of Dissent*.

64. Southern Baptists generally referred to the "priesthood of the believer" as opposed to the "priesthood of all believers," which did not become popular until the 1990s. Moreover, the legacy of Landmarkism, a nineteenth-century movement, also lingered in the states of the former frontier. Landmarkists exercised an extreme form of local church autonomy and shunned any denomination-wide program or venture. Not surprisingly, they staunchly opposed the WMU. For a history of the landmark movement, see Tull, *High-Church Baptists in the South*.

65. Leonard presents Southern Baptist theology as a quest for balance between competing beliefs and practices: biblical authority versus soul competency, the autonomous church versus the associational body, the priesthood of all believers versus ministerial authority, dramatic conversion versus ongoing regeneration, and religious freedom versus Christian citizenship and institutional obedience. See Leonard, *God's Last and Only Hope*, 74–98.

66. See ibid., 105–30.

67. Baptist and church historians will be well familiar with the events surrounding conservative ascendancy particularly as related to SBC agencies and seminaries. While I initially provided only a brief sketch of these episodes, directing readers to other histories of the controversy, some outside scholars asked for more details in order to better comprehend the analysis involving women.

Chapter 1

1. Durso and Durso, "'Cherish the Dream God Has Given You,'" 19. Davis's story, as told in this section, comes primarily from Durso and Durso, "'Cherish the Dream God Has Given You.'" See also Davis interview and Davis, "Called of God-Press On," Boyce Centennial Library and Archives.

2. Durso and Durso, "'Cherish the Dream God Has Given You,'" 20.

3. Ibid., 22–23.

4. Pierce, "Addie Davis, First Woman Ordained as Southern Baptist Pastor, Dies at 88," *Associated Baptist Press*, December 9, 2005.

5. "Church Ordains Woman to Pastoral Ministry," *Baptist Press*, August 12, 1964.

6. "Southern Baptists Tell Why 'Ministry Is for Men Only,'" *Detroit News*, May 24, 1966.

7. Morgan, *Southern Baptist Sisters*, 174.

8. Walter B. Shurden first used the image of synthesis to describe the SBC. It appears in much of his work, and others have utilized it as well. See Shurden, *Not an Easy Journey*.

9. Scholars of the South have debated endlessly the issue of postwar continuity and change. In 1965, the Southern Sociological Society and the Center for Southern Studies jointly published a groundbreaking collection of essays exploring the theme: McKinney and Thompson, *South in Continuity and Change*. Numerous works followed. During the early to mid-1970s, scholars emphasized continuity in change. John Shelton Reed became a leading spokesperson for this position. He argued that southern localism, southern violence, and southern religion forged a single culture. Differences between southerners and nonsoutherners persisted because these southern distinctions did not rest on tangible dissimilarities with other regions. See Reed, *Enduring South*. Charles P. Roland likewise argued the paradox of continuity in change. Roland linked the South's endurance to the stories and myths it told itself—stories of the Romantic South, the Tragic South, the Fundamentalist South, and the Benighted South. As Roland admitted, the South that spun those myths was solidly white. And the widely used term "Solid South" referred to both the white South's one-party politics and its Jim Crow segregation. See Roland, *Improbable Era*. As these systems collapsed, some scholars welcomed a newer New South. See, in particular, Lander and Calhoun, *Two Decades of Change*, and Noble and Thomas, *Rising South*.

By the 1980s and 1990s, most historians had become less optimistic. As Numan V. Bartley observed, sweeping change had occurred, but during the 1970s, a national recession hit, and the South's glory days ended. Consequently, old economic and racial problems resurfaced. See Bartley, *New South*. In *Lost Revolutions*, Pete Daniel also explored the radical potentials for change that had been squandered. Other scholars focused on the continuity of racism in reactionary politics. See Black and Black, *Politics and Society in the South*; Carter, *From George Wallace to Newt Gingrich*; and Carter, *Politics of Rage*. Some historians questioned the bedrock assumption of continuity and change: the solidity of a white South. As early as 1979, J. Wayne Flynt indicated that change had been uneven, leaving large areas of the rural South untouched and whites as well as blacks impoverished and frustrated; see Flynt, *Dixie's Forgotten People*. As scholars of both the Old and New South were discovering, ethnic, class, regional, and gender diversity were more far-reaching than earlier scholars had recognized. Moreover, the post–World War II Sunbelt generally included the Southwest, and southern prosperity depended on this new regional makeup, which in turn also brought new diversities to the states that had composed the Solid South.

As for religion, in 1967, Samuel S. Hill claimed that white evangelical Protestantism promoted the conservative status quo, thereby abetting white supremacy. The failure of white evangelical piety to address racism and its inability to sustain change underscored the crisis motif in the historiography of southern religion. See Hill, *Southern Churches in*

Crisis. Later scholars, though, questioned this motif. Beth Barton Schweiger challenged southern religious history's "preoccupation" with "establishing the South's uniqueness" (as quoted in Hill, *Southern Churches in Crisis Revisited*, xxi). See also Schweiger's contribution in "Forum: Southern Religion." David L. Chappell challenged the crisis motif as well by claiming that white supremacy did not muster the religious support needed to overcome change; see Chappell, *Stone of Hope.* Several other historians have argued that southern evangelicalism shifted its gaze from race to gender. See Dowland, "Defending Manhood"; Feldman, "Status Quo Society"; and Harvey, *Freedom's Coming.*

10. For an overview of economic change, see Wright, *Old South, New South.* Two significant works from the 1980s explored the decline of southern agriculture: Fite, *Cotton Fields No More*, and Kirby, *Rural Worlds Lost.* Studies that focused on industrialization included Cobb, *Selling of the South*, and Schulman, *From Cotton Belt to Sunbelt.* More recently, in *King Cotton*, Clayton Brown has argued that cotton culture in the postwar period was increasingly a national culture and industry and that cotton's move to the western states also created regional tensions in the Sunbelt.

11. Naylor and Clotfelter, *Strategies for Change in the South*, 223. The Bureau of the Census classifies areas with 2,500 or more residents as urban and areas with fewer than 2,500 residents as rural. See also Roland, *Improbable Era*, 23–25.

12. Ammerman, *Baptist Battles*, 54.

13. By 1970, the South's percentage of children and teenagers enrolled in public elementary and secondary day schools was nearly the same as that of the national average of 86, whereas the South's college enrollment figures, 41.7 percent of its college-age population, fell considerably below the 57.6 percent for the whole nation. See Naylor and Clotfelter, *Strategies for Change in the South*, 10, 132–33.

14. I appreciate the insight of an anonymous reviewer in making this observation.

15. Fletcher, *Southern Baptist Convention*, 196.

16. Ibid.

17. These included the Historical Commission (1947), the Southern Baptist Foundation (1947), the *Baptist Press* (1948), the Brotherhood Commission (1950), the Radio and Television Commission (1955), and the Stewardship Commission (1960).

18. See Leonard, *God's Last and Only Hope*, 58, and Hill epilogue, 206.

19. Leonard, *God's Last and Only Hope*, 2.

20. Ammerman, *Baptist Battles*, 60.

21. Ibid., 59. Others disagree, arguing that worship continued to foster differences in preaching styles and liturgical preferences.

22. Leonard, *God's Last and Only Hope*, 59.

23. Ammerman, *Baptist Battles*, 63.

24. Ibid., 62.

25. Spain, *At Ease in Zion.*

26. Ammerman, *Baptist Battles*, 62.

27. Ibid., 52; Fletcher, *Southern Baptist Convention*, 189.

28. Ammerman, *Baptist Battles*, 52; Baker, *Southern Baptist Convention and Its People*, 413; Fletcher, *Southern Baptist Convention*, 188.

29. For a history of the SBC's territorial expansion, see Ammerman, *Baptist Battles*,

50–53; Baker, *Southern Baptist Convention and Its People*, 355–88; and Fletcher, *Southern Baptist Convention*, 186–88.

30. For the debate surrounding the Americanization of the South, see Egerton, *Americanization of Dixie*; Gregory, *Southern Diaspora*; Dochuk, *From Bible Belt to Sunbelt*; and Shibley, *Resurgent Evangelicalism in the United States*. See also Introduction, n. 24.

31. For an account of the events leading to and surrounding this contest, see Wills, *Southern Baptist Theological Seminary*, 351–404. See also the insider view of McCall with Tonks, *Duke McCall*.

32. See, in particular, Ammerman, *Baptist Battles*, 64–65; Fletcher, *Southern Baptist Convention*, 205–10; Shurden, *Not an Easy Journey*, 215–26; and Shurden, *Not a Silent People*, 69–82. See also Elliott's later account of the event, *"Genesis Controversy."*

33. See, for example, the foreword to *"The Genesis Controversy,"* by Morris Ashcraft, Elliott's friend and colleague at Midwestern.

34. Elliott, *"Genesis Controversy,"* 15.

35. Ashcraft foreword, xii.

36. For a book-length study of Norris, see Hankins, *God's Rascal*.

37. Fletcher, *Southern Baptist Convention*, 142.

38. For a history of the 1963 Baptist Faith and Message and its possible interpretations, see Pool, *Sacred Mandates of Conscience*.

39. Jennings, "Southern Baptist Convention Speaks on Race, Evangelism," *Baptist Press*, June 7, 1965.

40. Jennings, "Commentary Too Liberal SBC Messengers Decide," *Baptist Press*, June 4, 1970.

41. Hill, *Southern Churches in Crisis*, 5. Hill later links the Southern Baptist battles that began in 1979 to changes during the postwar period; see Hill, "Story before the Story." So, too, do Ammerman, *Baptist Battles*, and Leonard, *God's Last and Only Hope*. See also Edward L. Queen, who supports this thesis though wrongly predicts the "eventual failure of the Fundamentalists" and a return to the "traditional position of accommodation" (*In the South the Baptists Are the Center of Gravity*, 117). See also Winston, "Southern Baptist Story." Timothy George maintains that as the South became more American, Southern Baptist conservatives made crucial links to the northern evangelical world. The Southern Baptist controversy, he argues, was part of a wider evangelical struggle. See George, "Toward an Evangelical Future." Barry Hankins makes a similar claim in *Uneasy in Babylon*.

42. The literature on civil rights is vast. For a historiographic overview, see the bibliographic essays in Chappell, *Stone of Hope*, 297–326, and Goldfield, *Black, White, and Southern*, 279–312. As for Southern Baptists, see Copeland, *Southern Baptist Convention and the Judgment of History*, 17–32; Hankins, *Uneasy in Babylon*, 240–72; Newman, *Getting Right with God*; Stricklin, *Genealogy of Dissent*, 48–81; and Willis, *All According to God's Plan*.

43. See Newman, *Getting Right with God*, 23–50.

44. Wills, *Southern Baptist Theological Seminary*, 416–17.

45. Jennings, "Southern Baptist Convention Speaks on Race, Evangelism."

46. As for the role of the WMU and missions, see Willis, *All According to God's Plan*.

47. O'Chester, "A Stand against Violence," *Baptist Press*, April 14, 1968.

48. Denominationalists also contrasted hard-line segregationists, who pulled from select Old Testament verses and argued for segregation as a divine mandate.

49. Jennings, "Southern Baptist Convention Speaks on Race, Evangelism."

50. Newman, *Getting Right with God*, 32.

51. See ibid., 29–33.

52. See n. 9 above. On Criswell, see Freeman, "'Never Had I Been So Blind.'"

53. Historians from the 1970s and 1980s generally agreed that as the metropolitan Sunbelt with its corporate interests became the South's new power center, a two-party system replaced Democratic Party dominance. See Bartley and Graham, *Southern Politics and the Second Reconstruction*; Grantham, *Life and Death of the Solid South*; and Lamis, *Two-Party South*. Later scholars questioned this interpretation, seeing a top-down Republican "southern strategy" as producing the Reagan era. As they argued, Republican Party strategists exploited a white southern backlash against ongoing civil rights legislation to create a Republican majority among white southern voters. See Aistrup, *Southern Strategy Revisited*; Applebome, *Dixie Rising*; Carter, *From George Wallace to Newt Gingrich*; and Carter, *Politics of Rage*. More recently, Brooks Flippen has explored the rise of the religious right in the Republican Party as a result of the moral and racial politics of Carter's presidency, which proved much to the dissatisfaction of the southern evangelicals who supported his election; see Flippen, *Jimmy Carter*.

54. This understanding of the 1950s nuclear family and its accompanying ideology of new domesticity comes from Chafe, *Paradox of Change*, 176, 187. See also Mintz and Kellogg, *Domestic Revolutions*, and May, *Homeward Bound*. These works set the postwar domestic ideal within cold war politics and anxieties. The paradox, says Chafe, was that the rapid development of the military industrial complex enabled the booming postwar economy and the euphemistic happy days of the 1950s.

55. Chafe, *Paradox of Change*, 181.

56. Mintz and Kellogg, *Domestic Revolutions*, 186–90.

57. DeHart, "New Feminism and the Dynamics of Social Change," 545; Mintz and Kellogg, *Domestic Revolutions*, 203. See also the essays in Meyerowitz, *Not June Cleaver*, as well as Coontz, *Strange Stirring*; Coontz, *Way We Never Were*; Degler, *At Odds*; and Stacey, *Brave New Family*.

58. Some of the more significant legislative victories included an executive order extending affirmative action to women (1967); California's "no-fault" divorce law (1969), which every state consequently adopted; Title X of the Public Health Service Act, which dealt with comprehensive family planning (1970); the joint congressional resolution establishing "Women's Equality Day" (1971); Title IX of the Education Amendments of 1972; the Women's Educational Equity Act (1975); the Equal Credit Opportunity Act (1974); and the Pregnancy Discrimination Act (1978).

59. See Roth, *Separate Roads to Feminism*.

60. See Echols, *Daring to Be Bad*.

61. Braude introduction.

62. Daly, *The Church and the Second Sex*; Daly *Beyond God the Father*. As early as 1960, Valerie Saiving argued that theology had been conceived through a male lens, virtually ignoring women's experience; see Saiving, "Human Situation." Her thesis, as revolution-

ary for the period, made *Time* magazine. During the 1970s, several women scholars rein-terpreted traditional theology by reading the Bible and church history through a female lens. Phyllis Trible, for example, emphasized biblical texts that celebrated women's gifts and reclaimed women in the Hebrew scriptures that biblical scholars had ignored; see Trible, *God and the Rhetoric of Sexuality*. Letty M. Russell and Rosemary Radford Ru-ether applied the biblical principle of liberation to those texts and traditions perpetuating sexism and patriarchy. Both have been prolific scholars. Earlier works by Russell included *Human Liberation in a Feminist Perspective* and *The Liberating Word*. Texts by Ruether included *Mary, the Feminine Face of the Church* and *New Woman, New Earth*. Finally, in the early 1980s, Elisabeth Schussler-Fiorenza highlighted the early church as a place of freedom and egalitarianism for women; see Schussler-Fiorenza, *In Memory of Her*. These works eventually influenced Southern Baptist women who were profeminist and lobbied for women's ordination.

63. Chaves, *Ordaining Women*, 64–83.

64. There is debate about the extent of openness in Wesleyan holiness and Pentecostal traditions. Letha Scanzoni and Nancy Hardesty first argued in 1974 that the churches and denominations associated with these traditions were far more willing to ordain women; see Scanzoni and Hardesty, *All We're Meant to Be*. Donald W. Dayton and Lucille Sider Dayton concurred; see Dayton and Dayton, "'Your Daughters Shall Prophesy'?" and "Women as Preachers: Evangelical Precedents," *Christianity Today*, May 23, 1975. Grant Wacker, however, has more recently held that the record was more mixed than the Day-tons, Scanzoni, Hardesty, and others recognized. While several high-profile women like Amy Semple McPherson or Katherine Kuhlman seemed to have experienced few limita-tions, the vast majority of women in these traditions found their voices to be squelched. Women's leadership and power in holiness and Pentecostal circles proved more an excep-tion to the norm and, after a brief period in their development, a short-lived phenom-enon. See Wacker, *Heaven Below*, 158–76.

65. Hunt, *Reflections from Alma Hunt*, 96. Later, Hunt did make known her opposition to the conservative movement, particularly its tenet of gracious submission.

66. Holcomb, "Mothering the South."

67. See Allen, *Century to Celebrate*, 153–55, 159, 280–82.

68. Mimicking the popular domestic magazines of the day, *Royal Service* also ran a se-ries during 1974 on Alma Hunt's "favorite things." The series highlighted Hunt's furniture style, china, and jewelry as heirlooms from her global mission travels now decorating her apartment.

69. Allen, *Century to Celebrate*, 340.

70. Ibid., 339–40.

71. Ibid.

72. "Church Withdraws Ordination from Baptist Woman Minister," *Baptist Press*, July 26, 1972. There is some discrepancy over the date of her ordination. While *Baptist Press* places it in October, most sources cite August. An article by Carter herself cites August 22, 1971. See Carter, "Woman's Self-Affirmation in the Ministry," 45.

73. Addie Davis, "A Dream to Cherish," *FOLIO*, Autumn 1985, 1, 8.

Chapter 2

1. "Non-Controversial Convention Predicted for Portland SBC," *Baptist Press*, May 24, 1973.

2. "Editorials Describe SBC as 'Rosy,' 'Harmonious,'" *Baptist Press*, June 26, 1973.

3. Southern Baptist Convention, Thursday morning session, June 13, 1973, SBHLA; Sappington, *From My Point of View*, 30, 34.

4. Resolution No. 12. Of course, as the debate demonstrates, the biblical text was not as explicit on the matter as conservatives like Sappington assumed. For a more detailed analysis of inerrancy, particularly as Southern Baptist conservatives understood it, see the section on this concept in Chapter 3.

5. Southern Baptist Convention, Thursday morning session, June 13, 1973, SBHLA.

6. See, for example, "Editorials Describe SBC as 'Rosy,' 'Harmonious,'" *Baptist Press*, June 26, 1973.

7. See Dowland, "'Family Values' and the Formation of a Christian Right Agenda," 3. Dowland cites a 1974 editorial in *Christianity Today* endorsing the ERA. The survey came from the same issue.

8. For a history of evangelical feminism, see Cochran, *Evangelical Feminism*.

9. Evangelical feminists with Wesleyan backgrounds tended to stress that non-egalitarian passages had to be read within their cultural context. They claimed that Christ had created a new order and that gospel liberation superseded Genesis and Pauline patterns of order. See, first, Scanzoni and Hardesty, *All We're Meant to Be*, as well as Dayton and Dayton, "The Bible among Evangelicals." Those from more Reformed traditions emphasized that Paul was too often misread and mistranslated. They argued that the widely accepted notion of male headship stemmed from a flawed interpretation of the Greek for head in 1 Corinthians 11:1–10 and Ephesians 5:21–24. See Gundry, *Women Be Free*; Kroeger, "Ancient Heresies and a Strange Greek Verb"; and Kroeger and Kroeger, "Pandemonium and Silence at Corinth" and "Sexual Identity in Corinth." Catherine Clark Kroeger served as director of the Evangelical Women's Caucus. When in 1987 the caucus adopted a resolution supporting homosexuality, she founded Christians for Biblical Equality. Profeminists among Southern Baptists eventually drew their arguments from evangelical feminists on both the Wesleyan and Reformed sides.

10. Dowland, "'Family Values' and the Formation of a Christian Right Agenda," 619.

11. Morgan, *Total Woman*, 69–70.

12. Again, see Dowland, "'Family Values' and the Formation of a Christian Right Agenda," 607.

13. For a history of evangelical women's involvement in the political far right, see Brown, *For a Christian America*.

14. Note the subtitle of Bryant's autobiography from this period: *The Anita Bryant Story: The Survival of Our Nation's Families and the Threat of Militant Homosexuality*.

15. See Dobson's work from this period: *Dare to Discipline, Prescriptions for a Tired Housewife*, and *What Wives Wish Their Husbands Knew about Women*.

16. This information comes from my ethnographic work and interviews with conservative Southern Baptist women. Numerous women's ministry leaders cited O'Chester as the major influence in their understanding of womanhood and development of a wom-

en's ministry to women church program. O'Chester has also received several awards for her retreat ministry, which, by the 1990s, boasted 20,000 women per year at her church alone.

17. Crumpler interview. Carolyn Weatherford changed her name to Carolyn Weatherford Crumpler when she married in 1989.

18. "Women Ordained," Christian Life Commission Resource Files, SBHLA.

19. Crumpler interview.

20. "Recommendation No. 1."

21. *Annual of the Southern Baptist Convention, Nineteen Hundred and Seventy-Four*, 68–69, 72 73.

22. Ibid., 62, 72.

23. "Editorials Measure Dallas Convention," *Baptist Press*, July 2, 1974. Not surprisingly, Sappington's resolution "Unisex and the Scriptures" remained in the committee on resolutions. See *Annual of the Southern Baptist Convention, Nineteen Hundred and Seventy-Four*, 63.

24. "Editorials Measure Dallas Convention."

25. Ibid.

26. Hollis preface.

27. Floyd Craig, "Wrap-up: Conferees Determined to Raise Consciousness on Women," *Baptist Press*, August 9, 1974, 2.

28. "SBC Action on Women Called Painful but Beneficial," *Baptist Press*, August 5, 1974.

29. Program Committee member Alan Neely, also a Southeastern professor, wrote Program Committee chair Bobbie Sorrill, a WMU executive, that "during most of the sessions a man is presiding." He offered to "step aside and let a woman preside" during his assigned session. Sorrill apparently accepted his offer, and the committee replaced the men with women. Neely also indicated that he had returned from a Fuller Seminary consultation titled "Women and the Ministries of Christ" and requested that he share "an enormous amount of material" with Sorrill. Evangelical feminism flourished at Fuller, and Neely's letter revealed the wider evangelical influences on Southern Baptist life. See Neely, letter to Sorrill, Consultation on Women Collection, SBHLA.

30. Johnson, "Consultation on Women in Church-Related Vocations," in *Findings of the Consultation on Women*, Consultation on Women Collection, SBHLA, 3.

31. Allen, "Background Information," Consultation on Women Collection, SBHLA, 2–3. A handwritten note on the otherwise typed page marked the date as September 25, 1978—three days after the consultation ended. The note also directed Allen's piece to Southern Baptist state newspapers. Most state newspapers, however, ran the summary by Johnni Johnson, the consultation's publicity chair. See Johnson, "Consultation on Women in Church-Related Vocations," in *Findings of the Consultation on Women*, Consultation on Women Collection, SBHLA.

32. Shurden, "Analysis of the Images of Women," in *Findings of the Consultation on Women*, Consultation on Women Collection, SBHLA, 53.

33. The concept of call in twentieth-century Southern Baptist life was second in significance to salvation only and part of the Southern Baptist emphasis on personal piety. If Southern Baptists agreed on anything, it was that God had a plan or path for each

individual to follow over the course of his or her life. Much of the literature directed at children, youth, and young adults in the postwar period emphasized discerning this path, which included momentous life decisions such as choosing a spouse. The specific language of call, however, was most often reserved for those who felt God's stirring in the direction of vocational ministry or a career in missions. For a Southern Baptist girl or woman who heard or felt a call from God, this usually predicted that she would serve as a missionary or a pastor's wife.

34. Weaver-Williams, "My Call," in *Findings of the Consultation on Women*, Consultation on Women Collection, SBHLA, 24.

35. Honeycutt, "Response," in *Findings of the Consultation on Women*, Consultation on Women Collection, SBHLA, 31.

36. "Responses from the Audience," in *Findings of the Consultation on Women*, Consultation on Women Collection, SBHLA, 33.

37. Ibid.

38. "Serving God Is Not a Matter of Gender," *Birmingham News*, September 30, 1978, 21.

39. Allen, " . . . and She Arose, and Ministered," in *Findings of the Consultation on Women*, Consultation on Women Collection, SBHLA, 43.

40. Ibid., 44.

41. Ibid., 45.

Chapter 3

1. Nancy Sehested, "We Have This Treasure," in *Proceedings of the 1983 Conference*, Women in Baptist Life Collection, SBHLA, 11.

2. Primer interview.

3. "Baptists Ready for Man-Wife Copastors," *Birmingham News*, September 30, 1978, 24.

4. Robison, "Satan's Subtle Attacks," 29.

5. For a more extended analysis of key differences, see the section titled "Southern Baptists, Evangelicals, and Sectarian America" in the Introduction.

6. Ironically, Separate Baptists were more open than Regular Baptists to women's full participation and authority in worship services, revival meetings, and general ecclesial life.

7. When Rogers retired in 2005, Bellevue's membership had reached 30,000.

8. As recorded in Hefley, *Conservative Resurgence*, 32.

9. Lindsell, *Battle for the Bible*, 104.

10. Carl L. Kell and L. Raymond Camp consider conservative preachers' mastery of the rhetoric of inerrancy; see Kell and Camp, *In the Name of the Father*. For a critical analysis of the hermeneutical concept behind the various terms, see Noll, *Between Faith and Criticism*. For an analysis of the concept as understood in Southern Baptist life, see Barnhart, "What's All the Fighting About?," and James and Dockery, *Beyond the Impasse*.

11. Resolution No. 16. They also passed Resolution No. 21: "On Women," which reaffirmed the equal worth of men and women but insisted that equal worth did not mean sameness, thus resolving that the SBC did not endorse the ERA. A resolution on wom-

en's ordination, however, was tabled as a local church matter. See *Annual of the Southern Baptist Convention, Nineteen Hundred and Eighty*, 53–56.

12. Kell and Camp, *In the Name of the Father*, 40.

13. Ammerman, *Baptist Battles*, 74–76. Clark Pinnock, once a staunch conservative who taught at New Orleans Baptist Seminary in the 1960s, suggested that the debate was "not between inerrancy and non-inerrancy but between an elaborate, structured view of inerrancy versus a simpler, experienced-based view" and thus encouraged moderates to claim the title. See Marv Knox, "Scholars Appraise Facets of Inerrancy," *Baptist Press*, May 8, 1987. In "What's All the Fighting About?," Joe E. Barnhart claims that it is more accurate to speak of Southern Baptist conservatives as supporting special revelation over general revelation. Special revelation held that God dictated the scriptures as a self-contained epistemological whole, while general revelation maintained that God revealed the Divine in multiple ways throughout history and nature. According to general revelation, extrabiblical sources were valid truths in understanding God's purposes, and historical, scientific, and critical factors were necessary tools in interpreting the Bible's essential truths. See Barnhart, "What's All the Fighting About?," 124–27.

14. Kell and Camp, *In the Name of the Father*, 52.

15. Sutton, *Baptist Reformation*, 83.

16. Kell and Camp, *In the Name of the Father*, 52.

17. See, for instance, Vestal interview.

18. Community Bible Study and Bible Study Fellowship were highly popular among many Southern Baptist women.

19. Maddox interview.

20. Information on the conference comes primarily from program material, Mid-Continent Women's Concerns Conference, Office of Women's Ministry, Bellevue Baptist Church, as well as Hawkins interview, Maddox interview, and "Beginnings of Women's Ministries," Rogers Papers.

21. "Beginnings of Women's Ministries," Rogers Papers.

22. Hawkins interview.

23. Rogers, *Wise Woman*, 77–78.

24. Ibid., 159–60.

25. Cecelia Wright, "Conference to Emphasize Bible's Role for Women," *Memphis Press-Scimitar*, April 26, 1980.

26. The quotation comes from a typed summary of Weatherford letter, Hunt Library and Archives. Weatherford changed her name to Carolyn Weatherford Crumpler when she married. More than twenty-five years after the 1980 conference, Crumpler contrasted it with the 1978 consultation, saying of the consultation that "those attending were primarily those who were 'women in church-related vocations.' . . . The 1980 conference was completely different. Those attending it were 'women in the church'—lay women—some WMU-ers among them, of course" (Crumpler interview). It is difficult to determine other demographic differences between women in the two groups. Both reflected the largely white, middle-class status of postwar Southern Baptists. Many of the women attending the 1978 consultation were seminary educated. While Rogers and Maddox did not hold seminary degrees, they were college graduates.

27. Early programs in women's ministry included First Baptist Church, Dallas; First

Baptist Church, Ft. Lauderdale; First Baptist Church, Merrit Island, Florida; Great Hills Baptist Church, Austin; Prestonwood Baptist Church, Plano, Texas; Second Baptist Church, Houston; and Two Rivers Baptist Church, Nashville.

28. Hawkins interview. Information regarding the development of women's ministry comes primarily from interviews with Hawkins and Maddox as well as conversations with conservative women that took place during my ethnographic participation in women's ministry. Many of these women had been active in women's ministry since its inception and easily recalled, mostly with great enthusiasm, its early days. Other interviews that were sources of information included those with Denise George and Linda Gregory. Both George and Gregory served on the 1992 SBC task force on women's ministry chaired by Hawkins and Maddox. See also "Beginnings of Women's Ministries," Rogers Papers.

29. Adrian Rogers, "Welcome to the Women's Concerns Conference," *Bellevue Messenger*, May 16, 1980, 1.

30. Robison, "Satan's Subtle Attacks," 29.

31. Sherman, "Overview of the Moderate Movement," 17.

32. See Sherman interview, 2. Sherman clarified that he viewed the descriptor as more appropriate to the preceding generation of Herschel Hobbs and Duke McCall. Others, conservative leaders as well as advocates of women in ministry, saw Sherman and his peers as part of the good old boy network, or at least groomed to continue its legacy.

33. Some, who wanted to assert themselves as theologically conservative, still preferred names like "loyalist" or "traditionalist." Seeing the struggle more in terms of institutional politics, they called themselves "Southern Baptists Committed." For the most part, though, the label "moderate" prevailed.

34. "News Story," 56.

35. Sherman interview, 3.

36. Dilday interview, 11.

37. Ibid. See also Cothen interview. In his interview (p. 11), Dilday stated that under his leadership, Southwestern Seminary had used the Chicago Conference on Inerrancy as a model for a similar retreat at Ridgecrest, in which they had invited many of the Chicago participants and leaders to meet and engage in a dialogue with Southwestern professors. Besides the Dilday and Cothen interviews, see also the interviews of Bennett, Fields, Honeycutt, Lolley, Parks, and Sherman. Throughout their interviews, these key moderate leaders asserted theological conservatism, even inerrancy, as the basic position of not only most Southern Baptists but themselves as well. Lolley stated he refused to use the word "inerrancy" in application to his own view primarily because it had become "tainted" by political machinations; see Lolley interview, 7. Again the term "inerrancy" remained slippery, and during the 1980s some accused Southern Baptist conservatives of applying it in ways that were inconsistent with its usage in the wider Protestant evangelical world.

38. Hinson, "Background to the Moderate Movement," 2.

39. Shurden, *Baptist Identity*. See also Leonard's analysis of the quest for balance in Southern Baptist belief and practice, in *God's Last and Only Hope*, 75–99.

40. Sherman, "Overview of the Moderate Movement," 39.

41. See Allen, "History of Baptists Committed"; Sherman, "Overview of the Moderate Movement"; Shurden, "Struggle for the Soul of the SBC"; and Slatton, "History of

the Political Network of the Moderate Movement." As some women later noted, their invisibility was particularly puzzling because many prominent moderates had attended the Consultation on Women in Church-Related Vocations. Denominational loyalists who were present pledged to support women in their search for ecclesial equality. Sherman had supported the 1974 "Freedom for Women" report, which included a bylaw stipulating one-fifth of all SBC-appointed board members, trustees, commissioners, and standing committee members be women. During his SBC presidency, Jimmy Allen publicly affirmed women's ordination and leadership, though he also argued that ordination had become overplayed in Southern Baptist life.

42. Sherman, "Overview of the Moderate Movement," 44.

43. Shortly after the 1978 Consultation on Women in Church-Related Vocations, Helen Lee Turner, an ordained pastor and University of Virginia doctoral student, began the newsletter *Called and Committed* as a resource for Southern Baptist women pursuing ordained ministry. Turner had never attended a Southern Baptist college or seminary and so was somewhat removed from denominational structures. The newsletter's location, first in Bristol and then in Charlottesville, added to its isolation. The venture folded after a year. Still, both the consultation and the newsletter identified the growing number of Southern Baptist women struggling in their call. Several issues of *Called and Committed* can be found in the Women in Baptist Life Collection, SBHLA.

44. Information regarding the dinner comes from program materials, Dinner for Women in Ministry, Women in Baptist Life Collection, SBHLA.

45. Anders, "Women in Ministry," Women in Baptist Life Collection, SBHLA.

46. Turner interview.

47. "Women in Ministry: Report from the Working Group," 14.

48. Information regarding the conference comes from minutes, Conference for Women in Ministry, SBC, Cobb Papers, and *Proceedings of the 1983 Conference*, Women in Baptist Life Collection, SBHLA. For a brief history of SBWIM's founding, see Betty McGary Pearce, "History of Women in Ministry, SBC," *FOLIO*, Summer 1985, 9.

49. Minutes, Conference for Women in Ministry, SBC, Cobb Papers.

50. Primer interview.

51. Interviews, again conducted through written and e-mail correspondence, from SBWIM's early founders, steering committee members, and participants included those with Sarah Frances Anders, Elizabeth S. Bellinger, Reba S. Cobb, Carolyn W [Weatherford] Crumpler, Diane Eubanks Hill, Marilyn A. Mayse, Helen Lee Turner, and Lynda Weaver-Williams. Anne Thomas Neil participated in a telephone interview. Crumpler's interview concentrated more on the WMU. SBWIM leaders from the 1990s also commented on the organization's founding and early years: Linda Hood Hicks, Karrie Oertli, and Terry Thomas Primer.

52. Mayse interview.

53. Weaver-Williams interview.

54. Molly Marshall-Green, "Women in Ministry: A Biblical Theology," *FOLIO*, Fall 1983, 1.

55. Mayse interview.

56. McGary memoirs, 47. Betty McGary Pearce dropped her married surname after she divorced.

57. Bellinger memoirs, 149–50.

58. Like other conservative and moderates, during the 1980s, they spoke of the priesthood of the believer. Later, they more readily referred to the priesthood of all believers.

59. Griffis-Woodberry, "Women in Ministry," in *Proceedings of the 1983 Conference*, Women in Baptist Life Collection, SBHLA, 6.

60. Weaver-Williams interview.

61. Nancy Sehested, "Guest Editorial," *FOLIO*, Summer 1983, 2.

62. Neil, "Servant Model," in *Proceedings of the 1983 Conference*, Women in Baptist Life Collection, SBHLA.

63. See, for example, McGary memoirs.

Chapter 4

1. James H. Cox, "Draper Reviews Presidency as Final Term Concluded," *Baptist Press*, March 2, 1984.

2. Henry belonged to Capitol Hill Baptist Church in Washington, D.C. Henry resided, however, in California. Like Billy Graham, who lived in North Carolina and held membership at First Baptist, Dallas, Henry's primary affiliations and activities fell outside denominational church life and within parachurch organizations.

3. Some scholars have seen Henry as remaining more neutral when it came to the religious right and its rhetoric regarding women. As one anonymous reviewer put it, Henry's role in the 1984 convention at least suggests that he was not as "above the fray" as might have been perceived. The denominational context allowed him to assume a brief but particularly prominent role and "then step back behind the curtain."

4. Resolution No. 3.

5. Southern Baptist Convention, Thursday morning session, June 14, 1984, SBHLA.

6. Linda Lawson, "Resolutions Cover Range of Issues," *Baptist Press*, June 14, 1984.

7. James H. Cox, "Draper Reviews Presidency as Final Term Concluded," *Baptist Press*, March 2, 1984.

8. See Chapter 1, n. 53, on the debate concerning the Republican Party's southern strategy.

9. Resolution No. 5.

10. William Reed, "Baptist Subjugation of Women Old Hat," *Tennessean*, July 1, 1984.

11. Barry Hankins likewise makes this argument in his study of Southern Baptist conservatives. See Hankins, *Uneasy in Babylon*.

12. Molly Marshall-Green, "Women in Ministry: A Biblical Theology," *FOLIO*, Fall 1983, 1. For a more in-depth analysis of Marshall-Green's theology of women in ministry, see the relevant sections in Chapters 3 and 5 on a Baptist theology of women in ministry.

13. Resolution No. 3.

14. References to the "Danvers Statement" come from Piper and Grudem, *Recovering Biblical Manhood and Womanhood*.

15. Randall Lolley, "Southeastern Seminary," *FOLIO*, Autumn 1984, 7.

16. Bill Leonard, "Forgiving Eve," *Christian Century*, November 7, 1984, 1039.

17. Following other evangelical feminists, they argued that rather than meaning authority or ruler, the Greek word indicated source or origin. See *FOLIO*, Autumn 1984.

18. For an overview of the Peace Committee, see Morgan, *New Crusades*, 74–82.

19. Ibid., 75.

20. See "Report of the Peace Committee."

21. Sherman, "Overview of the Moderate Movement," 41–42.

22. Surveys from this period included Price, "Survey of Southern Baptist Attitudes," Women in Baptist Life Collection, SBHLA. According to an article in *Baptist Press*, Price's initial findings matched two earlier surveys from 1970 and 1975, though the 1975 survey was somewhat more open to women in nontraditional roles. See Judy Touchton, "Women Ordination Favored for Non-Pastoral Roles," *Baptist Press*, November 2, 1977.

23. "Debate Continues but Women in Ministry Report Progress," *FOLIO*, Summer 1986, 8.

24. Ammerman, *Baptist Battles*, 96.

25. See Wills, *Democratic Religion*, 98–115. His study focuses primarily on Georgia.

26. Covering the years from 1945 to 1995, the online archives of the *Baptist Press* do not list "disfellowship" as a title heading until 1975, with most entries coming in 1984 and afterward. See http://www.sbhla.org/bp_archive/index.asp (July 27, 2011).

27. "Women Making News," *FOLIO*, Spring 1985, 5.

28. "Virginia Baptists Approve Ordination of Women: Reactions to Resolution Continue," *FOLIO*, Winter 1985, 3. See also Deweese, *Women Deacons and Deaconesses*, 33–40. *FOLIO* and *Baptist Press* regularly covered these incidents.

29. Although the Credentials Committee actually recommended delaying action against Prescott, messengers rejected the committee's guidelines. See "Association to Investigate Church," *Baptist and Reflector*, September 30, 1987, 6; "Briefs," *FOLIO*, Winter 1987, 7; and "Prescott Memorial Baptist Church, Memphis, Calls Nancy Hastings Sehested as Pastor," *FOLIO*, Fall 1987, 5. The Home Mission Board also withdrew its support from the Eleventh National Workshop on Christian-Jewish Relations because of Sehested's participation. According to the board, Southern Baptists on the program were not "representative." And Sehested, it stated, stood at the "center of a raging controversy within the SBC." See Nancy Sehested, "An Open Letter the Home Mission Board of the Southern Baptist Convention," *FOLIO*, Summer 1989, 1.

30. Sehested interview, 3–4.

31. Ibid., 5. Sehested left Prescott after eight years for a chaplaincy position near Asheville, North Carolina.

32. According to the sociologist and SBWIM participant Sarah Frances Anders, the "amount of publicity given to the Ardmore and Memphis churches' disfellowshipment seemed to minimize later attention to others" (Anders interview).

33. Anders reports that in 1997, roughly 25 percent of ordained Southern Baptist women served as chaplains. At the time, Sarah Frances Anders served as a sociologist at Louisiana College, a Southern Baptist school. By all accounts, well into the 1990s, she was the only scholar collecting firsthand data on Southern Baptist women's ordinations and placements. As late as 2005, the largest number of ordained women serving on church staffs in moderate congregations were preschool or children's ministers, representing 31 percent or nearly one-third of those surveyed in Campbell-Reed and Durso, *State of Women, 2005.* The next two categories were music minister and youth minister.

34. Henlee Barnette, as he appears in *Battle for the Minds*. Barnette was a professor in

Christian ethics at Southern Seminary, beginning his tenure there in 1951. He was also the mentor of several women seminarians active in founding SBWIM, including Lynda Weaver-Williams.

35. *Student*, February 1985.

36. Ammerman gives a brief account of this affair in *Baptist Battles*, 93.

37. Ibid.

38. For a more thorough account, see Morgan, *New Crusades*, 115–17.

39. One of conservatives' immediate acts was to revoke support for the Christian Life Commission's *Issues and Answers*, a pamphlet series that reflected progressive views in numerous areas, including the environment, biomedical ethics, and public education. One of the most controversial pamphlets was titled *Changing Roles for Women*, which cited leading evangelical feminists and referred back to the commission's 1973 publication *Christian Freedom for Women*. It insisted that Christ had liberated women to move beyond homemaking and pursue their gifts and talents. It urged readers to examine their church structures to see if "positions of power and decision-making" were "open to both men and women" and to make all family members "equally subject to each other" (*Issues and Answers*, 8). See also Libby S. Bellinger, "An Open Letter to the Christian Life Commission," *FOLIO*, Winter 1987, 2.

40. The incident was widely reported. For summaries, see *FOLIO*, Autumn 1985 and Winter 1986. Ammerman also reports the McGhee incident in *Baptist Battles*, 95.

41. Ammerman, *Baptist Battles*, 226–30.

42. See *Annual of the Southern Baptist Convention, Nineteen Hundred and Eighty-One*, 95.

43. See Bob Stanley, "FMB Dismisses Willett for 'Doctrinal Ambiguity,'" *Baptist Press*, July 22, 1988. Morgan gives a fairly detailed account of this event in *New Crusades*, 125–26.

44. "Oklahoma Candidates Rejected over Ordination," *Baptist Messenger*, July 6, 1989, 5. The Willett and Pennington incidents were widely publicized. See also "Women's Ordination Underlying Issue in Rejection of Oklahoma Couple by FMB," *FOLIO*, Autumn 1989, 1.

45. Morgan, *New Crusades*, 126.

46. "FMB Appoints Ordained Woman," *FOLIO*, Winter 1989, 1, 7; Robert O'Brien, "FMB Votes East Europe Aid, Appoints Ordained Woman," *Baptist Press*, December 14, 1989.

47. Both the Home Mission Board and the Foreign Mission Board later made exceptions for women serving in certain chaplain capacities. Conservative churches ordained them specifically as chaplains, not church ministers.

48. See Allen, "Shifting Sands for Southern Baptist Women in Missions."

49. Ibid., 124.

50. For a history of the seminary, see Wills, *Southern Baptist Theological Seminary*.

51. In 1983, Southern had 2,543 students to Southeastern's 1,092. Southwestern reported 4,337. As for other seminaries, New Orleans had about 1,390, and Golden Gate had 789, with Midwestern trailing at 573. In 1992, enrollment had dropped significantly in what had been considered the three major seminaries. Southwestern, still the largest, reported 3,364 students; Southern, 1,917; and Southeastern, only 628. Midwestern was down

to 472. Golden Gate increased slightly to 859 students, and New Orleans, home to many conservative leaders, reported remarkable growth, almost tripling with 3,311 students. This dramatic rise was largely attributed to New Orleans Seminary's eight extension campuses, with their part-time students. The number of students was reported each year to the convention and can be found in the corresponding *Annual Report*. So, too, can the number of trustees.

52. See Chapter 1 at n. 31.

53. Hill, "Story before the Story," 38–39.

54. "Debate Continues but Women in Ministry Report Progress," *FOLIO*, Summer 1986, 8. Approximately 11 percent attended non–Southern Baptist seminaries, and 4 percent attended no seminary at all.

55. Morgan, *New Crusades*, 141.

56. "Women as Full Partners," *FOLIO*, Summer 1985, 4.

57. Lolley interview, 120.

58. "Southeastern Board Elects First Woman Theology Prof," *Baptist Press*, March 13, 1987.

59. Ammerman, *Baptist Battles*, 249. Ammerman provides a brief overview of the affair, on 249–51. Also see Cothen, *What Happened to the Southern Baptist Convention?*, 279–95. Lolley provides his own side of the story in his interview.

60. Lolley interview, 22.

61. "Briefs," *FOLIO*, Winter 1987, 7.

62. See "New Administration Closes Southeastern's Women's Center," *FOLIO*, Winter 1988, 12.

63. See *Faith and Mission* 14, no. 1 (1996). The Southeastern-based journal devoted its fall 1996 issue to the history and theology of the seminary's women's studies program. Articles of particular interest are Jobes, "For Such a Time as This"; Kassian, "The Challenge of Feminism"; Kostenberger, "'The Crux of the Matter'"; and Patterson, "A Biblically Based Women's Studies Program."

64. Shaw, *God Speaks to Us, Too*, 159.

65. Ibid., 160.

66. For an examination of the accommodating route that Honeycutt took, see Hull, *Seminary in Crisis*. William E. Hull, a moderate and former provost of Southern, contrasts the "idealist" personality of Honeycutt with his more "realist" predecessor Duke McCall. Hull holds that McCall's experience and style of leadership could have enabled Southern's independence from the SBC and thus prevented moderates' loss of control over the seminary.

67. See Hankins, *Uneasy in Babylon*, 77.

68. Ibid., 96.

69. Honeycutt memoirs, 7.

70. Ibid., 8.

71. Ibid., 28. No other source verifies Honeycutt's claim, but his assumption demonstrates the extent to which moderates felt betrayed by both Al and Mary Mohler—and might have later exaggerated their former progressivism.

72. Ibid., 8.

73. Mohler memoirs, 15–16.

74. Ibid., 8, 12–13, 17, 30.

75. Ibid., 8. For Mohler's understanding of the relationship between the church and American culture, see Mohler, *Culture Shift*.

76. Despite some rumors to the contrary, Marshall did not divorce her husband, the family practitioner Douglass Green. She simply reverted back to her maiden name, as she had not changed it legally.

77. See "Marshall Leaves SBTS," *FOLIO*, Winter 1995, 1, 5. Other targeted professors had departed already. In 1991, Bill Leonard became chair of the undergraduate religion department at Samford University, a Southern Baptist college in Birmingham. A year later, Glenn Hinson went to the newly established and decidedly moderate Baptist Theological Seminary in Richmond. Both Leonard and Hinson had been outspoken in their support of women's ordination. Neither, then, was on faculty when the debacle broke out.

78. Mohler memoirs, 37.

79. See Hankins, *Uneasy in Babylon*, 82–94; Ingersoll, *Evangelical Christian Women*, 47–60; Wills, *Southern Baptist Theological Seminary*, 519–43.

80. See Mohler memoirs, 34–36.

81. Mohler claimed that he asked for Garland's resignation and Garland accepted. Garland maintained that she never acquiesced to his demand and was fired. As Hankins acknowledges, a forced resignation is akin to a firing.

82. *Battle for the Minds*. Lipscomb filmed the documentary during that spring 1994 and was present for the events of Black Wednesday. He was also there to visit his mother, a student at Southern, who had told him about the brewing tensions.

83. For faculty recollections of the account, see Newman memoirs, 12–13, and Gushee memoirs, 11–12.

84. Richard D. White, "What's Really Going on at Southern Seminary?," *Western Recorder*, April 18, 1995, 6. See also White's appearance in the documentary *Battle for the Minds*.

85. Newman memoirs, 20.

86. Mohler memoirs, 45.

87. In 1989, the number stood at 11 percent. See Sarah Frances Anders, "Has a Generation Really Passed?," *FOLIO*, Summer 1989, 5.

88. For this background information on Dorothy Patterson, see Patterson memoirs. Hankins and many others have likewise made the observation that with her education and background, Dorothy did not seem the candidate to promote homemaking and submission. In fact, moderate women often showed surprise when they learned of her credentials. Several with whom I spoke had assumed her degrees were honorary.

89. See Clanton, "Why I Believe Southern Baptists Should Ordain Women," and Patterson, "Why I Believe Southern Baptist Churches Should Not Ordain Women," Women in Baptist Life Collection, SBHLA. Edited versions of the papers can also be found in *Baptist History and Heritage* 23 (July 1998). The Southern Baptist Historical Library and Archives also holds a video of the debate. For additional analysis of the papers, see Hankins, *Uneasy in Babylon*, 205–13.

90. Patterson, "Why I Believe Southern Baptist Churches Should Not Ordain Women," Women in Baptist Life Collection, SBHLA, 2–3.

91. Ibid., 6–8.

92. Ibid., 7–8.

93. Patterson more briefly exegeted I Corinthians 14:33–35.

94. Clanton, "Why I Believe Southern Baptists Should Ordain Women," Women in Baptist Life Collection, SBHLA, 8.

95. Patterson, "Why I Believe Southern Baptist Churches Should Not Ordain Women," Women in Baptist Life Collection, SBHLA, 10–11.

96. Ibid., 12–13.

97. Ibid., 14.

98. Hankins, *Uneasy in Babylon*, 212. Hankins describes the atmosphere of the meeting as good-natured.

99. O'Brien interview. O'Brien served as WMU executive director from 1989 to 1999. Other interviews with WMU women again conducted through written and e-mail correspondence included Carolyn W [Weatherford] Crumpler (executive director, 1974–89); Barbara Massey (WMU editor, 1979–2002); Carolyn D. Miller (WMU president, 1991–96); and Carol Richardson (WMU executive committee, 1995–98). Unless otherwise indicated, information regarding the WMU during this period comes largely from these interviews as well as WMU surveys.

100. Patterson memoirs, 31.

101. *Christian Century*, April 21, 1993, 424. See also "Rogers Is Critical of Persons Speaking for Him," *Baptist Press*, March 11, 1993, 7.

102. *Christian Century*, February 17, 1993, 168. See also "Chapman: SBC Needs Clarification from WMU," *Baptist Press*, January 11, 1993, 3.

103. Both Barry Hankins and Emmanuel McCall place the SBC's 1995 resolution on racial reconciliation in this wider context. See Hankins, *Uneasy in Babylon*, 245, and McCall, *When All God's Children Get Together*, 128.

104. Kevin A. Miller, "NBEA Hears Promise Keepers' Message," *Christianity Today*, June 19, 1995. For a scholarly analysis, see Wadsworth, "Reconciliation Politics."

105. For a description of the convention events, see Hankins, *Uneasy in Babylon*, 246–47; McCall, *When All God's Children Get Together*, 135–36; and Newman, *Getting Right with God*, 201–4.

106. Resolution No. 1.

107. See McCall, *When All God's Children Get Together*, 136–37.

108. For a history of the reception of the resolution, see Hankins, *Uneasy in Babylon*, 248–55.

109. Ibid., 249.

110. Ibid., 248.

111. Michael Dabney, "Southern Baptist Church Apologizes to Blacks for Its Historic Role in Slavery," *Philadelphia Tribune*, July 21, 1995.

112. Timothy C. Morgan, "Southern Baptists Racist No More? Black Leaders Ask," *Christianity Today*, August 1, 1995.

113. Hankins, *Uneasy in Babylon*, 245–46.

114. Ibid., 246.

115. Keith Beene, "African American Fellowship Backs Racial Reconciliation," *Baptist Press*, June 20, 1995.

116. Hankins, *Uneasy in Babylon*, 246. See also the articles in *Baptist Press*, June 20, 1995.

117. Gustav Niebuhr, "Baptist Group Votes to Repent Stand on Slaves," *New York Times*, June 21, 1995.

118. See, for example, Dowland, "Defending Manhood," 195–96. Dowland draws from interviews with Southern Baptist conservatives.

119. Amy Green, "Southern Baptist Surprise!," *Christianity Today*, September 1, 2004. Green notes that if one compared the SBC's 3,000 predominantly black congregations to the National Baptist Convention's 5,000 congregations and the Progressive National Baptist Convention's 1,800, then the SBC, in 2004, was one of the largest black denominations in America. At the same time, SBC officials estimated that one-third of predominantly black SBC-affiliated churches were dually aligned with the National Baptist Convention, which means that they did not readily identify as Southern Baptist. See also Hankins, *Uneasy in Babylon*, 255–60.

120. While I link Southern Baptists who proved progressive on race to those who proved progressive on women, the situation regarding conservatives seems somewhat more nebulous and demands further research. Certainly, as previous chapters argue, when conservatives wrested power from moderates, a more restrained sense of women's ministry served to replace hardened concepts of race that had fallen out of favor after civil rights. Still, questions remain as to the nature of the relationship between Southern Baptist segregationists and those arguing later for women's submission.

121. For the amendment and commentary, see *Annual of the Southern Baptist Convention, Nineteen Hundred and Ninety-Eight*, 78–81.

122. "Clinton Balks at Submissive Wife Edict," *USA Today*, June 11, 1998, 6D.

123. Mary Otto, "Baptist Leader, Wife Promote Principle of Submission," *Spartanburg Herald-Journal*, July 12, 1998, B5. This article was syndicated and appeared in several newspapers.

124. Ibid.

125. For a copy of the changes as well as conservative explanation and commentary on each article, see Blount and Wooddell, *Baptist Faith and Message 2000*.

126. See Dilday, "Analysis of the Baptist Faith and Message, 2000."

127. See, as representative of the numerous articles that covered the event, Michelle Brummitt, "Firing Sprees," *Lynchburg News and Advance*, May 17, 2003; "Fired Missionaries Long Tenures with IMB," *Biblical Recorder*, May 16, 2003; and Mark Wingfield, "Loss of 43 Missionaries in a Day Called IMB Record," *Baptist Standard*, May 19, 2003. For a list of the missionaries and related articles, see http://www.mainstreambaptists.org/mob4/missionary_terminations.htm (October 15, 2010).

128. Dilday, "Analysis of the Baptist Faith and Message, 2000."

Chapter 5

1. Minutes, meeting of Concerned Southern Baptists, Office of the Baptist Alliance.
2. Neil, "Life's Greatest Adventure," Neil Papers, 6.
3. Minutes, meeting of the Southern Baptist Alliance, Office of the Baptist Alliance.
4. Neil, "Life's Greatest Adventure," Neil Papers, 13–14.
5. Ibid. Neil also recounted the incident in addressing the Alliance's 1996 convocation.

See minutes, meeting of the Southern Baptist Alliance Executive Committee, Office of the Baptist Alliance.

6. Molly Marshall-Green, "Toward Encompassing Theological Vision for Women in Light of Baptist Tradition," *FOLIO*, Autumn 1986, 1. As late as 2001, BWIM, which had dropped the "Southern" from its name, included Marshall-Green's brief article as part of its basic information packet.

7. Ibid., 2.

8. Elizabeth Barnes, "Envisioning God, Envisioning Humanity," *FOLIO*, Spring 1987, 1–2.

9. Sarah Frances Anders, "The Church as Redemptive Public Servant," *FOLIO*, Fall 1987, 1–2.

10. Jann Aldredge Clanton, "The Sin of Tolerance," *FOLIO*, Spring 1988, 11. See also Aldredge-Clanton, *Breaking Free*, 250–51, where she connected feminism to the Baptist free-church tradition. This linkage seemed typical of BWIM and Alliance Baptists.

11. Jann Aldredge Clanton, "The Sin of Tolerance," *FOLIO*, Spring 1988, 11.

12. Neely, "History of the Alliance of Baptists," 108. In 1992, the Alliance of Southern Baptists changed its name to the Alliance of Baptists.

13. Ibid., 109.

14. Chapter titles were "Freedom for Individual Interpretation," "Freedom of the Local Church," "Freedom to Participate in the Wider Community of Faith," "Freedom for Theological Education," "Freedom to be Servant Leaders," "Freedom to Work for Global Justice," and "Freedom for the Church in a Free State."

15. Neely introduction, v–vi.

16. See the Alliance of Baptists website, http://www.allianceofbaptists.org (October 15, 2010).

17. For a history of these statements, see again the Alliance of Baptists website. For a more updated history of the Alliance, as well as an examination of the statements, see Weaver, "Progressive Baptist Dissenters."

18. Neil, "Life's Greatest Adventure," Neil Papers, 5.

19. See Neil and Neely, *New Has Come*. Virginia Neely had been appointed, along with her husband, Alan Neely, as a missionary teacher by the Foreign Mission Board to Columbia, where she and Alan served thirteen years.

20. For example, one year after Neil's public rebuke, the Alliance elected her as its president. Elizabeth Bellinger served simultaneously as SBWIM president and chair of the Alliance's committee on women in the church. Nancy Sehested, Susan Lockwood Wright, and Lynda Weaver-Williams, all of whom were ordained ministers, served on both the SBWIM steering committee and the Alliance executive committee.

21. Neely, "History of the Alliance of Baptists," 125.

22. Mary Jane Welch, "Women May Pay the Price for Unity," *FOLIO*, Summer 1985, 4.

23. Neely, "History of the Alliance of Baptists," 125.

24. Information regarding the SBC Forum comes from the insider account of John H. Hewett, a leading moderate pastor in Missouri and North Carolina during the 1980s and early 1990s; see Hewett, "History of the Forum." Although the Forum did not dissolve until 1991, its most crucial years were the mid-1980s, when no formal moderate organization existed as a direct counter to conservative politics.

25. Forms of participation involved delivering a formal address, preaching a sermon, leading in prayer, or reading aloud from scripture.

26. These numbers come from Hewett, "History of the Forum," which lists the Forum's yearly program participants and steering committee members. Some of the seventy overlapped from year to year, but I could count no more than ten women.

27. Weaver-Williams interview. Information regarding SBWIM comes from *FOLIO*; interviews with founders, leaders, and participants; and ethnographic work. See the Introduction at n. 37 and Chapter 3, n. 51.

28. Information on Baptists Committed to the Southern Baptist Convention comes from the insider account of former SBC president Jimmy Allen. Allen, who was the last SBC president among the denominationalists-turned-moderates, helped spearhead Baptists Committed. In his account, Allen stated that the executive committee "included" the eighteen, roughly counted. If women served on the executive committee, he did not remember them, though the Texas chapter did have a woman serving as project director. See Allen, "History of Baptists Committed," 96.

29. In fact, the forces behind Baptists Committed to the Southern Baptist Convention eventually organized to become Texas Baptists Committed.

30. Moderates did not nominate a candidate in 1983.

31. Southcliff Baptist Church in Fort Worth, which Vestal served from 1972 to 1976, sided with the conservative Southern Baptist Convention of Texas, which broke away from the moderate-leaning General Baptist Convention of Texas. Others, such as the First Baptist in Midland and Tallowood Baptist Church in Houston, seemed to fall on the more traditional end of the moderate spectrum, which was reflective of the General Baptist Convention of Texas.

32. See Stinson memoirs, in which Stinson recounts her struggle for ordination from the congregation Vestal was serving. Vestal has addressed his change of mind regarding women's ordination in numerous venues. See, for example, Marv Knox, "Fellowship Focuses on Future, Not Past," *Baptist Standard*, July 9, 1997.

33. Vestal, "History of the Cooperative Baptist Fellowship," 253. See also Vestal interview, 10–12.

34. Vestal, "History of the Cooperative Baptist Fellowship," 254.

35. Crumpler interview.

36. Vestal, "History of the Cooperative Baptist Fellowship," 254. Again, for Vestal's more personal take on the election, see Vestal interview.

37. Neil interview. See also Sherman, "Ten Years Old," 18.

38. Sehested interview, 8.

39. The following critique comes primarily from interviews with SBWIM women as well as sustained conversations with SBWIM steering committee and board members from this period.

40. Stewart Newman, as quoted in Vestal, "History of the Cooperative Baptist Fellowship," 257. Newman was a retired seminary professor who had taught at both Southwestern and Southeastern.

41. Sherman, "Ten Years Old," 18.

42. Ibid.

43. Women echoed other moderates in speaking of themselves as prioritizing

the overarching message and themes of Jesus in the gospels over the dogmatism of biblicists.

44. "An Address to the Public." See also http://www.thefellowship.info (October 15, 2010).

45. Oertli interview. Southern Baptist Women in Ministry became Baptist Women in Ministry (BWIM) in 1995.

46. Anonymous woman, as quoted by Shaw and Lewis, "'Once There Was Camelot,'" 411.

47. Bellinger, "More Hidden Than Revealed," 146. Elizabeth Bellinger, who sometimes went by Libby, included the excerpt in her interview. Johnson offered a more extensive response to the question in "What Do Southern Baptist Women in Ministry Want?: An Absence of Reneging," *FOLIO*, Summer 1992, 8.

48. Sehested interview, 7.

49. Marv Knox, "Fellowship Focuses on Future, Not Past," *Baptist Standard*, July 9, 1997.

50. In 2000, these seminaries or divinity schools included Baptist Theological Seminary in Richmond, Truett School of Theology (Baylor University), Campbell University Divinity School, Central Baptist Theological Seminary, The Baptist House of Studies at Duke University Divinity School, The Baptist House of Studies at Candler School of Theology (Emory University), Gardner Webb School of Divinity, Logsdon School of Theology (Hardin Simmons University), McAfee School of Theology (Mercer University), and Brite Divinity School (Texas Christian University). While statistics from the 1990s are not readily available, a 2005 survey can be found in Campbell-Reed and Durso, *State of Women, 2005*, 6–7.

51. While this expression was used by one woman, others did seem to agree.

52. These comments and observations come from conversations with women active with BWIM during this period.

53. Sherman, "Ten Years Old," 19, 22.

54. Russell D. Moore, "CBF to Approve Funding for Pro-homosexual Groups," *Baptist Press*, June 30, 2000.

55. Art Toalston, "CBF Adopts Initial Stance on Homosexuality," *Baptist Press*, October 17, 2000. Vestal's statements were carried by both the *Baptist Press* and the moderate *Associated Baptist Press* as well as numerous state Baptist newspapers.

56. Mark Wingfield, "CBF Upholds Policy against Homosexuals," *Baptist Standard*, June 25, 2001. See also Bob Allen, "Divided CBF Upholds Ban on Funding of Pro-Gay Groups," *Associated Baptist Press*, July 12, 2001, and Russell D. Moore, "Analysis: Viva Le Chaos?," *Baptist Press*, July 3, 2001. Again, the event was reported on widely. This analysis comes largely from the printed sources listed here as well as my conversations with BWIM supporters present at the 2000 and 2001 CBF assemblies.

57. "Baptist Group Declines to Change Policy on Homosexuals," *Baptist Message*, July 19, 2001.

58. Sherman, "Ten Years Old," 18.

59. Ibid., 22.

60. Bill Leonard, "Good News at Wolf Creek," *FOLIO*, Summer 1984, 1.

61. "Profile: Ester Tye Perkins," *FOLIO*, Fall 1983, 5.

62. Betty Winstead McGary, "It's a Spiritual Thing," *FOLIO*, Winter 1989, 2.

63. Hays, "When God Calls People," 90.

64. Field notes, Baptist Women in Ministry panel, Cooperative Baptist Fellowship General Assembly, Memphis, Tenn., June, 19, 2008.

65. Ammerman, *Baptist Battles*, 94.

66. Sarah Frances Anders, "Historical Record-Keeping Essential for WIM," *FOLIO*, Fall 1997, 6. According to Anders, approximately 100 women served as associate pastors.

67. See Campbell-Reed and Durso, *State of Women*, 2005, 3.

68. Ibid., 3–4. See Epilogue, n. 28.

69. First Baptist had also undergone internal strife over its midtown location, and a large number, including Davis, left the congregation to plant another moderate-leaning church in the suburbs. During periodic trips to Memphis, I was able to visit the archives of both First Baptist and Prescott Memorial Baptist.

70. See also Richardson interview.

71. Primer interview. See also n. 27 above.

Epilogue

1. Field notes, Baptist Women in Ministry annual gathering and dinner, 2008.

2. See the section titled "From 'A Story to Tell' to Telling a Story" in the Introduction. For a list of the organized conferences, retreats, and meetings attended, see the Bibliography.

3. This admission comes from an informal conversation I had with a women's ministry director who requested that she remain anonymous.

4. Women's Enrichment Ministry was a division of Lifeway Christian Resources, the SBC's educational agency, and was devoted to helping local women's ministry programs. It included Women Reaching Women. Local churches adopted various names for their women's programs, but those used most often were Women's Ministry, Women's Ministry to Women, Women Reaching Women, and Women's Enrichment Ministry.

5. As she became successful, Beth Moore established Living Proof Ministries, with its headquarters in Houston. Still, her Bible study material is published by Lifeway Christian Resources, and Lifeway still handles much of her promotion.

6. See, for example, Moore, *Jesus* and *A Woman's Heart*. Moore has written more than two dozen Bible study series, almost all of which come with a leader kit and audiovisual resources.

7. Women's ministry surveys. The surveys were anonymous and did not distinguish between venues. Some women passed the surveys on to friends at their church or other women's ministry programs. In all, thirty-eight women in ministry participants responded to the surveys. See Introduction, n. 39.

8. Moore, "Beth's Passion," interview.

9. Lyons, "My Husband Wears the Cowboy Boots in Our Family." See also Sarah Pulliam Bailey, "Why Women Want Moore," *Christianity Today*, August 2010, 23.

10. Because the surveys were anonymous, and this woman mailed hers to me, I was not able to ask her to distinguish between preaching and prophesying.

11. Field notes, Women's Enrichment Ministry gathering and discipleship retreat, breakaway session, "How to Get Along with Male Staff."

12. When Tom Elliff, chairman of the Southern Baptist Council on Family Life, went on record in 2003 to say that the "husband should be vocationally focused" and the wife "not be burdened with the necessity of working outside the home," Jack Graham, president of the SBC, was quick to note "that would be the viewpoint of Dr. Elliff" and not necessarily the SBC. See Adelle M. Banks, "Baptist Convention Focuses on Women's Traditional Roles," *Durham Herald-Sun*, June 21, 2003, A11–A12.

13. Field notes, Women Reaching Women, regional training meeting and conference. See also Adams, *Women Reaching Women*, the more updated training material by the director of Women's Enrichment at Lifeway, as well as the Women Reaching Women website, http://blogs.lifeway.com/blog/women-ministry/about.html (October 15, 2010).

14. The women's programs included degrees, certificates, and even M.Div. tracks in women's studies, women's ministry, women's leadership, and ministers' wives training. They also worked with Lifeway Christian Resources and Women's Enrichment Ministry to host institutes and training seminars for female seminary students, women's ministry directors, and pastors' wives.

15. Patterson was prolific after 2000. Her books included *The Family*, *Handbook for Ministers' Wives*, *Handbook for Parents in Ministry*, and *Where's Mom?* She also served as general editor of *The Women's Studies Bible* and editor, with Rhonda Kelley, of the *Women's Evangelical Commentary*.

16. Kassian, "You've Come a Long Way, Baby!" To watch Kassian, read a transcript of her address, watch clips of the True Womanhood conferences, and consult the manifesto, see www.TrueWoman.com. See also Kassian, *Feminist Mistake*.

17. See, for example, Ken Walker, "A Kinder Gentler Conservatism," *Christianity Today*, June 28, 2006, http://www.christianitytoday.com/ct/2006/juneweb-only/126-32.0.html (October 15, 2010).

18. Greg Horton, "Pastor/Blogger Says Hebrew Prof's Gender Cost Her Tenure at Seminary," *Christianity Today*, January 23, 2007, http://www.christianitytoday.com/ct/2007/januaryweb-only/104-22.0.html (October 15, 2010). The Klouda affair generated a tremendous amount of local and Southern Baptist press. See Hannah Elliott, "Sheri Klouda Surprised at Fallout from Her 'Removal' at Southwestern," *Associated Baptist Press*, January 25, 2007; Sam Hodges, "Baptists at Odds over Removal of Female Professor," *Dallas Morning News*, January 19, 2006; and "Newspaper Reports Tenure Refusal for Southwestern Woman Prof.," *Baptist Press*, January 22, 2006. Bloggers Wade Burleson, Benjamin Cole, and Marty Duren helped break the story and, along with Denny Burk, who defended Southwestern, kept it circulating.

19. Hannah Elliott, "Sheri Klouda Surprised at Fallout from Her 'Removal' at Southwestern," *Associated Baptist Press*, January 25, 2007.

20. Ibid. See also Wade Burleson, "Sheri Klouda: Gender Discrimination, Federal Law, and the Law of Christ in the SBC and SWBTS," January 17, 2007, http://kerussocharis.blogspot.com/2007/01/sheri-klouda-gender-discrimination_17.html (October 15, 2010).

21. Again, the story was widely covered. See Katherine T. Phan, "Southern Baptist

Bookstores Pull Magazine featuring Female Pastors," *Christian Post*, September 20, 2008, http://www.christianpost.com/article/20080920/s-baptist-bookstores-pull-magazine-featuring-female-pastors (October 15, 2010).

22. Mary Otto, "Baptist Leader, Wife Promote Principle of Submission," *Spartanburg Herald-Journal*, 12 July 1998, B5. For Elliff's quote, see Adelle M. Banks, "Baptist Convention Focuses on Women's Traditional Roles," *Durham Herald-Sun*, June 21, 2003, A11–A12.

23. http://www.joshcrain.com/blog/files/sbc_hates_women.html (October 10, 2010).

24. Mark Wingfield, "Messengers Approve Family Proposal," *Arkansas Baptist Newsmagazine*, June 25, 1998, 9.

25. Al Mohler, "Palin Can Serve Family and Country," interview by Sally Quinn, *Washington Post*, September 5, 2010, http://newsweek.washingtonpost.com/onfaith/panelists/r_albert_mohler_jr/2008/09/a_tale_of_two_offices.html (October 15, 2010). See also David Kotter's four-part series, "Does Sarah Palin Present a Dilemma for Complementarians?," September 3–15, 2008, written for the Council on Biblical Manhood and Womanhood blog, http://www.cbmw.org/Blog/Posts/Does-Sarah-Palin-present-a-Dilemma-for-Complementarians-Part-1 (June 25, 2011).

26. Field notes, Baptist Women in Ministry sessions, Cooperative Baptist Fellowship General Assembly, 2008.

27. Campbell-Reed and Durso, *State of Women*, 2005, 3, and *State of Women*, 2007, 13–14.

28. Campbell-Reed and Durso, *State of Women*, 2005, 3–4. Numbers are difficult to obtain because the SBC, the CBF, and the Alliance do not keep exact statistics on church staff members. Of the 307 women who responded to Campbell-Reed and Durso's informal survey on ministerial positions other than church pastor, 31 percent served as children's minister, 16 percent as music minister, another 16 percent as youth minister, 11 percent as associate pastor, 9 percent as education minister, 4 percent as missions minister, 3 percent as senior adult minister, and the remaining 10 percent were such things as minister of congregational care, congregational health, counseling, family life, and spiritual formation.

29. This was true of both status reports, though it fell from the lowest six in 2005 to the lowest four in 2007.

30. Shaw, *God Speaks to Us, Too*, 180.

31. Campbell-Reed and Durso, *State of Women*, 2005, 6–7.

32. Mayse interview.

33. Durso related the incident through the BWIM blog. See Pamela R. Durso, "Options for our Baptist Daughters," May 3, 2010, http://www.bwim.info/category/pams blog/page/2/ (October 15, 2010).

34. Al Mohler, "Do SBC Moderates Really Believe Women Should Serve as Pastors?: An Important Research Project," August 21, 2006, http://www.conventionalthinking. org/?id=26. (October 15, 2010).

35. Durso and Durso, "'Cherish the Dream God Has Given You,'" 30, 22.

36. Global Women breakfast and presentation, 2005; Global Women luncheon and presentation, 2004.

37. Oklahoma Women in Baptist Life retreat, 2005.

Bibliography

Primary Sources

Archival Sources

James P. Boyce Centennial Library and Archives, Southern Baptist Theological
    Seminary, Louisville, Ky.
    Davis, Addie. "Called of God—Press On." Sermon audiotape. Chapel, Southern
        Baptist Theological Seminary, Louisville, Ky. March, 25, 1988.
Reba S. Cobb Personal Papers. In author's possession.
    Minutes. Conference for Women in Ministry, SBC. Pittsburgh, Pa. June 11–12, 1983.
Hunt Library and Archives, Woman's Missionary Union, Birmingham, Ala.
    Organizational Minutes. Woman's Missionary Union, Auxiliary to the SBC.
        May 11, 1888.
    Weatherford, Carolyn. Summary of letter. May 12, 1980.
Institute for Oral History, Baylor University, Waco, Tex.
Anne Thomas Neil Personal Papers. In author's possession.
    Neil, Anne Thomas. "Life's Greatest Adventure." March 15, 1996.
Office of the Baptist Alliance, Washington, D.C.
    Minutes. Meeting of Concerned Southern Baptists. Meredith College, Raleigh,
        N.C. September 23, 1986.
    Minutes. Meeting of the Southern Baptist Alliance. Charlotte, N.C. December
        1–2, 1986.
    Minutes. Meeting of the Southern Baptist Alliance Executive Committee.
        November 19–20, 1996.
Office of Women's Ministry, Bellevue Baptist Church, Cordova, Tenn.
    Program materials. Mid-Continent Women's Concerns Conference. Bellevue
        Baptist Church, Memphis, Tenn. May 15–17, 1980.
    Program materials. Women's Ministry. Bellevue Baptist Church, Cordova, Tenn.
        Conferences, 1980–2000.
Joyce Rogers Personal Papers. In author's possession.
    "Beginnings of Women's Ministries." Unpublished essay. 1995.

Southern Baptist Historical Library and Archives, Nashville, Tenn.
  Consultation on Women in Church-Related Vocations Collection
    Allen, Catherine. "Background Information."
    Findings of the Consultation on Women in Church-Related Vocations: Southern Baptist Convention. September 20–22, 1978.
      Allen, Jimmy. " . . . and She Arose, and Ministered." Pp. 42–45.
      Honeycutt, Roy. "Response." Pp. 30–31.
      Johnson, Johnni. "Consultation on Women in Church-Related Vocations." Pp. 2–5.
      "Responses from the Audience." Pp. 31–33.
      Shurden, Kay W. "An Analysis of the Images of Women in Selected Southern Baptist Literature." Pp. 49–55.
      Weaver-Williams, Lynda. "My Call." P. 24.
    Neely, Alan. Letter to Bobbie Sorrill. July 4, 1978.
  Southern Baptist Convention. Thursday morning session, June 13, 1973. Recording.
  Southern Baptist Convention. Thursday morning session, June 14, 1984. Video.
  Women in Baptist Life Collection
    Anders, Sarah Frances. "Women in Ministry: The Distaff of the Church in Action." Address at Dinner for Women in Ministry. Pittsburgh, Pa. June 13, 1982.
    Clanton, Jann Aldredge. "Why I Believe Southern Baptists Should Ordain Women." Paper delivered at the annual meeting of the Southern Baptist Historical Association. Nashville, Tenn. April 27, 1988.
    Patterson, Dorothy. "Why I Believe Southern Baptist Churches Should Not Ordain Women." Paper delivered at the annual meeting of the Southern Baptist Historical Association. Nashville, Tenn. April 27, 1988.
    Price, Clay Louis III. "A Survey of Southern Baptist Attitudes toward the Role of Women in Church and Society." Survey commissioned by the Home Mission Board, SBC, 1978.
    Proceedings of the 1983 Conference for Women in Ministry, SBC. Pittsburgh, Pa. June 11–12, 1983.
      Griffis-Woodberry, Debra. "Women in Ministry: Identifying the Issues." Pp. 5–7.
      Neil, Anne Thomas. "The Servant Model." Pp. 7–9.
      Sehested, Nancy Hastings. "We Have This Treasure." Pp. 9–11.
    Program materials. Dinner for Women in Ministry. Pittsburgh, Pa. June 13, 1982.

Conferences, Retreats, and National Meetings

Baptist Women in Ministry (BWIM)
  BWIM annual gathering and anniversary dinner. Cooperative Baptist Fellowship General Assembly, auxiliary event. Memphis, Tenn. June 18, 2008.

BWIM annual worship service and meeting. "Rooted in the Past: Grounded for the Future." Baptist Church of the Covenant, Birmingham, Ala. June 24, 2004.

BWIM annual worship service and meeting. "Vocare: Leading Lives Worthy of Calling." Gaylord Texas Resort, Grapevine, Tex. June 29, 2005.

BWIM board meeting. Baptist Church of the Covenant, Birmingham, Ala. June 23, 2004.

BWIM panel sessions. Cooperative Baptist Fellowship General Assembly. Memphis Convention Center, Memphis, Tenn. June 19, 2008.

Oklahoma Women in Baptist Life retreat. "Ordinary Women Doing Extraordinary Things." First Baptist Church, Oklahoma City. March 4–5, 2005.

CBF-affiliated

Cooperate Baptist Fellowship General Assembly. "Being the Presence of Christ: Today, Tomorrow, Together." Birmingham Convention Center, Birmingham, Ala. June 24–26, 2004.

Cooperative Baptist General Assembly. "Being the Presence of Christ in All the World." Gaylord Texas Resort, Grapevine, Tex. June 30–July 2, 2005.

Cooperative Baptist General Assembly. "Embracing the World." Memphis Convention Center, Memphis, Tenn. June 19–20, 2008.

Global Women

Global Women breakfast and presentation. Gaylord Texas Resort, Grapevine, Tex. July 1, 2005.

Global Women luncheon and presentation. Baptist Church of the Covenant, Birmingham, Ala. June 24, 2004.

SBC-affiliated

Southern Baptist Convention. "Kingdom Forever." Indianapolis, Ind. June 15–16, 2004.

Woman's Missionary Union (WMU)

National WMU annual meeting and missions celebration. "Christ Followers." Southern Baptist Convention, preconvention event. Indianapolis, Ind. June 13–14, 2004.

Sisters Who Care fall retreat. First Metropolitan Baptist Church, Houston, Tex. September 10–11, 2004.

Texas WMU leadership conference. Annual state WMU house party. "Christ Followers." Baylor University, Waco, Tex. June 22–24, 2004.

Women's Enrichment Ministry

Living Proof Live with Beth Moore. Alltel Arena, Little Rock, Ark. September 17–18, 2004.

Ministers' wives annual conference. Southern Baptist Convention. Indiana Convention Center, Indianapolis. June 15, 2004.

Women Reaching Women regional training meeting and conference. Sponsored by Lifeway Christian Resources, Women's Enrichment Ministry. Vista Ridge Baptist Church, Carrollton, Tex. August 21, 2004.

Women's Enrichment Ministry annual gathering and discipleship retreat. Sponsored by Lifeway Christian Resources, Women's Enrichment Ministry track. Ridgecrest, N.C. July 5–9, 2004.

Interviews

Anders, Sarah Frances. Interview by author, written correspondence. June 26, 2006.

Bellinger, Elizabeth Smith. Interview by author, written correspondence. April 2006.

———. Oral Memoirs. Interview by Rosalie Beck. August 20, November 19, 1986. Institute for Oral History, Baylor University, Waco, Tex.

Bennett, Harold. Oral History Interview by Bill Sumners. August 5, 1994. Southern Baptist Historical Library and Archives, Nashville, Tenn.

Cobb, Reba S. Interview by author, written correspondence. October 2006.

Cothen, Grady. Oral History Interview by Bill Sumners. September 16, 1994. Southern Baptist Historical Library and Archives, Nashville, Tenn.

Crumpler, Carolyn W [Weatherford]. Interview by author, written correspondence. April 18, 2006.

Davis, Addie. Interview by Eljee Bentley. June 9, 1985. Hunt Library and Archives, Woman's Missionary Union, Birmingham, Ala.

Dilday, Russell. Oral History Interview by Bill Sumners. September 9, 1994. Southern Baptist Historical Library and Archives, Nashville, Tenn.

Fields, W. C. Oral History Interview by Bill Sumners. July 8, 1994. Southern Baptist Historical Library and Archives, Nashville, Tenn.

George, Denise. Interview by author, written correspondence. July 1, 2006.

Gregory, Linda. Interview by author, written correspondence. June 28, 2006.

Gushee, David P. Oral Memoirs. Interview by Barry Hankins. June 16, 1999. Institute for Oral History, Baylor University, Waco, Tex.

Hawkins, Susie. Interview by author, written correspondence. May 2006.

Hicks, Linda Hood. Interview by author, written correspondence. July 19, 2006.

Hill, Diane Eubanks. Interview by author, written correspondence. April 6, 2006.

Honeycutt, Roy L. Oral History Interview by Bill Sumners. N.d. Southern Baptist Historical Library and Archives, Nashville, Tenn.

———. Oral Memoirs. Interview by Barry Hankins. September 5, 2000. Institute for Oral History, Baylor University, Waco, Tex.

Lolley, Randall. Oral History Interview by Bill Sumners. July 13, 1994. Southern Baptist Historical Library and Archives, Nashville, Tenn.

Maddox, Sarah O. Interview by author, written correspondence. May 25, 2006.

Massey, Barbara. Interview by author, written correspondence. April 11, 2006.

Mayse, Marilyn A. Interview by author, written correspondence. April 2, 2006.

McGary, Betty W. Oral Memoirs. Interview by Rosalie Beck. July 9, 1986. Institute for Oral History, Baylor University, Waco, Tex.

Miller, Carolyn D. Interview by author, written correspondence. April 17, 2006.

Mohler, R. Albert, Jr. Oral Memoirs. Interview by Barry Hankins. August 5, 1997, and August 13, 1999. Institute for Oral History, Baylor University, Waco, Tex.

Moore, Beth. "Beth's Passion." Interview by Jane Johnson Struck. *Christianity Today*, July 13, 2010. http://www.christianitytoday.com/biblestudies/articles/bibleinsights/bethspassion.html. October 15, 2010.

Neil, Anne Thomas. Interview by author, telephone. August 2006.

Newman, Carey Charles. Oral Memoirs. Interview by Barry Hankins. August 11, 1999. Institute for Oral History, Baylor University, Waco, Tex.

O'Brien, Dellanna. Interview by author, written correspondence. April 25, 2006.

Oertli, Karrie. Interview by author, written correspondence. July 6, 2006.

Parks, Keith. Oral History Interview by Bill Sumners. July 5, 1994. Southern Baptist Historical Library and Archives, Nashville, Tenn.

Patterson, Dorothy. Oral Memoirs. Interview by Barry Hankins. June 8, 1999. Institute for Oral History, Baylor University, Waco, Tex.

Primer, Terry Thomas. Self-recorded interview, responding to questions by author, and written correspondence. July 26, 2006.

Richardson, Carol. Interview by author, written correspondence. April 5, 2006.

Sehested, Nancy Hastings. Oral History Interview by Bill Sumners. 1994. Southern Baptist Historical Library and Archives, Nashville, Tenn.

Sherman, Cecil. Oral History Interview by Bill Sumners. July 6, 1994. Southern Baptist Historical Library and Archives, Nashville, Tenn.

Stinson, Deborah Whisnand. Oral Memoirs. Interview by Rosalie Beck. July 10, 1986. Institute for Oral History, Baylor University, Waco, Tex.

Turner, Helen Lee. Interview by author, written correspondence. June 26, 2006.

Vestal, Daniel. Oral History Interview by Bill Sumners. August 31, 1994. Southern Baptist Historical Library and Archives, Nashville, Tenn.

Weaver-Williams, Lynda. Interview by author, written correspondence. July 4, 2006.

Newspapers, Newsletters, and Periodicals

Alabama Baptist

Annual of the Southern Baptist Convention

Arkansas Baptist Newsmagazine

Associated Baptist Press releases

Baptist and Reflector

Baptist Basket

Baptist Courier

Baptist Index

Baptist Message

Baptist Messenger

Baptist Press releases

Baptist Standard

Baptists Today

Bellevue Messenger

Called and Committed

Christian Century

Christianity Today

Christian Post

Commission

Connections: Newsletter of the Alliance of Baptists

Facts and Trends

FOLIO

Home Missions

Missions Mosaic

Religious Herald

Royal Service

SBC Today

Student

Vocare

VOICES

Western Recorder

Word and Way

Published and Online Sources

Adams, Chris. *Women Reaching Women: Beginning and Building a Growing Women's Enrichment Ministry.* Nashville, Tenn.: Lifeway Christian Resources, 2005.

"An Address to the Public." Interim Steering Committee of the Cooperative Baptist Fellowship. May 9, 1991. In *Going for the Jugular: A Documentary History of the SBC*

Holy War, edited by Walter B. Shurden and Randy Shepley, 266–70. Macon, Ga.: Mercer University Press, 1996.

Aldredge-Clanton, Jann. *Breaking Free: The Story of a Feminist Baptist Pastor*. Austin, Tex.: Eakin Press, 2002.

Allen, Jimmy. "The History of Baptists Committed." In *The Struggle for the Soul of the SBC: Moderate Responses to the Fundamentalist Movement*, edited by Walter B. Shurden, 93–100. Macon, Ga.: Mercer University Press, 1996.

Ashcraft, Morris. Foreword to *"The Genesis Controversy" and Continuity in Southern Baptist Chaos: A Eulogy for a Great Tradition*. Macon, Ga.: Mercer University Press, 1992.

Bellinger, Libby. "More Hidden Than Revealed: The History of Southern Baptist Women in Ministry." In *The Struggle for the Soul of the SBC: Moderate Responses to the Fundamentalist Movement*, edited by Walter B. Shurden, 129–50. Macon, Ga.: Mercer University Press, 1996.

Blount, Douglas K., and Joseph D. Wooddell, eds. *Baptist Faith and Message 2000: Critical Issues in America's Largest Protestant Denomination*. Lanham, Md.: Rowman and Littlefield, 2007.

Bryant, Anita. *The Anita Bryant Story: The Survival of Our Nation's Families and the Threat of Militant Homosexuality*. Old Tappan, N.J.: Fleming H. Revell, 1977.

Burleson, Wade. "Sheri Klouda: Gender Discrimination, Federal Law, and the Law of Christ in the SBC and SWBTS." http://kerussocharis.blogspot.com/2007/01/sheri-klouda-gender%20discrimination_17.html. October 15, 2010.

Campbell-Reed, Eileen, and Pamela R. Durso. *The State of Women in Baptist Life, 2005*. Atlanta: Baptist Women in Ministry, 2006.

———. *The State of Women in Baptist Life, 2007*. Atlanta: Baptist Women in Ministry, 2008.

Carter, Shirley. "A Woman's Self-Affirmation in the Ministry." *Pastoral Psychology* 23, no. 3 (March 1972): 45–50.

Cothen, Grady C. *The New SBC: Fundamentalism's Impact on the Southern Baptist Convention*. Macon, Ga.: Smith and Helwys, 1995.

———. *What Happened to the Southern Baptist Convention?: A Memoir of the Controversy*. Macon, Ga.: Smith and Helwys, 1993.

Daly, Mary. *Beyond God the Father: Toward a Philosophy of Women's Liberation*. Boston, Mass.: Beacon Press, 1973.

———. *The Church and the Second Sex*. New York: Harper and Row, 1968.

"The Danvers Statement." In *Recovering Biblical Manhood and Womanhood: A Response to Evangelical Feminism*, edited by John Piper and Wayne Grudem, 469–72. Wheaton, Ill.: Crossway Books, 1991.

Dayton, Donald W., and Lucille Sider Dayton. "The Bible among Evangelicals: Some Aspects of Its Biblical Interpretation." *Explore* 2 (1976): 17–22.

Dilday, Russell. "An Analysis of the Baptist Faith and Message, 2000." April 2001. http://www.centerforbaptststudies.org/hotissues/dildayfm2000.htm. October 15, 2010.

Dobson, James. *Dare to Discipline*. Wheaton, Ill.: Tyndale House, 1972.

———. *Prescriptions for a Tired Housewife*. Wheaton, Ill.: Tyndale House, 1975.

———. *What Wives Wish Their Husbands Knew about Women*. Wheaton, Ill.: Tyndale House, 1975.

Elliot, Elisabeth. *Let Me Be a Woman: Notes on Womanhood for Valerie*. Wheaton, Ill.: Tyndale House, 1976.

Elliott, Ralph. *"The Genesis Controversy" and Continuity in Southern Baptist Chaos: A Eulogy for a Great Tradition*. Macon, Ga.: Mercer University Press, 1992.

Faith and Mission 14, no. 1 (1996).

Foh, Susan T. *Women and the Word of God: A Response to Biblical Feminism*. 1979. Grand Rapids, Mich.: Baker Book House, 1980.

Gundry, Patricia. *Women Be Free: The Clear Message of Scripture*. Grand Rapids, Mich.: Zondervan, 1977.

Hays, Ida Mae. "When God Calls People, He Calls Them to 'Preach the Gospel' to Everyone and in All Places." In *Courage and Hope: The Stories of Ten Baptist Women Ministers*, edited by Keith E. Durso and Pamela R. Durso, 76–94. Macon, Ga.: Mercer University Press, 2005.

Hewett, John. "A History of the Forum." In *The Struggle for the Soul of the SBC: Moderate Responses to the Fundamentalist Movement*, edited by Walter B. Shurden, 73–92. Macon, Ga.: Mercer University Press, 1996.

Hinson, E. Glenn. "Background to the Moderate Movement." In *The Struggle for the Soul of the SBC: Moderate Responses to the Fundamentalist Movement*, edited by Walter B. Shurden, 1–16. Macon, Ga.: Mercer University Press, 1996.

Hollis, Harry N., Jr. Preface to *Christian Freedom for Women and Other Human Beings*, by Harry N. Hollis Jr., Vera Mace, David Mace, and Sarah Frances Anders. Nashville, Tenn.: Broadman Press, 1975.

Hunt, Alma. *Reflections from Alma Hunt*. Birmingham, Ala.: Woman's Missionary Union, 1987.

Issues and Answers: Changing Roles of Women. Nashville, Tenn.: Christian Life Commission, 1981.

Kassian, Mary. *The Feminist Mistake: The Radical Impact of Feminism on Church and Culture*. Wheaton, Ill.: Crossway Books, 2005.

———. "You've Come a Long Way, Baby!" http://www.truewoman.com/?id=341. July 25, 2011.

Kell, Carl L., ed. *Exiled: Voices of the Southern Baptist Convention Holy War*. Knoxville: University of Tennessee Press, 2006.

Knight, George W. *The New Testament Teaching on the Role Relationship between Men and Women*. Grand Rapids, Mich.: Baker Book House, 1977.

Kroeger, Catherine Clark. "Ancient Heresies and a Strange Greek Verb." *Reformed Journal*, March 1979, 12–15.

Kroeger, Catherine Clark, and Richard Clark Kroeger. "Pandemonium and Silence at Corinth." *Reformed Journal*, June 1978, 6–10.

———. "Sexual Identity in Corinth." *Reformed Journal*, December 1978, 11–15.

Lindsell, Harold. *The Battle for the Bible*. Grand Rapids, Mich.: Zondervan, 1976.

McCall, Duke, with A. Ronald Tonks. *Duke McCall: An Oral History*. Brentwood, Tenn.: Baptist History and Heritage Society and Fields Publishing, 2001.

Mohler, Albert R., Jr. *Culture Shift: Engaging Current Issues with Timeless Truths.*
Portland, Oreg.: Multnomah, 2008.

Moore, Beth. *Jesus, the One and Only.* Nashville, Tenn.: Lifeway Christian Resources,
2000.

———. *A Woman's Heart: God's Dwelling Place.* Nashville, Tenn.: Lifeway Christian
Resources, 1997.

Morgan, Marabel. *Total Joy.* Old Tappan, N.J.: Fleming H. Revell, 1977.

———. *The Total Woman.* Old Tappan, N.J.: Fleming H. Revell, 1973.

Neely, Alan. "The History of the Alliance of Baptists." In *The Struggle for the Soul of
the SBC: Moderate Responses to the Fundamentalist Movement,* edited by Walter B.
Shurden, 101–28. Macon, Ga.: Mercer University Press, 1996.

———. Introduction to *Being Baptist Means Freedom,* edited by Alan Neely, v–vi.
Charlotte, N.C.: Southern Baptist Alliance, 1988.

Neil, Anne Thomas, and Virginia Garrett Neely, eds. *The New Has Come: Emerging
Roles among Southern Baptist Women.* Washington, D.C.: Southern Baptist Alliance,
1988.

"News Story: Pressler's 'Going for the Jugular' Statement." In *Going for the Jugular:
A Documentary History of the SBC Holy War,* edited by Walter B. Shurden and
Randy Shepley, 56–61. Macon, Ga.: Mercer University Press, 1996.

"Organizational Policy on Homosexual Behavior Related to Personnel and Funding."
http://www.thefellowship.info/documents/homosexuality.pdf. October 15, 2010.

Patterson, Dorothy. *The Family: Unchanging Principles for Changing Times.* Nashville,
Tenn.: Broadman Press, 2001.

———. *A Handbook for Ministers' Wives: Sharing the Blessings of Your Marriage, Family,
and Home.* Nashville, Tenn.: Broadman and Holman, 2002.

———. *Where's Mom?: The High Calling of Wives and Mothers.* Wheaton, Ill.: Crossway
Books, 2003.

Patterson, Dorothy, and Rhonda Kelley, eds. *Women's Evangelical Commentary: New
Testament.* Nashville, Tenn.: Broadman and Holman, 2005.

Patterson, Dorothy, and Armour Patterson. *A Handbook for Parents in Ministry:
Training Up a Child while Answering the Call.* Nashville, Tenn.: Broadman and
Holman, 2004.

Patterson, Paige. *Anatomy of a Reformation: The Southern Baptist Convention, 1978–2004.*
Fort Worth, Tex.: Seminary Hill Press, 2005.

Pressler, Paul. *A Hill on Which to Die: One Southern Baptist's Journey.* Nashville, Tenn.:
Broadman and Holman, 1999.

"Recommendation No. 1: Concerning Freedom for Women." In *Annual of the Southern
Baptist Convention, Nineteen Hundred and Seventy-Four,* 209–10. Nashville, Tenn.:
Executive Committee, Southern Baptist Convention, 1974.

"Report of the Peace Committee." In *Annual of the Southern Baptist Convention,
Nineteen Hundred and Eighty-Seven,* 233–42. Nashville, Tenn.: Executive
Committee, Southern Baptist Convention, 1987.

Resolution No. 1: "On Racial Reconciliation on the 150th Anniversary of the Southern
Baptist Convention." In *Annual of the Southern Baptist Convention, Nineteen*

Hundred and Ninety-Five, 80–81. Nashville, Tenn.: Executive Committee, Southern Baptist Convention, 1995.

Resolution No. 3: "On the Ordination and the Role of Women in Ministry." In *Annual of the Southern Baptist Convention, Nineteen Hundred and Eighty-Four*, 65. Nashville, Tenn.: Executive Committee, Southern Baptist Convention, 1984.

Resolution No. 5: "On the Priesthood of the Believer." In *Annual of the Southern Baptist Convention, Nineteen Hundred and Eighty-Eight*, 68–69. Nashville, Tenn.: Executive Committee, Southern Baptist Convention, 1988.

Resolution No. 8: "On Woman." In *Annual of the Southern Baptist Convention, Nineteen Hundred and Eighty-Three*, 70–71. Nashville, Tenn.: Executive Committee, Southern Baptist Convention, 1983.

Resolution No. 12: "On the Place of Women in Christian Service." In *Annual of the Southern Baptist Convention, Nineteen Hundred and Seventy-Three*, 87. Nashville, Tenn.: Executive Committee, Southern Baptist Convention, 1973.

Resolution No. 16: "On Doctrinal Integrity." In *Annual of the Southern Baptist Convention, Nineteen Hundred and Eighty*, 51. Nashville, Tenn.: Executive Committee, Southern Baptist Convention, 1980.

Resolution No. 21: "On Women." In *Annual of the Southern Baptist Convention, Nineteen Hundred and Eighty*, 53–54. Nashville, Tenn.: Executive Committee, Southern Baptist Convention, 1980.

Robison, James. "Satan's Subtle Attacks." In *Going for the Jugular: A Documentary History of the SBC Holy War*, edited by Walter B. Shurden and Randy Shepley, 24–38. Macon, Ga.: Mercer University Press, 1996.

Rogers, Joyce. *The Wise Woman . . . How to Be One in a Thousand*. Nashville, Tenn.: Broadman Press, 1980.

Ruether, Rosemary Radford. *Mary, the Feminine Face of the Church*. Philadelphia: Westminster Press, 1977.

———. *New Woman, New Earth: Sexist Ideologies and Human Liberation*. New York: Seabury Press, 1975.

Russell, Letty M. *Human Liberation in a Feminist Perspective: A Theology*. Philadelphia: Westminster Press, 1974.

———. *The Liberating Word: A Guide to Nonsexist Interpretation of the Bible*. Philadelphia: Westminster Press, 1976.

Saiving, Valerie. "The Human Situation: A Feminine View." *Journal of Religion* 40, no. 2 (April 1969): 100–112.

Sappington, Jessie Tillison. *From My Point of View on the Ordination Issue*. Houston, Tex.: M. and M. Printing, 1978.

Scanzoni, Letha, and Nancy Hardesty. *All We're Meant to Be: A Biblical Approach to Women's Liberation*. Waco, Tex.: Word Books, 1974.

Schussler-Fiorenza, Elisabeth. *In Memory of Her: A Feminist Theological Reconstruction of Christian Origins*. New York: Crossroad, 1983.

Sherman, Cecil E. *By My Own Reckoning*. Macon, Ga.: Smyth and Helwys, 2008.

———. "An Overview of the Moderate Movement." In *The Struggle for the Soul of the SBC: Moderate Responses to the Fundamentalist Movement*, edited by Walter B. Shurden, 17–46. Macon, Ga.: Mercer University Press, 1996.

———. "Ten Years Old: Cecil Sherman's Reflections on the Genesis of CBF." *Whitsitt Journal* 8, no. 1 (Spring 2001): 14–19, 21–23.

Shurden, Walter B. *The Baptist Identity: Four Fragile Freedoms*. Macon, Ga.: Smyth and Helwys, 1994.

———. "The Struggle for the Soul of the SBC: Reflections and Interpretations." In *The Struggle for the Soul of the SBC: Moderate Responses to the Fundamentalist Movement*, edited by Walter B. Shurden, 275–90. Macon, Ga.: Mercer University Press, 1996.

———, ed. *The Struggle for the Soul of the SBC: Moderate Responses to the Fundamentalist Movement*. Macon, Ga.: Mercer University Press, 1996.

Slatton, James H. "A History of the Political Network of the Moderate Movement." In *The Struggle for the Soul of the SBC: Moderate Responses to the Fundamentalist Movement*, edited by Walter B. Shurden, 47–72. Macon, Ga.: Mercer University Press, 1996.

Trible, Phyllis. *God and the Rhetoric of Sexuality*. Philadelphia: Fortress Press, 1978.

———. *Texts of Terror: Literary-Feminist Readings of Biblical Narratives*. Philadelphia: Fortress Press, 1984.

Vestal, Daniel. "The History of the Cooperative Baptist Fellowship." In *The Struggle for the Soul of the SBC: Moderate Responses to the Fundamentalist Movement*, edited by Walter B. Shurden, 253–74. Macon, Ga.: Mercer University Press, 1996.

"Women in Ministry: Report from the Working Group." In *Issues Affecting Women: A Report from the Theology Is a Verb Conference*. Chapel Hill, N.C.: Southern Baptists for the Family and Equal Rights, 1982.

Secondary Sources

Abu-Lughod, Lila. "The Romance of Resistance: Tracing Transformations of Power through Bedouin Women." *American Ethnologist* 17, no. 1 (February 1990): 41–55.

Aistrup, Joseph A. *The Southern Strategy Revisited: Republican Top-Down Advancement in the South*. Lexington: University Press of Kentucky, 1996.

Allen, Catherine B. *A Century to Celebrate: History of Woman's Missionary Union*. Birmingham, Ala.: Woman's Missionary Union, 1987.

———. *Laborers Together with God: 22 Great Women in Baptist Life*. Birmingham, Ala.: Woman's Missionary Union, 1987.

———. "Shifting Sands for Southern Baptist Women in Missions." In *Gospel Bearers, Gender Barriers: Missionary Women in the Twentieth Century*, edited by Dana L. Robert, 113–26. Maryknoll, N.Y.: Orbis Books.

Ammerman, Nancy Tatom. *Baptist Battles: Social Change and Religious Conflict in the Southern Baptist Convention*. 1990. New Brunswick, N.J.: Rutgers University Press, 1995.

Applebome, Peter. *Dixie Rising: How the South Is Shaping American Values, Politics, and Culture*. New York: Harcourt Brace, 1996.

Asad, Talal. *Genealogies of Religion: Discipline and Reasons of Power in Christianity and Islam*. Baltimore, Md.: Johns Hopkins University Press, 1993.

Baker, Robert A. *The Southern Baptist Convention and Its People, 1607–1972*. Nashville, Tenn.: Broadman Press, 1974.

Barnhart, Joe E. "What's All the Fighting About? Southern Baptists and the Bible."
In *Southern Baptists Observed: Multiple Perspectives on a Changing Denomination*,
edited by Nancy Tatom Ammerman, 124–43. Knoxville: University of Tennessee
Press, 1993.

Bartkowski, John P. *Remaking the Godly Marriage: Gender Negotiation in Godly
Families*. New Brunswick, N.J.: Rutgers University Press, 2001.

Bartley, Numan V. *The New South, 1945–1980*. Baton Rouge: Louisiana State University
Press, 1995.

Bartley, Numan V., and Hugh D. Graham. *Southern Politics and the Second
Reconstruction*. Baltimore, Md.: Johns Hopkins University Press, 1975.

Battle for the Minds. Directed by Steven Lipscomb. Documentary. Battle for the
Minds, Inc., 1997.

Bendroth, Margaret Lamberts. *Fundamentalism and Gender, 1875 to the Present*. New
Haven, Conn.: Yale University Press, 1993.

Bentley, Eljee. "Personal Responses to the Call to World Missions." *Baptist History and
Heritage* 27 (1992): 35–36.

Bivins, Jason C. *The Fracture of Good Order: Christian Antiliberalism and the Challenge to
American Politics*. Chapel Hill: University of North Carolina Press, 2003.

Black, Earl, and Merle Black. *Politics and Society in the South*. Cambridge, Mass.:
Harvard University Press, 1987.

Brasher, Brenda E. *Godly Women: Fundamentalism and Female Power*. New Brunswick,
N.J.: Rutgers University Press, 1998.

Braude, Ann. Introduction to *Transforming the Faith of Our Fathers: Women Who
Changed American Religion*, edited by Ann Braude, 1–12. New York: Palgrave
Macmillan, 2004.

———. "Women's History *Is* American Religious History." In *Retelling U.S. Religious
History*, edited by Thomas A. Tweed, 87–107. Berkeley: University of California
Press, 1997.

Brekus, Catherine A. "Searching for Women in Narratives of American Religious
History." In *The Religious History of American Women: Reimagining the Past*, edited
by Catherine A. Brekus, 1–50. Chapel Hill: University of North Carolina Press,
2007.

———. *Strangers and Pilgrims: Female Preaching in America, 1740–1845*. Chapel Hill:
University of North Carolina Press, 1998.

Brown, D. Clayton. *King Cotton: A Cultural, Political, and Economic History since 1945*.
Oxford: University Press of Mississippi, 2011.

Brown, Karen McCarthy. *Mama Lola: A Vodou Priestess in Brooklyn*. Berkeley:
University of California Press, 1991.

———. "Writing about the Other." *Chronicle of Higher Education*, April 15, 1992, A56.

Brown, Kathleen M. "Brave New Worlds: Women's and Gender History." *William
and Mary Quarterly*, 3rd ser., vol. 50, no. 2 (April 1993): 311–28.

Brown, Ruth Murray. *For a Christian America: A History of the Religious Right*.
New York: Prometheus Books, 2002.

Carpenter, Joel. *Revive Us Again: The Reawakening of American Fundamentalism*.
New York: Oxford University Press, 1997.

Carter, Dan T. *From George Wallace to Newt Gingrich: Race in the Conservative Counterrevolution, 1963–1994.* Baton Rouge: Louisiana State University Press, 1996.

———. *The Politics of Rage: George Wallace, the Origins of New Conservatism, and the Transformation of American Politics.* New York: Simon and Schuster, 1995.

Chafe, William. *The Paradox of Change: American Women in the Twentieth Century.* New York: Oxford University Press, 1991.

Chappell, David L. *A Stone of Hope: Prophetic Religion and the Death of Jim Crow.* Chapel Hill: University of North Carolina Press, 2004.

Chaves, Mark. *Ordaining Women: Culture and Conflict in Religious Organizations.* Cambridge, Mass.: Harvard University Press, 1997.

Clinton, Catherine. *The Plantation Mistress: Woman's World in the Old South.* New York: Pantheon, 1982.

———. *Tara Revisited: Women, War, and the Plantation Legend.* New York: Abbeville Press, 1995.

Cobb, James C. *The Selling of the South: The Southern Crusade for Industrial Development, 1936–1990.* 2nd ed. Urbana: University of Illinois Press, 1993.

Cochran, Pamela D. H. *Evangelical Feminism: A History.* New York: New York University Press, 2005.

Coontz, Stephanie. *A Strange Stirring: The Feminine Mystique and American Women at the Dawn of the 1960s.* New York: Basic Books, 2011.

———. *The Way We Never Were: American Families and the Nostalgia Trap.* New York: Basic Books, 1992.

Copeland, E. Luther. *The Southern Baptist Convention and the Judgment of History: The Taint of an Original Sin.* Lanham, Md.: University Press of America, 2002.

Cott, Nancy F. *The Bonds of Womanhood: "Woman's Sphere" in New England, 1780–1835.* New Haven, Conn.: Yale University Press, 1977.

Cromartie, Michael, ed. *No Longer Exiles: The Religious New Right in America.* Washington, D.C.: Ethics and Public Policy, 1993.

Daniel, Pete. *Lost Revolutions: The South in the 1950s.* Chapel Hill: University of North Carolina Press, 2000.

Davis, Natalie Zemon. *Society and Culture in Early Modern France: Eight Essays.* Stanford: Stanford University Press, 1975.

Dayton, Donald W. "Yet Another Layer of the Onion; Or, Opening the Ecumenical Door to Let the Riffraff In." *Ecumenical Review* 40 (January 1988): 87–110.

Dayton, Donald W., and Lucille Sider Dayton. "'Your Daughters Shall Prophesy'?: Feminism in the Holiness Movement." *Methodist History* 14 (January 1976): 67–92.

Dayton, Donald W., and Robert Johnson, eds. *The Variety of American Evangelicalism.* Knoxville: University of Tennessee Press, 1991.

DeBerg, Betty A. *Ungodly Women: Gender and the First Wave of American Fundamentalism.* Minneapolis: Fortress Press, 1990.

Degler, Carl N. *At Odds: Women and the Family in America from the Revolution to the Present.* New York: Oxford University Press, 1981.

DeHart, Jane Sherron. "The New Feminism and the Dynamics of Social Change." In *Women's America: Refocusing the Past,* edited by Linda K. Kerber and Jane Sherron DeHart, 589–617. New York: Oxford University Press, 1995.

DeWeese, Charles W. *Women Deacons and Deaconesses: 400 Years of Baptist Service.* Macon, Ga.: Mercer University Press, 2005.

Dochuk, Darren. *From Bible Belt to Sunbelt: Plain-folk Religion, Grassroots Politics, and the Rise of Evangelical Conservatism.* New York: Norton, 2011.

Dockery, David S., ed. *Southern Baptists and American Evangelicals: The Conversation Continues.* Nashville, Tenn.: Broadman and Holman, 1993.

Dowland, Seth A. "Defending Manhood: Gender, Social Order, and the Rise of the Christian Right in the South, 1965–1995." Ph.D. diss., Duke University, 2007.

———. "Family Values and the Formation of a Christian Right Agenda." *Church History* 78, no. 3 (September 2009): 606–31.

Durso, Keith E., and Pamela R. Durso. "'Cherish the Dream God Has Given You': The Story of Addie Davis." In *Courage and Hope: The Stories of Ten Baptist Women Ministers,* edited by Keith E. Durso and Pamela R. Durso, 17–30. Macon, Ga.: Mercer University Press, 2005.

Durso, Pamela R., and Keith E. Durso. "Baptist Women Ministers: Called and Gifted by God." In *Courage and Hope: The Stories of Ten Baptist Women Ministers,* edited by Keith E. Durso and Pamela R. Durso, 1–16. Macon, Ga.: Mercer University Press, 2005.

Echols, Alice. *Daring to Be Bad: Radical Feminism in America, 1967–1975.* Minneapolis: University of Minnesota Press, 1989.

Egerton, John. *The Americanization of Dixie: The Southernization of America.* New York: Harper's Magazine Press, 1974.

Eighmy, John Lee. *Churches in Cultural Captivity: A History of Social Attitudes of Southern Baptists.* Knoxville: University of Tennessee Press, 1972.

Epstein, Barbara L. *The Politics of Domesticity: Women, Evangelism, and Temperance in Nineteenth-Century America.* Middletown, Conn.: Wesleyan University Press, 1981.

Farnsley, Arthur Emery, II. *Southern Baptist Politics: Authority and Power in the Restructuring of an American Denomination.* University Park: Pennsylvania State University Press, 1994.

Faust, Drew Gilpin. *Mothers of Invention: Women of the Slaveholding South in the American Civil War.* Chapel Hill: University of North Carolina Press, 1996.

Feldman, Glenn. "The Status Quo Society, the Rope of Religion, and the New Racism." In *Politics and Religion in the White South,* edited by Glenn Feldman, 287–351. Lexington: University Press of Kentucky, 2005.

Fite, Gilbert C. *Cotton Fields No More: Southern Agriculture, 1865–1980.* Lexington: University Press of Kentucky, 1984.

Fletcher, Jesse C. *The Southern Baptist Convention: A Sesquicentennial History.* Nashville, Tenn.: Broadman and Holman, 1994.

Flippen, J. Brooks. *Jimmy Carter, the Politics of Family, and the Rise of the Religious Right.* Athens: University of Georgia Press, 2011.

Flowers, Betsy. "Southern Baptist Evangelicals or Social Gospel Liberals?: The Woman's Missionary Union and Social Reform, 1888–1928." *American Baptist Quarterly* 19, no. 2 (June 2000): 106–28.

Flynt, J. Wayne. *Dixie's Forgotten People: The South's Poor Whites.* Bloomington: University of Indiana Press, 1979.

———. "The Impact of Social Factors on Southern Baptist Expansion, 1800–1914." *Baptist History and Heritage* 17 (1982): 27–28.

———. "Southern Baptists: Rural to Urban Transition." *Baptist History and Heritage* 16 (1981): 24–34.

Fox-Genovese, Elizabeth. *Within the Plantation Household: Black and White Women of the Old South*. Chapel Hill: University of North Carolina Press, 1988.

Freeman, Curtis W. "'Never Had I Been So Blind': W. A. Criswell's 'Change' on Racial Segregation." *Journal of Southern Religion* 10 (2007): 1–11.

———. "Visionary Women among Early Baptists." *Baptist Quarterly* 43 (January 2010): 260–83.

Friedman, Jean E. *The Enclosed Garden: Women and Community in the Evangelical South, 1830–1900*. Chapel Hill: University of North Carolina Press, 1990.

Gallagher, Sally K. *Evangelical Identity and Gendered Family Life*. New Brunswick, N.J.: Rutgers University Press, 2003.

Garrett, James Leo, Jr., E. Glenn Hinson, and James E. Tull. *Are Southern Baptists "Evangelicals"?* Macon, Ga.: Mercer University Press, 1983.

Geertz, Clifford. "Religion as a Cultural System." In *Interpretation of Cultures: Selected Essays*, 87–125. New York: Basic Books, 1973.

George, Timothy. "Toward an Evangelical Future." In *Southern Baptists Observed: Multiple Perspectives on a Changing Denomination*, edited by Nancy Tatom Ammerman, 276–300. Knoxville: University of Tennessee Press, 1993.

Ginzberg, Lori D. *Women and the Work of Benevolence: Morality, Politics, and Class in the Nineteenth-Century United States*. New Haven, Conn.: Yale University Press, 1990.

Goldfield, David R. *Black, White, and Southern: Race Relations and Southern Culture, 1940 to the Present*. Baton Rouge: Louisiana State University Press, 1990.

Grantham, Dewey W. *The Life and Death of the Solid South: A Political History*. Lexington: University Press of Kentucky, 1988.

Gregory, James N. *The Southern Diaspora: How the Great Migrations of Black and White Southerners Transformed America*. Chapel Hill: University of North Carolina Press, 2005.

Griffith, R. Marie. *God's Daughters: Evangelical Women and the Power of Submission*. Berkeley: University of California Press, 1997.

Groothuis, Rebecca. *Women Caught in the Conflict: The Culture War between Traditionalism and Feminism*. Grand Rapids, Mich.: Baker Books, 1994.

Hankins, Barry. *God's Rascal: J. Frank Norris and the Beginnings of Southern Fundamentalism*. Lexington: University Press of Kentucky, 1996.

———. *Jesus and Gin: Evangelicalism, the Roaring Twenties, and Today's Culture Wars*. New York: Palgrave Macmillan, 2010.

———. *Uneasy in Babylon: Southern Baptist Conservatives and American Culture*. Tuscaloosa: University of Alabama Press, 2002.

Hardesty, Nancy A. *Women Called to Witness: Evangelical Feminists in the Nineteenth Century*. 2nd ed. Knoxville: University of Tennessee Press, 1999.

Harper, Keith. *The Quality of Mercy: Southern Baptists and Social Christianity, 1890–1920*. Tuscaloosa: University of Alabama Press, 1996.

Harvey, Paul. *Freedom's Coming: Religious Culture and the Shaping of the South from the Civil War through the Civil Rights Era*. Chapel Hill: University of North Carolina Press, 2005.

Hefley, James Carl. *The Conservative Resurgence in the Southern Baptist Convention*. Hannibal, Mo.: Hannibal Books, 1991.

———. *The Truth in Crisis: The Controversy in the Southern Baptist Convention*. 5 vols. Hannibal, Mo.: Hannibal Books, 1989–90.

Heyrman, Christine Leigh. *Southern Cross: The Beginnings of the Bible Belt*. New York: Knopf, 1997.

Hill, Patricia. *The World Their Household: The American Woman's Foreign Mission Movement and Cultural Transformation, 1870–1920*. Ann Arbor: University of Michigan Press, 1985.

Hill, Samuel S. Epilogue in *Churches in Cultural Captivity: A History of Social Attitudes of Southern Baptists*, by John Lee Eighmy, 200–210. Knoxville: University of Tennessee Press, 1972.

———. *Southern Churches in Crisis*. New York: Holt, Rinehart and Winston, 1967.

———. *Southern Churches in Crisis Revisited*. Tuscaloosa: University of Alabama Press, 1999.

———. "The Story before the Story: Southern Baptists since World War II." In *Southern Baptists Observed: Multiple Perspectives on a Changing Denomination*, edited by Nancy Tatom Ammerman, 30–40. Knoxville: University of Tennessee Press, 1993.

Holcomb, Carol Crawford. "Mothering the South: The Influence of Gender and the Social Gospel on the Social Views of the Leadership of the Woman's Missionary Union, Auxiliary to the Southern Baptist Convention, 1888–1930." Ph.D. diss., Baylor University, 1999.

Hull, William E. *Seminary in Crisis: The Strategic Response of the Southern Baptist Theological Seminary to the SBC Controversy*. Atlanta: Baptist History and Heritage Society, 2010.

Hunt, Alma. *History of Woman's Missionary Union*. Nashville, Tenn.: Convention Press, 1964.

Hunter, James Davison. *Culture Wars: The Struggle to Define America*. New York: Basic Books, 1991.

Hunter, Jane. *The Gospel of Gentility: American Women Missionaries in Turn-of-the-Century China*. New Haven, Conn.: Yale University Press, 1984.

Ingersoll, Julie. *Evangelical Christian Women: War Stories in the Gender Battles*. New York: New York University Press, 2003.

James, Robison B., and David S. Dockery, eds. *Beyond the Impasse: Scripture, Interpretation, and Theology in Baptist Life*. Nashville, Tenn.: Broadman Press, 1992.

Kell, Carl L., and L. Raymond Camp. *In the Name of the Father: Rhetoric in the New Southern Baptist Convention*. Carbondale: Southern Illinois Press, 1999.

Keller, Rosemary Skinner, Ann Braude, Maureen Ursenbach Beecher, and Elizabeth Fox-Genovese. "Forum: Female Experience in American Religion." *Religion and American Culture* 5, no. 1 (Winter 1995): 1–21.

Kerber, Linda. "Separate Spheres, Female World, Woman's Place: The Rhetoric of Women's History." *Journal of American History* 75, no. 1 (June 1988): 9–39.

Kirby, Jack Temple. *Rural Worlds Lost: The American South, 1920–1960.* Baton Rouge: Louisiana State University Press, 1987.

Knight, Walker L. "Race Relations: Changing Patterns and Practices." In *Southern Baptists Observed: Multiple Perspectives on a Changing Denomination,* edited by Nancy Tatom Ammerman, 165–81. Knoxville: University of Tennessee Press, 1993.

Lamis, Alexander P. *The Two-Party South.* New York: Oxford University Press, 1984.

Lander, Ernest M., and Richard J. Calhoun, eds. *Two Decades of Change: The South since the Supreme Court Desegregation Decision.* Columbia: University of South Carolina Press, 1974.

Lassiter, Matthew D. *The Silent Majority: Suburban Politics in the Sunbelt South.* Princeton, N.J.: Princeton University Press, 2004.

Leonard, Bill J. *God's Last and Only Hope: The Fragmentation of the Southern Baptist Convention.* Grand Rapids, Mich.: William B. Eerdman's, 1990.

Lienesch, Michael. *Redeeming America: Piety and Politics in the New Christian Right.* Chapel Hill: University of North Carolina Press, 1993.

Lofton, Kathryn. *Oprah: The Gospel of an Icon.* Berkeley: University of California Press, 2011.

Lublin, David. *The Republican South: Democratization and Partisan Change.* Princeton, N.J.: Princeton University Press, 2004.

Lyons, Courtney. "My Husband Wears the Cowboy Boots in Our Family." Unpublished paper delivered at the annual meeting of the Southwest Commission on Religious Studies. Irving, Tex. March 5, 2011.

Mach, Zdzislaw. *Symbols, Conflict, and Identity: Essays in Political Anthropology.* Albany: State University of New York Press, 1993.

Marsden, George. *Fundamentalism and American Culture: The Shaping of Twentieth-Century Evangelicalism.* New York: Oxford University Press, 1980.

Martin, William C. *With God on Our Side: The Rise of the Religious Right in America.* New York: Broadway Books, 1996.

Mathews, Donald G. *Religion in the Old South.* Chicago: University of Chicago Press, 1977.

May, Elaine Tyler. *Homeward Bound: American Families in the Cold War Era.* New York: Basic Books, 1988.

McBeth, H. Leon. *Women in Baptist Life.* Nashville, Tenn.: Broadman Press, 1979.

McCall, Emmanuel. *When All God's Children Get Together: A Memoir of Race and Baptists.* Macon, Ga.: Mercer University Press, 2007.

McKinney, John C., and Edgar T. Thompson, eds. *The South in Continuity and Change.* Durham, N.C.: Duke University Press, 1965.

Meyerowitz, Joanne, ed. *Not June Cleaver: Women and Gender in Postwar America, 1945–1960.* Philadelphia: Temple University Press, 1994.

Miller, Steven P. *Billy Graham and the Rise of the Republican South.* Philadelphia: University of Pennsylvania Press, 2009.

Mintz, Steve, and Susan Kellogg. *Domestic Revolutions: A Social History of the American Family.* New York: Free Press, 1988.

Morgan, David T. *The New Crusades, the New Holy Land: Conflict in the Southern Baptist Convention, 1969–1991*. Tuscaloosa: University of Alabama Press, 1996.

———. *Southern Baptist Sisters: In Search of Status, 1845–2000*. Macon, Ga.: Mercer University Press, 2003.

Naylor, Thomas H., and James Clotfelter. *Strategies for Change in the South*. Chapel Hill: University of North Carolina Press, 1975.

Newman, Mark. *Getting Right with God: Southern Baptists and Desegregation, 1945–1995*. Tuscaloosa: University of Alabama Press, 2001.

Noble, Donald R., and Joab L. Thomas, eds. *The Rising South: Changes and Issues*. Tuscaloosa: University of Alabama Press, 1976.

Noll, Mark A. *Between Faith and Criticism: Evangelicals, Scholarship, and the Bible in America*. 2nd ed. Grand Rapids, Mich.: Baker Book House, 1991.

O'Hanlon, Rosalind. "Recovering the Subject: Subaltern Studies and Histories of Resistance in Colonial South Asia." *Modern Asian Studies* 22, no. 1 (1988): 189–224.

Orsi, Robert. "Snakes Alive: Resituating the Moral in the Study of Religion." In *Women, Gender, Religion: A Reader*, edited by Elizabeth A. Castelli and Rosamond C. Rodman, 98–116. New York: Palgrave.

Pool, Jeff B., ed. *Sacred Mandates of Conscience: Interpretations of the Baptist Faith and Message*. Macon, Ga.: Smyth and Helwys, 1997.

Queen, Edward L., II. *In the South the Baptists Are the Center of Gravity: Southern Baptist and Social Change, 1930–1980*. Brooklyn, N.Y.: Carlson Publishing, 1991.

Rabkin, Jeremy. "The Culture War That Isn't." *Policy Review* 96 (August/September 1999): 3–19.

Reed, John Shelton. *The Enduring South: Subcultural Persistence in Mass Society*. Chapel Hill: University of North Carolina Press, 1976.

Robert, Dana. *American Women in Mission: A Social History of Their Thought and Practice*. Macon, Ga.: Mercer University Press, 1997.

Roland, Charles P. *The Improbable Era: The South since World War II*. Lexington: University Press of Kentucky, 1975.

Roth, Benita. *Separate Roads to Feminism: Black, Chicana, and White Feminist Movements in America's Second Wave*. New York: Cambridge University Press, 2004.

Ryan, Mary P. *Cradle of the Middle Class: The Family in Oneida County, New York, 1790–1865*. New York: Cambridge University Press, 1981.

Scales, Laine. *All That Fits a Woman: Training Southern Baptist Women for Charity and Mission, 1907–1926*. Macon, Ga.: Mercer University Press, 2000.

Schulman, Bruce J. *From Cotton Belt to Sunbelt: Federal Policy, Economic Development, and the Transformation of the South, 1938–1980*. New York: Oxford University Press, 1991.

———. *The Seventies: The Great Shift in American Culture, Society, and Politics*. New York: Free Press, 2001.

Schweiger, Beth Barton. "Forum: Southern Religion." *Religion and American Culture* 8, no. 2 (Summer 1998): 161–66.

Scott, Ann Firor. *The Southern Lady: From Pedestal to Politics, 1830–1930*. Chicago: University of Chicago Press, 1970.

Scott, Joan. "Gender: A Useful Category of Historical Analysis." *American Historical Review* 91, no. 5 (December 1986): 1067–68.

Shaw, Susan M. *God Speaks to Us, Too: Southern Baptist Women on Church, Home, and Society*. Lexington: University Press of Kentucky, 2008.

Shaw, Susan M., and Tisa Lewis. "'Once There Was Camelot': Women Doctoral Graduates of the Southern Baptist Theological Seminary, 1982–1992, Talk about the Seminary, the Fundamentalist Takeover, and Their Lives since SBTS." *Review and Expositer* 95, no. 3 (1998): 397–423.

Shibley, Mark. *Resurgent Evangelicalism in the United States*. Columbia: University of South Carolina Press, 1996.

Shurden, Walter B. *Not an Easy Journey: Some Transitions in Baptist Life*. Macon, Ga.: Mercer University Press, 2005.

———. *Not a Silent People: Controversies That Have Shaped Southern Baptists*. Macon, Ga.: Smyth and Helwys, 1995.

Smith, Christian. "The Myth of the Culture Wars." In *Cultural Wars in American Politics: Critical Reviews of a Popular Myth*, edited by Rhys H. Williams, 175–95. New York: Aldine de Gruyter, 1997.

Smith, Timothy L. "The Evangelical Kaleidoscope and the Call to Christian Unity." *Christian Scholars Review* 15 (1986): 125–40.

Smith-Rosenberg, Carroll. "Beauty, the Beast, and the Militant Woman." *American Quarterly* 23 (1971): 562–84.

———. "The Female World of Love and Ritual." *Signs: Journal of Women in Culture and Society* 1, no. 1 (Autumn 1975): 1–29.

Spain, Rufus. *At Ease in Zion: Social History of Southern Baptists, 1865–1900*. Nashville, Tenn.: Vanderbilt University Press, 1967.

Spruill, Marjorie Julian. "'Women for God, Country and Family': Religion, Politics and Antifeminism in 1970s America." Unpublished paper referenced in Stephen P. Miller, "The Politics of Decency: Billy Graham, Evangelicalism, and the End of the Solid South, 1950–1980." Ph.D. diss., Vanderbilt University, 2006.

Stacey, Judith. *Brave New Family: Stories of Domestic Upheaval in Late Twentieth-Century America*. 2nd ed. New York: Basic Books, 1998.

Stricklin, David. *A Genealogy of Dissent: Southern Baptist Protest in the Twentieth Century*. Lexington: University Press of Kentucky, 1999.

Sutton, Jerry. *The Baptist Reformation: The Conservative Resurgence in the Southern Baptist Convention*. Nashville, Tenn.: Broadman and Holman, 2000.

Sweeney, Douglas. "The Essential Evangelicalism Dialectic: The Historiography of the Early Neo-Evangelical Movement and the Observer-Participant Dilemma." *Church History* 60, no. 1 (March 1991): 70–84.

Sweet, Leonard I. "The Evangelical Tradition in America." In *The Evangelical Tradition in America*, edited by Leonard I. Sweet, 1–86. Macon, Ga.: Mercer University Press, 1983.

———. "Wise as Serpents, Innocent as Doves: The New Evangelical Historiography." *Journal of the American Academy of Religion* 56 (Fall 1988): 397–416.

Swidler, Ann. "Culture in Action: Symbols and Strategies." *American Sociological Review* 51 (April 1986): 273–86.

Tew, Delane. "From Local Society to Para-Denomination: Woman's Missionary Union, 1890–1930." Ph.D. diss., Auburn University, 2003.

Thompson, James J., Jr. *Tried as by Fire: Southern Baptists and the Religious Controversies of the 1920s.* Macon, Ga.: Mercer University Press, 1982.

Tull, James E. *High-Church Baptists in the South: The Origin, Nature, and Influence of Landmarkism.* Edited and with a preface by Morris Ashcroft. Macon, Ga.: Mercer University Press, 2000.

Tweed, Thomas A. *Crossing and Dwelling: A Theory of Religion.* Cambridge, Mass.: Harvard University Press, 2006.

———. "On Moving Across: Translocative Religion and the Interpreter's Position." *Journal of the American Academy of Religion* 70, no. 2 (June 2002): 253–72.

———. *Our Lady of the Exile: Diasporic Religion at a Cuban Catholic Shrine in Miami.* New York: Oxford University Press, 1997.

Wacker, Grant. *Heaven Below: Early Pentecostals and American Culture.* Cambridge, Mass.: Harvard University Press, 2001.

Wadsworth, Nancy D. "Reconciliation Politics: Conservative Evangelicals and the New Race Discourse." *Politics and Society* 25, no. 3 (1997): 341–76.

Weaver, Aaron Douglas. "Progressive Baptist Dissenters: A History of the Alliance of Baptists." http://www.sitemason.com/files/cQ4qR2/Alliance%20of%20Baptists%20History.pdf. July 26, 2011.

Welter, Barbara. "The Cult of True Womanhood, 1820–1860." *American Quarterly* 18 (Summer 1966): 151–74.

Whitfield, Stephen J. *The Culture of the Cold War.* Baltimore, Md.: Johns Hopkins University Press, 1991.

Wilcox, Clyde. *God's Warriors: The Religious Right in American Politics.* Baltimore, Md.: Johns Hopkins University Press, 1992.

Williams, Rhys H., ed. *Cultural Wars in American Politics.* New York: Aldine de Gruyter, 1997.

Willis, Alan Scott. *All According to God's Plan: Southern Baptist Missions and Race, 1945–1970.* Lexington: University Press of Kentucky, 2005.

Wills, Gregory A. *Democratic Religion: Freedom, Authority, and Church Discipline in the Baptist South, 1785–1900.* New York: Oxford University Press, 1997.

———. *Southern Baptist Theological Seminary, 1859–2009.* New York: Oxford University Press, 2009.

Winston, Diane. "The Southern Baptist Story." In *Southern Baptists Observed: Multiple Perspectives on a Changing Denomination,* edited by Nancy Tatom Ammerman, 12–29. Knoxville: University of Tennessee Press, 1993.

Wolfe, Margaret Ripley. *Daughters of Canaan: A Saga of Southern Women.* Lexington: University Press of Kentucky, 1995.

Wright, Gavin. *Old South, New South: Revolutions in the Southern Economy since the Civil War.* New York: Basic Books, 1986.

Wyatt-Brown, Bertram. *Southern Honor: Ethics and Behavior in the Old South.* New York: Oxford University Press, 1982.

Index

and conservatives, 141, 142, 143, 144; and the Alliance, 155

Civil Rights Act of 1964, 40

Clanton, Jann Aldredge, 132, 133, 134, 154

Clark, Caesar A. W., 142

Clinton, Bill, 129, 146, 162

Clinton, Hillary, 129, 162

Cobb, Reba, 93, 166

Commission on Efficiency, 23

Committee on Boards, 113

Committee on Committees, 113

Committee on Nominations, 113

Communion, 4, 22

Complementarianism, 25, 130–35, 145, 162, 180–89 passim

Concerned Women of American, 76

Conservatives, Southern Baptist: presidential victories of, 1–2, 69, 140, 149, 160, 161; and ascendency to denominational power, 1–5, 7–8, 23–25 102–48; on women's ordination, 2, 4, 102–8, 110–40 passim, 147, 162, 187, 188; as women, 2–3, 8, 15–18, 25, 52, 76–86, 105, 130–35, 179–89; and women's submission, 4, 5, 8, 20, 21, 24–25, 102–8, 130–35, 140, 145–48, 182–89 passim, 193; and race, 4, 75, 140–44, 222 (n. 120); scholarship regarding, 5–6, 196–97 (n. 14); and relationship to evangelicals, 10–11, 72, 127, 128, 134–35; and relationship to culture wars and religious right, 11, 69, 85, 127, 129; on Baptist history and distinctives, 18–21, 75, 132, 154; and feminism, 45, 76–86 passim, 137, 144, 186; and inerrancy, 52, 69, 73–76, 87, 110, 213 (n. 13), 214 (n. 37); and denominationalists, 69–70; formation and early agenda of, 69–86; and planning of resurgence and takeover, 72, 113; and Peace Committee, 108–10; and practice of disfellowshipping, 110–13, 162; and control of mission boards, 115–18; and Southeastern Seminary, 118–19, 120–22; and Southern Seminary, 118–20, 122–29; and takeover of seminaries, 118–29; and development of complementarianism, 130–35; and relationship to WMU, 135–40; and Resolution on Racial Reconciliation, 140–44; growth of black churches under, 143–44, 222 (n. 119); as progressives, 144; and revision of Baptist Faith and Message, 145–48, 188; and debate over women in post-2000 period, 180–89, 194; and Calvinism, 188 (n. 4); terminology regarding, 195 (n. 4)

Consultation on Women in Church-Related Vocations, 24, 61–67, 78, 85, 91, 190

Conversion, 9, 22, 23

Cooperative Baptist Fellowship (CBF): women's involvement in and leadership of, 152, 163, 164, 165, 166, 169–70; founding of, 161–63; and relationship to the Alliance, 162–63, 164, 168; and relationship to (S)BWIM, 162–67, 169–73, 177, 189–93; on women's ordination, 162–75 passim; compromising and centrist position of, 163–64, 167, 168, 172; and missions, 163–65; early years of, 163–67; on freedom, 164; and relationship to WMU, 164; and struggle for identity, 167–73; growth and size of, 168; changing position on women in ministry and ordination, 168–73, 174–75; seminaries as partner institutions of, 169, 189–90, 225 (n. 50); on homosexuality, 170–73; and women's ordination in affiliated congregations, 174–75, 189; fieldwork regarding, 179. *See also* Moderates, Southern Baptist

Cooperative Program, 23, 33, 70, 87

Cothen, Grady, 88

Council on Biblical Manhood and Womanhood, 83, 105, 107, 122, 134, 135, 143, 168

Covenant Renewal, 123–24, 126, 127, 128, 129

Creationism, 1

Creedalism, 36

Criswell, W. A., 37, 39, 70, 71, 146

18; ratification process of, 43, 52, 58; campaign of Schlafly against, 53, 58; early Southern Baptist support for, 65, 93; tensions between southern women over, 144

Executive board, 31

Falwell, Jerry, 9, 11, 69, 128
Family, nuclear, 18, 42–43
Family amendment, 145–46. *See also* Baptist Faith and Message
Family Research Council, 141
Family values, 72, 77, 80, 81, 82, 84, 105, 114
Faubus, Orval, 39
Fellowship!, 163
Feminine Mystique, 27, 43
Feminism, 38, 107; as impetus for post-1979 Southern Baptist controversy, 2, 3, 5, 24, 29, 76–86 passim; conservative resolutions against, 7; and religious right, 18, 69; and changes within movement, 25, 43–44, 92, 175–76; Southern Baptist support of, 25, 62, 114; and civil rights, 41, 144; development and history of, 42–45; and women's ordination, 44–45, 48–49, 105; and WMU, 45–48; and evangelical support for, 52–54; 1970s evangelical women's campaign against, 55, 58, 67; and 1970s SBC officials, 57; conservative women against, 76–86 passim, 144, 186; and conservative campaign, 84–86, 137, 144; and (S)BWIM, 92, 99, 100, 170; moderates' discomfort with, 157, 162, 170. *See also* Women's liberation; Women's rights
Feminist theology, 53, 62, 95–100 passim, 122, 133, 150, 152, 170, 208–9 (n. 62)
Findley, Kathy Manis, 171
First Baptist Church, Asheville, 86
First Baptist Church, Dallas, 37, 39, 72
First Baptist Church, Memphis, 175–76
First Baptist Church, Orlando, 178
Focus on the Family, 105, 168
FOLIO, 16, 94, 95, 97, 98, 99, 100, 106, 108, 152, 154, 170, 173

Foreign Mission Board, 98, 136, 167; early financial struggles of, 20; and Cauthen years, 31; and Lottie Moon offering, 46; growth of, 50, 116; conservative control over, 116–18, 129; moderates' support of, 162, 167
Forester, Donna, 152
Forum, SBC, 158–59
Freedom, as moderate Baptist concept: 8, 24–25, 69, 121; historic and definitional tensions over, 89–91; (S)BWIM's interpretation of, 95, 97, 151; in terms of women and CBF, 152, 170; and the Alliance, 155
Freedom conferences, 193
"Freedom for Women" report, 59
Friedan, Betty, 27, 43
Frost, Gary, 140, 141, 142
Fuller, Janet, 115
Fuller Theological Seminary, 72, 102, 128
Fundamentalist-modernist debates (1920s), 10, 35–36, 75, 199–200 (n. 26)
Fundamentalists, 35, 36, 37, 124, 160, 162, 195 (n. 4). *See also* Conservatives, Southern Baptist

Gambrell, James, 30
Gardner, LeAnne, 190
Garland, Diana, 126–27, 129
Garrett Evangelical Theological Seminary, 99–100, 150
Gatlinburg gang, 87–88, 91, 120, 158
Genesis crisis, 35–38
George, Denise, 139
Gibson, Eugene, 142
Gingrich, Newt, 162
Glendale Baptist Church, 174
Global Women, 14, 193
Glorieta Statement, 104, 108–10, 120–21, 157
Golden Gate Baptist Theological Seminary, 34, 117, 119, 120
Gordon College, 126
Gordon Theological Seminary, 128
Gore, Al, 162

89–91, 151, 152, 157, 158, 159, 160, 168; and
inerrancy, 4, 24, 88–89, 213 (n. 13), 214
(n. 37); and race, 4, 142; and debate over
women's submission, ordination, and
ministerial roles, 4–5, 8, 18–21, 24–25,
151–61 passim, 189–93; scholarship
regarding, 5; and concept of freedom,
8, 24–25, 69, 89–91, 151, 152; evangelical identity of, 10; and relationship to
evangelicals, 10–11; on Baptist history
and distinctives, 18–21, 132, 146, 147, 151,
152–54, 168; as theologically conservative, 75–76, 86–89, 160, 214 (n. 37); and
charges of liberalism, 75–76, 88, 89;
and hesitancy toward liberal issues, 85;
as denominationalists, 86–88, 90, 151;
formation and early response to conservatives, 86–92; on historic tensions,
89–91; as inheritors of compromises,
90, 151, 152, 168; and internal conflicts,
90–92, 129, 149–52, 157; as inheritors of
dissent, 91, 112, 152, 157–58, 159, 168; and
absence of women in leadership, 91–92,
158–60, 214–15 (n. 41); and relationship
to (S)BWIM, 92–99 passim, 151, 152,
159; and Kansas City Resolution, 103,
108; and Peace Committee, 109, 157; and
response to disfellowshipping, 113; and
Southern Baptist missions, 115, 116; and
culture wars, 129; and continued participation in the SBC, 145; and response
to 1998 family amendment, 145–46;
and 2000 Baptist Faith and Message,
146–48; as progressives, 152, 157–58; and
religious right, 158; and campaign for
SBC presidency, 158–62; and precur-
sor organizations to CBF, 158–62; as
centrists, 160; and struggle for identity,
168–73; in post-2000 period, 189–93;
terminology concerning, 195 (n. 4), 214
(n. 33). *See also* Alliance of Baptists;
Cooperative Baptist Fellowship
Mohler, Albert, Jr.: and hire as Southern
Seminary's president, 124, 167; theological shift to right, 124–25; and Marshall,

126; and Garland and Carver School,
126–27; and Black Wednesday, 127; on
Covenant Renewal hires, 128; conserva-
tive direction of Southern Seminary
under, 129; and involvement with
Racial Reconciliation Resolution, 142;
on women in political office, 188; on
ordained women in moderate church
life, 192
Mohler, Mary, 124, 129
Moon, Lottie, 16, 62; and related offering,
35, 45, 46, 137, 138
Moore, Beth, 139, 180–81, 183, 184, 188
Moore, Winfred, 157, 158
Moral Majority, 69, 105, 141
Morgan, Marabel, 54–55, 62, 181
Motherhood: fieldwork concerning, 15,
16, 181; and agenda of religious right, 18;
Friedan's critique of, 43; as tenet of tra-
ditional womanhood, 54; conservative
women's support of, 77, 78, 79, 82; and
women's ministry, 82; and Dorothy Pat-
terson, 131; and women in politics, 188
Mothers of Preschoolers, 193
Ms. Magazine, 43
Mullins, E. Y., 30, 36

National African American Fellowship,
143
National Association of Evangelicals, 9,
53, 140
National Baptists, 142, 143, 222 (n. 119)
National Council of Churches, 168
National Organization for Women, 43,
176
Neely, Alan, 155, 157
Neil, Ann Thomas: as first president of
(S)BWIM, 98–99; social justice vision
of, 100, 154; on women in the Alliance,
149–50; involvement in and leadership
of the Alliance, 149–50, 154, 156, 162; on
women's ordination and CBF, 162; and
twenty-fifth anniversary celebration of
(S)BWIM, 190; as inspiration, 194
Neil, Lloyd, 98

Nelson, Bailey Edwards, 191
New Domesticity, 42–43, 78. *See also* Domesticity
New Hampshire Confession of 1833, 36
New Orleans Baptist Theological Seminary, 34, 56, 71, 72, 118, 119, 120, 130
Newman, Carey, 124, 128
Nixon, Richard, 52
Norris, Frank, 35–36, 75
North: liberalism of, 2, 36, 37, 84; migration patterns regarding, 7, 30, 33; evangelicals in, 9, 10, 53, 75, 125; and women's missions, 20; in contrast to South, 29
North, Oliver, 129
North American Mission Board. *See* Home Mission Board
Northern Baptist Convention, 33
Northern Baptists, 19, 33, 75, 170
Northwest Baptist Church, 111

O'Brien, Bill, 136
O'Brien, Dellana, 135, 136, 138
O'Chester, Barbara, 56, 57, 58, 76, 130, 144
O'Chester, Harold, 40, 56, 57, 144
Oertli, Kerrie, 165
Oklahoma Women in Baptist Life, 193
Old Forest Road Baptist Church, 87
Oligarchs, 3, 30, 58. *See also* Denominationalists
Ordination (women's): as central to argument, 2, 4, 5; increasing number of Southern Baptist women seeking, 2, 24, 48–49, 58–59; and relationship to inerrancy, 5, 24; and relationship to feminism, 5, 25, 44–45, 48–49, 105; and fragmentation of Southern Baptist women, 8; early moderates' support of, 18, 151; and (S)BWIM, 25, 92–101 passim, 151–76 passim, 189–93; moderates' hesitancy toward and tensions over, 25, 113, 151–76 passim; of Addie Davis, 27–29, 49, 119; among mainstream Protestants, 44–45; and WMU, 47–48, 58–59, 92, 135–40 passim; of Shirley Carter, 48–49; and Sappington affair,

50–51; evangelical feminists' support of, 53; and Christian Liberation Conference, 59–61; as central issue at Consultation on Women in Church-Related Vocations, 61–68 passim; and Kansas City Resolution, 102–8; conservative rejection of, 102–48 passim, 187, 188; shifting attitudes toward, 110; as reason for disfellowshipping, 110–13; and SBC mission boards, 115–18; as issue at Southeastern Seminary, 120, 121–22; as issue at Southern Seminary, 124–29; in Patterson-Clanton debate, 131–35; Alliance's support of, 154–58 passim; and Forum, 158–59; and Vestal, 162; and CBF, 162–76 passim, 189–93 passim; in local moderate church life, 173–76, 189–93; attitude of conservative women post-2000 toward, 183–84; in Wesleyan holiness and Pentecostal traditions, 209 (n. 64)
Ordination Study Committee, 115
Organization men, 30, 35. *See* also Denominationalists
Our Bodies, Ourselves, 43
Owen, K. O., 35

Packer, J. I., 88
Palin, Sarah, 187, 188
Park Cities Baptist Church, 59
Parks, Keith, 116–17, 163, 167
Pastoral authority, 22, 106, 107, 132, 149, 153, 175
Pastor's Conference, 73, 86, 158
Patterson, Dorothy, 71, 194; and complementarianism, 104, 130–35, 185, 187; at Southeastern, 122; biography of, 130–31; in Baptist History and Heritage debate, 131–35, 143; on WMU, 136, 138, 139; and 1998 family amendment, 145, 146; and Beth Moore, 181; at Southwestern, 185, 186; on domesticity, 187–88; on asking husband's permission, 188
Patterson, Paige: and initial meeting with Pressler, 70–71, 161; and conser-

vative plan, 71–73, 84, 88; background
of, 72–73; on inerrancy, 75, 76; and
Sherman, 86, 87; and Honeycutt and
Southern Seminary, 123; as culture
warrior, 129; as SBC president, 146;
Southwestern Seminary under presi-
dency of, 185, 186, 188
Patterson, T. A., 72–73
Payne, Les, 141
Peace Committee, 103, 108–10, 121, 123,
157, 160
Pearce, Betty McGary, 93. *See also*
McGary, Betty
Pennington, Greg, 117
Pennington, Katrina, 111, 117
Pentecostalism, 45, 188
Perkins, Esther Tye, 174
Petrey, Dixie, 171
Pine Bluff Baptist Church, 174
Presbyterian Church, USA, 45
Prescott Memorial Baptist Church, 111–12,
175
Pressler, Paul: initial meeting with Patter-
son, 70–71, 161; and conservative plan,
71–73, 84, 88; background of, 72; and
Sherman, 86, 87; and Peace Commit-
tee, 110; and Honeycutt and Southern
Seminary, 123; as culture warrior, 129;
as Depression era senior, 142, 161
Priesthood of all believers. *See* Priesthood
of the believer
Priesthood of the believer, 89, 97, 106, 132,
146, 151, 204 (n. 64)
Primer, Terry Thomas, 68, 69, 94, 101, 167
Principe, Linda, 115
Promise Keepers, 140
Pulpit: as symbol of power, 2, 44–45;
conservative rejection of women in,
2, 103; as central to controversy, 2, 104;
women in missions early access of, 21;
and (S)BWIM, 25; and Addie Davis,
28; as dangerous, 49; women's call to,
92; as visually symbolic in Sehested's
disfellowshipping, 112; seminary professor's podium as, 126; lack of women

in moderate, 152, 189; women in least
desirable, 173
Pulpiteer, 22, 33, 39, 45, 70, 73, 86, 87, 88, 89

Race, 75: shift in attitude toward, 4, 38–41,
84, 125, 140–41, 154; and relationship to
gender, 5, 19, 41, 58, 66, 104, 127, 143–44,
156, 222 (n. 120); and conservatives, 104,
140–44; attitudes toward at Southern
Seminary, 127
Racial Reconciliation Resolution, 140–44
Ramsey, Brooks, 40
Reagan, Ronald, 104
Reagan era, 105
Redwood Empire Baptist Association, 111
Reformed tradition, 9, 200 (n. 28), 210
(n. 9)
Regent University, 128
Regular Baptists, 19, 212 (n. 6)
Religious right: in the South, 11; and
Falwell, 11, 69, 72; and Southern Baptist
conservatives, 11, 76, 83, 85, 105, 114,
127–29; and moderates, 11, 85, 158; and
attack on feminism, 18, 85, 170, 176; and
Moral Majority, 69; beginnings of, 69,
72; and issues that contrast Southern
Baptist controversy, 85; and Focus on
the Family, 105; and Richard Land,
114; and Al Mohler, 127–28; and family
values, 129, 170; and race, 141, 142; and
the Alliance, 156
Republican Party, 53, 105, 129, 141, 162, 172,
180, 187, 208 (n. 53)
Resolution No. 1: "On Racial Reconcili-
ation on the 150th Anniversary of the
Southern Baptist Convention." *See*
Racial Reconciliation Resolution
Resolution No. 3: "On the Ordination
and the Role of Women in Ministry."
See Kansas City Resolution
Revivalism, 74
Richardson, Carol McCall, 139, 175
Robertson, Pat, 72, 128
Robison, James, 86
Roe v. Wade, 43

Rogers, Adrian: and 1979 election as SBC president, 1, 67, 69, 70; and Mid-America Theological Seminary, 37, 116; as husband to Joyce, 51; as supportive of women's ministry, 81, 86; and attack on feminism, 86; as outsider to SBC elite and denominationalists, 87; and disfellowshipping of Prescott Memorial Baptist Church, 111–12; as culture warrior, 129; on WMU, 137; as Depression era senior, 142; and second presidential victory, 149

Rogers, Joyce: on Sappington's resolution, 51; in constructing biblical argument for women's submission, 56–58, 79–80, 95, 96, 107, 134, 181; and Women's Concerns Conference, 77, 78, 79–80, 81; and women's ministry, 81, 82, 130

Rosser, Anne, 51

Routh, Porter, 31, 35, 37

Royal Ambassadors, 31

Royal Service, 46, 47

Ruether, Rosemary Radford, 150

Russell, Letty, 98, 157

Sacramental authority, 45

Saiving, Valerie, 98

Salvation, 3, 9, 36, 53, 79, 89, 104, 123, 126, 164

Sappington, Jesse Tillison, 50–52, 54, 58, 59, 194

Save Our Children, 55

SBC Today, 117, 167. See also *Baptists Today*

Scalise, Pam, 127

Scanzoni, Letha, 53, 132

Schaeffer, Francis, 88

Schlafly, Phyllis, 52–53, 55, 76

Second Baptist Church, 40

Segregation, 7, 22, 38, 39, 41, 52, 75, 141, 143–44, 156

Sehested, Nancy: as founder of (S)BWIM, 92–93; and Baptist theology of women in ministry, 98, 99; social justice vision of, 99–100; and disfellowshipping of Prescott Memorial Baptist Church, 111–12; as pastor of Prescott Memorial Baptist Church, 111–12, 175; and the Alliance, 150, 156; on the relationship between CBF and (S)BWIM, 167; as inspiration for younger generation, 191, 194

Seminaries, Southern Baptist: and charges of liberalism, 1, 71, 104, 118–20; expansion of, 33–34; and increasing number of women seeking ordination, 58, 85; and lack of support for women seeking ministerial placements, 65; as home to denominationalists, 87; as supportive to women in ministry, 96; and (S)BWIM, 99; as progressive, 101; and Glorieta Statement, 104, 108–10, 119; demographics regarding, 118–19; conservatives' ascendency and control of, 118–29, 162; and contrasting attitudes toward women in ministry, 119; conservative women's ministry programs in relation to, 130, 162, 185; and 2000 Baptist Faith and Message, 147; size of, 218–19 (n. 51)

Seminary Wives Institute, 129

Separate Baptists, 19, 70, 97, 212 (n. 6)

Sexual Politics, 43

Shaw, Susan, 122–23

Shelby County Baptist Association, 111–12

Sherman, Bill, 172

Sherman, Cecil: and initial worry over conservatives' ascendency, 86–87; formation of Gatlinburg gang, 87–88; as SBC loyalist, 90; and frustration over lack of support for moderate cause, 91; and lack of women in early moderate leadership, 92; and resignation from Peace Committee, 109; and the moderate campaign, 119, 158, 160; and formation of CBF, 161; on CBF's relationship to the Alliance, 162; as CBF's first coordinator, 163, 164; on women in ministry, 170; on CBF, social issues, and centrist position, 172–73

Sherwood, David, 126